p. 52

SESAME AND LILIES

THREE LECTURES

Illustrated Cabinet Edition

Sesame and Lilies ❧ Unto This Last ❧ The Queen of the Air ❧ The Storm Cloud of the Nineteenth Century ❧ ❧ ❧ ❧ ❧ ❧ ❧ ❧ ❧ by John Ruskin

Boston ❧ ❧ ❧ ❧ ❧
Dana Estes & Company
❧ ❧ ❧ ❧ Publishers

160963

CONTENTS.

PREFACE.

BEING now fifty-one years old, and little likely to change my mind hereafter on any important subject of thought (unless through weakness of age), I wish to publish a connected series of such parts of my works as now seem to me right, and likely to be of permanent use. In doing so I shall omit much, but not attempt to mend what I think worth reprinting. A young man necessarily writes otherwise than an old one, and it would be worse than wasted time to try to recast the juvenile language : nor is it to be thought that I am ashamed even of what I cancel ; for great part of my earlier work was rapidly written for temporary purposes, and is now unnecessary, though true, even to truism. What I wrote about religion, was, on the contrary, painstaking, and, I think, forcible, as compared with most religious writing ; especially in its frankness and fearlessness : but it was wholly mistaken ; for I had been educated in the doctrines of a narrow sect, and had read history as obliquely as sectarians necessarily must.

Mingled among these either unnecessary or erroneous statements, I find, indeed, some that might be still of value ; but these, in my earlier books, disfigured by affected language, partly through the desire to be thought a fine writer, and partly, as in the second volume of *Modern Painters*, in the notion of returning as far as I could to what I thought the better style of old English literature, especially to that of my then favourite, in prose, Richard Hooker.

For these reasons, though, as respects either art, policy, or morality as distinct from religion, I not only still hold, but would even wish strongly to re-affirm the substance of what I said in my earliest books, I shall reprint scarcely anything in this series out of the first and second volumes of *Modern Painters ;* and shall omit much of the *Seven Lamps* and *Stones of Venice :* but all my books written within the last fifteen years will be republished without change, as new editions of them are called for, with here and there perhaps an additional note, and having their text divided, for convenient reference, into paragraphs consecutive through each volume. I shall also throw together the shorter fragments that bear on each other, and fill in with such unprinted lectures or studies as seem to me worth preserving, so as to keep the volumes, on an average, composed of about a hundred leaves each.

The first book of which a new edition is required chances to be *Sesame* and *Lilies,* from which I now detach the old preface, about the Alps, for use elsewhere ; and to which I add a lecture given in Ireland on a subject closely connected with that of the book itself. I am glad that it should be the first of the complete series, for many reasons ; though in now looking over these two lectures, I am painfully struck by the waste of good work in them. They cost me much thought, and much strong emotion ; but it was foolish to suppose that I could rouse my audiences in a little while to any sympathy with the temper into which I had brought myself by years of thinking over subjects full of pain ; while, if I missed my purpose at the time, it was little to be hoped I could attain it afterwards ; since phrases written for oral delivery become ineffective when quietly read. Yet I should only take away what good is in them if I tried to translate them into the language of books ; nor, indeed, could I at all have done so at the time of their delivery, my thoughts then habitually and impatiently putting themselves into forms fit only for emphatic speech ; and thus I am startled, in my review of them, to find that, though there is much, (forgive me the impertinence) which seems to me accurately and energetically said, there is scarcely anything put in a form to be generally convincing, or even easily intelligible ; and I can well imagine a reader laying down the book without being at all moved by it, still less guided, to any definite course of action.

I think, however, if I now say briefly and clearly what *I*

meant my hearers to understand, and what I wanted, and still would fain have, them to do, there may afterwards be found some better service in the passionately written text.

The first Lecture says, or tries to say, that, life being very short, and the quiet hours of it few, we ought to waste none of them in reading valueless books ; and that valuable books should, in a civilized country, be within the reach of every one, printed in excellent form, for a just price ; but not in any vile, vulgar, or, by reason of smallness of type, physically injurious form, at a vile price. For we none of us need many books, and those which we need ought to be clearly printed, on the best paper, and strongly bound. And though we are, indeed, now, a wretched and poverty-struck nation, and hardly able to keep soul and body together, still, as no person in decent circumstances would put on his table confessedly bad wine, or bad meat, without being ashamed, so he need not have on his shelves ill-printed or loosely and wretchedly-stitched books ; for, though few can be rich, yet every man who honestly exerts himself may, I think, still provide, for himself and his family, good shoes, good gloves, strong harness for his cart or carriage horses, and stout leather binding for his books. And I would urge upon every young man, as the beginning of his due and wise provision for his household, to obtain as soon as he can, by the severest economy, a restricted, serviceable, and steadily—however slowly—increasing, series of books for use through life ; making his little library, of all the furniture in his room, the most studied and decorative piece ; every volume having its assigned place, like a little statue in its niche, and one of the earliest and strictest lessons to the children of the house being how to turn the pages of their own literary possessions lightly and deliberately, with no chance of tearing or dogs' ears.

That is my notion of the founding of King's Treasuries ; and the first Lecture is intended to show somewhat the use and preciousness of their treasures : but the two following ones have wider scope, being written in the hope of awakening the youth of England, so far as my poor words might have any power with them, to take some thought of the purposes

of the life into which they are entering, and the nature of the world they have to conquer.

These two lectures are fragmentary and ill-arranged, but not, I think, diffuse or much compressible. The entire gist and conclusion of them, however, is in the last six paragraphs, 135 to the end, of the third lecture, which I would beg the reader to look over not once nor twice (rather than any other part of the book), for they contain the best expression I have yet been able to put in words of what, so far as is within my power, I mean henceforward both to do myself, and to plead with all over whom I have any influence, to do also according to their means: the letters begun on the first day of this year, to the workmen of England, having the object of originating, if possible, this movement among them, in true alliance with whatever trustworthy element of help they can find in the higher classes. After these paragraphs, let me ask you to read, by the fiery light of recent events, the fable at p. 116 (§ 117), and then §§ 129—131 ; and observe, my statement re-specting the famine at Orissa is not rhetorical, but certified by official documents as within the truth. Five hundred thou-sand persons, *at least*, died by starvation in our British domin-ions, wholly in consequence of carelessness and want of fore-thought. Keep that well in your memory ; and note it as the best possible illustration of modern political economy in true practice, and of the relations it has accomplished between Supply and Demand. Then begin the second lecture, and all will read clear enough, I think, to the end ; only, since that second lecture was written, questions have arisen respecting the education and claims of women which have greatly troubled simple minds and excited restless ones. I am some-times asked my thoughts on this matter, and I suppose that some girl readers of the second lecture may at the end of it desire to be told summarily what I would have them do and desire in the present state of things. This, then, is what I would say to any girl who had confidence enough in me to believe what I told her, or do what I ask her.

First, be quite sure of one thing, that, however much you may know, and whatever advantages you may possess, and however good you may be, you have not been singled out, by the God who made you, from all the other girls in the world, to be especially informed respecting His own nature and character. You have not been born in a luminous point upon the surface of the globe, where a perfect theology might be expounded to you from your youth up, and where everything you were taught would be true, and everything that was enforced upon you, right. Of all the insolent, all the foolish persuasions that by any chance could enter and hold your empty little heart, this is the proudest and foolishest,—that you have been so much the darling of the Heavens, and favourite of the Fates, as to be born in the very nick of time, and in the punctual place, when and where pure Divine truth had been sifted from the errors of the Nations ; and that your papa had been providentially disposed to buy a house in the convenient neighbourhood of the steeple under which that Immaculate and final verity would be beautifully proclaimed. Do not think it, child ; it is not so. This, on the contrary, is the fact,—unpleasant you may think it ; pleasant, it seems to *me*,—that you, with all your pretty dresses, and dainty looks, and kindly thoughts, and saintly aspirations, are not one whit more thought of or loved by the great Maker and Master than any poor little red, black, or blue savage, running wild in the pestilent woods, or naked on the hot sands of the earth : and that, of the two, you probably know less about God than she does ; the only difference being that she thinks little of Him that is right, and you, much that is wrong.

That, then, is the first thing to make sure of ;—that you are not yet perfectly well informed on the most abstruse of all possible subjects, and that, if you care to behave with modesty or propriety, you had better be silent about it.

The second thing which you may make sure of is, that however good you may be, you have faults ; that however dull you may be, you can find out what some of them are ; and that however slight they may be, you had better make some—not too painful, but patient—effort to get quit of them. And so far as you have confidence in me at all, trust me for this, that how many soever you may find or fancy your faults to be, there are only two that are of real consequence,—Idleness and Cruelty. Perhaps you may be proud. Well, we can get much good out of pride, if only it be not religious. Perhaps you may be vain : it is highly probable ; and very pleasant for the people who like to praise you. Perhaps you are a little en- vious : that is really very shocking ; but then—so is every- body else. Perhaps, also, you are a little malicious, which I am truly concerned to hear, but should probably only the more, if I knew you, enjoy your conversation. But whatever else you may be, you must not be useless, and you must not be cruel. If there is any one point which, in six thousand years of thinking about right and wrong, wise and good men have agreed upon, or successively by experience discovered, it is that God dislikes idle and cruel people more than any other ;—that His first order is, "Work while you have light ; " and His second, "Be merciful while you have mercy."

"Work while you have light," especially while you have the light of morning. There are few things more wonderful to me than that old people never tell young ones how precious their youth is. They sometimes sentimentally regret their own earlier days ; sometimes prudently forget them ; often fool- ishly rebuke the young, often more foolishly indulge, often most foolishly thwart and restrain ; but scarcely ever warn or watch them. Remember, then, that I, at least, have warned *you*, that the happiness of your life, and its power, and its part and rank in earth or in heaven, depend on the way you pass your days now. They are not to be sad days ; far from that, the first duty of young people is to be delighted and delightful ; but they are to be in the deepest sense solemn days. There is no solemnity so deep, to a rightly-thinking creature, as that of dawn. But not only in that beautiful sense, but in all their character and method, they are to be solemn days. Take your Latin dictionary, and look out " sol- lennis," and fix the sense of the word well in your mind, and remember that every day of your early life is ordaining irrev- ocably, for good or evil, the custom and practice of your soul ; ordaining either sacred customs of dear and lovely recurrence, or trenching deeper and deeper the furrows for seed of sor row. Now, therefore, see that no day passes in which you do not make yourself a somewhat better creature ; and in order to do that, find out, first, what you are now. Do not think vaguely about it ; take pen and paper, and write down as accurate a description of yourself as you can, with the date to it. If you dare not do so, find out why you dare not, and try to get strength of heart enough to look yourself fairly in the face, in mind as well as body. I do not doubt but that the mind is a less pleasant thing to look at than the face, and for that very reason it needs more looking at ; so always have two mirrors on your toilet table, and see that with proper care you dress body and mind before them daily. After the dressing is once over for the day, think no more about it : as your hair will blow about your ears, so your temper and thoughts will get ruffled with the day's work, and may need, sometimes, twice dressing ; but I don't want you to carry about a mental pocket-comb ; only to be smooth braided always in the morning.

Write down then, frankly, what you are, or, at least, what you think yourself, not dwelling upon those inevitable faults which I have just told you are of little consequence, and which the action of a right life will shake or smooth away ; but that you may determine to the best of your intelligence what you are good for, and can be made into. You will find that the mere resolve not to be useless, and the honest desire to help other people, will, in the quickest and delicatest ways, improve yourself. Thus, from the beginning, consider all your accomplishments as means of assistance to others ; read attentively, in this volume, paragraphs 74, 75, 19, and 79, and you will understand what I mean, with respect to languages and music. In music especially you will soon find what personal benefit there is in being serviceable : it is probable that, however limited your powers, you have voice and ear enough to sustain a note of moderate compass in a concerted piece ;— that, then, is the first thing to make sure you can do. Get your voice disciplined and clear, and think only of accuracy ; never of effect or expression : if you have any soul worth expressing it will show itself in your singing ; but most likely there are very few feelings in you, at present, needing any particular expression ; and the one thing you have to do is to make a clear-voiced little instrument of yourself, which other people can entirely depend upon for the note wanted. So, in drawing, as soon as you can set down the right shape of anything, and thereby explain its character to another person, or make the look of it clear and interesting to a child, you will begin to enjoy the art vividly for its own sake, and all your habits of mind and powers of memory will gain precision : but if you only try to make showy drawings for praise, or pretty ones for amusement, your drawing will have little of real interest for you, and no educational power whatever.

Then, besides this more delicate work, resolve to do every day some that is useful in the vulgar sense. Learn first thoroughly the economy of the kitchen ; the good and bad qualities of every common article of food, and the simplest and best modes of their preparation : when you have time, go and help in the cooking of poorer families, and show them how to make as much of everything as possible, and how to make little, nice ; coaxing and tempting them into tidy and pretty ways, and pleading for well-folded table-cloths, however coarse, and for a flower or two out of the garden to strew on them. If you manage to get a clean table-cloth, bright plates on it, and a good dish in the middle, of your own cooking, you may ask leave to say a short grace ; and let your religious ministries be confined to that much for the present.

Again, let a certain part of your day (as little as you choose, but not to be broken in upon) be set apart for making strong and pretty dresses for the poor. Learn the sound qualities of all useful stuffs, and make everything of the best you can get, whatever its price. I have many reasons for desiring you to do this,—too many to be told just now,—trust me, and be sure you get everything as good as can be : and if, in the villainous state of moderate trade, you cannot get it good at any price, buy its raw material, and set some of the poor women about you to spin and weave, till you have got stuff that can be trusted : and then, every day, make some little piece of useful clothing, sewn with your own fingers as strongly as it can be stitched ; and embroider it or otherwise beautify it moderately with fine needlework, such as a girl may be proud of having done. And accumulate these things by you until you hear of some honest persons in need of clothing, which may often too sorrowfully be ; and, even though you should be deceived, and give them to the dishonest, and hear of their being at once taken to the pawnbroker's, never mind that, for the pawnbroker must sell them to some one who has need of them. That is no business of yours ; what concerns you is only that when you see a half-naked child, you should have good and fresh clothes to give it, if its parents will let it be taught to wear them. If they will not, consider how they came to be of such a mind, which it will be wholesome for you beyond most subjects of inquiry to ascertain. And after you have gone on doing this a little while, you will begin to understand the meaning of at least one chapter of your Bible, Proverbs xxxi., without need of any laboured comment, sermon, or meditation.

In these, then (and of course in all minor ways besides, that you can discover in your own household), you must be to the best of your strength usefully employed during the greater part of the day, so that you may be able at the end of it to say, as proudly as any peasant, that you have not eaten the bread of idleness. Then, secondly, I said, you are not to be cruel. Perhaps you think there is no chance of your being so ; and indeed I hope it is not likely that you should be deliberately unkind to any creature ; but unless you are deliberately kind to every creature, you will often be cruel to many. Cruel, partly through want of imagination (a far rarer and weaker faculty in women than men), and yet more, at the present day, through the subtle encouragement of your selfishness by the religious doctrine that all which we now suppose to be evil will be brought to a good end ; doctrine practically issuing, not in less earnest efforts that the immediate unpleasantness may be averted from ourselves, but in our remaining satisfied in the contemplation of its ultimate objects, when it is inflicted on others.

It is not likely that the more accurate methods of recent mental education will now long permit young people to grow up in the persuasion that, in any danger or distress, they may expect to be themselves saved by the providence of God, while those around them are lost by His Improvidence : but they may be yet long restrained from rightly kind action, and long accustomed to endure both their own pain occasionally, and the pain of others always, with an unwise patience, by misconception of the eternal and incurable nature of real evil. Observe, therefore, carefully in this matter : there are degrees of pain, as degrees of faultfulness, which are altogether conquerable, and which seem to be merely forms of wholesome trial or discipline. Your fingers tingle when you go out on a frosty morning, and are all the warmer afterwards ; your limbs are weary with wholesome work, and lie down in the pleasanter rest ; you are tried for a little while by having to wait for some promised good, and it is all the sweeter when it comes. But you cannot carry the trial past a certain point. Let the cold fasten on your hand in an extreme degree, and your fingers will moulder from their sockets. Fatigue yourself, but once, to utter exhaustion, and to the end of life you shall not recover the former vigour of your frame. Let heart-sickness pass beyond a certain bitter point, and the heart loses its life forever.

Now, the very definition of evil is in this irremediableness. It means sorrow, or sin, which end in death ; and assuredly, as far as we know, or can conceive, there are many conditions both of pain and sin which cannot but so end. Of course we are ignorant and blind creatures, and we cannot know what seeds of good may be in present suffering, or present crime : but with what we cannot know, we are not concerned. It is conceivable that murderers and liars may in some distant world be exalted into a higher humanity than they could have reached without homicide or falsehood ; but the contingency is not one by which our actions should be guided. There is, indeed, a better hope that the beggar, who lies at our gates in misery, may, within gates of pearl be comforted ; but the Master, whose words are our only authority for thinking so,

never Himself inflicted disease as a blessing, nor sent away
the hungry unfed, or the wounded unhealed.

Believe me, then, the only right principle of action here, is
to consider good and evil as defined by our natural sense of
both ; and to strive to promote the one, and to conquer the
other, with as hearty endeavor as if there were, indeed, no
other world than this. Above all, get quit of the absurd idea
that Heaven will interfere to correct great errors, while allowing its laws to take their course in punishing small ones. If
you prepare a dish of food carelessly, you do not expect Providence to make it palatable ; neither, if, through years of folly,
you misguide your own life, need you expect Divine interference to bring round everything at last for the best. I tell
you, positively, the world is not so constituted : the consequences of great mistakes are just as sure as those of small
ones, and the happiness of your whole life, and of all the lives
over which you have power, depends as literally on your own
common sense and discretion as the excellence and order of
the feast of a day.

Think carefully and bravely over these things, and you will
find them true : having found them so, think also carefully
over your own position in life. I assume that you belong to
the middle or upper classes, and that you would shrink from
descending into a lower sphere. You may fancy you would
not : nay, if you are very good, strong-hearted, and romantic,
perhaps you really would not ; but it is not wrong that you
should. You have then, I suppose, good food, pretty rooms
to live in, pretty dresses to wear, power of obtaining every
rational and wholesome pleasure ; you are, moreover, probably gentle and grateful, and in the habit of every day thanking God for these things. But why do you thank Him ? Is
it because, in these matters, as well as in your religious knowledge, you think He has made a favourite of you ? Is the essential meaning of your thanksgiving, "Lord, I thank thee
that I am not as other girls are, not in that I fast twice in the
week while they feast, but in that I feast seven times a week,
while they fast," and are you quite sure this is a pleasing form
of thanksgiving to your Heavenly Father ? Suppose you saw

one of your own true earthly sisters, Lucy or Emily, cast **out**
of your mortal father's house, starving, helpless, heartbroken ;
and that every morning when you went into your father's
room, you said to him, "How good you are, father, to **give**
me what you don't give Lucy," are you sure that, whatever
anger your parent might have just cause for, against your
sister, he would be pleased by that thanksgiving, or flattered
by that praise ? Nay, are you even sure that you *are* so much
the favourite : suppose that, all this while, he loves poor Lucy
just as well as you, and is only trying you through her pain,
and perhaps not angry with her in anywise, but deeply angry
with you, and all the more for your thanksgivings ? Would
it not be well that you should think, and earnestly too over
this standing of yours : and all the more if you wish to believe that text, which clergymen so much dislike preaching
on, "How hardly shall they that have riches enter into the
Kingdom of God ?" You do not believe it now, or you would
be less complacent in your state ; and you cannot believe it
at all, until you know that the Kingdom of God means—" not
meat and drink, but justice, peace, and joy in the Holy Ghost,"
nor until you know also that such joy is not by any means,
necessarily, in going to church, or in singing hymns ; but
may be joy in a dance, or joy in a jest, or joy in anything you
have deserved to possess, or that you are willing to give ; but
joy in nothing that separates you, as by any strange favour,
from your fellow creatures, that exalts you through their
degradation—exempts you from their toil—or indulges you
in time of their distress.

Think, then, and some day, I believe, you will feel also—no
morbid passion of pity such as would turn you into a black
Sister of Charity, but the steady fire of perpetual kindness
which will make you a bright one. I speak in no disparage-
ment of them ; I know well how good the Sisters of Charity
are, and how much we owe to them ; but all these profes-
sional pieties (except so far as distinction or association may
be necessary for effectiveness of work) are in their spirit
wrong, and in practice merely plaster the sores of disease
that ought never have been permitted to exist ; encouraging

at the same time the herd of less excellent women in frivolity, by leading them to think that they must either be good up to the black standard, or cannot be good for anything. Wear a costume, by all means, if you like ; but let it be a cheerful and becoming one ; and be in your heart a Sister of Charity always, without either veiled or voluble declaration of it.

As I pause, before ending my preface—thinking of one or two more points that are difficult to write of—I find a letter in *The Times*, from a French lady, which says all I want so beautifully, that I will print it just as it stands :

SIR,—It is often said that one example is worth many sermons. Shall I be judged presumptuous if I point out one, which seems to me so striking just now, that, however painful, I cannot help dwelling upon it ?

It is the share, the sad and large share, that French society and its recent habits of luxury, of expenses, of dress, of indulgence in every kind of extravagant dissipation, has to lay to its own door in its actual crisis of ruin, misery, and humiliation. If our *ménagères* can be cited as an example to English housewives, so, alas ! can other classes of our society be set up as an example—*not* to be followed.

Bitter must be the feelings of many a French woman whose days of luxury and expensive habits are at an end : and whose bills of bygone splendour lie with a heavy weight on her conscience, if not on her purse !

With us the evil has spread high and low. Everywhere have the examples given by the highest ladies in the land been followed but too successfully.

Every year did dress become more extravagant, entertainments more costly, expenses of every kind more considerable. Lower and lower became the tone of society, its good breeding, its delicacy. More and more were *monde* and *demimonde* associated in newspaper accounts of fashionable doings, in scandalous gossip, on racecourses, in *premières représentations*, in imitation of each other's costumes, *mobiliers* and slang.

Living beyond one's means became habitual—almost necessary—for every one to keep up with, if not to go beyond, every one else.

What the result of all this has been we now see in the wreck of our prosperity, in the downfall of all that seemed brightest and highest.

Deeply and fearfully impressed by what my own country
has incurred and is suffering, I cannot help feeling sorrowful
when I see in England signs of our besetting sins appearing
also.   Paint and chignons, slang and vaudevilles, knowing
"Anonymas" by name, and reading doubtfully moral novels,
are in themselves small offences, although not many years ago
they would have appeared very heinous ones, yet they are
quick and tempting conveyances on a very dangerous high-
road.

I would that all Englishwomen knew how they are looked
up to from abroad—what a high opinion, what honour and
reverence we foreigners have for their principles, their truthfulness, the fresh and pure innocence of their daughters, the
healthy youthfulness of their lovely children.

May I illustrate this by a short example which happened
very near me ?   During the days of the *émeutes* of 1848, all
the houses in Paris were being searched for firearms by the
mob.   The one I was living in contained none, as the master
of the house repeatedly assured the furious and incredulous
Republicans.   They were going to lay violent hands on him,
when his wife, an English lady, hearing the loud discussion,
came bravely forward and assured them that no arms were
concealed.   "Vous êtes anglaise, nous vous croyons ; les
anglaises disent toujours la vérité," was the immediate answer,
and the rioters quietly left.

Now, Sir, shall I be accused of unjust criticism if, loving
and admiring your country, as these lines will prove, certain
new features strike me as painful discrepancies in English life ?

Far be it from me to preach the contempt of all that can
make life lovable and wholesomely pleasant.   I love nothing
better than to see a women nice, neat, elegant, looking her
best in the prettiest dress that her taste and purse can afford,
or your bright, fresh young girls fearlessly and perfectly sitting their horses, or adorning their houses as pretty [*sic* ; it is
not quite grammar, but it is better than if it were ;] as care,
trouble, and refinement can make them.

It is the degree *beyond* that which to us has proved so fatal,
and that I would our example could warn you from, as a
small repayment for your hospitality and friendliness to us in
our days of trouble.

May Engiishwomen accept this in a kindly spirit as a new
year's wish from

FRENCH LADY.

Dec. 29.

That, then, is the substance of what I would fain say con-
vincingly, if it might be, to my girl friends ; at all events,
with certainty in my own mind that I was thus far a safe
guide to them.

For other and older readers it is needful I should write
a few words more, respecting what opportunity I have had
to judge, or right I have to speak, of such things ; for, indeed, too much of what I have said about women has been
said in faith only.   A wise and lovely English lady told me,
when *Sesame and Lilies* first appeared, that she was sure the
Sesame would be useful, but that in the *Lilies* I had been
writing of what I knew nothing about.   Which was in a measure too true, and also that it is more partial than my writings
are usually ; for as Ellesmere spoke his speech on the —— in-
tervention, not indeed otherwise than he felt, but yet altogether
for the sake of Gretchen, so I wrote the *Lilies* to please one
girl ; and were it not for what I remember of her, and of few
besides, should now perhaps recast some of the sentences in
the *Lilies* in a very different tone : for as years have gone by,
it has chanced to me, untowardly in some respects, fortunately
in others (because it enables me to read history more clearly),
to see the utmost evil that is in women, while I have had but
to believe the utmost good.   The best women are indeed
necessarily the most difficult to know ; they are recognized
chiefly in the happiness of their husbands and the nobleness
of their children ; they are only to be divined, not discerned,
by the stranger ; and, sometimes, seem almost helpless except
in their homes ; yet without the help of one of them,* to
whom this book is dedicated, the day would probably have
come before now, when I should have written and thought no
more.

On the other hand, the fashion of the time renders whatever is forward, coarse or senseless, in feminine nature, too
palpable to all men :—the weak picturesqueness of my earlier
writings brought me acquainted with much of their emptiest
enthusiasm ; and the chances of later life gave me opportunities of watching women in states of degradation and vir

* φίλη.

2

dictiveness which opened to me the gloomiest secrets of Greek and Syrian tragedy. I have seen them betray their household charities to lust, their pledged love to devotion ; I have seen mothers dutiful to their children, as Medea ; and children dutiful to their parents, as the daughter of Herodias : but my trust is still unmoved in the preciousness of the natures that are so fatal in their error, and I leave the words of the *Lilies* unchanged ; believing, yet, that no man ever lived a right life who had not been chastened by a woman's love, strengthened by her courage, and guided by her discretion.

What I might myself have been, so helped, I rarely indulge in the idleness of thinking ; but what I am, since I take on me the function of a teacher, it is well that the reader should know, as far as I can tell him.

Not an unjust person ; not an unkind one; not a false one ; a lover of order, labor, and peace. That, it seems to me, is enough to give me right to say all I care to say on ethical subjects : more, I could only tell definitely through details of autobiography such as none but prosperous and (in the simple sense of the word) faultless, lives could justify ;— and mine has been neither. Yet, if any one, skilled in reading the torn manuscripts of the human soul, cares for more intimate knowledge of me, he may have it by knowing with what persons in past history I have most sympathy.

I will name three.

In all that is strongest and deepest in me,—that fits me for my work, and gives light or shadow to my being, I have sympathy with Guido Guinicelli.

In my constant natural temper, and thoughts of things and of people, with Marmontel.

In my enforced and accidental temper, and thoughts of things and of people, with Dean Swift.

Any one who can understand the natures of those three men, can understand mine ; and having said so much, I am content to leave both life and work to be remembered or forgotten, as their uses may deserve.

DENMARK HILL,
  1st January, 1871.

PREFACE—FIRST EDITION.

A PASSAGE in the fifty-fifth page of this book, referring to Alpine travellers, will fall harshly on the reader's ear since it has been sorrowfully enforced by the deaths on Mont Cervin. I leave it, nevertheless, as it stood, for I do not now write unadvisedly, and think it wrong to cancel what has once been thoughtfully said ; but it must not so remain without a few added words.

No blame ought to attach to the Alpine tourist for incurring danger. There is usually sufficient cause, and real reward, for all difficult work ; and even were it otherwise, some experience of distinct peril, and the acquirement of habits of quick and calm action in its presence, are necessary elements, at some period of life, in the formation of manly character. The blame of bribing guides into danger is a singular accusation, in behalf of a people who have made mercenary soldiers of themselves for centuries, without any one's thinking of giving their fidelity better employment : though, indeed, the piece of work they did at the gate of the Tuileries, however useless, was no unwise one ; and their lion of flawed molasse at Lucerne, worthless in point of art though it be, is nevertheless a better reward than much pay ; and a better ornament to the old town than the Schweizer Hof, or flat new quay, for the promenade of those travellers who do *not* take guides into danger. The British public are however, at home, so innocent of ever buying their fellow creatures' lives, that we may justly expect them to be punctilious abroad ! They do not, perhaps, often calculate how many souls flit annually, choked in fire-damp and sea-sand, from economically watched shafts, and economically manned

ships ; nor see the fiery ghosts writhe up out of every scut-
tleful of cheap coals : nor count how many threads of
girlish life are cut off and woven annually by painted
Fates, into breadths of ball-dresses ; or soaked away, like
rotten hemp-fibre, in the inlet of Cocytus which overflows
the Grassmarket where flesh is as grass. We need not, it
seems to me, loudly blame any one for paying a guide to
take a brave walk with him. Therefore, gentlemen of the
Alpine Club, as much danger as you care to face, by all
means ; but, if it please you, not so much talk of it. The
real ground of reprehension of Alpine climbing is that, with
less cause, it excites more vanity than any other athletic
skill. A good horseman knows what it has cost to make him
one ; everybody else knows it too, and knows that he is one ;
he need not ride at a fence merely to show his seat. But
credit for practice in climbing can only be claimed after success, which, though perhaps accidental and unmerited, must
yet be attained at all risks, or the shame of defeat borne
with no evidence of the difficulties encountered. At this
particular period, also, the distinction obtainable by first conquest of a peak is as tempting to a traveller as the discovery
of a new element to a chemist, or of a new species to a naturalist. Vanity is never so keenly excited as by competitions
which involve chance ; the course of science is continually
arrested, and its nomenclature fatally confused, by the eagerness of even wise and able men to establish their priority in
an unimportant discovery, or obtain vested right to a syllable
in a deformed word ; and many an otherwise sensible person
will risk his life for the sake of a line in future guide-books,
to the fact that "——horn was first ascended by Mr. X. in
the year ——" ;—never reflecting that of all the lines in the
page, the one he has thus wrought for will be precisely the
least interesting to the reader.

It is not therefore strange, however much to be regretted,
that while no gentleman boasts in other cases of his sagacity
or his courage—while no good soldier talks of the charge he
led, nor any good sailor of the helm he held,—every man
among the Alps seems to lose his senses and modesty with

the fall of the barometer, and returns from his Nephelo-coc-cygia brandishing his ice-axe in everybody's face. Whatever the Alpine Club have done, or may yet accomplish, is a sincere thirst for mountain knowledge, and in happy sense of youthful strength and play of animal spirit, they have done, and will do, wisely and well; but whatever they are urged to by mere sting of competition and itch of praise, they will do, as all vain things must be done for ever, foolishly and ill. It is a strange proof of that absence of any real national love of science, of which I have had occasion to speak in the text, that no entire survey of the Alps has yet been made by properly qualified men; and that, except of the chain of Chamouni, no accurate maps exist, nor any complete geological section even of that. But Mr. Reilly's survey of that central group, and the generally accurate information collected in the guide-book published by the Club, are honorable results of English adventure; and it is to be hoped that the continuance of such work will gradually put an end to the vulgar excitement which looked upon the granite of the Alps only as an unoccupied advertisement wall for chalking names upon.

Respecting the means of accomplishing such work with least risk, there was a sentence in the article of our leading public journal, which deserves, and requires expansion.

"Their" (the Alpine Club's) "ropes must not break."

Certainly not! nor any one else's ropes, if they may be rendered unbreakable by honesty of make; seeing that more lives hang by them on moving than on motionless seas. The records of the last gale at the Cape may teach us that economy in the manufacture of cables is not always a matter for exultation; and, on the whole, it might even be well in an honest country, sending out, and up and down, various lines east and west, that *nothing* should break; banks,—words,—nor dredging tackle.

Granting, however, such praise and such sphere of exertion as we thus justly may, to the spirit of adventure, there is one consequence of it, coming directly under my own cognizance, of which I cannot but speak with utter regret,—the loss

namely, of all real understanding of the character and beauty
of Switzerland, by the country's being now regarded as half
watering-place, half gymnasium. It is indeed true that under
the influence of pride which gives poignancy to the sensations
which others cannot share with us (and a not unjustifiable
zest to the pleasure which we have worked for), an ordinary
traveller will usually observe and enjoy more on a difficult
excursion than on an easy one ; and more in objects to which
he is unaccustomed than in those with which he is familiar.
He will notice with extreme interest that snow is white on
the top of a hill in June, though he would have attached little
importance to the same peculiarity in a wreath at the bottom
of a hill in January. He will generally find more to admire
in a cloud under his feet, than in one over his head ; and, oppressed by the monotony of a sky which is prevalently blue,
will derive extraordinary satisfaction from its approximation
to black. Add to such grounds of delight the aid given to the
effect of whatever is impressive in the scenery of the high Alps,
by the absence of ludicrous or degrading concomitants ; and
it ceases to be surprising that Alpine excursionists should be
greatly pleased, or that they should attribute their pleasure to
some true and increased apprehension of the nobleness of
natural scenery. But no impression can be more false. The
real beauty of the Alps is to be seen, and seen only, where all
may see it, the child, the cripple, and the man of gray hairs.
There is more true loveliness in a single glade of pasture
shadowed by pine, or gleam of rocky brook, or inlet of unsul-
lied lake among the lower Bernese and Savoyard hills, than in
the entire field of jagged gneiss which crests the central ridge
from the Shreckhorn to the Viso. The valley of Cluse, through
which unhappy travellers consent now to be invoiced, packed
in baskets like fish, so only that they may cheaply reach, in the
feverous haste which has become the law of their being, the
glen of Chamouni whose every lovely foreground rock has
now been broken up to build hotels for them, contains more
beauty in half a league of it, than the entire valley they have
devastated, and turned into a casino, did in its uninjured
pride ; and that passage of the Jura by Olten (between Basle

and Lucerne), which is by the modern tourist triumphantly effected through a tunnel in ten minutes, between two piggish trumpet grunts proclamatory of the ecstatic transit, used to show from every turn and sweep of its winding ascent, up which one sauntered, gathering wild-flowers, for half a happy day, diviner aspects of the distant Alps than ever were achieved by toil of limb, or won by risk of life.

There is indeed a healthy enjoyment both in engineers' work, and in school-boy's play ; the making and mending of roads has its true enthusiasms, and I have still pleasure enough in mere scrambling to wonder not a little at the supreme gravity with which apes exercise their superior powers in that kind, as if profitless to them. But neither macadamisation, nor tunnelling, nor rope ladders, will ever enable one human creature to understand the pleasure in natural scenery felt by Theocritus or Virgil ; and I believe the athletic health of our schoolboys might be made perfectly consistent with a spirit of more courtesy and reverence, both for men and things, than is recognisable in the behaviour of modern youth. Some year or two back, I was staying at the Montanvert to paint Alpine roses, and went every day to watch the budding of a favorite bed, which was rounding into faultless bloom beneath a cirque of rock, high enough, as I hoped, and close enough, to guard it from rude eyes and plucking hands. But,

> " Tra erto e piano era un sentiero ghembo,
> Che ne condusse in fianco del a lacca,"

and on the day it reached the fulness of its rubied fire, I was standing near when it was discovered by a forager on the flanks of a travelling school of English and German lads. He shouted to his companions, and they swooped down upon it ; threw themselves into it, rolled over and over in it, shrieked, hallooed, and fought in it, trampled it down, and tore it up by the roots ; breathless at last with rapture of ravage, they fixed the brightest of the remnant blossoms of it in their caps, and went on their way rejoicing.

They left me much to think upon ; partly respecting the es

sential power of the beauty which could so excite them, and
partly respecting the character of the youth which could only
be excited to destroy. But the incident was a perfect type of
that irreverence for natural beauty with respect to which I
said in the text, at the place already indicated, "You make
railroads of the aisles of the cathedrals of the earth, and eat
off their altars." For indeed all true lovers of natural beauty
hold it in reverence so deep, that they would as soon think of
climbing the pillars of the choir Beauvais for a gymnastic exercise, as of making a play-ground of Alpine snow : and they
would not risk one hour of their joy among the hill meadows
on a May morning, for the fame or fortune of having stood on
every pinnacle of the silver temple, and beheld the kingdoms
of the world from it. Love of excitement is so far from being
love of beauty, that it ends always in a joy in its exact reverse ; joy in destruction,—as of my poor roses,—or in actual
details of death ; until, in the literature of the day, "nothing
is too dreadful, or too trivial, for the greed of the public." *
And in politics, apathy, irreverence, and lust of luxury go
hand in hand, until the best solemnization which can be conceived for the greatest event in modern European history, the
crowning of Florence capital of Italy, is the accursed and ill-
omened folly of casting down her old walls, and surrounding
her with a "boulevard ;" and this at the very time when
every stone of her ancient cities is more precious to her than
the gems of a Urim breastplate, and when every nerve of her
heart and brain should have been strained to redeem her guilt
and fulfil her freedom. It is not by making roads round
Florence, but through Calabria, that she should begin her
Roman causeway work again ; and her fate points her march,
not on boulevards by Arno, but waist-deep in the lagoons at
Venice. Not yet, indeed, but five years of patience and discipline of her youth would accomplish her power, and sweep
the martello towers from the cliffs of Verona, and the ramparts
from the marsh of Mestre. But she will not teach her youth
that discipline on boulevards.

Strange, that while we both, French and English, can give

* *Pall Mall Gazette*, August 15th, article on the Forward murders.

lessons in war, we only corrupt other nations when they imitate either our pleasures or our industries. We English, had
we loved Switzerland indeed, should have striven to elevate,
but not to disturb, the simplicity of her people, by teaching
them the sacredness of their fields and waters, the honour of
their pastoral and burgher life, and the fellowship in glory of
the gray turreted walls round their ancient cities, with their
cottages in their fair groups by the forest and lake. Beautiful, indeed, upon the mountains, had been the feet of any who
had spoken peace to their children ;—who had taught those
princely peasants to remember their lineage, and their league
with the rocks of the field ; that so they might keep their
mountain waters pure, and their mountain paths peaceful, and
their traditions of domestic life holy. We have taught them
(incapable by circumstances and position of ever becoming a
great commercial nation) all the foulness of the modern lust
of wealth, without its practical intelligences ; and we have developed exactly the weakness of their temperament by which
they are liable to meanest ruin. Of the ancient architecture
and most expressive beauty of their country there is now little vestige left ; and it is one of the few reasons which console
me for the advance of life, that I am old enough to remember
the time when the sweet waves of the Reuss and Limmat (now
foul with the refuse of manufacture) were as crystalline as the
heaven above them, when her pictured bridges and embattled
towers ran unbroken round Lucerne ; when the Rhone flowed
in deep-green, softly dividing currents round the wooded ramparts of Geneva ; and when from the marble roof of the western vault of Milan, I could watch the Rose of Italy flush in
the first morning light, before a human foot had sullied its
summit, or the reddening dawn on its rocks taken shadow of
sadness from the crimson which long ago stained the ripples
of Otterburn.

SESAME AND LILIES.

LECTURE I.—SESAME.

OF KINGS' TREASURIES.

"You shall each have a cake of sesame,—and ten pound."
—LUCIAN: *The Fisherman.*

I BELIEVE, ladies and gentlemen, that my first duty this evening is to ask your pardon for the ambiguity of title under
which the subject of lecture has been announced; and for having endeavoured, as you may ultimately think, to obtain your
audiences under false pretences. For indeed I am not going
to talk of kings, known as regnant, nor of treasuries, understood to contain wealth; but of quite another order of royalty,
and material of riches, than those usually acknowledged. And I
had even intended to ask your attention for a little while on
trust, and (as sometimes one contrives in taking a friend to
see a favourite piece of scenery) to hide what I wanted most to
show, with such imperfect cunning as I might, until we had
unexpectedly reached the best point of view by winding paths.
But since my good plain-spoken friend, Canon Anson, has already partly anticipated my reserved "trot for the avenue"
in his first advertised title of subject, "How and What to
Read;"—and as also I have heard it said, by men practised
in public address, that hearers are never so much fatigued as
by the endeavour to follow a speaker who gives them no clue
to his purpose, I will take the slight mask off at once, and
tell you plainly that I want to speak to you about books; and
about the way we read them, and could, or should read them.
A grave subject, you will say; and a wide one! Yes; so wide

that I shall make no effort to touch the compass of it. I will try only to bring before you a few simple thoughts about reading, which press themselves upon me every day more deeply, as I watch the course of the public mind with respect to our daily enlarging means of education, and the answeringly wider spreading, on the levels, of the irrigation of literature. It happens that I have practically some connection with schools for different classes of youth ; and I receive many letters from parents respecting the education of their children. In the mass of these letters, I am always struck by the precedence which the idea of a "position in life " takes above all other thoughts in the parents'—more especially in the mothers'—minds. "The education befitting such and such a *station in life*"—this is the phrase, this the object, always. They never seek, as far as I can make out, an education good in itself ; the conception of abstract rightness in training rarely seems reached by the writers. But an education "which shall keep a good coat on my son's back ;—an education which shall enable him to ring with confidence the visitors' bell at double-belled doors ;—education which shall result ultimately in establishment of a double-belled door to his own house ; in a word, which shall lead to "advancement in life." It never seems to occur to the parents that there may be an education which, in itself, *is* advancement in Life ;—that any other than that may perhaps be advancement in Death ; and that this essential education might be more easily got, or given, than they fancy, if they set about it in the right way ; while it is for no price, and by no favour, to be got, if they set about it in the wrong.

Indeed, among the ideas most prevalent and effective in the mind of this busiest of countries, I suppose the first—at least that which is confessed with the greatest frankness, and put forward as the fittest stimulus to youthful exertion—is this of "advancement in life." My main purpose this evening is to determine, with you, what this idea practically includes, and what it should include.

Practically, then, at present, "advancement in life" means becoming conspicuous in life ;—obtaining a position which

shall be acknowledged by others to be respectable or honourable. We do not understand by this advancement, in
general, the mere making of money, but the being known to
have made it ; not the accomplishment of any great aim, but
the being seen to have accomplished it. In a word, we mean
the gratification of our thirst for applause. That thirst, if the
last infirmity of noble minds, is also the first infirmity of weak
ones ; and, on the whole, the strongest impulsive influence of
average humanity : the greatest efforts of the race have always
been traceable to the love of praise, as its greatest catastro-
phes to the love of pleasure.

I am not about to attack or defend this impulse. I want
you only to feel how it lies at the root of effort ; especially of
all modern effort. It is the gratification of vanity which is,
with us, the stimulus of toil, and balm of repose ; so closely
does it touch the very springs of life, that the wounding of
our vanity is always spoken of (and truly) as in its measure
mortal ; we call it "mortification," using the same expression
which we should apply to a gangrenous and incurable bodily
hurt. And although few of us may be physicians enough to
recognize the various effect of this passion upon health and
energy, I believe most honest men know and would at once
acknowledge, its leading power with them as a motive. The
seaman does not commonly desire to be made captain only
because he knows he can manage the ship better than any
other sailor on board. He wants to be made captain that he
may be *called* captain. The clergyman does not usually want
to be made a bishop only because he believes no other hand
can, as firmly as his, direct the diocese through its difficulties.
He wants to be made bishop primarily that he may be called
"My Lord." And a prince does not usually desire to enlarge,
or a subject to gain, a kingdom, because he believes that no
one else can as well serve the state upon the throne ; but,
briefly, because he wishes to be addressed as "Your Majesty,'
by as many lips as may be brought to such utterance.

This, then, being the main idea of advancement in life, the
force of it applies, for all of us, according to our station, par
ticularly to that secondary result of such advancement which

we call "getting into good society." We want to get into good society, not that we may have it, but that we may be seen in it ; and our notion of its goodness depends primarily on its conspicuousness.

Will you pardon me if I pause for a moment to put what I fear you may think an impertinent question ? I never can go on with an address unless I feel, or know, that my audience are either with me or against me : (I do not much care which, in beginning ;) but I must know where they are ; and I would fain find out, at this instant, whether you think I am putting the motives of popular action too low. I am resolved to-night, to state them low enough to be admitted as probable ; for whenever, in my writings on Political Economy, I assume that a little honesty, or generosity,—or what used to be called " virtue "—may be calculated upon as a human motive of action, people always answer me, saying, "You must not calculate on that : that is not in human nature : you must not assume anything to be common to men but acquisitiveness and jealousy ; no other feeling ever has influence on them, except accidentally, and in matters out of the way of business." I begin accordingly to-night low down in the scale of motives ; but I must know if you think me right in doing so. Therefore, let me ask those who admit the love of praise to be usually the strongest motive in men's minds in seeking advancement, and the honest desire of doing any kind of duty to be an entirely secondary one, to hold up their hands. (*About a dozen of hands held up—the audience partly not being sure the lecturer is serious, and partly shy of expressing opinion.*) I am quite serious—I really do want to know what you think ; however, I can judge by putting the reverse question. Will those who think that duty is generally the first, and love of praise the second motive, hold up their hands? (*One hand reported to have been held up, behind the lecturer.*) Very good ; I see you are with me, and that you think I have not begun too near the ground. Now, without teasing you by putting farther question, I venture to assume that you will admit duty as at least a secondary or tertiary motive. You think that the desire of doing something useful, or obtaining some

real good, is indeed an existent collateral idea, though a secondary one, in most men's desire of advancement. You will
grant that moderately honest men desire place and office, at
least in some measure, for the sake of their beneficent power ;
and would wish to associate rather with sensible and well-informed persons than with fools and ignorant persons, whether
they are seen in the company of the sensible ones or not.
And finally, without being troubled by repetition of any common truisms about the preciousness of friends, and the influence of companions, you will admit, doubtless, that according to the sincerity of our desire that our friends may be true,
and our companions wise,—and in proportion to the earnestness and discretion with which we choose both, will be the
general chances of our happiness and usefulness.

But, granting that we had both the will and the sense to
choose our friends well, how few of us have the power ! or, at
least, how limited, for most, is the sphere of choice ! Nearly
all our associations are determined by chance or necessity ;
and restricted within a narrow circle. We cannot know whom
we would ; and those whom we know, we cannot have at our
side when we most need them. All the higher circles of human intelligence are, to those beneath, only momentarily and
partially open. We may, by good fortune, obtain a glimpse
of a great poet, and hear the sound of his voice ; or put a
question to a man of science, and be answered good-humour-
edly. We may intrude ten minutes' talk on a cabinet minister, answered probably with words worse than silence, being
deceptive ; or snatch, once or twice in our lives, the privilege
of throwing a bouquet in the path of a Princess, or arresting
the kind glance of a Queen. And yet these momentary chances
we covet ; and spend our years, and passions, and powers in
pursuit of little more than these ; while, meantime, there is
a society continually open to us, of people who will talk to
us as long as we like, whatever our rank or occupation ;—talk
to us in the best words they can choose, and with thanks if
we listen to them. And this society, because it is so numerous and so gentle,—and can be kept waiting round us all day
long, not to grant audience, but to gain it ;—kings and states

men lingering patiently in those plainly furnished and narrow anterooms, our bookcase shelves,—we make no account of that company,—perhaps never listen to a word they would say, all day long!

You may tell me, perhaps, or think within yourselves, that the apathy with which we regard this company of the noble, who are praying us to listen to them, and the passion with which we pursue the company, probably of the ignoble, who despise us, or who have nothing to teach us, are grounded in this,—-that we can see the faces of the living men, and it is themselves, and not their sayings, with which we desire to become familiar. But it is not so. Suppose you never were to see their faces ;—suppose you could be put behind a screen in the statesman's cabinet, or the prince's chamber, would you not be glad to listen to their words, though you were forbidden to advance beyond the screen? And when the screen is only a little less, folded in two, instead of four, and you can be hidden behind the cover of the two boards that bind a book, and listen, all day long, not to the casual talk, but to the studied, determined, chosen addresses of the wisest of men ;—this station of audience, and honourable privy council, you despise!

But perhaps you will say that it is because the living people talk of things that are passing, and are of immediate interest to you, that you desire to hear them. Nay ; that cannot be so, for the living people will themselves tell you about passing matters, much better in their writings than in their careless talk. But I admit that this motive does influence you, so far as you prefer those rapid and ephemeral writings to slow and enduring writings—books, properly so called. For all books are divisible into two classes, the books of the hour, and the books of all time. Mark this distinction—it is not one of quality only. It is not merely the bad book that does not last, and the good one that does. It is a distinction of species. There are good books for the hour, and good ones for all time ; bad books for the hour, and bad ones for all time. I must define the two kinds before I go farther.

The good book of the hour, then,—I do not speak of the

bad ones—is simply the useful or pleasant talk of some person whom you cannot otherwise converse with, printed for
you.   Very useful often, telling you what you need to know ;
very pleasant often, as a sensible friend's present talk would
be.   These bright accounts of travels ; good-humoured and
witty discussions of question ; lively or pathetic story-telling
in the form of novel ; firm fact-telling, by the real agents concerned in the events of passing history ;—all these books of
the hour, multiplying among us as education becomes more
general, are a peculiar characteristic and possession of the
present age; we ought to be entirely thankful for them, and
entirely ashamed of ourselves if we make no good use of
them.   But we make the worst possible use, if we allow them
to usurp the place of true books : for, strictly speaking, they
are not books at all, but merely letters or newspapers in good
print.   Our friend's letter may be delightful, or necessary,
to-day : whether worth keeping or not, is to be considered.
The newspaper may be entirely proper at breakfast time, but
assuredly it is not reading for all day.   So, though bound up
in a volume, the long letter which gives you so pleasant an
account of the inns, and roads, and weather last year at such
a place, or which tells you that amusing story, or gives you
the real circumstances of such and such events, however valuable for occasional reference, may not be, in the real sense of
the word, a " book " at all, nor, in the real sense, to be
" read."   A book is essentially not a talked thing, but a written thing ; and written, not with the view of mere communication, but of permanence.   The book of talk is printed only
because its author cannot speak to thousands of people at
once ; if he could, he would—the volume is mere *multiplication* of his voice.   You cannot talk to your friend in India ; if
you could, you would ; you write instead : that is mere *conveyance* of voice.   But a book is written, not to multiply the
voice merely, not to carry it merely, but to preserve it.   The
author has something to say which he perceives to be true and
useful, or helpfully beautiful.   So far as he knows, no one
has yet said it ; so far as he knows, no one else can say it.
He is bound to say it clearly and melodiously if he may ;

clearly, at all events. In the sum of his life he finds this to be the thing, or group of things, manifest to him ;—this the piece of true knowledge, or sight, which his share of sun‑ shine and earth has permitted him to seize. He would fain set it down for ever ; engrave it on rock, if he could ; say‑ ing, "This is the best of me ; for the rest, I ate, and drank, and slept, loved, and hated, like another ; my life was as the vapour, and is not ; but this I saw and knew : this, if anything of mine, is worth your memory." That is his "writing ;" it is, in his small human way, and with whatever degree of true inspiration is in him, his inscription, or scripture. That is a "Book."

Perhaps you think no books were ever so written ?

But, again, I ask you, do you at all believe in honesty, or at all in kindness ? or do you think there is never any honesty or benevolence in wise people ? None of us, I hope, are so unhappy as to think that. Well, whatever bit of a wise man's work is honestly and benevolently done, that bit is his book, or his piece of art.* It is mixed always with evil fragments —ill-done, redundant, affected work. But if you read rightly, you will easily discover the true bits, and those *are* the book.

Now books of this kind have been written in all ages by their greatest men ;—by great leaders, great statesmen, and great thinkers. These are all at your choice ; and life is short. You have heard as much before ;—yet have you measured and mapped out this short life and its possibilities ? Do you know, if you read this, that you cannot read that—that what you lose to-day you cannot gain to-morrow ? Will you go and gossip with your housemaid, or your stable-boy, when you may talk with queens and kings ; or flatter yourselves that it is with any worthy consciousness of your own claims to re‑ spect that you jostle with the common crowd for *entrée* here, and audience there, when all the while this eternal court is open to you, with its society wide as the world, multitudinous as its days, the chosen, and the mighty, of every place and time ? Into that you may enter always ; in that you may take

* Note this sentence carefully, and compare the *Queen of the Air*, § 106.

fellowship and rank according to your wish ; from that, once entered into it, you can never be outcast but by your own fault ; by your aristocracy of companionship there, your own inherent aristocracy will be assuredly tested, and the motives with which you strive to take high place in the society of the living, measured, as to all the truth and sincerity that are in them, by the place you desire to take in this company of the Dead.

"The place you desire," and the place you *fit yourself for*, I must also say ; because, observe, this court of the past differs from all living aristocracy in this :—it is open to labour and to merit, but to nothing else. No wealth will bribe, no name overawe, no artifice deceive, the guardian of those Elysian gates. In the deep sense, no vile or vulgar person ever enters there. At the portières of that silent Faubourg St. Germain, there is but brief question, "Do you deserve to enter?" "Pass. Do you ask to be the companion of nobles? Make yourself noble, and you shall be. Do you long for the conversation of the wise? Learn to understand it, and you shall hear it. But on other terms?—no. If you will not rise to us, we cannot stoop to you. The living lord may assume courtesy, the living philosopher explain his thought to you with considerable pain ; but here we neither feign nor interpret ; you must rise to the level of our thoughts if you would be gladdened by them, and share our feelings, if you would recognize our presence."

This, then, is what you have to do, and I admit that it is much. You must, in a word, love these people, if you are to be among them. No ambition is of any use. They scorn your ambition. You must love them, and show your love in these two following ways.

I. First, by a true desire to be taught by them, and to enter into their thoughts. To enter into theirs, observe ; not to find your own expressed by them. If the person who wrote the book is not wiser than you, you need not read it ; if he be, he will think differently from you in many respects.

Very ready we are to say of a book, "How good this is—that's exactly what I think!" But the right feeling is, "How

strange that is! I never thought of that before, and yet I see
it is true ; or if I do not now, I hope I shall, some day." But
whether thus submissively or not, at least be sure that you go
to the author to get at *his* meaning, not to find yours. Judge
it afterwards, if you think yourself qualified to do so ; but as
certain it first. And be sure also, if the author is worth any.
thing, that you will not get at his meaning all at once ;—nay,
that at his whole meaning you will not for a long time arrive
in any wise. Not that he does not say what he means, and in
strong words too ; but he cannot say it all ; and what is more
strange, will not, but in a hidden way and in parables, in order that he may be sure you want it. I cannot quite see the
reason of this, nor analyse that cruel reticence in the breasts
of wise men which makes them always hide their deeper
thought. They do not give it to you by way of help, but of
reward, and will make themselves sure that you deserve it before they allow you to reach it. But it is the same with the
physical type of wisdom, gold. There seems, to you and me,
no reason why the electric forces of the earth should not carry
whatever there is of gold within it at once to the mountain
tops, so that kings and people might know that all the gold
they could get was there ; and without any trouble of digging, or anxiety, or chance, or waste of time, cut it away, and
coin as much as they needed. But Nature does not manage
it so. She puts it in little fissures in the earth, nobody knows
where : you may dig long and find none ; you must dig painfully to find any.

　　And it is just the same with men's best wisdom. When
you come to a good book, you must ask yourself, "Am I in-
clined to work as an Australian miner would? Are my pickaxes and shovels in good order, and am I in good trim myself,
my sleeves well up to the elbow, and my breath good, and
my temper?" And, keeping the figure a little longer, even
at cost of tiresomeness, for it is a thoroughly useful one, the
metal you are in search of being the author's mind or meaning, his words are as the rock which you have to crush and
smelt in order to get at it. And your pickaxes are your own
care, wit, and learning ; your smelting-furnace is your own

thoughtful soul. Do not hope to get at any good author's meaning without those tools and that fire ; often you will need sharpest, finest chiselling, and patientest fusing, before you can gather one grain of the metal.

And, therefore, first of all, I tell you, earnestly and authoritatively, (I *know* I am right in this,) you must get into the habit of looking intensely at words, and assuring yourself of their meaning, syllable by syllable—nay letter by letter. For though it is only by reason of the opposition of letters in the function of signs, to sounds in functions of signs, that the study of books is called "literature," and that a man versed in it is called, by the consent of nations, a man of letters instead of a man of books, or of words, you may yet connect with that accidental nomenclature this real principle ;—that you might read all the books in the British Museum (if you could live long enough), and remain an utterly "illiterate," uneducated person ; but that if you read ten pages of a good book, letter by letter,—that is to say, with real accuracy,—you are for evermore in some measure an educated person. The entire difference between education and non-education (as regards the merely intellectual part of it), consists in this accuracy. A well-educated gentleman may not know many languages,—may not be able to speak any but his own,—may have read very few books. But whatever language he knows, he knows precisely ; whatever word he pronounces he pronounces rightly ; above all, he is learned in the *peerage* of words ; knows the words of true descent and ancient blood at a glance, from words of modern canaille ; remembers all their ancestry—their inter-marriages, distantest relationships, and the extent to which they were admitted, and offices they held, among the national noblesse of words at any time, and in any country. But an uneducated person may know by memory any number of languages, and talk them all, and yet truly know not a word of any,—not a word even of his own. An ordinarily clever and sensible seaman will be able to make his way ashore at most ports ; yet he has only to speak a sentence of any language to be known for an illiterate person : so also the accent, or turn of expression of a single sentence will at once mark a scholar. And this is so strongly felt, so conclusively admitted by educated persons, that a false accent or a mistaken syllable is enough, in the parliament of any civilized nation, to assign to a man a certain degree of inferior standing for ever. And this is right ; but it is a pity that the accuracy insisted on is not greater, and required to a serious purpose. It is right that a false Latin quantity should excite a smile in the House of Commons ; but it is wrong that a false English meaning should *not* excite a frown there. Let the accent of words be watched, by all means, but let their meaning be watched more closely still, and fewer will do the work. A few words well chosen and well distinguished, will do work that a thousand cannot, when every one is acting, equivocally, in the function of another. Yes ; and words, if they are not watched, will do deadly work sometimes. There are masked words droning and skulking about us in Europe just now,— (there never were so many, owing to the spread of a shallow, blotching, blundering, infectious "information," or rather deformation, everywhere, and to the teaching of catechisms and phrases at schools instead of human meanings)—there are masked words abroad, I say, which nobody understands, but which everybody uses, and most people will also fight for, live for, or even die for, fancying they mean this, or that, or the other, of things dear to them : for such words wear chamæleon cloaks—"groundlion" cloaks, of the colour of the ground of any man's fancy : on that ground they lie in wait, and rend him with a spring from it. There were never creatures of prey so mischievous, never diplomatists so cunning, never poisoners so deadly, as these masked words ; they are the unjust stewards of all men's ideas : whatever fancy or favourite instinct a man most cherishes, he gives to his favourite masked word to take care of for him ; the word at last comes to have an infinite power over him,—you cannot get at him but by its ministry. And in languages so mongrel in breed as the English, there is a fatal power of equivocation put into men's hands, almost whether they will or no, in being able to use Greek or Latin forms for a word when they want it to be respectable, and Saxon or otherwise common forms

when they want to discredit it. What a singular and salutary
effect, for instance, would be produced on the minds of people who are in the habit of taking the Form of the words
they live by, for the Power of which those words tell them, if
we always either retained, or refused, the Greek form " bib-
los," or " biblion," as the right expression for "book"—instead of employing it only in the one instance in which we
wish to give dignity to the idea, and translating it everywhere
else. How wholesome it would be for the many simple persons who worship the Letter of God's Word instead of its
Spirit, (just as other idolaters worship His picture instead of
His presence,) if, in such places (for instance) as Acts xix. 19
we retained the Greek expression, instead of translating it,
and they had to read—"Many of them also which used curious arts, brought their Bibles together, and burnt them before all men ; and they counted the price of them, and found
it fifty thousand pieces of silver!" Or if, on the other hand,
we translated instead of retaining it, and always spoke of
" The Holy Book," instead of " Holy Bible," it might come
into more heads than it does at present that the Word of
God, by which the heavens were, of old, and by which they
are now kept in store,* cannot be made a present of to anybody in morocco binding ; nor sown on any wayside by help
either of steam plough or steam press ; but is nevertheless
being offered to us daily, and by us with contumely refused ;
and sown in us daily, and by us as instantly as may be,
choked.

So, again, consider what effect has been produced on the
English vulgar mind by the use of the sonorous Latin form
"damno," in translating the Greek κατακρίνω, when people
charitably wish to make it forcible ; and the substitution of
the temperate " condemn " for it, when they choose to keep
it gentle. And what notable sermons have been preached by
illiterate clergymen on—"He that believeth not shall be
damned ; " though they would shrink with horror from translating Heb. xi. 7, "The saving of his house, by which he
damned the world ;" or John viii. 12, "Woman, hath no man

* 2 Peter iii. 5–7.

damned thee? She saith, No man, Lord. Jesus answered her, Neither do I damn thee : go and sin no more." And divisions in the mind of Europe, which have cost seas of blood, and in the defence of which the noblest souls of men have been cast away in frantic desolation, countless as forest leaves —though, in the heart of them, founded on deeper causes— have nevertheless been rendered practicably possible, namely, by the European adoption of the Greek word for a public meeting, to give peculiar respectability to such meetings, when held for religious purposes ; and other collateral equivocations, such as the vulgar English one of using the word "priest" as a contraction for "presbyter."

Now, in order to deal with words rightly, this is the habit you must form. Nearly every word in your language has been first a word of some other language—of Saxon, German, French, Latin, or Greek (not to speak of eastern and primitive dialects). And many words have been all these ;—that is to say, have been Greek first, Latin next, French or German next, and English last : undergoing a certain change of sense and use on the lips of each nation ; but retaining a deep vital meaning which all good scholars feel in employing them, even at this day. If you do not know the Greek alphabet, learn it ; young or old—girl or boy—whoever you may be, if you think of reading seriously (which, of course, implies that you have some leisure at command), learn your Greek alphabet ; then get good dictionaries of all these languages, and whenever you are in doubt about a word, hunt it down patiently. Read Max Müller's lectures thoroughly, to begin with ; and, after that, never let a word escape you that looks suspicious. It is severe work ; but you will find it, even at first, interesting, and at last, endlessly amusing. And the general gain to your character, in power and precision, will be quite incalculable.

Mind, this does not imply knowing, or trying to know, Greek, or Latin, or French. It takes a whole life to learn any language perfectly. But you can easily ascertain the meanings through which the English word has passed ; and those which in a good writer's work it must still bear.

And now, merely for example's sake, I will, with your permission, read a few lines of a true book with you, carefully;
and see what will come out of them. I will take a book perfectly known to you all; No English words are more familiar
to us, yet nothing perhaps has been less read with sincerity
I will take these few following lines of Lycidas:

> " Last came, and last did go,
>   The pilot of the Galilean lake ;
>   Two massy keys he bore of metals twain,
>   (The golden opes, the iron shuts amain),
>   He shook his mitred locks, and stern bespake,
>   How well could I have spar'd for thee, young swain,
>   Enow of such as for their bellies' sake
>   Creep and intrude, and climb into the fold :
>   Of other care they little reckoning make,
>   Than how to scramble at the shearers' feast,
>   And shove away the worthy bidden guest ;
>   Blind mouths ! that scarce themselves know how to hold
>   A sheep-hook, or have learn'd aught else, the least
>   That to the faithful herdsman's art belongs !
>   What recks it them ? What need they ? They are sped ;
>   And when they list, their lean and flashy songs
>   Grate on their scrannel pipes of wretched straw ;
>   The hungry sheep look up, and are not fed,
>   But, swoln with wind, and the rank mist they draw,
>   Rot inwardly, and foul contagion spread ;
>   Besides what the grim wolf with privy paw
>   Daily devours apace, and nothing said."

Let us think over this passage, and examine its words.

First, is it not singular to find Milton assigning to St. Peter,
not only his full episcopal function, but the very types of it
which Protestants usually refuse most passionately? His
" mitred" locks ! Milton was no Bishop-lover; how comes
St. Peter to be " mitred ? " " Two massy keys he bore." Is
this, then, the power of the keys claimed by the Bishops of
Rome, and is it acknowledged here by Milton only in a poeti
cal licence, for the sake of its picturesqueness, that he may
get the gleam of the golden keys to help his effect? Do not
think it. Great men do not play stage tricks with doctrines
of life and death : only little men do that. Milton means what

he says ; and means it with his might too—is going to put the
whole strength of his spirit presently into the saying of it.
For though not a lover of false bishops, he *was* a lover of true
ones ; and the Lake-pilot is here, in his thoughts, the type
and head of true episcopal power. For Milton reads that
text, "I will give unto thee the keys of the kingdom of
Heaven" quite honestly. Puritan though he be, he would not
blot it out of the book because there have been bad bishops ;
nay, in order to understand him, we must understand that
verse first ; it will not do to eye it askance, or whisper it under
our breath, as if it were a weapon of an adverse sect. It is a
solemn, universal assertion, deeply to be kept in mind by all
sects. But perhaps we shall be better able to reason on it if
we go on a little farther, and come back to it. For clearly,
this marked insistance on the power of the true episcopate is
to make us feel more weightily what is to be charged against
the false claimants of episcopate ; or generally, against false
claimants of power and rank in the body of the clergy ; they
who, "for their bellies' sake, creep, and intrude, and climb
into the fold."

Do not think Milton uses those three words to fill up his
verse, as a loose writer would. He needs all the three ; specially those three, and no more than those—"creep," and
"intrude," and "climb ;" no other words would or could
serve the turn, and no more could be added. For they exhaustively comprehend the three classes, correspondent to the
three characters, of men who dishonestly seek ecclesiastical
power. First, those who "*creep*" into the fold ; who do not
care for office, nor name, but for secret influence, and do all
things occultly and cunningly, consenting to any servility of
office or conduct, so only that they may intimately discern,
and unawares direct, the minds of men. Then those who
"intrude" (thrust, that is) themselves into the fold, who by
natural insolence of heart, and stout eloquence of tongue, and
fearlessly perseverant self-assertion, obtain hearing and authority with the common crowd. Lastly, those who "climb," who
by labor and learning, both stout and sound, but selfishly ex-
rted in the cause of their own ambition, gain high dignities

and authorities, and become "lords over the heritage," though not "ensamples to the flock."

Now go on :—

> " Of other care they little reckoning make,
>   Than how to scramble at the shearers' feast.
>   *Blind mouths—*"

I pause again, for this is a strange expression ; a broken metaphor, one might think, careless and unscholarly.

Not so : its very audacity and pithiness are intended to make us look close at the phrase and remember it. Those two monosyllables express the precisely accurate contraries of right character, in the two great offices of the Church—those of bishop and pastor.

A Bishop means a person who sees.

A Pastor means one who feeds.

The most unbishoply character a man can have is therefore to be Blind.

The most unpastoral is, instead of feeding, to want to be fed,—to be a Mouth.

Take the two reverses together, and you have "blind mouths." We may advisably follow out this idea a little. Nearly all the evils in the Church have arisen from bishops desiring *power* more than *light*. They want authority, not outlook. Whereas their real office is not to rule ; though it may be vigorously to exhort and rebuke ; it is the king's office to rule ; the bishop's office is to *oversee* the flock ; to number it, sheep by sheep ; to be ready always to give full account of it. Now it is clear he cannot give account of the souls, if he has not so much as numbered the bodies of his flock. The first thing, therefore, that a bishop has to do is at least to put himself in a position in which, at any moment, he can obtain the history from childhood of every living soul in his diocese, and of its present state. Down in that back street, Bill, and Nancy, knocking each other's teeth out !— Does the bishop know all about it ? Has he his eye upon them ? Has he *had* his eye upon them ? Can he circumstantially explain to us how Bill got into the habit of beating

Nancy about the head? If he cannot, he is no bishop,
though he had a mitre as high as Salisbury steeple; he is no
bishop,—he has sought to be at the helm instead of the mast-
head; he has no sight of things. "Nay," you say, it is not
his duty to look after Bill in the back street. What! the
fat sheep that have full fleeces—you think it is only those he
should look after, while (go back to your Milton) "the hungry
sheep look up, and are not fed, besides what the grim wolf,
with privy paw" (bishops knowing nothing about it) "daily
devours apace, and nothing said?"

"But that's not our idea of a bishop."* Perhaps not; but
it was St. Paul's; and it was Milton's. They may be right, or
we may be; but we must not think we are reading either one
or the other by putting our meaning into their words.

I go on.

"But, swollen with wind, and the rank mist they draw."

This is to meet the vulgar answer that "if the poor are not
looked after in their bodies, they are in their souls; they have
spiritual food."

And Milton says, "They have no such thing as spiritual
food; they are only swollen with wind." At first you may
think that is a coarse type, and an obscure one. But again,
it is a quite literally accurate one. Take up your Latin and
Greek dictionaries, and find out the meaning of "Spirit." It
is only a contraction of the Latin word "breath," and an indistinct translation of the Greek word for "wind." The same
word is used in writing, "The wind bloweth where it listeth;"
and in writing, "So is every one that is born of the Spirit;"
born of the *breath*, that is; for it means the breath of God, in
soul and body. We have the true sense of it in our words
"inspiration" and "expire." Now, there are two kinds of
breath with which the flock may be filled; God's breath, and
man's. The breath of God is health, and life, and peace to
them, as the air of heaven is to the flocks on the hills; but
man's breath—the word which *he* calls spiritual,—is disease
and contagion to them, as the fog of the fen. They rot in-

* Compare the 13th Letter in *Time and Tide*

wardly with it; they are puffed up by it, as a dead body by the vapours of its own decomposition. This is literally true of all false religious teaching; the first and last, and fatalest sign of it is that "puffing up." Your converted children, who teach their parents; your converted convicts, who teach honest men; your converted dunces, who, having lived in cretinous stupefaction half their lives, suddenly awakening to the fact of there being a God, fancy themselves therefore His peculiar people and messengers; your sectarians of every species, small and great, Catholic or Protestant, of high church or low, in so far as they think themselves exclusively in the right and others wrong; and pre-eminently, in every sect, those who hold that men can be saved by thinking rightly instead of doing rightly, by word instead of act, and wish instead of work:—these are the true fog children—clouds, these, without water; bodies, these, of putrescent vapour and skin, without blood or flesh: blown bag-pipes for the fiends to pipe with—corrupt, and corrupting,—" Swollen with wind, and the rank mist they draw."

Lastly, let us return to the lines respecting the power of the keys, for now we can understand them. Note the difference between Milton and Dante in their interpretation of this power: for once, the latter is weaker in thought; he supposes *both* the keys to be of the gate of heaven; one is of gold, the other of silver: they are given by St. Peter to the sentinel angel; and it is not easy to determine the meaning either of the substances of the three steps of the gate, or of the two keys. But Milton makes one, of gold, the key of heaven; the other, of iron, the key of the prison, in which the wicked teachers are to be bound who "have taken away the key of knowledge, yet entered not in themselves."

We have seen that the duties of bishop and pastor are to see, and feed; and, of all who do so, it is said, "He that watereth, shall be watered also himself." But the reverse is truth also. He that watereth not, shall be *withered* himself, and he that seeth not, shall himself be shut out of sight,— shut into the perpetual prison-house. And that prison opens here, as well as hereafter: he who is to be bound in heaven must first be bound on earth. That command to the strong angels, of which the rock-apostle is the image, "Take him, and bind him hand and foot, and cast him out," issues, in its measure, against the teacher, for every help withheld, and for every truth refused, and for every falsehood enforced ; so that he is more strictly fettered the more he fetters, and farther outcast, as he more and more misleads, till at last the bars of the iron cage close upon him, and as "the golden opes, the iron shuts amain."

We have got something out of the lines, I think, and much more is yet to be found in them ; but we have done enough by way of example of the kind of word-by-word examination of your author which is rightly called "reading ;" watching every accent and expression, and putting ourselves always in the author's place, annihilating our own personality, and seeking to enter into his, so as to be able assuredly to say, "Thus Milton thought," not "Thus I thought, in mis-reading Milton." And by this process you will gradually come to attach less weight to your own "Thus I thought" at other times. You will begin to perceive that what *you* thought was a matter of no serious importance ;—that your thoughts on any subject are not perhaps the clearest and wisest that could be arrived at thereupon :—in fact, that unless you are a very singular person, you cannot be said to have any "thoughts" at all ; that you have no materials for them, in any serious matters ; *—no right to "think," but only to try to learn more of the facts. Nay, most probably all your life (unless, as I said, you are a singular person) you will have no legitimate right to an "opinion" on any business, except that instantly under your hand. What must of necessity be done, you can always find out, beyond question, how to do. Have you a house to keep in order, a commodity to sell, a field to plough, a ditch to cleanse ? There need be no two opinions about these proceedings ; it is at your peril if you have not much more than an "opinion" on the way to manage such matters.

* Modern "Education" for the most part signifies giving people the faculty of thinking wrong on every conceivable subject of importance to them.

And also, outside of your own business, there are one or two
subjects on which you are bound to have but one opinion.
That roguery and lying are objectionable, and are instantly
to be flogged out of the way whenever discovered ;—that
covetousness and love of quarrelling are dangerous dispositions even in children, and deadly dispositions in men and
nations ;—that in the end, the God of heaven and earth loves
active, modest, and kind people, and hates idle, proud, greedy,
and cruel ones ;—on these general facts you are bound to
have but one and that a very strong, opinion. For the rest,
respecting religions, governments, sciences, arts, you will find
that, on the whole, you can know NOTHING,—judge nothing ;
that the best you can do, even though you may be a well-
educated person, is to be silent, and strive to be wiser every
day, and to understand a little more of the thoughts of others,
which so soon as you try to do honestly, you will discover
that the thoughts even of the wisest are very little more than
pertinent questions. To put the difficulty into a clear shape,
and exhibit to you the grounds for *in*decision, that is all they
can generally do for you !—and well for them and for us, if
indeed they are able "to mix the music with our thoughts,
and sadden us with heavenly doubts." This writer, from
whom I have been reading to you, is not among the first or
wisest : he sees shrewdly as far as he sees, and therefore it is
easy to find out his full meaning ; but with the greater men,
you cannot fathom their meaning ; they do not even wholly
measure it themselves,—it is so wide. Suppose I had asked
you, for instance, to seek for Shakespeare's opinion, instead of
Milton's, on this matter of Church authority?—or for Dante's?
Have any of you, at this instant, the least idea what either
thought about it ? Have you ever balanced the scene with
the bishops in Richard III. against the character of Cranmer ?
the description of St. Francis and St. Dominic against that
of him who made Virgil wonder to gaze upon him,—"disteso,
tanto vilmente, nell' eterno esilio ;" or of him whom Dante
stood beside, "come 'l frate che confessa lo perfido assassin ?" * Shakespeare and Alighieri knew men better than

* Inf. xix. 71 ; xxiii. 117.

most of us, I presume ! They were both in the midst of the main struggle between the temporal and spiritual powers. They had an opinion, we may guess? But where is it? Bring it into court ! Put Shakespeare's or Dante's creed into articles, and send *that* up into the Ecclesiastical Courts !

You will not be able, I tell you again, for many and many a day, to come at the real purposes and teaching of these great men ; but a very little honest study of them will enable you to perceive that what you took for your own "judgment" was mere chance prejudice, and drifted, helpless, entangled weed of castaway thought : nay, you will see that most men's minds are indeed little better than rough heath wilderness, neglected and stubborn, partly barren, partly overgrown with pestilent brakes and venomous wind-sown herbage of evil surmise ; that the first thing you have to do for them, and yourself, is eagerly and scornfully to set fire to *this ;* burn all the jungle into wholesome ash heaps, and then plough and sow. All the true literary work before you, for life, must begin with obedience to that order, "Break up your fallow ground, and *sow not among thorns.*"

II. Having then faithfully listened to the great teachers, that you may enter into their Thoughts, you have yet this higher advance to make ;—you have to enter into their Hearts. As you go to them first for clear sight, so you must stay with them that you may share at last their just and mighty Passion. Passion, or "sensation." I am not afraid of the word ; still less of the thing. You have heard many outcries against sensation lately ; but, I can tell you, it is not less sensation we want, but more. The ennobling difference between one man and another,—between one animal and another,—is precisely in this, that one feels more than another. If we were sponges, perhaps sensation might not be easily got for us ; if we were earth-worms, liable at every instant to be cut in two by the spade, perhaps too much sensation might not be good for us. But, being human creatures, *it is* good for us ; nay, we are only human in so far as we are sensit: and our honour is precisely in proportion to our passion.

You know I said of that great and pure society of the dead, that it would allow "no vain or vulgar person to enter there." What do you think I meant by a "vulgar" person? What do you yourselves mean by "vulgarity?" You will find it a fruitful subject of thought; but, briefly, the essence of all vulgarity lies in want of sensation. Simple and innocent vulgarity is merely an untrained and undeveloped bluntness of body and mind; but in true inbred vulgarity, there is a deathful callousness, which, in extremity, becomes capable of every sort of bestial habit and crime, without fear, without pleasure, without horror, and without pity. It is in the blunt hand and the dead heart, in the diseased habit, in the hardened conscience, that men become vulgar; they are for ever vulgar, precisely in proportion as they are incapable of sympathy,—of quick understanding,—of all that, in deep insistance on the common, but most accurate term, may be called the "tact" or touch-faculty of body and soul; that tact which the Mimosa has in trees, which the pure woman has above all creatures;—fineness and fulness of sensation, beyond reason;—the guide and sanctifier of reason itself. Reason can but determine what is true:—it is the God-given passion of humanity which alone can recognize what God has made good.

We come then to the great concourse of the Dead, not merely to know from them what is True, but chiefly to feel with them what is Righteous. Now, to feel with them, we must be like them; and none of us can become that without pains. As the true knowledge is disciplined and tested knowledge,—not the first thought that comes,—so the true passion is disciplined and tested passion—not the first passion that comes. The first that come are the vain, the false, the treacherous; if you yield to them they will lead you wildly and far in vain pursuit, in hollow enthusiasm, till you have no true purpose and no true passion left. Not that any feeling possible to humanity is in itself wrong, but only wrong when undisciplined. Its nobility is in its force and justice; it is wrong when it is weak, and felt for paltry cause. There is a mean wonder as of a child who sees a juggler tossing golden balls, and this is base, if you will. But do you think that the wonder is ignoble, or the sensation less, with which every human soul is called to watch the golden balls of heaven tossed through the night by the Hand that made them? There is a mean curiosity, as of a child opening a forbidden door, or a servant prying into her master's business;—and a noble curiosity, questioning, in the front of danger, the source of the great river beyond the sand—the place of the great continents beyond the sea;—a nobler curiosity still, which questions of the source of the River of Life, and of the space of the Continent of Heaven,— things which "the angels desire to look into." So the anxiety is ignoble, with which you linger over the course and catastrophe of an idle tale; but do you think the anxiety is less, or greater, with which you watch, or *ought* to watch, the dealings of fate and destiny with the life of an agonized nation? Alas! is is the narrowness, selfishness, minuteness, of your sensation that you have to deplore in England at this day;—sensation which spends itself in bouquets and speeches; in revellings and junketings; in sham fights and gay puppet shows, while you can look on and see noble nations murdered, man by man, woman by woman, child by child, without an effort, or a tear.

I said "minuteness" and "selfishness" of sensation, but in a word, I ought to have said "injustice" or "unrighteousness" of sensation. For as in nothing is a gentleman better to be discerned from a vulgar person, so in nothing is a gentle nation (such nations have been) better to be discerned from a mob, than in this,—that their feelings are constant and just, results of due contemplation, and of equal thought. You can talk a mob into anything; its feelings may be—usually are—on the whole generous and right; but it has no foundation for them, no hold of them; you may tease or tickle it into any, at your pleasure; it thinks by infection, for the most part, catching a passion like a cold, and there is nothing so little that it will not roar itself wild about, when the fit is on;—nothing so great but it will forget in an hour, when the fit is past. But a gentleman's or a gentle nation's, passions are just, measured and continuous. A great nation, for instance, does not spend its entire national wits for a couple of months in weighing evidence of a single ruffian's having done a single murder ; and for a couple of years, see its own children murder each other by their thousands or tens of thousands a day, considering only what the effect is likely to be on the price of cotton, and caring nowise to determine which side of battle is in the wrong. Neither does a great nation send its poor little boys to jail for stealing six walnuts and allow its bankrupts to steal their hundreds or thousands with a bow, and its bankers, rich with poor men's savings, to close their doors " under circumstances over which they have no control," with a " by your leave ;" and large landed estates to be bought by men who have made their money by going with armed steamers up and down the China Seas, selling opium at the cannon's mouth, and altering, for the benefit of the foreign nation, the common highwayman's demand of "your money *or* your life," into that of "your money *and* your life." Neither does a great nation allow the lives of its innocent poor to be parched out of them by fog fever, and rotted out of them by dunghill plague, for the sake of sixpence a life extra per week to its landlords ; * and then debate,

---

* See the evidence in the Medical officer's report to the Privy Council, just published. There are suggestions in its preface which will make some stir among us, I fancy, respecting which let me note these points following :—

There are two theories on the subject of land now abroad, and in contention ; both false.

The first is that by Heavenly law, there have always existed, and must continue to exist, a certain number of hereditarily sacred persons, to whom the earth, air, and water of the world belong, as personal property ; of which earth, air and water these persons may, at their pleasure, permit, or forbid, the rest of the human race to eat, breathe, or to drink. This theory is not for many years longer tenable. The adverse theory is that a division of the land of the world among the mob of the world would immediately elevate the said mob into sacred personages ; that houses would then build themselves, and corn grow of itself ; and that everybody would be able to live, without doing any work for his living. This theory would also be found highly untenable in practice.

It will, however, require some rough experiments, and rougher catas-

with drivelling tears, and diabolical sympathies, whether it
ought not piously to save, and nursingly cherish, the lives of
its murderers. Also, a great nation having made up its mind
that hanging is quite the wholesomest process for its homicides in general, can yet with mercy distinguish between the
degrees of guilt in homicides ; and does not yelp like a pack
of frost-pinched wolf-cubs on the blood-track of an unhappy
crazed boy, or grey-haired clodpate Othello, " perplexed i' the
extreme," at the very moment that it is sending a Minister of
the Crown to make polite speeches to a man who is bayonet-
ing young girls in their father's sight, and killing noble youths
in cool blood, faster than a country butcher kills lambs in
spring. And, lastly, a great nation does not mock Heaven

trophes, even in this magnesium-lighted epoch, before the generality of
persons will be convinced that no law concerning anything, least of all
concerning land, for either holding or dividing it, or renting it high, or
renting it low, would be of the smallest ultimate use to the people, so
long as the general contest for life, and for the means of life, remains
one of mere brutal competition. That contest, in an unprincipled nation, will take one deadly form or another, whatever laws you make for
it. For instance, it would be an entirely wholesome law for England,
if it could be carried, that maximum limits should be assigned to incomes
according to classes ; and that every nobleman's income should be paid to
him as a fixed salary or pension by the nation ; and not squeezed by him
in a variable sum, at discretion, out of the tenants of his land. But if
you could get such a law passed to-morrow ; and if, which would be
farther necessary, you could fix the value of the assigned incomes by
making a given weight of pure wheat-flour legal tender for a given sum,
a twelve-month would not pass before another currency would have
been tacitly established, and the power of accumulative wealth would
have re-asserted itself in some other article, or some imaginary sign.
Forbid men to buy each other's lives for sovereigns, and they will for
shells, or slates. There is only one cure for public distress — and that is
public education, directed to make men thoughtful, merciful, and just.
There are, indeed, many laws conceivable which would gradually better and strengthen the national temper ; but, for the most part, they are
such as the national temper must be much bettered before it would bear.
A nation in its youth may be helped by laws, as a weak child by back-
boards, but when it is old, it cannot that way straighten its crooked
spine.

And besides, the problem of land, at its worst, is a bye one ; distribute the lth as you will, the principal question remains inexorable, —

and its Powers, by pretending belief in a revelation which as-
serts the love of money to be the root of *all* evil, and declaring,
at the same time, that it is actuated, and intends to be actuated,
in all chief national deeds and measures, by no other love.

My friends, I do not know why any of us should talk about
reading. We want some sharper discipline than that of reading ; but, at all events, be assured, we cannot read. No reading is possible for a people with its mind in this state. No
sentence of any great writer is intelligible to them. It is
simply and sternly impossible for the English public, at this
moment, to understand any thoughtful writing,—so incapable of thought has it become in its insanity of avarice. Happily, our disease is, as yet, little worse than this incapacity of

Who is to dig it ? Which of us, in brief words, is to do the hard and
dirty work for the rest—and for what pay ? Who is to do the pleasant
and clean work, and for what pay ? Who is to do no work, and for
what pay ? And there are curious moral and religious questions connected with these. How far is it lawful to suck a portion of the soul
out of a great many persons, in order to put the abstracted psychical
quantities together, and make one very beautiful or ideal soul ? If we had
to deal with mere blood, instead of spirit, and the thing might literally
be done (as it has been done with infants before now) so that it were possible, by taking a certain quantity of blood from the arms of a given
number of the mob, and putting it all into one person, to make a more
azure-blooded gentleman of him, the thing would of course be managed ;
but secretly, I should conceive. But now, because it is brain and soul
that we abstract, not visible blood, it can be done quite openly ; and we
live, we gentlemen, on delicatest prey, after the manner of weasels ;
that is to say, we keep a certain number of clowns digging and ditch-
ing, and generally stupefied, in order that we, being fed gratis, may have
all the thinking and feeling to ourselves. Yet there is a great deal to
be said for this. A highly-bred and trained English, French, Austrian
or Italian gentleman (much more a lady) is a great production ; a better
production than most statues ; being beautifully coloured as well as
shaped, and plus all the brains ; a glorious thing to look at, a wonderful
thing to talk to ; and you cannot have it, any more than a pyramid or a
church, but by sacrifice of much contributed life. And it is, perhaps,
better to build a beautiful human creature than a beautiful dome or
steeple, and more delightful to look up reverently to a creature far above
us, than to a wall ; only the beautiful human creature will have some
duties to do in return—duties of living belfry and rampart—of which
presently.

thought; it is not corruption of the inner nature; we ring true
still, when anything strikes home to us; and though the idea
that everything should "pay" has infected our every purpose
so deeply, that even when we would play the good Samaritan,
we never take out our twopence and give them to the host,
without saying, "When I come again, thou shalt give me
fourpence," there is a capacity of noble passion left in our
hearts' core.   We show it in our work—in our war,—even in
those unjust domestic affections which make us furious at a
small private wrong, while we are polite to a boundless public
one : we are still industrious to the last hour of the day,
though we add the gambler's fury to the labourer's patience ;
we are still brave to the death, though incapable of discerning true cause for battle, and are still true in affection to our
own flesh, to the death, as the sea-monsters are, and the rock-
eagles.   And there is hope for a nation while this can be still
said of it.   As long as it holds its life in its hand, ready to
give it for its honour (though a foolish honour), for its love
(though a selfish love), and for its business (though a base
business), there is hope for it.   But hope only ; for this instinctive, reckless virtue cannot last.   No nation can last,
which has made a mob of itself, however generous at heart.
It must discipline its passions, and direct them, or they will
discipline it, one day, with scorpion whips.   Above all, a nation cannot last as a money-making mob : it cannot with im-
punity,—it cannot with existence,—go on despising literature,
despising science, despising art, despising nature, despising
compassion, and concentrating its soul on Pence.   Do you
think these are harsh or wild words?   Have patience with me
but a little longer.   I will prove their truth to you, clause by
clause.

   I.   I say first we have despised literature.   What do we, as
a nation, care about books?   How much do you think we
spend altogether on our libraries, public or private, as compared with what we spend on our horses?   If a man spends
lavishly on his library, you call him mad—a biblio-maniac.
But you never call any one a horse-maniac, though men ruin
themselves every day by their horses, and you do not hear of

people ruining themselves by their books. Or, to go lower still, how much do you think the contents of the book-shelves of the United Kingdom, public and private, would fetch, as compared with the contents of its wine-cellars? What position would its expenditure on literature take, as compared with its expenditure on luxurious eating? We talk of food for the mind, as of food for the body : now a good book contains such food inexhaustibly ; it is a provision for life, and for the best part of us ; yet how long most people would look at the best book before they would give the price of a large turbot for it ! Though there have been men who have pinched their stomachs and bared their backs to buy a book, whose libraries were cheaper to them, I think, in the end, than most men's dinners are. We are few of us put to such trial, and more the pity ; for, indeed, a precious thing is all the more precious to us if it has been won by work or economy ; and if public libraries were half as costly as public dinners, or books cost the tenth part of what bracelets do, even foolish men and women might sometimes suspect there was good in reading, as well as in munching and sparkling ; whereas the very cheapness of literature is making even wise people forget that if a book is worth reading, it is worth buying. No book is worth anything which is not worth *much ;* nor is it serviceable, until it has been read, and reread, and loved, and loved again ; and marked, so that you can refer to the passages you want in it, as a soldier can seize the weapon he needs in an armoury, or a housewife bring the spice she needs from her store. Bread of flour is good : but there is bread, sweet as honey, if we would eat it, in a good book ; and the family must be poor indeed which, once in their lives, cannot, for such multipliable barley-loaves, pay their baker's bill. We call ourselves a rich nation, and we are filthy and foolish enough to thumb each other's books out of circulating libraries !

II. I say we have despised science. "What!" (you exclaim) "are we not foremost in all discovery, and is not the whole world giddy by reason, or unreason, of our inventions?" Yes ; but do you suppose that is national work? That work is all done in spite of the nation ; by private people's zeal and money. We are glad enough, indeed, to make our profit of science; we snap up anything in the way of a scientific bone that has meat on it, eagerly enough; but if the scientific man comes for a bone or a crust to *us*, that is another story. What have we publicly done for science? We are obliged to know what o'clock it is, for the safety of our ships, and there-fore we pay for an observatory; and we allow ourselves, in the person of our Parliament, to be annually tormented into doing something, in a slovenly way, for the British Museum; sullenly apprehending that to be a place for keeping stuffed birds in, to amuse our children. If anybody will pay for their own telescope, and resolve another nebula, we cackle over the discernment as if it were our own; if one in ten thousand of our hunting squires suddenly perceives that the earth was indeed made to be something else than a portion for foxes, and burrows in it himself, and tells us where the gold is, and where the coals, we understand that there is some use in that; and very properly knight him: but is the accident of his having found out how to employ himself usefully any credit to *us*? (The negation of such discovery among his brother squires may perhaps be some *dis*credit to us, if we would consider of it.) But if you doubt these gen-eralities, here is one fact for us all to meditate upon, illus-trative of our love of science. Two years ago there was a collection of the fossils of Solenhofen to be sold in Bavaria; the best in existence, containing many specimens unique for perfectness, and one, unique as an example of a species (a whole kingdom of unknown living creatures being announced by that fossil). This collection, of which the mere market worth, among private buyers, would probably have been some thousand or twelve hundred pounds, was offered to the Eng-lish nation for seven hundred: but we would not give seven hundred, and the whole series would have been in the Munich Museum at this moment, if Professor Owen * had not, with

---

* I state this fact without Professor Owen's permission: which of course he could not with propriety have granted, had I asked it; but I consider it so important that the public should be aware of the fact that I do what seems to be right though rude.

loss of his own time, and patient tormenting of the British public in person of its representatives, got leave to give four hundred pounds at once, and himself become answerable for the other three ! which the said public will doubtless pay him eventually, but sulkily, and caring nothing about the matter all the while ; only always ready to cackle if any credit comes of it. Consider, I beg of you, arithmetically, what this fact means. Your annual expenditure for public purposes (a third of it for military apparatus) is at least fifty millions. Now 700*l* is to 50,000,000*l*. roughly, as seven pence to two thousand pounds. Suppose then, a gentlemen of unknown income, but whose wealth was to be conjectured from the fact that he spent two thousand a year on his park-walls and footmen only, professes himself fond of science ; and that one of his servants comes eagerly to tell him that an unique collection of fossils, giving clue to a new era of creation, is to be had for the sum of seven pence sterling ; and that the gentleman, who is fond of science, and spends two thousand a year on his park, answers, after keeping his servant waiting several months, " Well ! I'll give you four pence for them, if you will be answerable for the extra three pence yourself, till next year ! "

III. I say you have despised Art ! " What ! " you again answer, " have we not Art exhibitions, miles long ? and do we not pay thousands of pounds for single pictures ? and have we not Art schools and institutions, more than ever nation had before ? " Yes, truly, but all that is for the sake of the shop. You would fain sell canvas as well as coals, and crockery as well as iron ; you would take every other nation's bread out of its mouth if you could ; * not being able to do that, your ideal of life is to stand in the thoroughfares of the world, like Ludgate apprentices, screaming to every passer-by, " What d'ye lack ? " You know nothing of your own faculties or circumstances ; you fancy that, among your damp, flat, fields of clay, you can have as quick art-fancy as

---

* That was our real idea of " Free Trade "—" All the trade to my-self." You find now that by " competition " other people can manage to sell something as well as you—and now we call for Protection again. Wretches !

the Frenchman among his bronzed vines, or the Italian under his volcanic cliffs ;—that Art may be learned as book-keeping is, and when learned will give you more books to keep.   You care for pictures, absolutely, no more than you do for the bills pasted on your dead walls.   There is always room on the walls for the bills to be read,—never for the pictures to be seen.   You do not know what pictures you have (by repute) in the country, nor whether they are false or true, nor whether they are taken care of or not ; in foreign countries, you calmly see the noblest existing pictures in the world rotting in abandoned wreck—(and, in Venice, with the Austrian guns deliberately pointed at the palaces containing them), and if you heard that all the Titians in Europe were made sand-bags to-morrow on the Austrian forts, it would not trouble you so much as the chance of a brace or two of game less in your own bags in a day's shooting.   That is your national love of Art.

IV. You have despised nature ; that is to say, all the deep and sacred sensations of natural scenery.   The French revolutionists made stables of the cathedrals of France ; you have made racecourses of the cathedrals of the earth.   Your *one* conception of pleasure is to drive in railroad carriages round their aisles, and eat off their altars.*   You have put a railroad bridge over the fall of Schaffhausen.   You have tunnelled the cliffs of Lucerne by Tell's chapel ; you have destroyed the Clarens shore of the Lake of Geneva; there is not a quiet valley in England that you have not filled with bellowing fire ; there is no particle left of English land which you have not trampled coal ashes into—nor any foreign city in which the spread of your presence is not marked among its fair old streets and happy gardens by a consuming white leprosy of new hotels and perfumers' shops : the Alps themselves, which your own poets used to love so reverently, you look upon as soaped poles in a bear-garden, which you set

---

* I meant that the beautiful places of the world—Switzerland, Italy, South Germany, and so on—are, indeed, the truest cathedrals—places to be reverent in, and to worship in ; and that we only care to drive through them : and to eat and drink at their most sacred places.

yourselves to climb, and slide down again, with "shrieks of delight." When you are past shrieking, having no human articulate voice to say you are glad with, you fill the quietude of their valleys with gunpowder blasts, and rush home, red with cutaneous eruption of conceit, and voluble with con- vulsive hiccough of self-satisfaction. I think nearly the two sorrowfullest spectacles I have ever seen in humanity, taking the deep inner significance of them, are the English mobs in the valley of Chamouni, amusing themselves with firing rusty howitzers ; and the Swiss vintagers of Zurich expressing their Christian thanks for the gift of the vine, by assembling in knots in the "towers of the vineyards," and slowly loading and firing horse-pistols from morning till evening. It is pitiful to have dim conceptions of beauty ; more pitiful, it seems to me, to have conceptions like these, of mirth.

Lastly. You despise compassion. There is no need of words of mine for proof of this. I will merely print one of the newspaper paragraphs which I am in the habit of cutting out and throwing into my store-drawer ; here is one from a *Daily Telegraph* of an early date this year ; date which though by me carelessly left unmarked, is easily discoverable, for on the back of the slip there is the announcement that "yesterday the seventh of the special services of this year was performed by the Bishop of Ripon in St. Paul's ; " and there is a pretty piece of modern political economy besides, worth preserving note of, I think, so I print it in the note below.* But my business is with the main paragraph, relating one of such facts as happen now daily, which, by chance, has taken a form in which it came before the coroner. I will print the paragraph in

---

* It is announced that an arrangement has being concluded between the Ministry of Finance and the Bank of Credit for the payment of the eleven millions which the State has to pay to the National Bank by the 14th inst. This sum will be raised as follows :—The eleven commercial members of the committee of the Bank of Credit will each borrow a million of florins for three months of this bank, which will accept their bills, which again will be discounted by the National Bank. By this arrangement *the National Bank will itself furnish the funds with which it will be paid.*

red.* Be sure, the facts themselves are written in that color, in a book which we shall all of us, literate or illiterate, have to read our page of, some day.

"An inquiry was held on Friday by Mr. Richards, deputy coroner, at the White Horse Tavern, Christ Church, Spital-fields, respecting the death of Michael Collins, aged 58 years. Mary Collins, a miserable-looking woman, said that she lived with the deceased and his son in a room at 2, Cobb's court, Christ Church. Deceased was a 'translator' of boots. Wit-ness went out and bought old boots; deceased and his son made them into good ones, and then witness sold them for what she could get at the shops, which was very little indeed. Deceased and his son used to work night and day to try and get a little bread and tea, and pay for the room (2s. a week), so as to keep the home together. On Friday night week de-ceased got up from his bench and began to shiver. He threw down the boots, saying, 'Somebody else must finish them when I am gone, for I can do no more.' There was no fire, and he said, 'I would be better if I was warm.' Witness therefore took two pairs of translated boots† to sell at the shop, but she could only get 14d. for the two pairs, for the people at the shop said, 'We must have our profit.' Witness got 14lb. of coal, and a little tea and bread. Her son sat up the whole night to make the 'translations,' to get money, but deceased died on Saturday morning. The family never had enough to eat.—Coroner: 'It seems to me deplorable that you did not go into the workhouse.'—Witness: 'We wanted the comforts of our little home.' A juror asked what the com-forts were, for he only saw a little straw in the corner of the room, the windows of which were broken. The witness began to cry, and said that they had a quilt and other little things. The deceased said he never would go into the workhouse. In summer, when the season was good, they sometimes made as much as 10s. profit in the week. They then always saved

---

* The following extract was printed in *red* in the English edition.

† One of the things which we must very resolutely enforce, for the good of all classes, in our future arrangements, must be that they wear no "translated" articles of dress. See the preface.

towards the next week, which was generally a bad one. In winter they made not half so much. For three years they had been getting from bad to worse.—Cornelius Collins said that he had assisted his father since 1847. They used to work so far into the night that both nearly lost their eyesight. Witness now had a film over his eyes. Five years ago deceased applied to the parish for aid. The relieving officer gave him a 4lb. loaf, and told him if he came again he should 'get the stones.'* That disgusted deceased, and he would have nothing to do with them since. They got worse and worse until last Friday week, when they had not even a halfpenny to buy a candle. Deceased then lay down on the straw, and said he could not live till morning.—A juror : You are dying of starvation yourself, and you ought to go into the house until the summer. Witness : If we went in we should die.

* This abbrevaition of the penalty of useless labour is curiously coincident in verbal form with a certain passage which some of us may remember. It may perhaps be well to preserve beside this paragraph another cutting out of my store-drawer, from the *Morning Post,* of about a parallel date, Friday, March 10th, 1865 :—" The *salons* of Mme. C——, who did the honours with clever imitative grace and elegance, were crowded with princes, dukes, marquises, and counts—in fact, with the same *male* company as one meets at the parties of the Princess Metternich and Madame Drouyn de Lhuys. Some English peers and members of Parliament were present, and appeared to enjoy the animated and dazzlingly improper scene. On the second floor the supper tables were loaded with every delicacy of the season. That your readers may form some idea of the dainty fare of the Parisian demi monde, I copy the menu of the supper, which was served to all the guests (about 200) seated at four o'clock. Choice Yquem, Johannisberg, Laffitte, Tokay, and Champagne of the finest vintages were served most lavishly through out the morning. After supper dancing was resumed with increased animation, and the ball terminated with a *chaîne diabolique* and a *can-can d'enfer* at seven in the morning. (Morning service—' Ere the fresh lawns appeared, under the opening eyelids of the Morn.—') Here is the menu : —' Consommé de volaille à la Bagration ; 16 hors-d'œuvres variés. Bouchées à la Talleyrand. Saumons froids, sauce Ravigote. Filets de bœuf en Bellevue, timbales milanaises chaudfroid de gibier. Dindes truffées. Pâtés de foies gras, buissons d'écrevisses, salades vénétiennes, gelées blanches aux fruits, gateaux mancini, parisiens et parisiennes. Fromages glacés Ananas. Dessert.' "

When we come out in the summer we should be like people dropped from the sky. No one would know us, and we would not have even a room. I could work now if I had food, for my sight would get better. Dr. G. P. Walker said deceased died from syncope, from exhaustion, from want of food. The deceased had had no bedclothes. For four months he had had nothing but bread to eat. There was not a particle of fat in the body. There was no disease, but if there had been medical attendance, he might have survived the syncope or fainting. The coroner having remarked upon the painful nature of the case, the jury returned the following verdict, 'That deceased died from exhaustion from want of food and the common necessaries of life; also through want of medical aid.'"

"Why would witness not go into the workhouse?" you ask. Well, the poor seem to have a prejudice against the workhouse which the rich have not; for of course every one who takes a pension from Government goes into the workhouse on a grand scale : only the workhouses for the rich do not involve the idea of work, and should be called playhouses. But the poor like to die independently, it appears; perhaps if we made the play-houses for them pretty and pleasant enough, or gave them their pensions at home, and allowed them a little introductory peculation with the public money, their minds might be reconciled to it. Meantime, here are the facts : we make our relief either so insulting to them, or so painful, that they rather die than take it at our hands ; or, for third alternative, we leave them so untaught and foolish that they starve like brute creatures, wild and dumb, not knowing what to do, or what to ask. I say, you despise compassion ; if you did not, such a newspaper paragraph would be as impossible in a Christian country as a deliberate assassination permitted in its public streets.* "Christian "

* I am heartily glad to see such a paper as the *Pall Mall Gazette* established ; for the power of the press in the hands of highly-educated men, in independent position, and of honest purpose, may indeed become all that it has been hitherto vainly vaunted to be. Its editor will therefore, I doubt not, pardon me, in that, by very reason of my respect

did I say? Alas, if we were but wholesomely un-Christian, it would be impossible: it is our imaginary Christianity that helps us to commit these crimes, for we revel and luxuriate in our faith, for the lewd sensation of it; dressing *it* up, like everything else, in fiction. The dramatic Christianity of the organ and aisle, of dawn-service and twilight-revival—the Christianity which we do not fear to mix the mockery of, pictorially, with our play about the devil, in our Satanellas,—Roberts,—Fausts, chanting hymns through traceried windows for back-ground effect, and artistically modulating the "Dio" through variation on variation of mimicked prayer: (while we distribute tracts, next day, for the benefit of uncultivated swearers, upon what we suppose to be the signification of the Third Commandment;)—this gas-lighted, and gas-inspired, Christianity, we are triumphant in, and draw back

for the journal, I do not let pass unnoticed an article in its third number, page 5, which was wrong in every word of it, with the intense wrongness which only an honest man can achieve who has taken a false turn of thought in the outset, and is following it, regardless of consequences. It contained at the end this notable passage:—

"The bread of affliction, and the water of affliction—aye, and the bedsteads and blankets of affliction, are the very utmost that the law ought to give to *outcasts merely as outcasts.*" I merely put beside this expression of the gentlemanly mind of England in 1865, a part of the message which Isaiah was ordered to "lift up his voice like a trumpet" in declaring to the gentlemen of his day: "Ye fast for strife, and to smite with the fist of wickedness. Is not this the fast that I have chosen, to deal thy bread to the hungry, and that thou bring the poor *that are cast out* (margin 'afflicted') to *thy* house." The falsehood on which the writer had mentally founded himself, as previously stated by him, was this: "To confound the functions of the dispensers of the poor-rates with those of the dispensers of a charitable institution is a great and pernicious error." This sentence is so accurately and exquisitely wrong, that its substance must be thus reversed in our minds before we can deal with any existing problem of national distress. "To understand that the dispensers of the poor-rates are the almoners of the nation, and should distribute its alms with a gentleness and freedom of hand as much greater and franker than that possible to individual charity, as the collective national wisdom and power may be supposed greater than those of any single person, is the foundation of all law respecting pauperism."

the hem of our robes from the touch of the heretics who dispute it. But to do a piece of common Christian righteousness in a plain English word or deed ; to make Christian law
any rule of life, and found one National act or hope thereon,
—we know too well what our faith comes to for that ! You
might sooner get lightning out of incense smoke than true
action or passion out of your modern English religion. You
had better get rid of the smoke, and the organ pipes, both :
leave them, and the Gothic windows, and the painted glass, to
the property man ; give up your carburetted hydrogen ghost
in one healthy expiration, and look after Lazarus at the door-
step. For there is a true Church wherever one hand meets
another helpfully, and that is the only holy or Mother Church
which ever was, or ever shall be.

All these pleasures, then, and all these virtues, I repeat,
you nationally despise. You have, indeed, men among you
who do not ; by whose work, by whose strength, by whose
life, by whose death, you live, and never thank them. Your
wealth, your amusement, your pride, would all be alike impossible, but for those whom you scorn or forget. The po-
liceman, who is walking up and down the black lane all night
to watch the guilt you have created there, and may have his
brains beaten out and be maimed for life at any moment, and
never be thanked ; the sailor wrestling with the sea's rage ;
the quiet student poring over his book or his vial ; the common worker, without praise, and nearly without bread, fulfill-
ing his task as your horses drag your carts, hopeless, and
spurned of all : these are the men by whom England lives ;
but they are not the nation ; they are only the body and
nervous force of it, acting still from old habit in a convulsive
perseverance, while the mind is gone. Our National mind
and purpose are to be amused ; our National religion, the
performance of church ceremonies, and preaching of soporific
truths (or untruths) to keep the mob quietly at work, while
we amuse ourselves ; and the necessity for this amusement is
fastening on us as a feverous disease of parched throat and
wandering eyes—senseless, dissolute, merciless. When men
are rightly occupied, their amusement grows out of their

work, as the colour-petals out of a fruitful flower;—when
they are faithfully helpful and compassionate, all their emotions become steady, deep, perpetual, and vivifying to the
soul as the natural pulse to the body. But now, having no
true business, we pour our whole masculine energy into the
false business of money-making ; and having no true emotion, we must have false emotions dressed up for us to play
with, not innocently, as children with dolls, but guiltily and
darkly, as the idolatrous Jews with their pictures on cavern
walls, which men had to dig to detect. The justice we do
not execute, we mimic in the novel and on the stage ; for the
beauty we destroy in nature, we substitute the metamorphosis
of the pantomime, and (the human nature of us imperatively
requiring awe and sorrow of *some* kind) for the noble grief
we should have borne with our fellows, and the pure tears
we should have wept with them, we gloat over the pathos of
the police court, and gather the night-dew of the grave.

It is difficult to estimate the true significance of these things ;
the facts are frightful enough ;—the measure of national fault
involved in them is perhaps not as great as it would at first
seem. We permit, or cause, thousands of deaths daily, but
we mean no harm ; we set fire to houses, and ravage peasants'
fields ; yet we should be sorry to find we had injured anybody. We are still kind at heart ; still capable of virtue,
but only as children are. Chalmers, at the end of his long
life, having had much power with the public, being plagued
in some serious matter by a reference to "public opinion,"
uttered the impatient exclamation, "The public is just a great
baby !" And the reason that I have allowed all these graver
subjects of thought to mix themselves up with an inquiry into
methods of reading, is that, the more I see of our national
faults and miseries, the more they resolve themselves into
conditions of childish illiterateness, and want of education in
the most ordinary habits of thought. It is, I repeat, not vice,
not selfishness, not dulness of brain, which we have to lament ;
but an unreachable schoolboy's recklessness, only differing
from the true schoolboy's in its incapacity of being helped,
because it acknowledges no master. There is a curious type

of us given in one of the lovely, neglected works of the last of our great painters. It is a drawing of Kirkby Lonsdale churchyard, and of its brook, and valley, and hills, and folded morning sky beyond. And unmindful alike of these, and of the dead who have left these for other valleys and for other skies, a group of schoolboys have piled their little books upon a grave, to strike them off with stones. So do we play with the words of the dead that would teach us, and strike them far from us with our bitter, reckless will, little thinking that those leaves which the wind scatters had been piled, not only upon a gravestone, but upon the seal of an enchanted vault— nay, the gate of a great city of sleeping kings, who would awake for us, and walk with us, if we knew but how to call them by their names. How often, even if we lift the marble entrance gate, do we but wander among those old kings in their repose, and finger the robes they lie in, and stir the crowns on their foreheads ; and still they are silent to us, and seem but a dusty imagery ; because we know not the incanta- tion of the heart that would wake them ;—which, if they once heard, they would start up to meet us in their power of long ago, narrowly to look upon us, and consider us ; and, as the fallen kings of Hades meet the newly fallen, saying, " Art thou also become weak as we—art thou also become one of us ?" so would these kings, with their undimmed, unshaken dia- dems, meet us, saying, " Art thou also become pure and mighty of heart as we ? art thou also become one of us ? "

Mighty of heart, mighty of mind—"magnanimous "—to be this, is indeed to be great in life ; to become this increasingly, is, indeed, to " advance in life,"—in life itself—not in the trappings of it. My friends, do you remember that old Scythian custom, when the head of a house died ? How he was dressed in his finest dress, and set in his chariot, and carried about to his friends' houses ; and each of them placed him at his table's head, and all feasted in his presence ? Sup- pose it were offered to you, in plain words, as it *is* offered to you in dire facts, that you should gain this Scythian honour, gradually, while you yet thought yourself alive. Suppose the offer were this : " You shall die slowly ; your blood shall daily grow cold, your flesh petrify, your heart beat at last only **as a** rusted group of iron valves. Your life shall fade from you, and sink through the earth into the ice of Caina ; but, day by day, your body shall be dressed more gaily, and set in higher chariots, and have more orders on its breast—crowns on **its** head, if you will. Men shall bow before it, stare and shout round it, crowd after it up and down the streets ; build **pal** aces for it, feast with it at their tables' heads all the night long ; your soul shall stay enough within it to know what they do, and feel the weight of the golden dress on its shoulders, and the furrow of the crown-edge on the skull ;—no more. Would you take the offer, verbally made by the death-angel? Would the meanest among us take it, think you? Yet practically and verily we grasp at it, every one of us, in a measure ; many of us grasp at it in its fulness of horror. Every man accepts it, who desires to advance in life without knowing what life is ; who means only that he is to get more horses, and more footmen, and more fortune, and more public honour, and—*not* more personal soul. He only is advancing in life, whose heart is getting softer, whose blood warmer, whose brain quicker, whose spirit is entering into Living * peace. And the men who have this life in them are the true lords or kings of the earth—they, and they only. All other kingships, so far as they are true, are only the practical issue and expression of theirs ; if less than this, they are either dramatic royalties,—costly shows, with real jewels instead of tinsel—the toys of nations ; or else, they are no royalties at all, but tyrannies, or the mere active and practical issue of national folly ; for which reason I have said of them elsewhere, " Visible governments are the toys of some nations, the diseases of others, the harness of some, the burdens of more."

But I have no words for the wonder with which I hear Kinghood still spoken of, even among thoughtful men, as if governed nations were a personal property, and might be bought and sold, or otherwise acquired, as sheep, of whose flesh their king was to feed, and whose fleece he was to gather ; as if Achilles' indignant epithet of base kings, "peo

* " το δὲ φρόνημα του πνεύματος ζωὴ και ειρήνη."

ple-eating," were the constant and proper title of all mon-
archs ; and enlargement of a king's dominion meant the same
thing as the increase of a private man's estate ! Kings who
think so, however powerful, can no more be the true kings of
the nation than gad-flies are the kings of a horse ; they suck
it, and may drive it wild, but do not guide it. They, and
their courts, and their armies are, if one could see clearly,
only a large species of marsh mosquito, with bayonet pro-
boscis and melodious, band-mastered, trumpeting in the summer air ; the twilight being, perhaps, sometimes fairer, but
hardly more wholesome, for its glittering mists of midge com-
panies. The true kings, meanwhile, rule quietly, if at all, and
hate ruling ; too many of them make "il gran refiûto ;" and
if they do not, the mob, as soon as they are likely to become
useful to it, is pretty sure to make *its* "gran refiûto " of *them.*

Yet the visible king may also be a true one, some day, if
ever day comes when he will estimate his dominion by the
force of it,—not the geographical boundaries. It matters
very little whether Trent cuts you a cantel out here, or Rhine
rounds you a castle less there. But it does matter to you,
king of men, whether you can verily say to this man, "Go,"
and he goeth ; and to another, "Come," and he cometh.
Whether you can turn your people as you can Trent—and
where it is that you bid them come, and where go. It matters to you, king of men, whether your people hate you, and
die by you, or love you, and live by you. You may measure
your dominion by multitudes better that by miles ; and count
degrees of love latitude, not from, but to, a wonderfully warm
and infinite equator. Measure ! nay you cannot measure. Who
shall measure the difference between the power of those who
"do and teach," and who are greatest in the kingdoms of
earth, as of heaven—and the power of those who undo, and
consume—whose power, at the fullest, is only the power of
the moth and rust? Strange ! to think how the Moth-
kings lay up treasures for the moth, and the Rust-kings, who
are to their peoples' strength as rust to armour, lay up treasures for the rust ; and the Robber-kings, treasures for the
robber ; but how few kings have ever laid up treasures that

needed no guarding—treasures of which, the more thieves there were, the better! Broidered robe, only to be rent—helm and sword, only to be dimmed ; jewel and gold, only to be scattered—there have been three kinds of kings who have gathered these. Suppose there ever should arise a Fourth order of kings, who had read, in some obscure writing of long ago, that there was a Fourth kind of treasure, which the jewel and gold could not equal, neither should it be valued with pure gold. A web more fair in the weaving, by Athena's shuttle ; an armour, forged in diviner fire by Vulcanian force—a gold only to be mined in the sun's red heart, where he sets over the Delphian cliffs ;—deep-pictured tissue, impenetrable armour, potable gold !—the three great Angels of Conduct, Toil, and Thought, still calling to us, and waiting at the posts of our doors, to lead us, if we would, with their winged power, and guide us, with their inescapable eyes, by the path which no fowl knoweth, and which the vulture's eye has not seen! Suppose kings should ever arise, who heard and believed this word, and at last gathered and brought forth treasures of—Wisdom —for their people ?

Think what an amazing business *that* would be ! How inconceivable, in the state of our present national wisdom. That we should bring up our peasants to a book exercise instead of a bayonet exercise !—organize, drill, maintain with pay, and good generalship, armies of thinkers, instead of armies of stabbers !—find national amusement in reading-rooms as well as rifle-grounds ; give prizes for a fair shot at a fact, as well as for a leaden splash on a target. What an absurd idea it seems, put fairly in words, that the wealth of the capitalists of civilized nations should ever come to support literature instead of war ! Have yet patience with me, while I read you a single sentence out of the only book, properly to be called a book, that I have yet written myself, the one that will stand, (if anything stand,) surest and longest of all work of mine.

"It is one very awful form of the operation of wealth in Europe that it is entirely capitalists' wealth which supports unjust wars. Just wars do not need so much money to support them ; for most of the men who wage such, wage them gratis ; but for an unjust war, men's bodies and souls have both to be bought ; and the best tools of war for them besides, which makes such war costly to the maximum ; not to speak of the cost of base fear, and angry suspicion, between nations which have not grace nor honesty enough in all their multitudes to buy an hour's peace of mind with ; as, at present France and England, purchasing of each other ten millions' sterling worth of consternation, annually (a remarkably light crop, half thorns and half aspen leaves, sown, reaped, and granaried by the 'science' of the modern political economist, teaching covetousness instead of truth). And, all unjust war being supportable, if not by pillage of the enemy, only by loans from capitalists, these loans are repaid by subsequent taxation of the people, who appear to have no will in the matter, the capitalists' will being the primary root of the war ; but its real root is the covetousness of the whole nation, rendering it incapable of faith, frankness, or justice, and bringing about, therefore, in due time, his own separate loss and punishment to each person."

France and England literally, observe, buy *panic* of each other ; they pay, each of them, for ten thousand thousand pounds' worth of terror, a year. Now suppose, instead of buying these ten millions' worth of panic annually, they made up their minds to be at peace with each other, and buy ten millions' worth of knowledge annually ; and that each nation spent its ten thousand thousand pounds a year in founding royal libraries, royal art galleries, royal museums, royal gardens, and places of rest. Might it not be better somewhat for both French and English ?

It will be long, yet, before that comes to pass. Nevertheless, I hope it will not be long before royal or national libraries will be founded in every considerable city, with a royal series of books in them ; the same series in every one of them, chosen books, the best in every kind, prepared for that national series in the most perfect way possible ; their text printed all on leaves of equal size, broad of margin, and divided into pleasant volumes, light in the hand, beautiful, and strong, and thorough as examples of binders' work ; and that these great libraries will be accessible to all clean and orderly persons at all times of the day and evening ; strict law being enforced for this cleanliness and quietness.

I could shape for you other plans, for art-galleries, and for natural history galleries, and for many precious, many, it seems to me, needful, things ; but this book plan is the easi- est and needfullest, and would prove a considerable tonic to what we call our British constitution, which has fallen dropsi- cal of late, and has an evil thirst, and evil hunger, and wants healthier feeding. You have got its corn laws repealed for it ; try if you cannot get corn laws established for it, dealing in a better bread ;—bread made of that old enchanted Arabian grain, the Sesame, which opens doors ;—doors, not of robbers,' but of Kings' Treasuries.

Friends, the treasuries of true kings are the streets of their cities ; and the gold they gather, which for others is as the mire of the streets, changes itself, for them and their people, into a crystalline pavement for evermore.

LECTURE II.—LILIES.

" Be thou glad, oh thirsting Desert ; let the desert be made cheerful, and bloom as the lily ; and the barren places of Jordan shall run wild with wood."—ISAIAH 35, i. (Septuagint.)

IT will, perhaps, be well, as this Lecture is the sequel of one previously given, that I should shortly state to you my general intention in both. The questions specially proposed to you in the first, namely, How and What to Read, rose out of a far deeper one, which it was my endeavour to make you propose earnestly to yourselves, namely, *Why* to Read. I want you to feel, with me, that whatever advantages we possess in the present day in the diffusion of education and of literature, can only be rightly used by any of us when we have apprehended clearly what education is to lead to, and literature to teach. I wish you to see that both well-directed moral training and well-chosen reading lead to the possession of a power over the ill-guided and illiterate, which is, according to the measure of it, in the truest sense, *kingly ;* conferring indeed the purest kingship that can exist among men : too many other kingships (however distinguished by visible insignia or material power) being either spectral, or tyrannous ;—Spectral—that is to say, aspects and shadows only of royalty, hollow as death, and which only the "Likeness of a kingly crown have on ; " or else tyrannous—that is to say, substituting their own will for the law of justice and love by which all true kings rule.

There is, then, I repeat—and as I want to leave this idea with you, I begin with it, and shall end with it—only one pure kind of kingship ; an inevitable and eternal kind, crowned or not : the kingship, namely, which consists in a stronger moral state, and a truer thoughtful state, than that

of others ; enabling you, therefore, to guide, or to raise them.
Observe that word " State ; " we have got into a loose way of
using it. It means literally the standing and stability of a
thing ; and you have the full force of it in the derived word
" statue "—" the immoveable thing." A king's majesty or
" state," then, and the right of his kingdom to be called a
state, depends on the movelessness of both :—without tremor,
without quiver of balance ; established and enthroned upon
a foundation of eternal law which nothing can alter nor over-
throw.

Believing that all literature and all education are only useful so far as they tend to confirm this calm, beneficent, and
therefore kingly, power—first, over ourselves, and, through
ourselves, over all around us, I am now going to ask you to
consider with me farther, what special portion or kind of
this royal authority, arising out of noble education, may
rightly be possessed by women ; and how far they also are
called to a true queenly power. Not in their households
merely, but over all within their sphere. And in what sense,
if they rightly understood and exercised this royal or gracious influence, the order and beauty induced by such benig-
nant power would justify us in speaking of the territories
over which each of them reigned, as " Queens' Gardens."

And here, in the very outset, we are met by a far deeper
question, which—strange though this may seem—remains
among many of us yet quite undecided, in spite of its infinite
importance.

We cannot determine what the queenly power of women
should be, until we are agreed what their ordinary power
should be. We cannot consider how education may fit them
for any widely extending duty, until we are agreed what is
their true constant duty. And there never was a time when
wilder words were spoken, or more vain imagination permitted, respecting this question—quite vital to all social happiness. The relations of the womanly to the manly nature,
their different capacities of intellect or of virtue, seem never
to have been yet measured with entire consent. We hear of
the mission and of the rights of Woman, as if these could

ever be separate from the mission and the rights of Man ;—
as if she and her lord were creatures of independent kind
and of irreconcileable claim. This, at least, is wrong. And
not less wrong—perhaps even more foolishly wrong (for I
will anticipate thus far what I hope to prove)—is the idea
that woman is only the shadow and attendant image of her
lord, owing him a thoughtless and servile obedience, and supported altogether in her weakness by the pre-eminence of his
fortitude.

This, I say, is the most foolish of all errors respecting her
who was made to be the helpmate of man. As if he could be
helped effectively by a shadow, or worthily by a slave!

Let us try, then, whether we cannot get at some clear and
harmonious idea (it must be harmonious if it is true) of what
womanly mind and virtue are in power and office, with respect to man's; and how their relations, rightly accepted,
aid, and increase, the vigour, and honour, and authority of
both.

And now I must repeat one thing I said in the last lecture
namely, that the first use of education was to enable us to
consult with the wisest and the greatest men on all points of
earnest difficulty. That to use books rightly, was to go to
them for help: to appeal to them, when our own knowledge
and power of thought failed; to be led by them into wider
sight, purer conception than our own, and receive from them
the united sentence of the judges and councils of all time,
against our solitary and unstable opinion.

Let us do this now. Let us see whether the greatest, the
wisest, the purest-hearted of all ages are agreed in any wise
on this point: let us hear the testimony they have left respecting what they held to be the true dignity of woman, and her
mode of help to man.

And first let us take Shakespeare.

Note broadly in the outset, Shakespeare has no heroes ;—
he has only heroines. There is not one entirely heroic figure
in all his plays, except the slight sketch of Henry the Fifth,
exaggerated for the purposes of the stage ; and the still slighter
Valentine in The Two Gentlemen of Verona. In his laboured

and perfect plays you have no hero. Othello would have been one, if his simplicity had not been so great as to leave him the prey of every base practice round him ; but he is the only example even approximating to the heroic type. Coriolanus —Cæsar—Antony, stand in flawed strength, and fall by their vanities ;—Hamlet is indolent, and drowsily speculative ; Romeo an impatient boy ; the Merchant of Venice languidly submissive to adverse fortune ; Kent, in King Lear, is entirely noble at heart, but too rough and unpolished to be of true use at the critical time, and he sinks into the office of a servant only. Orlando, no less noble, is yet the despairing toy of chance, followed, comforted, saved, by Rosalind. Whereas there is hardly a play that has not a perfect woman in it, stead-fast in grave hope, and errorless purpose ; Cordelia, Desde-mona, Isabella, Hermione, Imogen, Queen Katherine, Perdita, Sylvia, Viola, Rosalind, Helena, and last, and perhaps loveli-est, Virgilia, are all faultless ; conceived in the highest heroic type of humanity.

Then observe, secondly,

The catastrophe of every play is caused always by the folly or fault of a man ; the redemption, if there be any, is by the wisdom and virtue of a woman, and failing that, there is none. The catastrophe of King Lear is owing to his own want of judgment, his impatient vanity, his misunderstanding of his children ; the virtue of his one true daughter would have saved him from all the injuries of the others, unless he had cast her away from him ; as it is, she all but saves him.

Of Othello I need not trace the tale ;—nor the one weak-ness of his so mighty love ; nor the inferiority of his percep-tive intellect to that even of the second woman character in the play, the Emilia who dies in wild testimony against his error :—" Oh, murderous coxcomb ! What should such a fool Do with so good a wife ? "

In Romeo and Juliet, the wise and entirely brave stratagem of the wife is brought to ruinous issue by the reckless impa-tience of her husband. In Winter's Tale, and in Cymbeline, the happiness and existence of two princely households, lost through long years, and imperilled to the death by the folly and obstinacy of the husbands, are redeemed at last by the queenly patience and wisdom of the wives. In Measure for Measure, the injustice of the judges, and the corrupt cowardice of the brother, are opposed to the victorious truth and adamantine purity of a woman. In Coriolanus, the mother's counsel, acted upon in time, would have saved her son from all evil; his momentary forgetfulness of it is his ruin; her prayer at last granted, saves him—not, indeed, from death but from the curse of living as the destroyer of his country.

And what shall I say of Julia, constant against the fickleness of a lover who is a mere wicked child?—of Helena, against the petulance and insult of a careless youth?—of the patience of Hero, the passion of Beatrice, and the calmly devoted wisdom of the "unlessoned girl," who appears among the helplessness, the blindness, and the vindictive passions of men, as a gentle angel, to save merely by her presence, and defeat the worst intensities of crime by her smile?

Observe, further, among all the principal figures in Shakespeare's plays, there is only one weak woman—Ophelia; and it is because she fails Hamlet at the critical moment, and is not, and cannot in her nature be, a guide to him when he needs her most, that all the bitter catastrophe follows. Finally, though there are three wicked women among the principal figures, Lady Macbeth, Regan, and Goneril, they are felt at once to be frightful exceptions to the ordinary laws of life; fatal in their influence also in proportion to the power for good which they have abandoned.

Such, in broad light, is Shakespeare's testimony to the position and character of women in human life. He represents them as infallibly faithful and wise counsellors,—incorruptibly just and pure examples—strong always to sanctify, even when they cannot save.

Not as in any wise comparable in knowledge of the nature of man,—still less in his understanding of the causes and courses of fate,—but only as the writer who has given us the broadest view of the conditions and modes of ordinary thought in modern society, I ask you next to receive the witness of Walter Scott.

I put aside his merely romantic prose writings as of no
value : and though the early romantic poetry is very beautiful,
its testimony is of no weight, other than that of a boy's ideal.
But his true works, studied from Scottish life, bear a true
witness, and in the whole range of these there are but three
men who reach the heroic type *—Dandie Dinmont, Rob Roy,
and Claverhouse : of these, one is a border farmer ; another
a freebooter ; the third a soldier in a bad cause. And these
touch the ideal of heroism only in their courage and faith,
together with a strong, but uncultivated, or mistakenly applied, intellectual power ; while his younger men are the gentlemanly playthings of fantastic fortune, and only by aid (or
accident) of that fortune, survive, not vanquish, the trials they
involuntarily sustain. Of any disciplined, or consistent character, earnest in a purpose wisely conceived, or dealing with
forms of hostile evil, definitely challenged, and resolutely subdued, there is no trace in his conceptions of men. Whereas
in his imaginations of women,—in the characters of Ellen
Douglas, of Flora MacIvor, Rose Bradwardine, Catherine Sey-
ton, Diana Vernon, Lilias Redgauntlet, Alice Bridgenorth,
Alice Lee, and Jeanie Deans,—with endless varieties of grace,
tenderness, and intellectual power we find in all a quite infallible and inevitable sense of dignity and justice ; a fearless,
instant, and untiring self-sacrifice to even the appearance of
duty, much more to its real claims ; and, finally, a patient wisdom of deeply restrained affection, which does infinitely more
than protect its objects from a momentary error ; it gradually
forms, animates, and exalts the characters of the unworthy
lovers, until, at the close of the tale, we are just able, and no
more, to take patience in hearing of their unmerited success.

* I ought, in order to make this assertion fully understood, to have
noted the various weaknesses which lower the ideal of other great characters of men in the Waverley novels—the selfishness and narrowness of
thought in Redgauntlet, the weak religious enthusiasm in Edward Glen-
denning, and the like ; and I ought to have noticed that there are several quite perfect characters sketched sometimes in the backgrounds :
three—let us accept joyously this courtesy to England and her soldiers
—are English officers: Colonel Gardiner, Colonel Talbot, and Colonel
Mannering.

So that in all cases, with Scott as with Shakespeare, it is the woman who watches over, teaches, and guides the youth ; it is never, by any chance, the youth who watches over or educates his mistress.

Next, take, though more briefly, graver and deeper testimony—that of the great Italians and Greeks. You know well the plan of Dante's great poem—that it is a love-poem to his dead lady, a song of praise for her watch over his soul. Stooping only to pity, never to love, she yet saves him from destruction—saves him from hell. He is going eternally astray in despair ; she comes down from heaven to his help, and throughout the ascents of Paradise is his teacher, interpreting for him the most difficult truths, divine and human, and leading him, with rebuke upon rebuke, from star to star.

I do not insist upon Dante's conception ; if I began I could not cease : besides, you might think this a wild imagination of one poet's heart. So I will rather read to you a few verses of the deliberate writing of a knight of Pisa to his living lady, wholly characteristic of the feeling of all the noblest men of the thirteenth century, preserved among many other such records of knightly honour and love, which Dante Rossetti has gathered for us from among the early Italian poets.

> For lo ! thy law is passed
> That this my love should manifestly be
> To serve and honour thee :
> And so I do ; and my delight is full,
> Accepted for the servant of thy rule.
>
> Without almost, I am all rapturous,
> Since thus my will was set
> To serve, thou flower of joy, thine excellence :
> Nor ever seems it anything could rouse
> A pain or regret,
> But on thee dwells mine every thought and sense :
> Considering that from thee all virtues spread
> As from a fountain head,—
> *That in thy gift is wisdom's best avail,*
> *And honour without fail ;*
> With whom each sovereign good dwells separate,
> Fulfilling the perfection of thy state

Lady, since I conceived
Thy pleasurable aspect in my heart,
My life has been apart
In shining brightness and the place of truth;
Which till that time, good sooth,
Groped among shadows in a darken'd place,
Where many hours and days
It hardly ever had remember'd good.
But now my servitude
Is thine, and I am full of joy and rest.
A man from a wild beast
Thou madest me, since for thy love I lived.

You may think, perhaps, a Greek knight would have had a lower estimate of women than this Christian lover. His own spiritual subjection to them was indeed not so absolute ; but as regards their own personal character, it was only because you could not have followed me so easily, that I did not take the Greek women instead of Shakespeare's ; and instance, for chief ideal types of human beauty and faith, the simple mother's and wife's heart of Andromache ; the divine, yet rejected wisdom of Cassandra; the playful kindness and simple princess-life of happy Nausicaa ; the housewifely calm of that of Penelope, with its watch upon the sea ; the ever patient, fearless, hopelessly devoted piety of the sister, and daughter, in Antigone ; the bowing down of Iphigenia, lamb-like and silent ; and, finally, the expectation of the resurrection, made clear to the soul of the Greeks in the return from her grave of that Alcestis, who, to save her husband, had passed calmly through the bitterness of death.

Now I could multiply witness upon witness of this kind upon you if I had time. I would take Chaucer, and show you why he wrote a Legend of Good Women ; but no Legend of Good Men. I would take Spenser, and show you how all his fairy knights are sometimes deceived and sometimes vanquished ; but the soul of Una is never darkened, and the spear of Britomart is never broken. Nay, I could go back into the mythical teaching of the most ancient times, and show you how the great people,—by one of whose princesses it was appointed that the Lawgiver of all the earth should be

educated, rather than by his own kindred ;—how that great
Egyptian people, wisest then of nations, gave to their Spirit
of Wisdom the form of a woman ; and into her hand, for a
symbol, the weaver's shuttle : and how the name and the
form of that spirit, adopted, believed, and obeyed by the
Greeks, became that Athena of the olive-helm, and cloudy
shield, to whose faith you owe, down to this date, whatever
you hold most precious in art, in literature, or in types of national virtue.

But I will not wander into this distant and mythical element ; I will only ask you to give its legitimate value to the
testimony of these great poets and men of the world,—consistent as you see it is on this head.   I will ask you whether
it can be supposed that these men, in the main work of their
lives, are amusing themselves with a fictitious and idle view
of the relations between man and woman ;—nay, worse than
fictitious or idle ; for a thing may be imaginary, yet desirable,
if it were possible ; but this, their ideal of women, is, according to our common idea of the marriage relation, wholly un-
desirable.   The woman, we say, is not to guide, nor even to
think, for herself.   The man is always to be the wiser ; he is
to be the thinker, the ruler, the superior in knowledge and
discretion, as in power.   Is it not somewhat important to
make up our minds on this matter ?   Are all these great men
mistaken, or are we ?   Are Shakespeare and Æschylus, Dante
and Homer, merely dressing dolls for us ; or, worse than
dolls, unnatural visions, the realization of which, were it possible, would bring anarchy into all households and ruin into
all affections ?   Nay, if you could suppose this, take lastly the
evidence of facts, given by the human heart itself.   In all
Christian ages which have been remarkable for their purity
or progress, there has been absolute yielding of obedient devotion, by the lover, to his mistress.   I say *obedient*—not
merely enthusiastic and worshipping in imagination, but entirely subject, receiving from the beloved woman, however
young, not only the encouragement, the praise, and the reward of all toil, but so far as any choice is open, or any question difficult of decision. the *direction* of all toil.   That chiv

alry, to the abuse and dishonour of which are attributable primarily whatever is cruel in war, unjust in peace, or corrupt and ignoble in domestic relations; and to the original purity and power of which we owe the defence alike of faith, of law, and of love;—that chivalry, I say, in its very first conception of honourable life, assumes the subjection of the young knight to the command—should it even be the command in caprice—of his lady. It assumes this, because its masters knew that the first and necessary impulse of every truly taught and knightly heart is this of blind service to its lady; that where that true faith and captivity are not, all wayward and wicked passions must be; and that in this rapturous obedience to the single love of his youth, is the sanctification of all man's strength, and the continuance of all his purposes. And this, not because such obedience would be safe, or honourable, were it ever rendered to the unworthy; but because it ought to be impossible for every noble youth—it *is* impossible for every one rightly trained—to love any one whose gentle counsel he cannot trust, or whose prayerful command he can hesitate to obey.

I do not insist by any farther argument on this, for I think it should commend itself at once to your knowledge of what has been and to your feelings of what should be. You cannot think that the buckling on of the knight's armour by his lady's hand was a mere caprice of romantic fashion. It is the type of an eternal truth—that the soul's armour is never well set to the heart unless a woman's hand has braced it; and it is only when she braces it loosely that the honour of manhood fails. Know you not those lovely lines—I would they were learned by all youthful ladies of England :—

> " Ah, wasteful woman!—she who may
> On her sweet self set her own price,
> Knowing he cannot choose but pay—
> How has she cheapen'd Paradise!
> How given for nought her priceless gift,
> How spoiled the bread and spill'd the wine,
> Which, spent with due, respective thrift,
> Had made brutes men, and men divine* "

* Coventry Patmore.

This much, then, respecting the relations of lovers I believe you will accept. But what we too often doubt is the fitness of the continuance of such a relation throughout the whole of human life. We think it right in the lover and mistress, not in the husband and wife. That is to say, we think that a reverent and tender duty is due to one whose affection we still doubt, and whose character we as yet do but partially and distantly discern ; and that this reverence and duty are to be withdrawn when the affection has become wholly and limitlessly our own, and the character has been so sifted and tried that we fear not to entrust it with the happiness of our lives. Do you not see how ignoble this is, as well as how unreasonable ? Do you not feel that marriage—when it is marriage at all,—is only the seal which marks the vowed transition of temporary into untiring service, and of fitful into eternal love ?

But how, you will ask, is the idea of this guiding function of the woman reconcileable with a true wifely subjection? Simply in that it is a *guiding*, not a determining, function. Let me try to show you briefly how these powers seem to be rightly distinguishable.

We are foolish, and without excuse foolish, in speaking of the " superiority " of one sex to the other, as if they could be compared in similar things. Each has what the other has not : each completes the other, and is completed by the other : they are in nothing alike, and the happiness and perfection of both depends on each asking and receiving from the other what the other only can give.

Now their separate characters are briefly these. The man's power is active, progressive, defensive. He is eminently the doer, the creator, the discoverer, the defender. His intellect is for speculation and invention ; his energy for adventure, for war, and for conquest, wherever war is just, wherever conquest necessary. But the woman's power is for rule, not for battle,—and her intellect is not for invention or creation, but for sweet ordering, arrangement and decision. She sees the qualities of things, their claims and their places. Her great function is Praise : she enters into no contest, but infallibly judges the crown of contest. By her office, and place, she is protected from all danger and temptation. The man, in his rough work in open world, must encounter all peril and trial : —to him, therefore, the failure, the offence, the inevitable error : often he must be wounded, or subdued, often misled, and *always* hardened. But he guards the woman from all this ; within his house, as ruled by her, unless she herself has sought it, need enter no danger, no temptation, no cause of error or offence. This is the true nature of home—it is the place of Peace ; the shelter, not only from all injury, but from all terror, doubt, and division. In so far as it is not this, it is not home : so far as the anxieties of the outer life penetrate into it, and the inconsistently-minded, unknown, unloved, or hostile society of the outer world is allowed by either husband or wife to cross the threshold, it ceases to be home ; it is then only a part of that outer world which you have roofed over, and lighted fire in. But so far as it is a sacred place, a vestal temple, a temple of the hearth watched over by Household Gods, before whose faces none may come but those whom they can receive with love,—so far as it is this, and roof and fire are types only of a nobler shade and light,—shade as of the rock in a weary land, and light as of the Pharos in the stormy sea ;—so far it vindicates the name, and fulfils the praise, of home.

And wherever a true wife comes, this home is always round her. The stars only may be over her head ; the glow-worm in the night-cold grass may be the only fire at her foot : but home is yet wherever she is ; and for a noble woman it stretches far round her, better than ceiled with cedar, or painted with vermilion, shedding its quiet light far, for those who else were homeless.

This, then, I believe to be,—will you not admit it to be,— the woman's true place and power ? But do not you see that to fulfil this, she must—as far as one can use such terms of a human creature—be incapable of error ? So far as she rules, all must be right, or nothing is. She must be enduringly, incorruptibly good ; instinctively, infallibly wise—wise, not for self-development, but for self-renunciation : wise, not that she may set herself above her husband, but that she may never fail from his side : wise, not with the narrowness of in-solent and loveless pride, but with the passionate gentleness of an infinitely variable, because infinitely applicable, modesty of service—the true changefulness of woman. In that great sense—"La donna e mobile," not "Qual piùm' al vento ;" no, nor yet "Variable as the shade, by the light quivering aspen made ;" but variable as the *light*, manifold in fair and serene division, that it may take the color of all that it falls upon, and exalt it.

II.   I have been trying, thus far, to show you what should be the place, and what the power of woman. Now, secondly, we ask, What kind of education is to fit her for these ?

And if you indeed think this a true conception of her office and dignity, it will not be difficult to trace the course of edu-cation which would fit her for the one, and raise her to the other.

The first of our duties to her—no thoughtful persons now doubt this,—is to secure for her such physical training and exercise as may confirm her health, and perfect her beauty, the highest refinement of that beauty being unattainable with-out splendor of activity and of delicate strength.   To perfect her beauty, I say, and increase its power ; it cannot be too powerful, nor shed its sacred light too far : only remember that all physical freedom is vain to produce beauty without a corresponding freedom of heart.   There are two passages of that poet who is distinguished, it seems to me, from all others —not by power, but by exquisite *right*ness—which point you to the source, and describe to you, in a few syllables, the com-pletion of womanly beauty.   I will read the introductory stan-zas, but the last is the one I wish you specially to notice .

> " Three years she grew in sun and shower,
>   Then Nature said, a lovelier flower
>   On earth was never sown.
>   This child I to myself will take ;
>   She shall be mine, and I will make
>   A lady of my own.

" Myself will to my darling be
    Both law and impulse ; and with **me**
        The girl, in rock and plain,
    In earth and heaven, in glade and **bower,**
    Shall feel an overseeing power
        To kindle, or restrain.

" The floating clouds their state shall **lend**
    To her, for her the willow bend ;
        Nor shall she fail to see
    Even in the motions of the storm,
    Grace that shall mould the maiden's **form**
        By silent sympathy.

" And *vital feelings of delight*
    Shall rear her form to stately height,—
        Her virgin bosom swell.
    Such *thoughts* to Lucy I will give,
    While she and I together live,
        Here in this happy dell. "

" *Vital* feelings of delight," observe.   There are deadly feelings of delight ; but the natural ones are vital, necessary to very life.

And they must be feelings of delight, if they are to be vital. Do not think you can make a girl lovely, if you do not make her happy.   There is not one restraint you put on a good girl's nature—there is not one check you give to her instincts of affection or of effort—which will not be indelibly written on her features, with a hardness which is all the more painful because it takes away the brightness from the eyes of innocence, and the charm from the brow of virtue.

This for the means : now note the end.   Take from the same poet, in two lines, a perfect description of womanly beauty—

" A countenance in which did meet
    Sweet records, promises as sweet. "

The perfect loveliness of a woman's countenance can only consist in that majestic peace, which is founded in the memory of happy and useful years,—full of sweet records ; and from the joining of this with that yet more majestic childish ness, which is still full of change and promise ;—opening always—modest at once, and bright, with hope of better things to be won, and to be bestowed. There is no old age where there is still that promise—it is eternal youth.

Thus, then, you have first to mould her physical frame, and then, as the strength she gains will permit you, to fill and temper her mind with all knowledge and thoughts which tend to confirm its natural instincts of justice, and refine its natural tact of love.

All such knowledge should be given her as may enable her to understand, and even to aid, the work of men : and yet it should be given, not as knowledge,—not as if it were, or could be, for her an object to know ; but only to feel, and to judge. It is of no moment, as a matter of pride or perfect ness in herself, whether she knows many languages or one ; but it is of the utmost, that she should be able to show kindness to a stranger, and to understand the sweetness of a stranger's tongue. It is of no moment to her own worth or dignity that she should be acquainted with this science or that ; but it is of the highest that she should be trained in habits of ac curate thought ; that she should understand the meaning, the inevitableness, and the loveliness of natural laws, and follow at least some one path of scientific attainment, as far as to the threshold of that bitter Valley of Humiliation, into which only the wisest and bravest of men can descend, owning themselves forever children, gathering pebbles on a bound less shore. It is of little consequence how many positions of cities she knows, or how many dates of events, or how many names of celebrated persons—it is not the object of education to turn a woman into a dictionary ; but it is deeply necessary that she should be taught to enter with her whole personality into the history she reads ; to picture the passages of it vitally in her own bright imagination ; to apprehend, with her fine instincts, the pathetic circumstances and dramatic relations, which the historian too often only eclipses by his reasoning, and disconnects by his arrangement : it is for her to trace the hidden equities of divine reward, and catch sight, through the darkness, of the fateful threads of woven fire that connect error with its retribution. But, chiefly of all, she is to be taught to extend the limits of her sympathy with respect to that history which is being for her determined, as the moments pass in which she draws her peaceful breath : and to the contemporary calamity which, were it but rightly mourned by her, would recur no more hereafter. She is to exercise herself in imagining what would be the effects upon her mind and conduct, if she were daily brought into the presence of the suffering which is not the less real because shut from her sight. She is to be taught somewhat to understand the nothingness of the proportion which that little world in which she lives and loves, bears to the world in which God lives and loves ;—and solemnly she is to be taught to strive that her thoughts of piety may not be feeble in proportion to the number they embrace, nor her prayer more languid than it is for the momentary relief from pain of her husband or her child, when it is uttered for the multitudes of those who have none to love them,—and is, "for all who are desolate and oppressed."

Thus far, I think, I have had your concurrence ; perhaps you will not be with me in what I believe is most needful for me to say. There *is* one dangerous science for women—one which let them indeed beware how they profanely touch— that of theology. Strange, and miserably strange, that while they are modest enough to doubt their powers, and pause at the threshold of sciences where every step is demonstrable and sure, they will plunge headlong, and without one thought of incompetency, into that science in which the greatest men have trembled, and the wisest erred. Strange, that they will complacently and pridefully bind up whatever vice or folly there is in them, whatever arrogance, petulance, or blind incomprehensiveness, into one bitter bundle of consecrated myrrh. Strange, in creatures born to be Love visible, that where they can know least, they will condemn first, and think to recommend themselves to their Master by scrambling up the steps of His judgment throne, to divide it with Him. Most strange, that they should think they were led by the Spirit of the

Comforter into habits of mind which have become in them the unmixed elements of home discomfort ; and that they dare to turn the Household Gods of Christianity into ugly idols of their own—spiritual dolls, for them to dress accord-ing to their caprice ; and from which their husbands must turn away in grieved contempt, lest they should be shrieked at for breaking them.

I believe, then, with this exception, that a girl's education should be nearly, in its course and material of study, the same as a boy's ; but quite differently directed. A woman, in any rank of life, ought to know whatever her husband is likely to know, but to know it in a different way. His com-mand of it should be foundational and progressive, hers, general and accomplished for daily and helpful use. Not but that it would often be wiser in men to learn things in a womanly sort of way, for present use, and to seek for the dis-cipline and training of their mental powers in such branches of study as will be afterwards fittest for social service ; but, speaking broadly, a man ought to know any language or science he learns, thoroughly, while a woman ought to know the same language, or science, only so far as may enable her to sympathise in her husband's pleasures, and in those of his best friends.

Yet, observe, with exquisite accuracy as far as she reach-es. There is a wide difference between elementary knowledge and superficial knowledge—between a firm beginning, and a feeble smattering. A woman may always help her husband by what she knows, however little ; by what she half-knows, or mis-knows, she will only teaze him.

And, indeed, if there were to be any difference between a girl's education and a boy's, I should say that of the two the girl should be earlier led, as her intellect ripens faster, into deep and serious subjects ; and that her range of lit-erature should be, not more, but less frivolous, calculated to add the qualities of patience and seriousness to her nat-ural poignancy of thought and quickness of wit ; and also to keep her in a lofty and pure element of thought. I enter not now into any question of choice of books ; only be sure that her books are not heaped up in her lap as they fall out of the package of the circulating library, wet with the last and lightest spray of the fountain of folly.

Or even of the fountain of wit; for with respect to that sore temptation of novel-reading, it is not the badness of a novel that we should dread, but its over-wrought interest. The weakest romance is not so stupefying as the lower forms of religious exciting literature, and the worst romance is not so corrupting as false history, false philosophy, or false political essays. But the best romance becomes dangerous, if, by its excitement, it renders the ordinary course of life uninteresting, and increases the morbid thirst for useless acquaintance with scenes in which we shall never be called upon to act.

I speak therefore of good novels only; and our modern literature is particularly rich in types of such. Well read, indeed, these books have serious use, being nothing less than treatises on moral anatomy and chemistry; studies of human nature in the elements of it. But I attach little weight to this function: they are hardly ever read with earnestness enough to permit them to fulfil it. The utmost they usually do is to enlarge somewhat the charity of a kind reader, or the bitterness of a malicious one; for each will gather, from the novel, food for her own disposition. Those who are naturally proud and envious will learn from Thackeray to despise humanity; those who are naturally gentle, to pity it; those who are naturally shallow, to laugh at it. So, also, there might be a serviceable power in novels to bring before us, in vividness, a human truth which we had before dimly conceived; but the temptation to picturesqueness of statement is so great, that often the best writers of fiction cannot resist it; and our views are rendered so violent and one-sided, that their vitality is rather a harm than good.

Without, however, venturing here on any attempt at decision how much novel-reading should be allowed, let me at least clearly assert this, that whether novels, or poetry, or history be read, they should be chosen, not for what is *out* of them, but for what is *in* them. The chance and scattered

evil that may here and there haunt, or hide itself in, a powerful book, never does any harm to a noble girl; but the
emptiness of an author oppresses her, and his amiable folly
degrades her. And if she can have access to a good library of
old and classical books, there need be no choosing at all.
Keep the modern magazine and novel out of your girl's way:
turn her loose into the old library every wet day, and let her
alone. She will find what is good for her; you cannot: for
there is just this difference between the making of a girl's
character and a boy's—you may chisel a boy into shape, as
you would a rock, or hammer him into it, if he be of a better
kind, as you would a piece of bronze. But you cannot hammer a girl into anything. She grows as a flower does,—she
will wither without sun; she will decay in her sheath, as the
narcissus does, if you do not give her air enough; she may
fall, and defile her head in dust, if you leave her without help
at some moments of her life; but you cannot fetter her; she
must take her own fair form and way, if she take any, and in
mind as in body, must have always

> " Her household motions light and free
> And steps of virgin liberty."

Let her loose in the library, I say, as you do a fawn in a field.
It knows the bad weeds twenty times better than you; and
the good ones too, and will eat some bitter and prickly ones,
good for it, which you had not the slightest thought were
good.

Then, in art, keep the finest models before her, and let her
practice in all accomplishments be accurate and thorough, so
as to enable her to understand more than she accomplishes.
I say the finest models—that is to say, the truest, simplest,
usefullest. Note those epithets; they will range through all
the arts. Try them in music, where you might think them
the least applicable. I say the truest, that in which the notes
most closely and faithfully express the meaning of the words,
or the character of intended emotion; again, the simplest,
that in which the meaning and melody are attained with the
fewest and most significant notes possible; and, finally, the

usefullest, that music which makes the best words most beau-tiful, which enchants them in our memories each with its own glory of sound, and which applies them closest to the heart at the moment we need them.

And not only in the material and in the course, but yet more earnestly in the spirit of it, let a girl's education be as serious as a boy's. You bring up your girls as if they were meant for sideboard ornament, and then complain of their frivolity. Give them the same advantages that you give their brothers—appeal to the same grand instincts of virtue in them ; teach *them* also that courage and truth are the pillars of their being : do you think that they would not answer that appeal, brave and true as they are even now, when you know that there is hardly a girl's school in this Christian kingdom where the children's courage or sincerity would be thought of half so much importance as their way of coming in at a door ; and when the whole system of society, as re-spects the mode of establishing them in life, is one rotten plague of cowardice and imposture—cowardice, in not daring to let them live, or love, except as their neighbours choose ; and imposture, in bringing, for the purpose of our own pride, the full glow of the world's worst vanity upon a girl's eyes, at the very period when the whole happiness of her future ex-istence depends upon her remaining undazzled ?

And give them, lastly, not only noble teachings, but noble teachers. You consider somewhat, before you send your boy to school, what kind of a man the master is ;—whatsoever kind of a man he is, you at least give him full authority over your son, and show some respect for him yourself ; if he comes to dine with you, you do not put him at a side table ; you know also that, at his college, your child's immediate tutor will be under the direction of some still higher tutor, for whom you have absolute reverence. You do not treat the Dean of Christ Church or the Master of Trinity as your in-feriors.

But what teachers do you give your girls, and what rever-ence do you show to the teachers you have chosen ? Is a girl likely to think her own conduct, or her own intellect, of much

importance, when you trust the entire formation of her char‑
acter, moral and intellectual, to a person whom you let your
servants treat with less respect than they do your housekeeper
(as if the soul of your child were a less charge than jams and
groceries), and whom you yourself think you confer an hon‑
our upon by letting her sometimes sit in the drawing-room in
the evening?

Thus, then, of literature as her help, and thus of art.
There is one more help which we cannot do without—one
which, alone, has sometimes done more than all other influ‑
ences besides,—the help of wild and fair nature. Hear this
of the education of Joan of Arc :

"The education of this poor girl was mean according to
the present standard ; was ineffably grand, according to a
purer philosophic standard ; and only not good for our age,
because for us it would be unattainable. * * *

"Next after her spiritual advantages, she owed most to the
advantages of her situation. The fountain of Domrémy was
on the brink of a boundless forest ; and it was haunted to
that degree by fairies, that the parish priest (*curé*) was obliged
to read mass there once a year, in order to keep them in any
decent bounds. * * *

"But the forests of Domrémy—those were the glories of the
land, for in them abode mysterious powers and ancient secrets
that towered into tragic strength. 'Abbeys there were, and
abbey windows,'—'like Moorish temples of the Hindoos,' that
exercised even princely power both in Touraine and in the
German Diets. These had their sweet bells that pierced the
forests for many a league at matins or vespers, and each its
own dreamy legend. Few enough, and scattered enough,
were these abbeys, so as in no degree to disturb the deep soli‑
tude of the region ; yet many enough to spread a network or
awning of Christian sanctity over what else might have seemed
a heathen wilderness." *

Now, you cannot, indeed, have here in England, woods
eighteen miles deep to the centre ; but you can, perhaps, keep
a fairy or two for your children yet, if you wish to keep them.

* "Joan of Arc : in reference to M. Michelet's History of France.'
De Quincey's Works. Vol. iii. p 217.

But *do* you wish it? Suppose you had each, at the back of your houses, a garden large enough for your children to play in, with just as much lawn as would give them room to run, —no more—and that you could not change your abode; but that, if you chose, you could double your income, or quadruple it, by digging a coal shaft in the middle of the lawn, and turning the flower-beds into heaps of coke. Would you do it? I think not. I can tell you, you would be wrong if you did, though it gave you income sixty-fold instead of four-fold.

Yet this is what you are doing with all England. The whole country is but a little garden, not more than enough for your children to run on the lawns of, if you would let them *all* run there. And this little garden you will turn into furnace-ground, and fill with heaps of cinders, if you can; and those children of yours, not you, will suffer for it. For the fairies will not be all banished; there are fairies of the furnace as of the wood, and their first gifts seem to be " sharp arrows of the mighty;" but their last gifts are " coals of juniper."

And yet I cannot—though there is no part of my subject that I feel more—press this upon you; for we made so little use of the power of nature while we had it that we shall hardly feel what we have lost. Just on the other side of the Mersey you have your Snowdon, and your Menai Straits, and that mighty granite rock beyond the moors of Anglesea, splendid in its heatherly crest, and foot planted in the deep sea, once thought of as sacred—a divine promontory, looking westward; the Holy Head or Headland, still not without awe when its red light glares first through storm. These are the hills, and these the bays and blue inlets, which, among the Greeks, would have been always loved, always fateful in influence on the national mind. That Snowdon is your Parnassus; but where are its Muses? That Holyhead mountain is your Island of Ægina, but where is its Temple to Minerva?

Shall I read you what the Christian Minerva had achieved under the shadow of our Parnassus, up to the year 1848?— Here is a little account of a Welsh School, from page 261 of the report on Wales, published by the Committee of Council

on Education. This is a School close to a town containing
5,000 persons :—

" I then called up a larger class, most of whom had recently
come to the school.   Three girls repeatedly declared they had
never heard of Christ, and two that they had never heard of
God.   Two out of six thought Christ was on earth now ('they
might have had a worse thought, perhaps') ; three knew nothing about the crucifixion.   Four out of seven did not know
the names of the months, nor the number of days in a year.
They had no notion of addition beyond two and two, or three
and three ; their minds were perfect blanks."

Oh, ye women of England ! from the Princess of that Wales
to the simplest of you, do not think your own children can be
brought into their true fold of rest while these are scattered
on the hills, as sheep having no shepherd.   And do not think
your daughters can be trained to the truth of their own human
beauty, while the pleasant places, which God made at once for
their school-room and their play-ground, lie desolate and defiled.   You cannot baptize them rightly in those inch-deep
fonts of yours, unless you baptize them also in the sweet
waters which the great Lawgiver strikes forth forever from
the rocks of your native land—waters which a Pagan would
have worshipped in their purity, and you only worship with
pollution.   You cannot lead your children faithfully to those
narrow axe-hewn church altars of yours, while the dark azure
altars in heaven—the mountains that sustain your island
throne,—mountains on which a Pagan would have seen the
powers of heaven rest in every wreathed cloud—remain for
you without inscription ; altars built, not to, but by, an Unknown God.

III. Thus far, then, of the nature, thus far of the teaching,
of woman, and thus of her household office, and queenliness.
We come now to our last, our widest question,—What is her
queenly office with respect to the state ?

Generally we are under an impression that a man's duties
are public, and a woman's private.   But this is not altogether
so.   A man has a personal work or duty relating to his own

home, and a public work or duty, which is the expansion of the other, relating to the state. So a woman has a personal work and duty, relating to her own home, and a public work and duty, which is also the expansion of that.

Now the man's work for his own home is, as has been said, to secure its maintenance, progress, and defence ; the woman's to secure its order, comfort and loveliness.

Expand both these functions. The man's duty, as a member of a commonwealth, is to assist in the maintenance, in the advance, in the defence of the state. The woman's duty, as a member of the commonwealth, is to assist in the ordering, in the comforting, and in the beautiful adornment of the state.

What the man is at his own gate, defending it, if need be, against insult and spoil, that also, not in a less, but in a more devoted measure, he is to be at the gate of his country, leaving his home, if need be, even to the spoiler, to do his more incumbent work there.

And, in like manner, what the woman is to be within her gates, as the centre of order, the balm of distress, and the mirror of beauty ; that she is also to be without her gates, where order is more difficult distress more imminent, loveliness more rare.

And as within the human heart there is always set an instinct for all its real duties,—an instinct which you cannot quench, but only warp and corrupt if you withdraw it from its true purpose ;—as there is the intense instinct of love, which, rightly disciplined, maintains all the sanctities of life and, misdirected, undermines them ; and *must* do either the one or the other ; so there is in the human heart an inextinguishable instinct, the love of power, which, rightly directed, maintains all the majesty of law and life, and misdirected, wrecks them.

Deep rooted in the innermost life of the heart of man, and of the heart of woman, God set it there, and God keeps it there. Vainly, as falsely, you blame or rebuke the desire of power !—For Heaven's sake, and for Man's sake, desire it all you can. But *what* power ? That is all the question. Power to destroy ? the lion's limb, and the dragon's breath ? Not so. Power to heal, to redeem, to guide and to guard. Power of the sceptre and shield; the power of the royal hand that heals in touching,—that binds the fiend and looses the captive; the throne that is founded on the rock of Justice, and descended from only by steps of mercy. Will you not covet such power as this, and seek such a throne as this, and be no more housewives, but queens?

It is now long since the women of England arrogated, universally, a title which once belonged to nobility only, and having once been in the habit of accepting the simple title of gentlewoman, as correspondent to that of gentleman, insisted on the privilege of assuming the title of "Lady,"* which properly corresponds only to the title of "Lord."

I do not blame them for this; but only for their narrow motive in this. I would have them desire and claim the title of Lady, provided they claim, not merely the title, but the office and duty signified by it. Lady means "bread-giver" or "loaf-giver," and Lord means "maintainer of laws," and both titles have reference, not to the law which is maintained in the house, nor to the bread which is given to the household; but to law maintained for the multitude, and to bread broken among the multitude. So that a Lord has legal claim only to his title in so far as he is the maintainer of the justice of the Lord of Lord's; and a Lady has legal claim to her title, only so far as she communicates that help to the poor representatives of her Master, which women once, ministering to Him of their substance, were permitted to extend to that Master Himself; and when she is known, as He Himself once was, in breaking of bread.

And this beneficent and legal dominion, this power of the Dominus, or House Lord, and of the Domina, or House-Lady,

---

* I wish there were a true order of chivalry instituted for our English youth of certain ranks, in which both boy and girl should receive, at a given age, their knighthood and ladyhood by true title; attainable only by certain probation and trial both of character and accomplishment; and to be forfeited. on conviction, by their peers of any dishonorable act. Such an institution would be entirely, and with all noble results, possible, in a nation which loved honour. That it would not be possible among us is not to the discredit of the scheme

is great and venerable, not in the number of those through whom it has lineally descended, but in the number of those whom it grasps within its sway ; it is always regarded with reverent worship wherever its dynasty is founded on its duty, and its ambition corelative with its beneficence. Your fancy is pleased with the thought of being noble ladies, with a train of vassals. Be it so : you cannot be too noble, and your train cannot be too great ; but see to it that your train is of vassals whom you serve and feed, not merely of slaves who serve and feed *you ;* and that the multitude which obeys you is of those whom you have comforted, not oppressed,—whom you have redeemed, not led into captivity.

And this, which is true of the lower or household dominion, is equally true of the queenly dominion ;—that highest dignity is open to you, if you will also accept that highest duty. Rex et Regina—Roi et Reine—"*Right*-doers ;" they differ but from the Lady and Lord, in that their power is supreme over the mind as over the person—that they not only feed and clothe, but direct and teach. And whether consciously or not, you must be, in many a heart, enthroned: there is no putting by that crown ; queens you must always be ; queens to your lovers ; queens to your husbands and your sons ; queens of higher mystery to the world beyond, which bows itself, and will for ever bow, before the myrtle crown, and the stainless sceptre, of womanhood. But, alas ! you are too often idle and careless queens, grasping at majesty in the least things, while you abdicate it in the greatest ; and leaving misrule and violence to work their will among men, in defiance of the power, which, holding straight in gift from the Prince of all Peace, the wicked among you betray, and the good forget.

"Prince of Peace." Note that name. When kings rule in that name, and nobles, and the judges of the earth, they also, in their narrow place, and mortal measure, receive the power of it. There are no other rulers than they : other rule than theirs is but *mis*rule ; they who govern verily "Dei gratiâ" are all princes, yes, or princesses, of peace. There is not a war in the world, no, nor an injustice, but you women are answerable for it ; not in that you have provoked, but in that you have not hindered. Men, by their nature, are prone to fight; they will fight for any cause, or for none. It is for you to choose their cause for them, and to forbid them when there is no cause. There is no suffering, no injustice, no misery in the earth, but the guilt of it lies lastly with you. Men can bear the sight of it, but you should not be able to bear it. Men may tread it down without sympathy in their own struggle; but men are feeble in sympathy, and contracted in hope; it is you only who can feel the depths of pain; and conceive the way of its healing. Instead of trying to do this, you turn away from it; you shut yourselves within your park walls and garden gates; and you are content to know that there is beyond them a whole world in wilderness—a world of secrets which you dare not penetrate; and of suffering which you dare not conceive.

I tell you that this is to me quite the most amazing among the phenomena of humanity. I am surprised at no depths to which, when once warped from its honor, that humanity can be degraded. I do not wonder at the miser's death, with his hands, as they relax, dropping gold. I do not wonder at the sensualist's life, with the shroud wrapped about his feet. I do not wonder at the single-handed murder of a single victim, done by the assassin in the darkness of the railway, or reed-shadow of the marsh. I do not even wonder at the myriad-handed murder of multitudes, done boastfully in the daylight, by the frenzy of nations, and the immeasurable, unimaginable guilt, heaped up from hell to heaven, of their priests, and kings. But this is wonderful to me—oh, how wonderful!—to see the tender and delicate woman among you, with her child at her breast, and a power, if she would wield it, over it, and over its father, purer than the air of heaven, and stronger than the seas of earth—nay, a magnitude of blessing which her husband would not part with for all that earth itself, though it were made of one entire and perfect chrysolite:—to see her abdicate this majesty to play at precedence with her next-door neighbor! This is wonderful—oh, wonderful!—to see her, with every innocent feeling fresh within her, go out in the morning into her garden to play with the fringes of its guarded flowers, and lift their heads when they are drooping, with her happy smile upon her face, and no cloud upon her brow, because there is a little wall around her place of peace : and yet she knows, in her heart, if she would only look for its knowledge, that, outside of that little rose-covered wall, the wild grass, to the horizon, is torn up by the agony of men, and beat level by the drift of their life-blood.

Have you ever considered what a deep under meaning there lies, or at least may be read, if we choose, in our custom of strewing flowers before those whom we think most happy? Do you suppose it is merely to deceive them into the hope that happiness is always to fall thus in showers at their feet? —that wherever they pass they will tread on herbs of sweet scent, and that the rough ground will be made smooth for them by depth of roses? So surely as they believe that, they will have, instead, to walk on bitter herbs and thorns ; and the only softness to their feet will be of snow. But it is not thus intended they should believe ; there is a better meaning in that old custom. The path of a good woman is indeed strewn with flowers : but they rise behind her steps, not before them. "Her feet have touched the meadows, and left the daisies rosy." You think that only a lover's fancy ;—false and vain ! How if it could be true? You think this also, perhaps, only a poet's fancy—

> " Even the light harebell raised its head
> Elastic from her airy tread."

But it is little to say of a woman, that she only does not destroy where she passes. She should revive ; the harebells should bloom, not stoop, as she passes. You think I am going into wild hyperbole? Pardon me, not a whit—I mean what I say in calm English, spoken in resolute truth. You have heard it said—(and I believe there is more than fancy even in that saying, but let it pass for a fanciful one)—that flowers only flourish rightly in the garden of some one who loves them. I know you would like that to be true ; you would think it a pleasant magic if you could flush your flow ers into brighter bloom by a kind look upon them : nay more, if your look had the power, not only to cheer, but to guard them—if you could bid the black blight turn away, and the knotted caterpillar spare—if you could bid the dew fall upon them in the drought, and say to the south wind, in frost —"Come, thou south, and breathe upon my garden, that the spices of it may flow out." This you would think a great thing? And do you think it not a greater thing, that all this (and how much more than this !) you *can* do, for fairer flowers than these—flowers that could bless you for having blessed them, and will love you for having loved them ;—flowers that have eyes like yours, and thoughts like yours, and lives like yours ; which, once saved, you save for ever? Is this only a little power? Far among the moorlands and the rocks,— far in the darkness of the terrible streets,—these feeble florets are lying, with all their fresh leaves torn, and their stems broken—will you never go down to them, nor set them in order in their little fragrant beds, nor fence them in their shuddering from the fierce wind? Shall morning follow morning, for you, but not for them ; and the dawn rise to watch, far away, those frantic Dances of Death ; * but no dawn rise to breathe upon these living banks of wild violet, and wood-bine, and rose ; nor call to you, through your casement,— call, (not giving you the name of the English poet's lady, but the name of Dante's great Matilda, who on the edge of happy Lethe, stood, wreathing flowers with flowers,) saying :—

> " Come into the garden, Maud,
>   For the black bat, night, has flown,
>   And the woodbine spices are wafted abroad
>   And the musk of the roses blown ? "

Will you not go down among them ?—among those sweet living things, whose new courage, sprung from the earth with the deep colour of heaven upon it, is starting up in strength of goodly spire ; and whose purity, washed from the dust, is opening, bud by bud, into the flower of promise ;—and still

* See note, p. 57.

they turn to you, and for you, " The Larkspur listens—I hear, I hear ! And the Lily whispers—I wait."

Did you notice that I missed two lines when I read you that first stanza ; and think that I had forgotten them? **Hear them now :—**

> " Come into the garden, Maud,
>   For the black bat, night, has flown :
>   Come into the garden, Maud,
>   I am here at the gate, alone."

Who is it, think you, who stands at the gate of this sweeter garden, alone, waiting for you? Did you ever hear, not of a Maude, but a Madeleine, who went down to her garden in the dawn, and found one waiting at the gate, whom she sup-posed to be the gardener? Have you not sought Him often ; —sought Him in vain, all through the night ;—sought Him in vain at the gate of that old garden where the fiery sword is set? He is never there ; but at the gate of *this* garden He is waiting always—waiting to take your hand—ready to go down to see the fruits of the valley, to see whether the vine has flourished, and the pomegranate budded. There you shall see with Him the little tendrils of the vines that His hand is guiding—there you shall see the pomegranate spring-ing where His hand cast the sanguine seed ;—more : you shall see the troops of the angel keepers, that, with their wings, wave away the hungry birds from the pathsides where He has sown, and call to each other between the vineyard rows, " Take us the foxes, the little foxes, that spoil the vines, for our vines have tender grapes." Oh--you queens—you queens ! among the hills and happy greenwood of this land of yours, shall the foxes have holes, and the birds of the air have nests ; and in your cities, shall the stones cry out against you, that they are the only pillows where the Son of Man can lay His head?

LECTURE III.

Lecture delivered in the theatre of the Royal College of Science, Dublin, 1868.

96. WHEN I accepted the privilege of addressing you to-day, I was not aware of a restriction with respect to the topics of discussion which may be brought before this Society *—a restriction which, though entirely wise and right under the circumstances contemplated in its introduction, would necessarily have disabled me, thinking as I think, from preparing any lecture for you on the subject of art in a form which might be permanently useful. Pardon me, therefore, in so far as I must transgress such limitation; for indeed my infringement will be of the letter—not of the spirit—of your commands. In whatever I may say touching the religion which has been the foundation of art, or the policy which has contributed to its power, if I offend one, I shall offend all; for I shall take no note of any separations in creeds, or antagonisms in parties : neither do I fear that ultimately I shall offend any, by proving—or at least stating as capable of positive proof—the connection of all that is best in the crafts and arts of man, with the simplicity of his faith, and the sincerity of his patriotism.

97. But I speak to you under another disadvantage, by which I am checked in frankness of utterance, not here only, but everywhere; namely, that I am never fully aware how far my audiences are disposed to give me credit for real knowledge of my subject, or how far they grant me attention only because I have been sometimes thought an ingenious or pleasant essayist upon it. For I have had what, in many respects, I boldly call the misfortune, to set my words some-

---

* That no reference should be made to religious questions.

times prettily together; not without a foolish vanity in the poor knack that I had of doing so; until I was heavily punished for this pride, by finding that many people thought of the words only, and cared nothing for their meaning. Happily, therefore, the power of using such pleasant language—if indeed it ever were mine—is passing away from me; and whatever I am now able to say at all, I find myself forced to say with great plainness. For my thoughts have changed also, as my words have; and whereas in earlier life, what little influence I obtained was due perhaps chiefly to the enthusiasm with which I was able to dwell on the beauty of the physical clouds, and of their colours in the sky; so all the influence I now desire to retain must be due to the earnestness with which I am endeavouring to trace the form and beauty of another kind of cloud than those; the bright cloud, of which it is written—

"What is your life? It is even as a vapour that appeareth for a little time, and then vanisheth away."

98. I suppose few people reach the middle or latter period of their age, without having, at some moment of change or disappointment, felt the truth of those bitter words; and been startled by the fading of the sunshine from the cloud of their life, into the sudden agony of the knowledge that the fabric of it was as fragile as a dream, and the endurance of it as transient as the dew. But it is not always that, even at such times of melancholy surprise, we can enter into any true perception that this human life shares, in the nature of it, not only the evanescence, but the mystery of the cloud; that its avenues are wreathed in darkness, and its forms and courses no less fantastic, than spectral and obscure; so that not only in the vanity which we cannot grasp, but in the shadow which we cannot pierce, it is true of this cloudy life of ours, that "man walketh in a vain shadow, and disquieteth himself in vain."

99. And least of all, whatever may have been the eagerness of our passions. or the height of our pride, are we able to understand in its depth the third and most solemn character in which our life is like those clouds of heaven; that to it be-

longs not only their transience, not only their mystery, but
also their power ; that in the cloud of the human soul there
is a fire stronger than the lightning, and a grace more
precious than the rain ; and that though of the good and evil
it shall one day be said alike, that the place that knew them
knows them no more, there is an infinite separation between
those whose brief presence had there been a blessing, like
the mist of Eden that went up from the earth to water the
garden, and those whose place knew them only as a drifting
and changeful shade, of whom the heavenly sentence is, that
they are "wells without water ; clouds that are carried with
a tempest, to whom the mist of darkness is reserved for
ever?"

100. To those among us, however, who have lived long
enough to form some just estimate of the rate of the changes
which are, hour by hour in accelerating catastrophe, mani-
festing themselves in the laws, the arts, and the creeds of
men, it seems to me, that now at least, if never at any former
time, the thoughts of the true nature of our life, and of its
powers and responsibilities, should present themselves with
absolute sadness and sternness.

And although I know that this feeling is much deepened in
my own mind by disappointment, which, by chance, has attended the greater number of my cherished purposes, I do
not for that reason distrust the feeling itself, though I am on
my guard against an exaggerated degree of it : nay, I rather
believe that in periods of new effort and violent change,
disappointment is a wholesome medicine ; and that in the
secret of it, as in the twilight so beloved by Titian, we may
see the colours of things with deeper truth than in the most
dazzling sunshine.   And because these truths about the works
of men, which I want to bring to-day before you, are most of
them sad ones, though at the same time helpful ; and because also I believe that your kind Irish hearts will answer
more gladly to the truthful expression of a personal feeling,
than to the exposition of an abstract principle, I will permit
myself so much unreserved speaking of my own causes of regret, as may enable you to make just allowance for what, so

cording to your sympathies, you will call either the bitter-ness, or the insight, of a mind which has surrendered its best hopes, and been foiled in its favorite aims.

101. I spent the ten strongest years of my life, (from twenty to thirty,) in endeavoring to show the excellence of the work of the man whom I believed, and rightly believed, to be the greatest painter of the schools of England since Reynolds. I had then perfect faith in the power of every great truth or beauty to prevail ultimately, and take its right place in usefulness and honour; and I strove to bring the painter's work into this due place, while the painter was yet alive. But he knew, better than I, the uselessness of talking about what people could not see for themselves. He always discouraged me scornfully, even when he thanked me—and he died before even the superficial effect of my work was visible. I went on, however, thinking I could at least be of use to the public, if not to him, in proving his power. My books got talked about a little. The prices of modern pic-tures, generally, rose, and I was beginning to take some pleasure in a sense of gradual victory, when, fortunately or unfortunately, an opportunity of perfect trial undeceived me at once, and for ever. The Trustees of the National Gallery commissioned me to arrange the Turner drawings there, and permitted me to prepare three hundred examples of his studies from nature, for exhibition at Kensington. At Ken-sington they were and are, placed for exhibition; but they are not exhibited, for the room in which they hang is always empty.

102. Well—this showed me at once, that those ten years of my life had been, in their chief purpose, lost. For that, I did not so much care; I had, at least, learned my own busi-ness thoroughly, and should be able, as I fondly supposed, after such a lesson, now to use my knowledge with better effect. But what I did care for, was the—to me frightful—discovery, that the most splendid genius in the arts might be permitted by Providence to labour and perish uselessly; that in the very fineness of it there might be something rendering it invisible to ordinary eyes; but, that with this strange ex-

cellence, faults might be mingled which would be as deadly
as its virtues were vain ; that the glory of it was perishable,
as well as invisible, and the gift and grace of it might be to
us, as snow in summer, and as rain in harvest.

103. That was the first mystery of life to me. But, while
my best energy was given to the study of painting, I had put
collateral effort, more prudent, if less enthusiastic, into that
of architecture ; and in this I could not complain of meeting
with no sympathy. Among several personal reasons which
caused me to desire that I might give this my closing lecture
on the subject of art here, in Ireland, one of the chief was,
that in reading it, I should stand near the beautiful building,
—the engineers' school of your college,—which was the first
realization I had the joy to see, of the principles I had, until
then, been endeavouring to teach ; but which alas, is now, to
me, no more than the richly canopied monument of one of
the most earnest souls that ever gave itself to the arts, and
one of my truest and most loving friends, Benjamin Woodward. Nor was it here in Ireland only that I received the
help of Irish sympathy and genius.   When, to another friend,
Sir Thomas Deane, with Mr. Woodward, was entrusted the
building of the museum at Oxford, the best details of the work
were executed by scupltors who had been born and trained
here ; and the first window of the façade of the building, in
which was inaugurated the study of natural science in England, in true fellowship with literature, was carved from my
design by an Irish sculptor.

104. You may perhaps think that no man ought to speak
of disappointment, to whom, even in one branch of labour, so
much success was granted. Had Mr. Woodward now been
beside me, I had not so spoken ; but his gentle and passionate
spirit was cut off from the fulfilment of its purposes, and the
work we did together is now become vain. It may not be so
in future ; but the architecture we endeavoured to introduce
is inconsistent alike with the reckless luxury, the deforming
mechanism, and the squalid misery of modern cities ; among
the formative fashions of the day, aided, especially in England,
by ecclesiastical sentiment, it indeed obtained notoriety ; and

sometimes behind an engine furnace, or a railroad bank, you may detect the pathetic discord of its momentary grace, and, with toil, decipher its floral carvings choked with soot. I felt answerable to the schools I loved, only for their injury. I perceived that this new portion of my strength had also been spent in vain ; and from amidst streets of iron, and palaces of crystal, shrank back at last to the carving of the mountain and colour of the flower.

105. And still I could tell of failure, and failure repeated as years went on ; but I have trespassed enough on your patience to show you, in part, the causes of my discouragement. Now let me more deliberately tell you its results. You know there is a tendency in the minds of many men, when they are heavily disappointed in the main purposes of their life, to feel, and perhaps in warning, perhaps in mockery, to declare, that life itself is a vanity. Because it has disappointed them, they think its nature is of disappointment always, or at best, of pleasure that can be grasped by imagination only ; that the cloud of it has no strength nor fire within ; but is a painted cloud only, to be delighted in, yet despised. You know how beautifully Pope has expressed this particular phase of thought :—

> " Meanwhile opinion gilds, with varying rays,
> These painted clouds that beautify our days ;
> Each want of happiness by hope supplied,
> And each vacuity of sense, by pride.
>
> Hope builds as fast as Knowledge can destroy ;
> In Folly's cup, still laughs the bubble joy.
> One pleasure past, another still we gain,
> And not a vanity is given in vain."

But the effect of failure upon my own mind has been just the reverse of this. The more that my life disappointed me, the more solemn and wonderful it became to me. It seemed, contrarily to Pope's saying, that the vanity of it *was* indeed given in vain ; but that there was something behind the veil of it, which was not vanity. It became to me not a painted cloud, but a terrible and impenetrable one : not a mirage,

which vanished as I drew near, but a pillar of darkness, to
which I was forbidden to draw near. For I saw that both my
own failure, and such success in petty things as in its poor
triumph seemed to me worse than failure, came from the want
of sufficiently earnest effort to understand the whole law and
meaning of existence, and to bring it to noble and due end;
as, on the other hand, I saw more and more clearly that all
enduring success in the arts, or in any other occupation, had
come from the ruling of lower purposes, not by a conviction
of their nothingness, but by a solemn faith in the advancing
power of human nature, or in the promise, however dimly apprehended, that the mortal part of it would one day be swallowed up in immortality; and that, indeed, the arts themselves
never had reached any vital strength or honour but in the
effort to proclaim this immortality, and in the service either
of great and just religion, or of some unselfish patriotism, and
law of such national life as must be the foundation of religion.

106. Nothing that I have ever said is more true or necessary—nothing has been more misunderstood or misapplied—
than my strong assertion, that the arts can never be right
themselves, unless their motive is right. It is misunderstood
this way : weak painters, who have never learned their business, and cannot lay a true line, continually come to me, cry-
ing out—" Look at this picture of mine; it *must* be good, I
had such a lovely motive. I have put my whole heart into it,
and taken years to think over its treatment." Well, the only
answer for these people is—if one had the cruelty to make it
—" Sir, you cannot think over *any*thing in any number of
years,—you haven't the head to do it; and though you had
fine motives, strong enough to make you burn yourself in a
slow fire, if only first you could paint a picture, you can't
paint one, nor half an inch of one; you haven't the hand to
do it."

But, far more decisively we have to say to the men who *do*
know their business, or may know it if they choose—" Sir,
you have this gift and a mighty one; see that you serve your
nation faithfully with it. It is a greater trust than ships and
armies : you might cast *them* away, if you were their captain,

with less treason to your people than in casting your own glorious power away, and serving the devil with it instead of men. Ships and armies you may replace if they are lost, but a great intellect, once abused, is a curse to the earth for ever.'

107. This, then, I meant by saying that the arts must have noble motive. This also I said respecting them, that they never had prospered, nor could prosper, but when they had such true purpose, and were devoted to the proclamation of divine truth or law. And yet I saw also that they had always failed in this proclamation—that poetry, and sculpture, and painting, though only great when they strove to teach us something about the gods, never had taught us anything trustworthy about the gods, but had always betrayed their trust in the crisis of it, and, with their powers at the full reach, became ministers to pride and to lust. And I felt also, with increasing amazement, the unconquerable apathy in ourselves the hearers, no less than in these the teachers; and that, while the wisdom and rightness of every act and art of life could only be consistent with a right understanding of the ends of life, we were all plunged as in a languid dream— our heart fat, and our eyes heavy, and our ears closed, lest the inspiration of hand or voice should reach us—lest we should see with our eyes, and understand with our hearts, and be healed.

108. This intense apathy in all of us is the first great mystery of life; it stands in the way of every perception, every virtue. There is no making ourselves feel enough astonishment at it. That the occupations or pastimes of life should have no motive, is understandable; but—That life itself should have no motive—that we neither care to find out what it may lead to, nor to guard against its being for ever taken away from us—here is a mystery indeed. For, just suppose I were able to call at this moment to any one in this audience by name, and to tell him positively that I knew a large estate had been lately left to him on some curious conditions; but that, though I knew it was large, I did not know how large, nor even where it was—whether in the East Indies or the West, or in England, or at the Antipodes. I only knew it

was a vast estate, and that there was a chance of his losing it altogether if he did not soon find out on what terms it had been left to him. Suppose I were able to say this positively to any single man in this audience, and he knew that I did not speak without warrant, do you think that he would rest content with that vague knowledge, if it were anywise possible to obtain more? Would he not give every energy to find some trace of the facts, and never rest till he had ascertained where this place was, and what it was like? And suppose he were a young man, and all he could discover by his best endeavour was, that the estate was never to be his at all unless he persevered, during certain years of probation, in an, orderly and industrious life; but that, according to the rightness of his conduct, the portion of the estate assigned to him would be greater or less, so that it literally depended on his behaviour from day to day whether he got ten thousand a year, or thirty thousand a year, or nothing whatever—would you not think it strange if the youth never troubled himself to satisfy the conditions in any way, nor even to know what was required of him, but lived exactly as he chose, and never inquired whether his chances of the estate were increasing or passing away? Well, you know that this is actually and literally so with the greater number of the educated persons now living in Christian countries. Nearly every man and woman, in any company such as this, outwardly professes to believe—and a large number unquestionably think they believe—much more than this; not only that a quite unlimited estate is in prospect for them if they please the Holder of it, but that the infinite contrary of such a possession—an estate of perpetual misery, is in store for them if they displease this great Land-Holder, this great Heaven-Holder. And yet there is not one in a thousand of these human souls that cares to think, for ten minutes of the day, where this estate is, or how beautiful it is, or what kind of life they are to lead in it, or what kind of life they must lead to obtain it.

109. You fancy that you care to know this: so little do you care that, probably, at this moment many of you are displeased with me for talking of the matter! You came to hear

about the Art of this world, not about the Life of the next, and you are provoked with me for talking of what you can hear any Sunday in church. But do not be afraid. I will tell you something before you go about pictures, and carvings, and pottery, and what else you would like better to hear of than the other world. Nay, perhaps you say, "We want you to talk of pictures and pottery, because we are sure that you know something of them, and you know nothing of the other world." Well—I don't. That is quite true. But the very strangeness and mystery of which I urge you to take notice is in this—that I do not ;—nor you either. Can you answer a single bold question unflinchingly about that other world— Are you sure there is a heaven ? Sure there is a hell ? Sure that men are dropping before your faces through the pavements of these streets into eternal fire, or sure that they are not ? Sure that at your own death you are going to be delivered from all sorrow, to be endowed with all virtue, to be gifted with all felicity, and raised into perpetual companionship with a King, compared to whom the kings of the earth are as grasshoppers, and the nations as the dust of His feet? Are you sure of this ? or, if not sure, do any of us so much as care to make it sure ? and, if not, how can anything that we do be right—how can anything we think be wise ; what honor can there be in the arts that amuse us, or what profit in the possessions that please ?

Is not this a mystery of life ?

110. But farther, you may, perhaps, think it a beneficent ordinance for the generality of men that they do not, with earnestness or anxiety, dwell on such questions of the future ; because the business of the day could not be done if this kind of thought were taken by all of us for the morrow. Be it so : but at least we might anticipate that the greatest and wisest of us, who were evidently the appointed teachers of the rest, would set themselves apart to seek out whatever could be surely known of the future destinies of their race ; and to teach this in no rhetorical or ambiguous manner, but in the plainest and most severely earnest words.

Now, the highest representatives of men who have thus en-

deavoured, during the Christian era, to search out these deep
things, and relate them, are Dante and Milton.   There are
none who for earnestness of thought, for mastery of word,
can be classed with these.   I am not at present, mind you,
speaking of persons set apart in any priestly or pastoral office, to deliver creeds to us, or doctrines ; but of men who
try to discover and set forth, as far as by human intellect is
possible, the facts of the other world.   Divines may perhaps
teach us how to arrive there, but only these two poets have in
any powerful manner striven to discover, or in any definite
words professed to tell, what we shall see and become there :
or how those upper and nether worlds are, and have been, inhabited.

111.   And what have they told us ?   Milton's account of the
most important event in his whole system of the universe, the
fall of the angels, is evidently unbelievable to himself ; and
the more so, that it is wholly founded on, and in a great part
spoiled and degraded from, Hesiod's account of the decisive
war of the younger gods with the Titans.   The rest of his
poem is a picturesque drama, in which every artifice of invention is visibly and consciously employed, not a single fact
being, for an instant, conceived as tenable by any living faith.
Dante's conception is far more intense, and, by himself, for
the time, not to be escaped from ; it is indeed a vision, but a
vision only, and that one of the wildest that ever entranced a
soul—a dream in which every grotesque type or phantasy of
heathen tradition is renewed, and adorned ; and the destinies
of the Christian Church, under their most sacred symbols, become literally subordinate to the praise, and are only to be
understood by the aid, of one dear Florentine maiden.

112.   I tell you truly that, as I strive more with this strange
lethargy and trance in myself, and awake to the meaning and
power of life, it seems daily more amazing to me that men
such as these should dare to play with the most precious
truths (or the most deadly untruths), by which the whole
human race listening to them could be informed, or deceived ;
—all the world their audiences for ever, with pleased ear, and
passionate heart ;—and yet, to this submissive infinitude of

souls, and evermore succeeding and succeeding multitude, hungry for bread of life, they do but play upon sweetly modulated pipes ; with pompous nomenclature adorn the councils of hell ; touch a troubadour's guitar to the courses of the suns ; and fill the openings of eternity, before which prophets have veiled their faces, and which angels desire to look into, with idle puppets of their scholastic imagination, and melancholy lights of frantic faith in their lost mortal love.

Is not this a mystery of life ?

113. But more. We have to remember that these two great teachers were both of them warped in their temper, and thwarted in their search for truth. They were men of intellectual war, unable, through darkness of controversy, or stress of personal grief, to discern where their own ambition modified their utterances of the moral law ; or their own agony mingled with their anger at its violation. But greater men than these have been—innocent-hearted—too great for contest. Men, like Homer and Shakespeare, of so unrecognized personality, that it disappears in future ages, and becomes ghostly, like the tradition of a lost heathen god. Men, therefore, to whose unoffended, uncondemning sight, the whole of human nature reveals itself in a pathetic weakness, with which they will not strive ; or in mournful and transitory strength, which they dare not praise. And all Pagan and Christian civilization thus becomes subject to them. It does not matter how little, or how much, any of us have read, either of Homer or Shakespeare : everything round us, in substance, or in thought, has been moulded by them. All Greek gentlemen were educated under Homer. All Roman gentlemen, by Greek literature. All Italian, and French, and English gentlemen, by Roman literature, and by its principles. Of the scope of Shakespeare, I will say only, that the intellectual measure of every man since born, in the domains of creative thought, may be assigned to him, according to the degree in which he has been taught by Shakespeare. Well, what do these two men, centres of moral intelligence, deliver to us of conviction respecting what it most behoves that intelligence to grasp? What is their hope; their crown of rejoicing !

8

what manner of exhortation have they for us, or of rebuke? what lies next their own hearts, and dictates their undying words? Have they any peace to promise to our unrest—any redemption to our misery?

114. Take Homer first, and think if there is any sadder image of human fate than the great Homeric story. The main features in the character of Achilles are its intense desire of justice, and its tenderness of affection. And in that bitter song of the Iliad, this man, though aided continually by the wisest of the gods, and burning with the desire of justice in his heart, becomes yet, through ill-governed passion, the most unjust of men : and, full of the deepest tenderness in his heart, becomes yet, through ill-governed passion, the most cruel of men. Intense alike in love and in friendship, he loses, first his mistress, and then his friend ; for the sake of the one, he surrenders to death the armies of his own land ; for the sake of the other, he surrenders all. Will a man lay down his life for his friend? Yea—even for his *dead* friend, this Achilles, though goddess-born, and goddess-taught, gives up his kingdom, his country, and his life—casts alike the innocent and guilty, with himself, into one gulf of slaughter, and dies at last by the hand of the basest of his adversaries. Is not this a mystery of life?

115. But what, then, is the message to us of our own poet, and searcher of hearts, after fifteen hundred years of Christian faith have been numbered over the graves of men? Are his words more cheerful than the heathen's—is his hope more near—his trust more sure—his reading of fate more happy? Ah, no! He differs from the Heathen poet chiefly in this—that he recognizes, for deliverance, no gods nigh at hand ; and that, by petty chance—by momentary folly—by broken message—by fool's tyranny—or traitor's snare, the strongest and most righteous are brought to their ruin, and perish without word of hope. He indeed, as part of his rendering of character, ascribes the power and modesty of habitual devotion, to the gentle and the just. The death-bed of Katharine is bright with vision of angels ; and the great soldier-king, standing by his few dead, acknowledges the pres

ence of the hand that can save alike by many or by few. But observe that from those who with deepest spirit, meditate, and with deepest passion, mourn, there are no such words as these ; nor in their hearts are any such consolations. Instead of the perpetual sense of the helpful presence of the Deity, which, through all heathen tradition, is the source of heroic strength, in battle, in exile, and in the valley of the shadow of death, we find only in the great Christian poet, the consciousness of a moral law, through which " the gods are just, and of our pleasant vices make instruments to scourge us ;" and of the resolved arbitration of the destinies, that conclude into precision of doom what we feebly and blindly began ; and force us, when our indiscretion serves us, and our deepest plots do pall, to the confession, that "there's a divinity that shapes our ends, rough hew them how we will."

Is not this a mystery of life ?

116. Be it so then. About this human life that is to be, or that is, the wise religious men tell us nothing that we can trust ; and the wise contemplative men, nothing that can give us peace. But there is yet a third class, to whom we may turn—the wise practical men. We have sat at the feet of the poets who sang of heaven, and they have told us their dreams. We have listened to the poets who sang of earth, and they have chanted to us dirges, and words of despair. But there is one class of men more :—men, not capable of vision, nor sensitive to sorrow, but firm of purpose—practised in busi-ness : learned in all that can be, (by handling,—) known. Men whose hearts and hopes are wholly in this present world, from whom, therefore, we may surely learn, at least, how, at present, conveniently to live in it. What will *they* say to us, or show us by example ? These kings—these councillors—these statesmen and builders of kingdoms—these capitalists and men of business, who weigh the earth, and the dust of it, in a balance. They know the world, surely ; and what is the mystery of life to us, is none to them. They can surely show us how to live, while we live, and to gather out of the present world what is best.

117 I think I can best tell you their answer, by telling you

a dream I had once. For though I am no poet, I have dreams
sometimes :—I dreamed I was at a child's May-day party, in
which every means of entertainment had been provided for
them, by a wise and kind host. It was in a stately house,
with beautiful gardens attached to it ; and the children had
been set free in the rooms and gardens, with no care whatever but how to pass their afternoon rejoicingly.' They did
not, indeed, know much about what was to happen next
day ; and some of them, I thought, were a little frightened,
because there was a chance of their being sent to a new school
where there were examinations ; but they kept the thoughts
of that out of their heads as well as they could, and resolved
to enjoy themselves. The house, I said, was in a beautiful garden, and in the garden were all kinds of flowers ; sweet grassy
banks for rest ; and smooth lawns for play ; and pleasant
streams and woods ; and rocky places for climbing. And the
children were happy for a little while, but presently they
separated themselves into parties; and then each party declared, it would have a piece of the garden for its own, and that
none of the others should have anything to do with that piece.
Next, they quarrelled violently, which pieces they would have ;
and at last the boys took up the thing, as boys should do,
"practically," and fought in the flower-beds till there was
hardly a flower left standing ; then they trampled down each
other's bits of the garden out of spite ; and the girls cried till
they could cry no more ; and so they all lay down at last
breathless in the ruin, and waited for the time when they
were to be taken home in the evening.*

118. Meanwhile, the children in the house had been making
themselves happy also in their manner. For them, there had
been provided every kind of in-doors pleasure : there was
music for them to dance to ; and the library was open, with
all manner of amusing books ; and there was a museum, full
of the most curious shells, and animals, and birds ; and there
was a workshop, with lathes and carpenter's tools, for the in-

---

* I have sometimes been asked what this means. I intended it to set
forth the wisdom of men in war contending for kingdoms, and what follows to set forth their wisdom in peace, contending for wealth.

genious boys; and there were pretty fantastic dresses, for the girls to dress in; and there were microscopes, and kaleido-scopes; and whatever toys a child could fancy; and a table, in the dining-room, loaded with everything nice to eat.

But, in the midst of all this, it struck two or three of the more "practical" children, that they would like some of the brass-headed nails that studded the chairs; and so they set to work to pull them out. Presently, the others, who were read-ing, or looking at shells, took a fancy to do the like; and, in a little while, all the children nearly, were spraining their fin-gers, in pulling out brass-headed nails. With all that they could pull out, they were not satisfied; and then, everybody wanted some of somebody else's. And at last the really prac-tical and sensible ones declared, that nothing was of any real consequence, that afternoon, except to get plenty of brass-headed nails; and that the books, and the cakes, and the mi-croscopes were of no use at all in themselves, but only, if they could be exchanged for nail-heads. And, at last they began to fight for nail-heads, as the others fought for the bits of garden. Only here and there, a despised one shrank away into a corner, and tried to get a little quiet with a book, in the midst of the noise; but all the practical ones thought of nothing else but counting nail-heads all the afternoon—even though they knew they would not be allowed to carry so much as one brass knob away with them. But no—it was—"who has most nails? I have a hundred, and you have fifty; or, I have a thousand and you have two. I must have as many as you before I leave the house, or I cannot possibly go home in peace." At last, they made so much noise that I awoke, and thought to myself, "What a false dream that is, of *children.*" The child is the father of the man; and wiser. Children never do such foolish things. Only men do.

119. But there is yet one last class of persons to be inter-rogated. The wise religious men we have asked in vain; the wise contemplative men, in vain; the wise worldly men, in vain. But there is another group yet. In the midst of this vanity of empty religion—of tragic contemplation—of wrath-ful and wretched ambition, and dispute for dust, there is yet

one great group of persons, by whom all these disputers live —the persons who have determined, or have had it by a beneficent Providence determined for them, that they will do something useful ; that whatever may be prepared for them hereafter, or happen to them here, they will, at least, deserve the food that God gives them by winning it honourably ; and that, however fallen from the purity, or far from the peace, of Eden, they will carry out the duty of human dominion, though they have lost its felicity ; and dress and keep the wilderness, though they no more can dress or keep the garden.

These,—hewers of wood, and drawers of water—these bent under burdens, or torn of scourges—these, that dig and weave—that plant and build ; workers in wood, and in marble, and in iron—by whom all food, clothing, habitation, furniture, and means of delight are produced, for themselves, and for all men beside ; men, whose deeds are good, though their words may be few ; men, whose lives are serviceable, be they never so short, and worthy of honour, be they never so humble ;—from these, surely at least, we may receive some clear message of teaching : and pierce, for an instant, into the mystery of life, and of its arts.

120. Yes ; from these, at last, we do receive a lesson. But I grieve to say, or rather—for that is the deeper truth of the matter—I rejoice to say—this message of theirs can only be received by joining them—not by thinking about them.

You sent for me to talk to you of art ; and I have obeyed you in coming. But the main thing I have to tell you is,— that art must not be talked about. The fact that there is talk about it all, signifies that it is ill done, or cannot be done. No true painter ever speaks, or ever has spoken, much of his art. The greatest speak nothing. Even Reynolds is no exception, for he wrote of all that he could not himself do, and was utterly silent respecting all that he himself did.

The moment a man can really do his work, he becomes speechless about it. All words become idle to him—all theories.

121. Does a bird need to theorize about building its nest, or boast of it when built? All good work is essentially done that way—without hesitation, without difficulty, without boasting; and in the doers of the best, there is an inner and involuntary power which approximates literally to the instinct of an animal—nay, I am certain that in the most perfect human artists, reason does *not* supersede instinct, but is added to an instinct as much more divine than that of the lower animals as the human body is more beautiful than theirs; that a great singer sings not with less instinct than the nightingale, but with more—only more various, applicable, and governable; that a great architect does not build with less instinct than the beaver or the bee, but with more—with an innate cunning of proportion that embraces all beauty, and a divine ingenuity of skill that improvises all construction. But be that as it may —be the instinct less or more than that of inferior animals— like or unlike theirs, still the human art is dependent on that first, and then upon an amount of practice, of science,—and of imagination disciplined by thought, which the true possessor of it knows to be incommunicable, and the true critic of it, inexplicable, except through long process of laborious years. That journey of life's conquest, in which hills over hills, and Alps on Alps arose, and sank,—do you think you can make another trace it painlessly, by talking? Why, you cannot even carry us up an Alp, by talking. You can guide us up it, step by step, no otherwise—even so, best silently. You girls, who have been among the hills, know how the bad guide chatters and gesticulates, and it is "put your foot here," and "mind how you balance yourself there;" but the good guide walks on quietly, without a word, only with his eyes on you when need is, and his arm like an iron bar, if need be.

122. In that slow way, also, art can be taught—if you have faith in your guide, and will let his arm be to you as an iron bar when need is. But in what teacher of art have you such faith? Certainly not in me; for, as I told you at first, I know well enough it is only because you think I can talk, not because you think I know my business, that you let me speak to you at all. If I were to tell you anything that seemed

to you strange, you would not believe it, and yet it would only
be in telling you strange things that I could be of use to you.
I could be of great use to you—infinite use, with brief saying,
if you would believe it ; but you would not, just because the
thing that would be of real use would displease you.   You
are all wild, for instance, with admiration of Gustave Doré.
Well, suppose I were to tell you in the strongest terms I could
use, that Gustave Doré's art was bad—bad, not in weakness,
—not in failure,—but bad with dreadful power—the power of
the Furies and the Harpies mingled, enraging, and polluting ;
that so long as you looked at it, no perception of pure or
beautiful art was possible for you.   Suppose I were to tell
you that !   What would be the use ?   Would you look at Gustave Doré less ?   Rather more, I fancy.   On the other hand,
I could soon put you into good humour with me, if I chose.
I know well enough what you like, and how to praise it to
your better liking.   I could talk to you about moonlight, and
twilight, and spring flowers, and autumn leaves, and the Ma-
donnas of Raphael—how motherly ! and the Sibyls of Michael
Angelo—how majestic ! and the saints of Angelico—how
pious ! and the Cherubs of Correggio—how delicious !   Old
as I am, I could play you a tune on the harp yet, that you would
dance to.   But neither you nor I should be a bit the better
or wiser ; or, if we were, our increased wisdom could be of
no practical effect.   For, indeed, the arts, as regards teach-
ableness, differ from the sciences also in this, that their power
is founded not merely on facts which can be communicated,
but on dispositions which require to be created.   Art is
neither to be achieved by effort of thinking, nor explained by
accuracy of speaking.   It is the instinctive and necessary result of powers which can only be developed through the mind
of successive generations, and which finally burst into life
under social conditions as slow of growth as the faculties they
regulate.   Whole æras of mighty history are summed, and the
passions of dead myriads are concentrated, in the existence of
a noble art ; and if that noble art were among us, we should
feel it and rejoice ; not caring in the least to hear lectures on
it ; and since it is not among us, be assured we have to go

back to the root of it, or, at least, to the place where the stock of it is yet alive, and the branches began to die.

123. And now, may I have your pardon for pointing out, partly with reference to matters which are at this time of greater moment than the arts—that if we undertook such recession to the vital germ of national arts that have decayed, we should find a more singular arrest of their power in Ireland than in any other European country. For in the eighth century, Ireland possessed a school of art in her manuscripts and sculpture, which, in many of its qualities—apparently in all essential qualities of decorative invention—was quite without rival ; seeming as if it might have advanced to the highest triumphs in architecture and in painting. But there was one fatal flaw in its nature, by which it was stayed, and stayed with a conspicuousness of pause to which there is no parallel : so that, long ago, in tracing the progress of European schools from infancy to strength, I chose for the students of Kensington, in a lecture since published, two characteristic examples of early art, of equal skill ; but in the one case, skill which was progressive—in the other, skill which was at pause. In the one case, it was work receptive of correction—hungry for correction—and in the other, work which inherently rejected correction. I chose for them a corrigible Eve, and an incorrigible Angel, and I grieve to say that the incorrigible Angel was also an Irish angel ! *

124. And the fatal difference lay wholly in this. In both pieces of art there was an equal falling short of the needs of fact ; but the Lombardic Eve knew she was in the wrong, and the Irish Angel thought himself all right. The eager Lombardic sculptor, though firmly insisting on his childish idea, yet showed in the irregular broken touches of the features, and the imperfect struggle for softer lines in the form, a perception of beauty and law that he could not render ; there was the strain of effort, under conscious imperfection, in every line. But the Irish missal-painter had drawn his angel with no sense of failure, in happy complacency, and put red dots into the palms of each hand, and rounded the eyes into

* See *The Two Paths,* p. 27.

perfect circles, and, I regret to say, left the mouth out altogether, with perfect satisfaction to himself.

125. May I without offence ask you to consider whether this mode of arrest in ancient Irish art may not be indicative of points of character which even yet, in some measure, arrest your national power? I have seen much of Irish character, and have watched it closely, for I have also much loved it. And I think the form of failure to which it is most liable is this, that being generous-hearted, and wholly intending always to do right, it does not attend to the external laws of right, but thinks it must necessarily do right because it means to do so, and therefore does wrong without finding it out; and then when the consequences of its wrong come upon it, or upon others connected with it, it cannot conceive that the wrong is in anywise of its causing or of its doing, but flies into wrath, and a strange agony of desire for justice, as feeling itself wholly innocent, which leads it farther astray, until there is nothing that it is not capable of doing with a good conscience.

126. But mind, I do not mean to say that, in past or present relations between Ireland and England, you have been wrong, and we right. Far from that, I believe that in all great questions of principle, and in all details of administration of law, you have been usually right, and we wrong; sometimes in misunderstanding you, sometimes in resolute iniquity to you. Nevertheless, in all disputes between states, though the strongest is nearly always mainly in the wrong, the weaker is often so in a minor degree; and I think we sometimes admit the possibility of our being in error, and you never do.

127. And now, returning to the broader question what these arts and labours of life have to teach us of its mystery, this is the first of their lessons—that the more beautiful the art, the more it is essentially the work of people who *feel themselves wrong;*—who are striving for the fulfilment of a law, and the grasp of a loveliness, which they have not yet attained, which they feel even farther and farther from attaining, the more they strive for it. And yet, in still deeper

sense, it is the work of people who know also that they are right. The very sense of inevitable error from their purpose marks the perfectness of that purpose, and the continued sense of failure arises from the continued opening of the eyes more clearly to all the sacredest laws of truth.

128. This is one lesson. The second is a very plain, and greatly precious one, namely :—that whenever the arts and labours of life are fulfilled in this spirit of striving against misrule, and doing whatever we have to do, honourably and perfectly, they invariably bring happiness, as much as seems possible to the nature of man. In all other paths, by which that happiness is pursued, there is disappointment, or destruction : for ambition and for passion there is no rest—no fruition ; the fairest pleasures of youth perish in a darkness greater than their past light ; and the loftiest and purest love too often does but inflame the cloud of life with endless fire of pain. But, ascending from lowest to highest, through every scale of human industry, that industry worthily followed, gives peace. Ask the labourer in the field, at the forge, or in the mine ; ask the patient, delicate-fingered artisan, or the strong-armed, fiery-hearted worker in bronze, and in marble, and with the colours of light ; and none of these, who are true workmen, will ever tell you, that they have found the law of heaven an unkind one—that in the sweat of their face they should eat bread, till they return to the ground ; nor that they ever found it an unrewarded obedience, if, indeed, it was rendered faithfully to the command—"Whatsoever thy hand findeth to do—do it with thy might."

129. These are the two great and constant lessons which our labourers teach us of the mystery of life. But there is another, and a sadder one, which they cannot teach us, which we must read on their tombstones.

"Do it with thy might." There have been myriads upon myriads of human creatures who have obeyed this law—who have put every breath and nerve of their being into its toil— who have devoted every hour, and exhausted every faculty— who have bequeathed their unaccomplished thoughts at death

—who being dead, have yet spoken, by majesty of memory and strength of example. And, at last, what has all this "Might" of humanity accomplished, in six thousand years of labour and sorrow? What has it *done?* Take the three chief occupations and arts of men, one by one, and count their achievements. Begin with the first—the lord of them all— agriculture. Six thousand years have passed since we were set to till the ground, from which we were taken. How much of it is tilled? How much of that which is, wisely or well? In the very centre and chief garden of Europe—where the two forms of parent Christianity have had their fortresses— where the noble Catholics of the Forest Cantons, and the noble Protestants of the Vaudois valleys, have maintained, for dateless ages, their faiths and liberties—there the unchecked Alpine rivers yet run wild in devastation : and the marshes, which a few hundred men could redeem with a year's labour, still blast their helpless inhabitants into fevered idiotism. That is so, in the centre of Europe! While, on the near coast of Africa, once the Garden of the Hesperides, an Arab woman, but a few sunsets since, ate her child, for famine. And, with all the treasures of the East at our feet, we, in our own dominion, could not find a few grains of rice, for a people that asked of us no more; but stood by, and saw five hundred thousand of them perish of hunger.

130. Then, after agriculture, the art of kings, take the next head of human arts—weaving ; the art of queens, honoured of all noble Heathen women, in the person of their virgin goddess—honoured of all Hebrew women, by the word of their wisest king—" She layeth her hands to the spindle, and her hands hold the distaff ; she stretcheth out her hand to the poor. She is not afraid of the snow for her household, for all her household are clothed with scarlet. She maketh herself covering of tapestry, her clothing is silk and purple. She maketh fine linen, and selleth it, and delivereth girdles to the merchant." What have we done in all these thousands of years with this bright art of Greek maid and Christian matron ? Six thousand years of weaving, and have we learned to weave? Might not every naked wall have been purple

with tapestry, and every feeble breast fenced with sweet colours from the cold? What have we done? Our fingers are too few, it seems, to twist together some poor covering for our bodies. We set our streams to work for us, and choke the air with fire, to turn our spinning-wheels—and,— *are we yet clothed?* Are not the streets of the capitals of Europe foul with the sale of cast clouts and rotten rags? Is not the beauty of your sweet children left in wretchedness of disgrace, while, with better honour, nature clothes the brood of the bird in its nest, and the suckling of the wolf in her den? And does not every winter's snow robe what you have not robed, and shroud what you have not shrouded ; and every winter's wind bear up to heaven its wasted souls, to witness against you hereafter, by the voice of their Christ,— "I was naked, and ye clothed me not?"

131. Lastly—take the Art of Building—the strongest— proudest—most orderly—most enduring of the arts of man, that, of which the produce is in the surest manner accumulative, and need not perish, or be replaced; but if once well done, will stand more strongly than the unbalanced rocks— more prevalently than the crumbling hills. The art which is associated with all civic pride and sacred principle; with which men record their power—satisfy their enthusiasm— make sure their defence—define and make dear their habitation. And, in six thousand years of building, what have we done? Of the greater part of all that skill and strength, *no* vestige is left, but fallen stones, that encumber the fields and impede the streams. But, from this waste of disorder, and of time, and of rage, what *is* left to us? Constructive and progressive creatures, that we are, with ruling brains, and forming hands, capable of fellowship, and thirsting for fame, can we not contend, in comfort, with the insects of the forest, or, in achievement, with the worm of the sea. The white surf rages in vain against the ramparts built by poor atoms of scarcely nascent life ; but only ridges of formless ruin mark the places where once dwelt our noblest multitudes. The ant and the moth have cells for each of their young, but our little ones lie in festering heaps, in homes that consume them

like graves ; and night by night, from the corners of our streets, rises up the cry of the homeless—"I was a stranger, and ye took me not in."

132. Must it be always thus? Is our life for ever to be without profit—without possession? Shall the strength of its generations be as barren as death ; or cast away their labour, as the wild figtree casts her untimely figs? Is it all a dream then—the desire of the eyes and the pride of life—or, if it be, might we not live in nobler dream than this? The poets and prophets, the wise men, and the scribes, though they have told us nothing about a life to come, have told us much about the life that is now. They have had—they also,—their dreams, and we have laughed at them. They have dreamed of mercy, and of justice ; they have dreamed of peace and good-will ; they have dreamed of labour undisappointed, and of rest undisturbed ; they have dreamed of fulness in harvest, and overflowing in store ; they have dreamed of wisdom in council, and of providence in law ; of gladness of parents, and strength of children, and glory of grey hairs. And at these visions of theirs we have mocked, and held them for idle and vain, unreal and unaccomplishable. What have we accomplished with our realities? Is this what has come of our worldly wisdom, tried against their folly? this our mightiest possible, against their impotent ideal? or have we only wandered among the spectra of a baser felicity, and chased phantoms of the tombs, instead of visions of the Almighty ; and walked after the imaginations of our evil hearts, instead of after the counsels of Eternity, until our lives—not in the likeness of the cloud of heaven, but of the smoke of hell—have become "as a vapour, that appeareth for a little time, and then vanisheth away ?"

133. *Does* it vanish then? Are you sure of that?—sure, that the nothingness of the grave will be a rest from this troubled nothingness ; and that the coiling shadow, which disquiets itself in vain, cannot change into the smoke of the torment that ascends for ever? Will any answer that they *are* sure of it, and that there is no fear, nor hope, nor desire, nor labour, whither they go? Be it so : will you not, then

make as sure of the Life, that now is, as you are of the Death that is to come? Your hearts are wholly in this world—will you not give them to it wisely, as well as perfectly? And see, first of all, that you *have* hearts, and sound hearts, too, to give. Because you have no heaven to look for, is that any reason that you should remain ignorant of this wonderful and infinite earth, which is firmly and instantly given you in possession? Although your days are numbered, and the following darkness sure, is it necessary that you should share the degradation of the brute, because you are condemned to its mortality; or live the life of the moth, and of the worm, because you are to companion them in the dust? Not so; we may have but a few thousands of days to spend, perhaps hundreds only—perhaps tens; nay, the longest of our time and best, looked back on, will be but as a moment, as the twinkling of an eye; still, we are men, not insects; we are living spirits, not passing clouds. "He maketh the winds His messengers; the momentary fire, His minister;" and shall we do less than *these?* Let us do the work of men while we bear the form of them; and, as we snatch our narrow portion of time out of Eternity, snatch also our narrow inheritance of passion out of Immortality—even though our lives *be* as a vapour, that appeareth for a little time, and then vanisheth away.

134. But there are some of you who believe not this—who think this cloud of life has no such close—that it is to float, revealed and illumined, upon the floor of heaven, in the day when He cometh with clouds, and every eye shall see Him. Some day, you believe, within these five, or ten, or twenty years, for every one of us the judgment will be set, and the books opened. If that be true, far more than that must.be true. Is there but one day of judgment? Why, for us every day is a day of judgment—every day is a Dies Iræ, and writes its irrevocable verdict in the flame of its West. Think you that judgment waits till the doors of the grave are opened? It waits at the doors of your houses—it waits at the corners of your streets; we are in the midst of judgment—the insects that we crush are our judges—the moments we fret away are

our judges—the elements that feed us, judge, as they min
ister—and the pleasures that deceive us, judge as they indulge.   Let us, for our lives, do the work of Men while we
bear the Form of them, if indeed those lives are *Not* as a
vapour, and do *Not* vanish away.

135. "The work of men"—and what is that?   Well, we
may any of us know very quickly, on the condition of being
wholly ready to do it.   But many of us are for the most part
thinking, not of what we are to do, but of what we are to get ;
and the best of us are sunk into the sin of Ananias, and it is
a mortal one—we want to keep back part of the price ; and we
continually talk of taking up our cross, as if the only harm in
a cross was the *weight* of it—as if it was only a thing to be
carried, instead of to be—crucified upon.   "They that are
His have crucified the flesh, with the affections and lusts."
Does that mean, think you, that in time of national distress,
of religious trial, of crisis for every interest and hope of
humanity—none of us will cease jesting, none cease idling,
none put themselves to any wholesome work, none take so
much as a tag of lace off their footman's coats, to save the
world?   Or does it rather mean, that they are ready to leave
houses, lands and kindreds—yes, and life, if need be ?   Life !
—some of us are ready enough to throw that away, joyless as
we have made it.   But "*station* in Life"—how many of us
are ready to quit *that ?*   Is it not always the great objection,
where there is question of finding something useful to do—
"We cannot leave our stations in Life ? "

Those of us who really cannot—that is to say, who can only
maintain themselves by continuing in some business or
salaried office, have already something to do ; and all that
they have to see to, is that they do it honestly and with all
their might.   But with most people who use that apology,
"remaining in the station of life to which Providence has
called them," means keeping all the carriages, and all the
footmen and large houses they can possibly pay for ; and,
once for all, I say that if ever Providence *did* put them into
stations of that sort—which is not at all a matter of certainty
—Providence is just now very distinctly calling them out

again. Levi's station in life was the receipt of custom ; and Peter's, the shore of Galilee ; and Paul's, the ante-chambers of the High Priest,—which " station in life" each had to leave, with brief notice.

And, whatever our station in life may be, at this crisis, those of us who mean to fulfill our duty ought, first, to live on as little as we can ; and, secondly, to do all the wholesome work for it we can, and to spend all we can spare in doing all the sure good we can.

And sure good is first in feeding people, then in dressing people, then in lodging people, and lastly in rightly pleasing people, with arts, or sciences, or any other subject of thought.

136. I say first in feeding ; and, once for all, do not let yourselves be deceived by any of the common talk of " indiscriminate charity." The order to us is not to feed the deserving hungry, nor the industrious hungry, nor the amiable and well-intentioned hungry, but simply to feed the hungry. It is quite true, infallibly true, that if any man will not work, neither should he eat—think of that, and every time you sit down to your dinner, ladies and gentlemen, say solemnly, before you ask a blessing, " How much work have I done to-day for my dinner ? " But the proper way to enforce that order on those below you, as well as on yourselves, is not to leave vagabonds and honest people to starve together, but very distinctly to discern and seize your vagabond ; and shut your vagabond up out of honest people's way, and very sternly than see that, until he has worked, he does *not* eat. But the first thing is to be sure you have the food to give; and, therefore, to enforce the organization of vast activities in agriculture and in commerce, for the production of the wholesomest food, and proper storing and distribution of it, so that no famine shall any more be possible among civilized beings. There is plenty of work in this business alone, and at once, for any number of people who like to engage in it.

137. Secondly, dressing people—that is to say, urging every one within reach of your influence to be always neat and clean, and giving them means of being so. In so far as they

absolutely refuse, you must give up the effort with respect to them, only taking care that no children within your sphere of influence shall any more be brought up with such habits; and that every person who is willing to dress with propriety shall have encouragement to do so. And the first absolutely necessary step towards this is the gradual adoption of a consistent dress for different ranks of persons, so that their rank shall be known by their dress; and the restriction of the changes of fashion within certain limits. All which appears for the present quite impossible ; but it is only so far as even difficult as it is difficult to conquer our vanity, frivolity, and desire to appear what we are not. And it is not, nor ever shall be, creed of mine, that these mean and shallow vices are unconquerable by Christian women.

138. And then, thirdly, lodging people, which you may think should have been put first, but I put it third, because we must feed and clothe people where we find them, and lodge them afterwards. And providing lodgment for them means a great deal of vigorous legislation, and cutting down of vested interests that stand in the way, and after that, or before that, so far as we can get it, thorough sanitary and remedial action in the houses that we have ; and then the building of more, strongly, beautifully, and in groups of limited extent, kept in proportion to their streams, and walled round, so that there may be no festering and wretched suburb anywhere, but clean and busy street within, and the open country without, with a belt of beautiful garden and orchard round the walls, so that from any part of the city perfectly fresh air and grass, and sight of far horizon might be reachable in a few minutes' walk. This the final aim ; but in immediate action every minor and possible good to be instantly done, when, and as, we can ; roofs mended that have holes in them—fences patched that have gaps in them— walls buttressed that totter—and floors propped that shake : cleanliness and order enforced with our own hands and eyes, till we are breathless, every day. And all the fine arts will healthily follow. I myself have washed a flight of stone stairs all down, with bucket and broom, in a Savoy inn, where they

hadn't washed their stairs since they first went up them ? and
I never made a better sketch than that afternoon.

139. These, then, are the three first needs of civilized life;
and the law for every Christian man and woman is, that they
shall be in direct service towards one of these three needs, as
far as is consistent with their own special occupation, and if
they have no special business, then wholly in one of these
services. And out of such exertion in plain duty all other
good will come ; for in this direct contention with material
evil, you will find out the real nature of all evil ; you will discern by the various kinds of resistance, what is really the
fault and main antagonism to good ; also you will find the
most unexpected helps and profound lessons given, and truths
will come thus down to us which the speculation of all our
lives would never have raised us up to. You will find nearly
every educational problem solved, as soon as you truly want
to do something ; everybody will become of use in their own
fittest way, and will learn what is best for them to know in
that use. Competitive examination will then, and not till
then, be wholesome, because it will be daily, and calm, and
in practice ; and on these familiar arts, and minute, but certain and serviceable knowledges, will be surely edified and
sustained the greater arts and splendid theoretical sciences.

140. But much more than this. On such holy and simple
practice will be founded, indeed, at last, an infallible religion.
The greatest of all the mysteries of life, and the most terrible,
is the corruption of even the sincerest religion, which is not
daily founded on rational, effective, humble, and helpful
action. Helpful action, observe! for there is just one law,
which obeyed, keeps all religions pure—forgotten, makes
them all false. Whenever in any religious faith, dark or
bright, we allow our minds to dwell upon the points in which
we differ from other people, we are wrong, and in the devil's
power. That is the essence of the Pharisee's thanksgiving—
"Lord, I thank thee that I am not as other men are." At
every moment of our lives we should be trying to find out,
not in what we differ with other people, but in what we agree
with them ; and the moment we find we can agree as to any

thing that should be done, kind or good, (and who but fools couldn't?) then do it; push at it together; you can't quarrel in a side-by-side push; but the moment that even the best men stop pushing, and begin talking, they mistake their pugnacity for piety, and it's all over. I will not speak of the crimes which in past times have been committed in the name of Christ, nor of the follies which are at this hour held to be consistent with obedience to Him; but I *will* speak of the morbid corruption and waste of vital power in religious sentiment, by which the pure strength of that which should be the guiding soul of every nation, the splendour of its youthful manhood, and spotless light of its maidenhood, is averted or cast away. You may see continually girls who have never been taught to do a single useful thing thoroughly; who cannot sew, who cannot cook, who cannot cast an account, nor prepare a medicine, whose whole life has been passed either in play or in pride; you will find girls like these when they are earnest-hearted, cast all their innate passion of religious spirit, which was meant by God to support them through the irksomeness of daily toil, into grievous and vain meditation over the meaning of the great Book, of which no syllable was ever yet to be understood but through a deed; all the instinctive wisdom and mercy of their womanhood made vain, and the glory of their pure consciences warped into fruitless agony concerning questions which the laws of common serviceable life would have either solved for them in an instant, or kept out of their way. Give such a girl any true work that will make her active in the dawn, and weary at night, with the consciousness that her fellow-creatures have indeed been the better for her day, and the powerless sorrow of her enthusiasm will transform itself into a majesty of radiant and beneficent peace.

So with our youths. We once taught them to make Latin verses, and called them educated; now we teach them to leap and to row, to hit a ball with a bat, and call them educated. Can they plow, can they sow, can they plant at the right time, or build with a steady hand? Is it the effort of their lives to be chaste, knightly, faithful, holy in thought, lovely in word and deed? Indeed it is, with some, nay with many, and the strength of England is in them, and the hope; but we have to turn their courage from the toil of war to the toil of mercy; and their intellect from dispute of words to discernment of things; and their knighthood from the errantry of adventure to the state and fidelity of a kingly power. And then, indeed, shall abide, for them, and for us an incorruptible felicity, and an infallible religion; shall abide for us Faith, no more to be assailed by temptation, no more to be defended by wrath and by fear;—shall abide with us Hope, no more to be quenched by the years that overwhelm, or made ashamed by the shadows that betray; shall abide for us, and with us, the greatest of these; the abiding will, the abiding name, of our Father. For the greatest of these, is Charity.

UNTO THIS LAST

FOUR ESSAYS

ON THE FIRST PRINCIPLES OF

POLITICAL ECONOMY

"FRIEND, I DO THEE NO WRONG. DID'ST NOT THOU AGREE WITH ME FOR A PENNY? TAKE THAT THINE IS, AND GO THY WAY. I WILL GIVE UNTO THIS LAST EVEN AS UNTO THEE."

———

"IF YE THINK GOOD, GIVE ME MY PRICE; AND IF NOT, FORBEAR SO THEY WEIGHED FOR MY PRICE THIRTY PIECES OF SILVER."

PREFACE.

THE four following essays were published eighteen months ago in the *Cornhill Magazine*, and were reprobated in a violent manner, as far as I could hear, by most of the readers they met with.

Not a whit the less, I believe them to be the best, that is to say, the truest, rightest-worded, and most serviceable things I have ever written ; and the last of them, having had especial pains spent on it, is probably the best I shall ever write.

" This," the reader may reply, " it might be, yet not therefore well written." Which, in no mock humility, admitting, I yet rest satisfied with the work, though with nothing else that I have done ; and purposing shortly to follow out the subjects opened in these papers, as I may find leisure, I wish the introductory statements to be within the reach of any one who may care to refer to them. So I republish the essays as they appeared. One word only is changed, correcting the estimate of a weight ; and no word is added.

Although, however, I find nothing to modify in these papers, it is matter of regret to me that the most startling of all the statements in them,—that respecting the necessity of the organization of labour, with fixed wages,—should have found its way into the first essay ; it being quite one of the least important, though by no means the least certain, of the positions to be defended. The real gist of these papers, their central meaning and aim, is to give, as I believe for the first time in plain English,—it has often been incidentally given in good Greek by Plato and Xenophon, and good Latin by Cicero and Horace,—a logical definition of WEALTH : such definition being absolutely needed for a basis of economical science. The most reputed essay on that subject which has appeared in modern times, after opening with the statement that " writers on political economy profess to teach, or to investigate,* the nature of wealth," thus follows up the declaration of its thesis—" Every one has a notion, sufficiently correct for common purposes, of what is meant by wealth." . . . "It is is no part of the design of this treatise to aim at metaphysical nicety of definition.† "

Metaphysical nicety, we assuredly do not need ; but physical nicety, and logical accuracy, with respect to a physical subject, we as assuredly do.

Suppose the subject of inquiry, instead of being House law (*Oikonomia*), had been Star-law (*Astronomia*), and that, ignoring distinction between stars fixed and wandering, as here between wealth radiant and wealth reflective, the writer had begun thus : "Every one has a notion, sufficiently correct for common purposes, of what is meant by stars. Metaphysical nicety in the definition of a star is not the object of this treatise ; "—the essay so opened might yet have been far more true in its final statements, and a thousand-fold more serviceable to the navigator, than any treatise on wealth, which founds its conclusions on the popular conception of wealth, can ever become to the economist.

It was, therefore, the first object of these following papers to give an accurate and stable definition of wealth. Their second object was to show that the acquisition of wealth was finally possible only under certain moral conditions of society, of which quite the first was a belief in the existence and even, for practical purposes, in the attainability of honesty.

Without venturing to pronounce—since on such a matter human judgment is by no means conclusive—what is, or is not, the noblest of God's works, we may yet admit so much of Pope's assertion as that an honest man is among His best works presently visible, and, as things stand, a somewhat rare

* Which ? for where investigation is necessary, teaching is impossible.

† *Principles of Political Economy.* By J. S. Mill. Preliminary remarks, p. 2.

one ; but not an incredible or miraculous work ; still less **an** abnormal one. Honesty is not a disturbing force, which de- ranges the orbits of economy ; but a consistent and command- ing force, by obedience to which—and by no other obedience —those orbits can continue clear of chaos.

It is true, I have sometimes heard Pope condemned for the lowness, instead of the height, of his standard :—" Honesty is indeed a respectable virtue ; but how much higher may men attain ! Shall nothing more be asked of us than that we be honest ? "

For the present, good friends, nothing. It seems that in our aspirations to be more than that, we have to some extent lost sight of the propriety of being so much as that. What else we may have lost faith in, there shall be here no question : but assuredly we have lost faith in common honesty, and in the working power of it. And this faith, with the facts on which it may rest, it is quite our first business to recover and keep : not only believing, but even by experience assuring ourselves, that there are yet in the world men who can be re- strained from fraud otherwise than by the fear of losing em- ployment ; * nay, that it is even accurately in proportion to the number of such men in any State, that the said State does or can prolong its existence.

To these two points, then, the following essays are mainly directed. The subject of the organization of labour is only casually touched upon ; because, if we once can get a suffi- cient quantity of honesty in our captains, the organization of labour is easy, and will develop itself without quarrel or diffi- culty ; but if we cannot get honesty in our captains, the or- ganization of labour is for evermore impossible.

The several conditions of its possibility I purpose to exam- ine at length in the sequel. Yet, lest the reader should be alarmed by the hints thrown out during the following in- vestigation of first principles, as if they were leading him into

* " The effectual discipline which is exercised over a workman is not that of his corporation, but of his customers. It is the fear of losing their employment which restrains his frauds, and corrects his negli- gence." (*Wealth of Nations,* Book I. chap. 10.)

unexpectedly dangerous ground, I will, for his better assurance, state at once the worst of the political creed at which I wish him to arrive.

1. First,—that there should be training schools for youth established, at Government cost,* and under Government discipline, over the whole country ; that every child born in the country should, at the parent's wish, be permitted (and, in certain cases, be under penalty required) to pass through them ; and that, in these schools, the child should (with other minor pieces of knowledge hereafter to be considered) imperatively be taught, with the best skill of teaching that the country could produce, the following three things :—

(*a*) the laws of health, and the exercises enjoined by them ;

(*b*) habits of gentleness and justice ; and

(*c*) the calling by which he is to live.

2. Secondly,—that, in connection with these training schools, there should be established, also entirely under Government regulation, manufactories and workshops, for the production and sale of every necessary of life, and for the exercise of every useful art. And that, interfering no whit with private enterprise, nor setting any restraints or tax on private trade, but leaving both to do their best, and beat the Government if they could,—there should, at these Government manufactories and shops, be authoritatively good and exemplary work done, and pure and true substance sold ; so that a man could be sure, if he chose to pay the Government price, that he got for his money bread that was bread, ale that was ale, and work that was work.

3. Thirdly,—that any man, or woman, or boy, or girl, out of employment, should be at once received at the nearest

* It will probably be inquired by near-sighted persons, out of what funds such schools could be supported. The expedient modes of direct provision for them I will examine hereafter ; indirectly, they would be far more than self-supporting. The economy in crime alone, quite one of the most costly articles of luxury in the modern European market,' which such schools would induce, would suffice to support them ten times over. Their economy of labour would be pure gain, and that too large to be presently calculable.

Government school, and set to such work as it appeared, on trial, they were fit for, at a fixed rate of wages determinable every year :—that, being found incapable of work through ignorance, they should be taught, or being found incapable of work through sickness, should be tended ; but that being found objecting to work, they should be set, under compulsion of the strictest nature, to the more painful and degrading forms of necessary toil, especially to that in mines and other places of danger (such danger being, however, diminished to the utmost by careful regulation and discipline) and the due wages of such work be retained—cost of compulsion first abstracted—to be at the workman's command, so soon as he has come to sounder mind respecting the laws of employment.

4. Lastly,—that for the old and destitute, comfort and home should be provided ; which provision, when misfortune had been by the working of such a system sifted from guilt, would be honourable instead of disgraceful to the receiver. For (I repeat this passage out of my *Political Economy of Art*, to which the reader is referred for farther detail *) " a 'abourer serves his country with his spade, just as a man in the middle ranks of life serves it with sword, pen, or lancet. If the service be less, and, therefore, the wages during health less, then the reward when health is broken may be less, but not less honourable ; and it ought to be quite as natural and straightforward a matter for a labourer to take his pension from his parish, because he has deserved well of his parish, as for a man in higher rank to take his pension from his country, because he has deserved well of his country."

To which statement, I will only add, for conclusion, respecting the discipline and pay of life and death, that, for both high and low, Livy's last words touching Valerius Publicola, " *de publico est elatus*," † ought not to be a dishonourable close of epitaph.

---

* Addenda, p. 102.

† " P. Valerius, omnium consensu princeps belli pacisque artibus, anno post moritur ; gloriâ ingenti, copiis familiaribus adeo exiguis, ut funeri sumtus deesset : de publico est elatus. Luxére matronæ ut Brutum."—Lib. II. c. xvi.

These things, then, I believe, and am about, as I find power, to explain and illustrate in their various bearings; following out also what belongs to them of collateral inquiry. Here I state them only in brief, to prevent the reader casting about in alarm for my ultimate meaning ; yet requesting him, for the present, to remember, that in a science dealing with so subtle elements as those of human nature, it is only possible to answer for the final truth of principles, not for the direct success of plans : and that in the best of these last, what can be immediately accomplished is always questionable, and what can be finally accomplished, inconceivable.

Denmark Hill, 10*th May,* 1862.

CONTENTS.

"UNTO THIS LAST."

ESSAY I.

THE ROOTS OF HONOUR.

AMONG the delusions which at different periods have possessed themselves of the minds of large masses of the human race, perhaps the most curious—certainly the least creditable—is the modern *soi-disant* science of political economy, based on the idea that an advantageous code of social action may be determined irrespectively of the influence of social affection.

Of course, as in the instances of alchemy, astrology, witchcraft, and other such popular creeds, political economy has a plausible idea at the root of it. "The social affections," says the economist, "are accidental and disturbing elements in human nature; but avarice and the desire of progress are constant elements. Let us eliminate the inconstants, and, considering the human being merely as a covetous machine, examine by what laws of labour, purchase, and sale, the greatest accumulative result in wealth is attainable. Those laws once determined, it will be for each individual afterwards to introduce as much of the disturbing affectionate element as he chooses, and to determine for himself the result on the new conditions supposed."

This would be a perfectly logical and successful method of analysis, if the accidentals afterwards to be introduced were of the same nature as the powers first examined. Supposing a body in motion to be influenced by constant and inconstant forces, it is usually the simplest way of examining its course to trace it first under the persistent conditions, and afterwards introduce the causes of variation. But the disturbing elements in the social problem are not of the same nature as the constant ones; they alter the essence of the creature under examination the moment they are added; they operate, not mathematically, but chemically, introducing conditions which render all our previous knowledge unavailable. We made learned experiments upon pure nitrogen, and have convinced ourselves that it is a very manageable gas: but behold! the thing which we have practically to deal with is its chloride; and this, the moment we touch it on our established principles, sends us and our apparatus through the ceiling.

Observe, I neither impugn nor doubt the conclusions of the science, if its terms are accepted. I am simply uninterested in them, as I should be in those of a science of gymnastics which assumed that men had no skeletons. It might be shown, on that supposition, that it would be advantageous to roll the students up into pellets, flatten them into cakes, or stretch them into cables; and that when these results were effected, the re-insertion of the skeleton would be attended with various inconveniences to their constitution. The reasoning might be admirable, the conclusions true, and the science deficient only in applicability. Modern political economy stands on a precisely similar basis. Assuming, not that the human being has no skeleton, but that it is all skeleton, it founds an ossifiant theory of progress on this negation of a soul; and having shown the utmost that may be made of bones, and constructed a number of interesting geometrical figures with death's-heads and humeri, successfully proves the inconvenience of the reappearance of a soul among these corpuscular structures. I do not deny the truth of this theory: I simply deny its applicability to the present phase of the world.

This inapplicability has been curiously manifested during the embarrassment caused by the late strikes of our workmen. Here occurs one of the simplest cases, in a pertinent and positive form, of the first vital problem which political economy has to deal with (the relation between employer and employed); and at a severe crisis, when lives in multitudes, and

wealth in masses, are at stake, the political economists are
helpless—practically mute ; no demonstrable solution of the
difficulty can be given by them, such as may convince or
calm the opposing parties. Obstinately the masters take one
view of the matter ; obstinately the operatives another ; and
no political science can set them at one.

It would be strange if it could, it being not by " science "
of any kind that men were ever intended to be set at one.
Disputant after disputant vainly strives to show that the interests of the masters are, or are not, antagonistic to those of
the men : none of the pleaders ever seeming to remember
that it does not absolutely or always follow that the persons
must be antagonistic because their interests are. If there is
only a crust of bread in the house, and mother and children
are starving, their interests are not the same. If the mother
eats it, the children want it ; if the children eat it, the mother
must go hungry to her work. Yet it does not necessarily follow that there will be " antagonism " between them, that they
will fight for the crust, and that the mother, being strongest,
will get it, and eat it. Neither, in any other case, whatever
the relations of the persons may be, can it be assumed for
certain that, because their interests are diverse, they must
necessarily regard each other with hostility, and use violence
or cunning to obtain the advantage.

Even if this were so, and it were as just as it is convenient
to consider men as actuated by no other moral influences
than those which affect rats or swine, the logical conditions of
the question are still indeterminable. It can never be shown
generally either that the interests of master and labourer are
alike, or that they are opposed ; for, according to circumstances, they may be either. It is, indeed, always the interest of both that the work should be rightly done, and a
just price obtained for it ; but, in the division of profits, the
gain of the one may or may not be the loss of the other. It
is not the master's interest to pay wages so low as to leave
the men sickly and depressed, nor the workman's interest to
be paid high wages if the smallness of the master's profit
hinders him from enlarging his business, or conducting it in

a safe and liberal way. A stoker ought not to desire high pay if the company is too poor to keep the engine-wheels in repair.

And the varieties of circumstances which influence these reciprocal interests are so endless, that all endeavour to deduce rules of action from balance of expediency is in vain. And it is meant to be in vain. For no human actions ever were intended by the Maker of men to be guided by balances of expediency, but by balances of justice. He has therefore rendered all endeavours to determine expediency futile for evermore. No man ever knew, or can know, what will be the ultimate result to himself, or to others, of any given line of conduct. But every man may know, and most of us do know, what is a just and unjust act. And all of us may know also, that the consequences of justice will be ultimately the best possible, both to others and ourselves, though we can neither say what *is* best, nor how it is likely to come to pass.

I have said balances of justice, meaning, in the term justice, to include affection,—such affection as one man *owes* to another. All right relations between master and operative, and all their best interests, ultimately depend on these.

We shall find the best and simplest illustration of the relations of master and operative in the position of domestic servants.

We will suppose that the master of a household desires only to get as much work out of his servants as he can, at the rate of wages he gives. He never allows them to be idle ; feeds them as poorly and lodges them as ill as they will endure, and in all things pushes his requirements to the exact point beyond which he cannot go without forcing the servant to leave him. In doing this, there is no violation on his part of what is commonly called "justice." He agrees with the domestic for his whole time and service, and takes them ; the limits of hardship in treatment being fixed by the practice of other masters in his neighbourhood ; that is to say, by the current rate of wages for domestic labour. If the servant can get a better place, he is free to take one, and the master can only tell what is the real market value of his labour, by requiring as much as he will give.

This is the politico-economical view of the case, according to the doctors of that science ; who assert that by this procedure the greatest average of work will be obtained from the servant, and therefore, the greatest benefit to the community, and through the community, by reversion, to the servant himself.

That, however, is not so. It would be so if the servant were an engine of which the motive power was steam, magnetism, gravitation, or any other agent of calculable force. But he being, on the contrary, an engine whose motive power is a Soul, the force of this very peculiar agent, as an unknown quantity, enters into all the political economist's equations, without his knowledge, and falsifies every one of their results. The largest quantity of work will not be done by this curious engine for pay, or under pressure, or by help of any kind of fuel which may be applied by the chaldron. It will be done only when the motive force, that is to say, the will or spirit of the creature, is brought to its greatest strength by its own proper fuel ; namely, by the affections.

It may indeed happen, and does happen often, that if the master is a man of sense and energy, a large quantity of material work may be done under mechanical pressure, enforced by strong will and guided by wise method ; also it may happen, and does happen often, that if the master is indolent and weak (however good-natured), a very small quantity of work, and that bad, may be produced by the servant's undirected strength, and contemptuous gratitude. But the universal law of the matter is that, assuming any given quantity of energy and sense in master and servant, the greatest material result obtainable by them will be, not through antagonism to each other, but through affection for each other ; and that if the master, instead of endeavouring to get as much work as possible from the servant, seeks rather to render his appointed and necessary work beneficial to him, and to forward his interests in all just and wholesome ways, the real amount of work ultimately done, or of good rendered, by the person so cared for, will indeed be the greatest possible.

Observe, I say, "of good rendered," for a servant's work is not necessarily or always the best thing he can give his master. But good of all kinds, whether in material service, in protective watchfulness of his master's interest and credit, or in joyful readiness to seize unexpected and irregular occasions of help.

Nor is this one whit less generally true because indulgence will be frequently abused, and kindness met with ingratitude. For the servant who, gently treated, is ungrateful, treated ungently, will be revengeful; and the man who is dishonest to a liberal master will be injurious to an unjust one.

In any case, and with any person, this unselfish treatment will produce the most effective return. Observe, I am here considering the affections wholly as a motive power; not at all as things in themselves desirable or noble, or in any other way abstractedly good. I look at them simply as an anomalous force, rendering every one of the ordinary political economist's calculations nugatory; while, even if he desired to introduce this new element into his estimates, he has no power of dealing with it; for the affections only become a true motive power when they ignore every other motive and condition of political economy. Treat the servant kindly, with the idea of turning his gratitude to account, and you will get, as you deserve, no gratitude, nor any value for your kindness; but treat him kindly without any economical purpose, and all economical purposes will be answered; in this, as in all other matters, whosoever will save his life shall lose it, and whoso loses it shall find it.*

* The difference between the two modes of treatment, and between their effective material results, may be seen very accurately by a comparison of the relations of Esther and Charlie in *Bleak House*, with those of Miss Brass and the Marchioness in *Master Humphrey's Clock*.

The essential value and truth of Dickens's writings have been unwisely lost sight of by many thoughtful persons, merely because he presents his truth with some colour of caricature. Unwisely, because Dickens's caricature, though often gross, is never mistaken. Allowing for his manner of telling them, the things he tells us are always true. I wish

The next clearest and simplest example of relation between master and operative is that which exists between the commander of a regiment and his men.

Supposing the officer only desires to apply the rules of discipline so as, with least trouble to himself, to make the regiment most effective, he will not be able, by any rules, or administration of rules, on this selfish principle, to develop the full strength of his subordinates. If a man of sense and firmness, he may, as in the former instance, produce a better result than would be obtained by the irregular kindness of a weak officer; but let the sense and firmness be the same in both cases, and assuredly the officer who has the most direct personal relations with his men, the most care for their interests, and the most value for their lives, will develop their effective strength, through their affection for his own person, and trust in his character, to a degree wholly unattainable by other means. The law applies still more stringently as the numbers concerned are larger; a charge may often be successful, though the men dislike their officers; a battle has rarely been won, unless they loved their general.

Passing from these simple examples to the more complicated relations existing between a manufacturer and his workmen, we are met first by certain curious difficulties, resulting,

that he could think it right to limit his brilliant exaggeration to works written only for public amusement; and when he takes up a subject of high national importance, such as that which he handled in *Hard Times*, that he would use severer and more accurate analysis. The usefulness of that work (to my mind, in several respects, the greatest he has written) is with many persons seriously diminished because Mr. Bounderby is a dramatic monster, instead of a characteristic example of a worldly master; and Stephen Blackpool a dramatic perfection, instead of a characteristic example of an honest workman. But let us not lose the use of Dickens's wit and insight, because he chooses to speak in a circle of stage fire. He is entirely right in his main drift and purpose in every book he has written; and all of them, but especially *Hard Times*, should be studied with close and earnest care by persons interested in social questions. They will find much that is partial, and, because partial, apparently unjust; but if they examine all the evidence on the other side, which Dickens seems to overlook, it will appear, after all their trouble, that his view was the finally right one, grossly and sharply told.

apparently, from a harder and colder state of moral elements.
It is easy to imagine an enthusiastic affection existing among
soldiers for the colonel.   Not so easy to imagine an enthusiastic affection among cotton-spinners for the proprietor of the
mill.   A body of men associated for purposes of robbery (as a
Highland clan in ancient times) shall be animated by perfect
affection, and every member of it be ready to lay down his life
for the life of his chief.   But a band of men associated for
purposes of legal production and accumulation is usually animated, it appears, by no such emotions, and none of them are
in anywise willing to give his life for the life of his chief.
Not only are we met by this apparent anomaly, in moral
matters, but by others connected with it, in administration of
system.   For a servant or a soldier is engaged at a definite
rate of wages, for a definite period ; but a workman at a rate
of wages variable according to the demand for labour, and
with the risk of being at any time thrown out of his situation
by chances of trade.   Now, as, under these contingencies, no
action of the affections can take place, but only an explosive
action of *dis*affections, two points offer themselves for consideration in the matter.

The first—How far the rate of wages may be so regulated
as not to vary with the demand for labour.

The second—How far it is possible that bodies of workmen
may be engaged and maintained at such fixed rate of wages
(whatever the state of trade may be), without enlarging or
diminishing their number, so as to give them permanent interest in the establishment with which they are connected,
like that of the domestic servants in an old family, or an *esprit
de corps*, like that of the soldiers in a crack regiment.

The first question is, I say, how far it may be possible to
fix the rate of wages irrespectively of the demand for labour.

Perhaps one of the most curious facts in the history of
human error is the denial by the common political economist
of the possibility of thus regulating wages ; while for all the
important, and much of the unimportant, labour on the earth,
wages are already so regulated.

We do not sell our prime-ministership by Dutch auction ;

nor, on the decease of a bishop, whatever may be the general
advantages of simony, do we (yet) offer his diocese to the
clergyman who will take the episcopacy at the lowest contract.
We (with exquisite sagacity of political economy !) do indeed
sell commissions, but not openly, generalships : sick, we do
not inquire for a physician who takes less than a guinea ; li-
tigious, we never think of reducing six-and-eightpence to four-
and-sixpence ; caught in a shower, we do not canvass the cab-
men, to find out who values his driving at less than sixpence
a mile.

It is true that in all these cases there is, and in every conceivable case there must be, ultimate reference to the presumed difficulty of the work, or number of candidates for the
office.   If it were thought that the labour necessary to make
a good physician would be gone through by a sufficient number of students with the prospect of only half-guinea fees,
public consent would soon withdraw the unnecessary half-
guinea.   In this ultimate sense, the price of labour is indeed
always regulated by the demand for it ; but so far as the
practical and immediate administration of the matter is regarded, the best labour always has been, and is, as *all* labour
ought to be, paid by an invariable standard.

"What !" the reader, perhaps, answers amazedly : "pay
good and bad workmen alike ?"

Certainly.   The difference between one prelate's sermons
and his successor's,—or between one physician's opinion and
another's,—is far greater, as respects the qualities of mind involved, and far more important in result to you personally,
than the difference between good and bad laying of bricks
(though that is greater than most people suppose).   Yet you
pay with equal fee, contentedly, the good and bad workmen
upon your soul, and the good and bad workmen upon your
body ; much more may you pay, contentedly, with equal fees,
the good and bad workmen upon your house.

"Nay, but I choose my physician and (?) my clergyman,
thus indicating my sense of the quality of their work."   By
all means, also, choose your bricklayer ; that is the proper reward of the good workman, to be "chosen."   The natural and

right system respecting all labour is, that it should be paid at a fixed rate, but the good workman employed, and the bad workman unemployed. The false, unnatural, and destructive system is when the bad workman is allowed to offer his work at half-price, and either take the place of the good, or force him by his competition to work for an inadequate sum.

This equality of wages, then, being the first object towards which we have to discover the directest available road; the second is, as above stated, that of maintaining constant numbers of workmen in employment, whatever may be the accidental demand for the article they produce.

I believe the sudden and extensive inequalities of demand which necessarily arise in the mercantile operations of an active nation, constitute the only essential difficulty which has to be overcome in a just organization of labour. The subject opens into too many branches to admit of being investigated in a paper of this kind; but the following general facts bearing on it may be noted.

The wages which enable any workman to live are necessarily higher, if his work is liable to intermission, than if it is assured and continuous; and however severe the struggle for work may become, the general law will always hold, that men must get more daily pay if, on the average, they can only calculate on work three days a week, than they would require if they were sure of work six days a week. Supposing that a man cannot live on less than a shilling a day, his seven shillings he must get, either for three days' violent work, or six days' deliberate work. The tendency of all modern mercantile operations is to throw both wages and trade into the form of a lottery, and to make the workman's pay depend on intermittent exertion, and the principal's profit on dexterously used chance.

In what partial degree, I repeat, this may be necessary, in consequence of the activities of modern trade, I do not here investigate; contenting myself with the fact, that in its fatallest aspects it is assuredly unnecessary, and results merely from love of gambling on the part of the masters, and from ignorance and sensuality in the men. The masters cannot bear to let any opportunity of gain escape them, and frantically rush at every gap and breach in the walls of Fortune, raging to be rich, and affronting, with impatient covetousness, every risk of ruin ; while the men prefer three days of violent labour, and three days of drunkenness, to six days of moderate work and wise rest.   There is no way in which a principal, who really desires to help his workmen, may do it more effectually than by checking these disorderly habits both in himself and them ; keeping his own business operations on a scale which will enable him to pursue them securely, not yielding to temptations of precarious gain ; and, at the same time, leading his workmen into regular habits of labour and life, either by inducing them rather to take low wages in the form of a fixed salary, than high wages, subject to the chance of their being thrown out of work ; or, if this be impossible, by discouraging the system of violent exertion for nominally high day wages, and leading the men to take lower pay for more regular labour.

In effecting any radical changes of this kind, doubtless there would be great inconvenience and loss incurred by all the originators of movement.   That which can be done with perfect convenience and without loss, is not always the thing that most needs to be done, or which we are most imperatively required to do.

I have already alluded to the difference hitherto existing between regiments of men associated for purposes of violence, and for purposes of manufacture ; in that the former appear capable of self-sacrifice—the latter, not ; which singular fact is the real reason of the general lowness of estimate in which the profession of commerce is held, as compared with that of arms.   Philosophically, it does not, at first sight, appear reasonable (many writers have endeavoured to prove it unreasonable) that a peaceable and rational person, whose trade is buying and selling, should be held in less honour than an unpeaceable and often irrational person, whose trade is slaying. Nevertheless, the consent of mankind has always, in spite of the philosophers, given precedence to the soldier.

And this is right.

For the soldier's trade, verily and essentially, is not slaying, but being slain. This, without well knowing its own meaning, the world honours it for. A bravo's trade is slaying; but the world has never respected bravos more than merchants: the reason it honours the soldier is, because he holds his life at the service of the State. Reckless he may be —fond of pleasure or of adventure—all kinds of bye-motives and mean impulses may have determined the choice of his profession, and may affect (to all appearance exclusively) his daily conduct in it; but our estimate of him is based on this ultimate fact—of which we are well assured—that, put him in a fortress breach, with all the pleasures of the world behind him, and only death and his duty in front of him, he will keep his face to the front; and he knows that this choice may be put to him at any moment, and has beforehand taken his part—virtually takes such part continually—does, in reality, die daily.

Not less is the respect we pay to the lawyer and physician, founded ultimately on their self-sacrifice. Whatever the learning or acuteness of a great lawyer, our chief respect for him depends on our belief that, set in a judge's seat, he will strive to judge justly, come of it what may. Could we suppose that he would take bribes, and use his acuteness and legal knowledge to give plausibility to iniquitous decisions, no degree of intellect would win for him our respect. Nothing will win it, short of our tacit conviction, that in all important acts of his life justice is first with him; his own interest, second.

In the case of a physician, the ground of the honour we render him is clearer still. Whatever his science, we should shrink from him in horror if we found him regard his patients merely as subjects to experiment upon; much more, if we found that, receiving bribes from persons interested in their deaths, he was using his best skill to give poison in the mask of medicine.

Finally, the principle holds with utmost clearness as it respects clergymen. No goodness of disposition will excuse want of science in a physician or of shrewdness in an advocate; but a clergyman, even though his power of intellect be small, is respected on the presumed ground of his unselfishness and serviceableness.

Now there can be no question but that the tact, foresight, decision, and other mental powers, required for the successful management of a large mercantile concern, if not such as could be compared with those of a great lawyer, general, or divine, would at least match the general conditions of mind required in the subordinate officers of a ship, or of a regiment, or in the curate of a country parish. If, therefore, all the efficient members of the so-called liberal professions are still, somehow, in public estimate of honour, preferred before the head of a commercial firm, the reason must lie deeper than in the measurement of their several powers of mind.

And the essential reason for such preference will be found to lie in the fact that the merchant is presumed to act always selfishly. His work may be very necessary to the community; but the motive of it is understood to be wholly personal. The merchant's first object in all his dealings must be (the public believe) to get as much for himself, and leave as little to his neighbour (or customer) as possible. Enforcing this upon him, by political statute, as the necessary principle of his action; recommending it to him on all occasions, and themselves reciprocally adopting it; proclaiming vociferously, for law of the universe, that a buyer's function is to cheapen, and a seller's to cheat,—the public, nevertheless, involuntarily condemn the man of commerce for his compliance with their own statement, and stamp him for ever as belonging to an inferior grade of human personality.

This they will find, eventually, they must give up doing. They must not cease to condemn selfishness; but they will have to discover a kind of commerce which is not exclusively selfish. Or, rather, they will have to discover that there never was, or can be, any other kind of commerce; that this which they have called commerce was not commerce at all, but cozening; and that a true merchant differs as much from a merchant according to laws of modern political economy, as the hero of the *Excursion* from Autolycus. They will find that commerce is an occupation which gentlemen will every day see more need to engage in, rather than in the businesses of talking to men, or slaying them; that, in true com merce, as in true preaching, or true fighting, it is necessary to admit the idea of occasional voluntary loss ;—that sixpences have to be lost, as well as lives, under a sense of duty ; that the market may have its martyrdoms as well as the pulpit ; and trade its heroisms, as well as war.

May have—in the final issue, must have—and only has not had yet, because men of heroic temper have always been misguided in their youth into other fields, not recognizing what is in our days, perhaps, the most important of all fields ; so that, while many a zealous person loses his life in trying to teach the form of a gospel, very few will lose a hundred pounds in showing the practice of one.

The fact is, that people never have had clearly explained to them the true functions of a merchant with respect to other people. I should like the reader to be very clear about this.

Five great intellectual professions, relating to daily necessities of life, have hitherto existed—three exist necessarily, in every civilized nation :

The Soldier's profession is to *defend* it.

The Pastor's, to *teach* it.

The Physician's, to *keep it in health.*

The Lawyer's, to *enforce justice.*

The Merchant's, to *provide* for it.

And the duty of all these men is, on due occasion, to *die* for it.

" On due occasion," namely :—

The Soldier, rather than leave his post in battle.

The Physician, rather than leave his post in plague.

The Pastor, rather than teach Falsehood.

The Lawyer, rather than countenance Injustice.

The Merchant—What is *his* " due occasion " of death ?

It is the main question for the merchant, as for all of us. For, truly, the man who does not know when to die, does not know how to live.

Observe, the merchant's function (or manufacturer's, for in the broad sense in which it is here used the word must be understood to include both) is to provide for the nation. It is no more his function to get profit for himself out of that provision than it is a clergyman's function to get his stipend. The stipend is a due and necessary adjunct, but not the object, of his life, if he be a true clergyman, any more than his fee (or *honorarium*) is the object of life to a true physician. Neither is his fee the object of life to a true merchant. All three, if true men, have a work to be done irrespective of fee —to be done even at any cost, or for quite the contrary of fee ; the pastor's function being to teach, the physician's to heal, and the merchant's, as I have said, to provide. That is to say, he has to understand to their very root the qualities of the thing he deals in, and the means of obtaining or producing it ; and he has to apply all his sagacity and energy to the producing or obtaining it in perfect state, and distributing it at the cheapest possible price where it is most needed.

And because the production or obtaining of any commodity involves necessarily the agency of many lives and hands, the merchant becomes in the course of his business the master and governor of large masses of men in a more direct, though less confessed way, than a military officer or pastor ; so that on him falls, in great part, the responsibility for the kind of life they lead : and it becomes his duty, not only to be always considering how to produce what he sells in the purest and cheapest forms, but how to make the various employments involved in the production, or transference of it, most beneficial to the men employed.

And as into these two functions, requiring for their right exercise the highest intelligence, as well as patience, kindness, and tact, the merchant is bound to put all his energy, so for their just discharge he is bound, as soldier or physician is bound, to give up, if need be, his life, in such way as may be demanded of him. Two main points he has in his providing function to maintain: first, his engagements (faithfulness to engagements being the real root of all possibilities in commerce) ; and, secondly, the perfectness and purity of the thing provided ; so that, rather than fail in any engagement, or consent to any deterioration, adulteration, or unjust and exorbitant price of that which he provides, he is bound to meet fearlessly any form of distress, poverty, or labour, which may, through maintenance of these points, come upon him.

Again : in his office as governor of the men employed by him, the merchant or manufacturer is invested with a distinctly paternal authority and responsibility. In most cases, a youth entering a commercial establishment is withdrawn altogether from home influence ; his master must become his father, else he has, for practical and constant help, no father at hand : in all cases the master's authority, together with the general tone and atmosphere of his business, and the character of the men with whom the youth is compelled in the course of it to associate, have more immediate and pressing weight than the home influence, and will usually neutralize it either for good or evil; so that the only means which the master has of doing justice to the men employed by him is to ask himself sternly whether he is dealing with such subordinate as he would with his own son, if compelled by circumstances to take such a position.

Supposing the captain of a frigate saw it right, or were by any chance obliged, to place his own son in the position of a common sailor ; as he would then treat his son, he is bound always to treat every one of the men under him. So, also, supposing the master of a manufactory saw it right, or were by any chance obliged, to place his own son in the position of an ordinary workman ; as he would then treat his son, he is bound always to treat every one of his men. This is the only effective, true, or practical RULE which can be given on this point of political economy.

And as the captain of a ship is bound to be the last man to leave his ship in case of wreck, and to share his last crust with the sailors in case of famine, so the manufacturer, in any commercial crisis or distress, is bound to take the suffering of it with his men, and even to take more of it for himself than he allows his men to feel ; as a father would in a famine, shipwreck, or battle, sacrifice himself for his son.

All which sounds very strange ; the only real strangeness

in the matter being, nevertheless, that it should so sound.
For all this is true, and that not partially nor theoretically,
but everlastingly and practically : all other doctrine than this
respecting matters political being false in premises, absurd in
deduction, and impossible in practice, consistently with any
progressive state of national life ; all the life which we now
possess as a nation showing itself in the resolute denial and
scorn, by a few strong minds and faithful hearts, of the
economic principles taught to our multitudes, which principles, so far as accepted, lead straight to national destruction.
Respecting the modes and forms of destruction to which they
lead, and, on the other hand, respecting the farther practical
working of true polity, I hope to reason further in a following
paper.

ESSAY II.

THE answer which would be made by any ordinary political economist to the statements contained in the preceding paper, is in few words as follows :—

"It is indeed true that certain advantages of a general nature may be obtained by the development of social affections. But political economists never professed, nor profess, to take advantages of a general nature into consideration. Our science is simply the science of getting rich. So far from being a fallacious or visionary one, it is found by experience to be practically effective. Persons who follow its precepts do actually become rich, and persons who disobey them become poor. Every capitalist of Europe has acquired his fortune by following the known laws of our science, and increases his capital daily by an adherence to them. It is vain to bring forward tricks of logic, against the force of accomplished facts. Every man of business knows by experience how money is made, and how it is lost."

Pardon me. Men of business do indeed know how they themselves made their money, or how, on occasion, they lost it. Playing a long-practised game, they are familiar with the chances of its cards, and can rightly explain their losses and gains. But they neither know who keeps the bank of the gambling-house, nor what other games may be played with the same cards, nor what other losses and gains, far away among the dark streets, are essentially, though invisibly, dependent on theirs in the lighted rooms. They have learned a few, and only a few, of the laws of mercantile economy; but not one of those of political economy.

Primarily, which is very notable and curious, I observe that men of business rarely know the meaning of the word

"rich." At least if they know, they do not in their reason-
ings allow for the fact, that it is a relative word, implying its
opposite " poor " as positively as the word "north" implies
its opposite "south." Men nearly always speak and write as
if riches were absolute, and it were possible, by following
certain scientific precepts, for everybody to be rich. Whereas
riches are a power like that of electricity, acting only through
inequalities or negations of itself. The force of the guinea
you have in your pocket depends wholly on the default of a
guinea in your neighbour's pocket. If he did not want it, it
would be of no use to you ; the degree of power it possesses
depends accurately upon the need or desire he has for it,—
and the art of making yourself rich, in the ordinary mercantile economist's sense, is therefore equally and necessarily the
art of keeping your neighbour poor.

I would not contend in this matter (and rarely in any matter), for the acceptance of terms. But I wish the reader
clearly and deeply to understand the difference between the
two economies, to which the terms " Political " and "Mercantile " might not unadvisably be attached.

Political economy (the economy of a State, or of citizens)
consists simply in the production, preservation, and distribution, at fittest time and place, of useful or pleasurable things.
The farmer who cuts his hay at the right time ; the ship-
wright who drives his bolts well home in sound wood ; the
builder who lays good bricks in well-tempered mortar ; the
housewife who takes care of her furniture in the parlour, and
guards against all waste in her kitchen ; and the singer who
rightly disciplines, and never overstrains her voice : are all
political economists in the true and final sense ; adding continually to the riches and well-being of the nation to which
they belong.

But mercantile economy, the economy of "merces " or of
"pay," signifies the accumulation, in the hands of individuals,
of legal or moral claim upon, or power over, the labour of
others ; every such claim implying precisely as much poverty
or debt on one side, as it implies riches or right on the other.

It does not, therefore, necessarily involve an addition to

the actual property, or well-being, of the State in which it exists. But since this commercial wealth, or power over labour, is nearly always convertible at once into real property, while real property is not always convertible at once into power over labour, the idea of riches among active men in civilized nations, generally refers to commercial wealth ; and in estimating their possessions, they rather calculate the value of their horses and fields by the number of guineas they could get for them, than the value of their guineas by the number of horses and fields they could buy with them.

There is, however, another reason for this habit of mind ; namely, that an accumulation of real property is of little use to its owner, unless, together with it, he has commercial power over labour. Thus, suppose any person to be put in possession of a large estate of fruitful land, with rich beds of gold in its gravel, countless herds of cattle in its pastures ; houses, and gardens, and storehouses full of useful stores, but suppose, after all, that he could get no servants ? In order that he may be able to have servants, some one in his neighbourhood must be poor, and in want of his gold—or his corn. Assume that no one is in want of either, and that no servants are to be had. He must, therefore, bake his own bread, make his own clothes, plough his own ground, and shepherd his own flocks. His gold will be as useful to him as any other yellow pebbles on his estate. His stores must rot, for he cannot consume them. He can eat no more than another man could eat, and wear no more than another man could wear. He must lead a life of severe and common labour to procure even ordinary comforts ; he will be ultimately unable to keep either houses in repair, or fields in cultivation ; and forced to content himself with a poor man's portion of cottage and garden, in the midst of a desert of waste land, trampled by wild cattle, and encumbered by ruins of palaces, which he will hardly mock at himself by calling "his own."

The most covetous of mankind, with small exultation, I presume, accept riches of this kind on these terms. What is really desired, under the name of riches, is, essentially, power over men ; in its simplest sense, the power of obtaining for our own advantage the labour of servant, tradesman, and artist ; in wider sense, authority of directing large masses of the nation to various ends (good, trivial, or hurtful, according to the mind of the rich person). And this power of wealth of course is greater or less in direct proportion to the poverty of the men over whom it is exercised, and in inverse proportion to the number of persons who are as rich as ourselves, and who are ready to give the same price for an article of which the supply is limited. If the musician is poor, he will sing for small pay, as long as there is only one person who can pay him ; but if there be two or three, he will sing for the one who offers him most. And thus the power of the riches of the patron (always imperfect and doubtful, as we shall see presently, even when most authoritative) depends first on the poverty of the artist, and then on the limitation of the number of equally wealthy persons, who also want seats at the concert. So that, as above stated, the art of becoming " rich," in the common sense, is not absolutely nor finally the art of accumulating much money for ourselves, but also of contriving that our neighbours shall have less. In accurate terms, it is " the art of establishing the maximum inequality in our own favour."

Now the establishment of such inequality cannot be shown in the abstract to be either advantageous or disadvantageous to the body of the nation. The rash and absurd assumption that such inequalities are necessarily advantageous, lies at the root of most of the popular fallacies on the subject of political economy. For the eternal and inevitable law in this matter is, that the beneficialness of the inequality depends, first, on the methods by which it was accomplished, and, secondly, on the purposes to which it is applied. Inequalities of wealth, unjustly established, have assuredly injured the nation in which they exist during their establishment ; and, unjustly directed, injure it yet more during their existence. But inequalities of wealth justly established, benefit the nation in the course of their establishment ; and nobly used, aid it yet more by their existence. That is to say, among every active and well-governed people, the various strength of individuals, tested by full exertion and specially applied to various need, issues in unequal, but harmonious results, receiving reward or authority according to its class and service ;* while in the inactive or ill-governed nation, the gradations of decay and the victories of treason work out also their own rugged system of subjection and success ; and substitute, for the melodious inequalities of concurrent power, the iniquitous dominances and depressions of guilt and misfortune.

Thus the circulation of wealth in a nation resembles that of the blood in the natural body. There is one quickness of the current which comes of cheerful emotion or wholesome exercise ; and another which comes of shame or of fever.

---

* I have been naturally asked several times, with respect to the sentence in the first of these papers, "the bad workmen unemployed," "But what are you to do with your bad unemployed workmen ? " Well, it seems to me the question might have occurred to you before. Your housemaid's place is vacant—you give twenty pounds a year—two girls come for it, one neatly dressed, the other dirtily ; one with good recommendations, the other with none. You do not, under these circumstances, usually ask the dirty one if she will come for fifteen pounds, or twelve; and, on her consenting, take her instead of the well-recommended one. Still less do you try to beat both down by making them bid against each other, till you can hire both, one at twelve pounds a year, and the other at eight. You simply take the one fittest for the place, and send away the other, not perhaps concerning yourself quite as much as you should with the question which you now impatiently put to me, " What is to become of her ? " For all that I advise you to do, is to deal with workmen as with servants ; and verily the question is of weight : " Your bad workman, idler, and rogue—what are you to do with him ? "

We will consider of this presently : remember that the administration of a complete system of national commerce and industry cannot be explained in full detail within the space of twelve pages. Meantime, consider whether, there being confessedly some difficulty in dealing with rogues and idlers, it may not be advisable to produce as few of them as possible. If you examine into the history of rogues, you will find they are as truly manufactured articles as anything else, and it is just because our present system of political economy gives so large a stimulus to that manufacture that you may know it to be a false one. We had better seek for a system which will develop honest men, than for one which will deal cunningly with vagabonds. Let us reform our schools, and we shall find little reform needed in our prisons.

There is a flush of the body which is full of warmth and life; and another which will pass in to putrefaction.

The analogy will hold, down even to minute particulars. For as diseased local determination of the blood involves depression of the general health of the system, all morbid local action of riches will be found ultimately to involve a weakening of the resources of the body politic.

The mode in which this is produced may be at once understood by examining one or two instances of the development of wealth in the simplest possible circumstances.

Suppose two sailors cast away on an uninhabited coast, and obliged to maintain themselves there by their own labour for a series of years.

If they both kept their health, and worked steadily, and in amity with each other, they might build themselves a convenient house, and in time come to possess a certain quantity of cultivated land, together with various stores laid up for future use. All these things would be real riches or property; and supposing the men both to have worked equally hard, they would each have right to equal share or use of it. Their political economy would consist merely in careful preservation and just division of these possessions. Perhaps, however, after some time one or other might be dissatisfied with the results of their common farming; and they might in consequence agree to divide the land they had brought under the spade into equal shares, so that each might thenceforward work in his own field and live by it. Suppose that after this arrangement had been made, one of them were to fall ill, and be unable to work on his land at a critical time— say of sowing or harvest.

He would naturally ask the other to sow or reap for him.

Then his companion might say, with perfect justice, "I will do this additional work for you; but if I do it, you must promise to do as much for me at another time. I will count how many hours I spend on your ground, and you shall give me a written promise to work for the same number of hours on mine, whenever I need your help, and you are able to give it."

Suppose the disabled man's sickness to continue, and that under various circumstances, for several years, requiring the help of the other, he on each occasion gave a written pledge to work, as soon as he was able, at his companion's orders, for the same number of hours which the other had given up to him. What will the positions of the two men be when the invalid is able to resume work?

Considered as a "Polis," or state, they will be poorer than they would have been otherwise: poorer by the withdrawal of what the sick man's labour would have produced in the interval. His friend may perhaps have toiled with an energy quickened by the enlarged need, but in the end his own land and property must have suffered by the withdrawal of so much of his time and thought from them; and the united property of the two men will be certainly less than it would have been if both had remained in health and activity.

But the relations in which they stand to each other are also widely altered. The sick man has not only pledged his labour for some years, but will probably have exhausted his own share of the accumulated stores, and will be in consequence for some time dependent on the other for food, which he can only "pay" or reward him for by yet more deeply pledging his own labour.

Supposing the written promises to be held entirely valid (among civilized nations their validity is secured by legal measures *), the person who had hitherto worked for both

---

* The disputes which exist respecting the real nature of money arise more from the disputants examining its functions on different sides, than from any real dissent in their opinions. All money, properly so called, is an acknowledgment of debt; but as such, it may either be considered to represent the labour and property of the creditor, or the idleness and penury of the debtor. The intricacy of the question has been much increased by the (hitherto necessary) use of marketable commodities, such as gold, silver, salt, shells, &c., to give intrinsic value or security to currency; but the final and best definition of money is that it is a documentary promise ratified and guaranteed by the nation to give or find a certain quantity of labour on demand. A man's labour for a day is a better standard of value than a measure of any produce, because no produce ever maintains a consistent rate of productibility.

might now, if he chose, rest altogether, and pass his time in idleness, not only forcing his companion to redeem all the engagements he had already entered into, but exacting from him pledges for further labour, to an arbitrary amount, for what food he had to advance to him.

There might not, from first to last, be the least illegality (in the ordinary sense of the word) in the arrangement; but if a stranger arrived on the coast at this advanced epoch of their political economy, he would find one man commercially Rich; the other commercially Poor. He would see, perhaps with no small surprise, one passing his days in idleness; the other labouring for both, and living sparely, in the hope of recovering his independence, at some distant period.

This is, of course, an example of one only out of many ways in which inequality of possession may be established between different persons, giving rise to the mercantile forms of Riches and Poverty. In the instance before us, one of the men might from the first have deliberately chosen to be idle, and to put his life in pawn for present ease; or he might have mismanaged his land, and been compelled to have recourse to his neighbour for food and help, pledging his future labour for it. But what I want the reader to note especially is the fact, common to a large number of typical cases of this kind, that the establishment of the mercantile wealth which consists in a claim upon labour, signifies a political diminution of the real wealth which consists in substantial possessions.

Take another example, more consistent with the ordinary course of affairs of trade. Suppose that three men, instead of two, formed the little isolated republic, and found themselves obliged to separate in order to farm different pieces of land at some distance from each other along the coast; each estate furnishing a distinct kind of produce, and each more or less in need of the material raised on the other. Suppose that the third man, in order to save the time of all three, undertakes simply to superintend the transference of commodities from one farm to the other; on condition of receiving some sufficiently remunerative share of every parcel of goods conveyed, or of some other parcel received in exchange for it.

If this carrier or messenger always brings to each estate, from the other, what is chiefly wanted, at the right time, the operations of the two farmers will go on prosperously, and the largest possible result in produce, or wealth, will be attained by the little community. But suppose no intercourse between the land owners is possible, except through the travelling agent ; and that, after a time, this agent, watching the course of each man's agriculture, keeps back the articles with which he has been entrusted, until there comes a period of extreme necessity for them, on one side or other, and then exacts in exchange for them all that the distressed farmer can spare of other kinds of produce ; it is easy to see that by ingeniously watching his opportunities, he might possess himself regularly of the greater part of the superfluous produce of the two estates, and at last, in some year of severest trial or scarcity, purchase both for himself, and maintain the former proprietors thenceforward as his labourers or his servants.

This would be a case of commercial wealth acquired on the exactest principles of modern political economy. But more distinctly even than in the former instance, it is manifest in this that the wealth of the State, or of the three men considered as a society, is collectively less than it would have been had the merchant been content with juster profit. The operations of the two agriculturists have been cramped to the utmost ; and the continual limitations of the supply of things they wanted at critical times, together with the failure of courage consequent on the prolongation of a struggle for mere existence, without any sense of permanent gain, must have seriously diminished the effective results of their labour ; and the stores finally accumulated in the merchant's hands will not in anywise be of equivalent value to those which, had his dealings been honest, would have filled at once the granaries of the farmers and his own.

The whole question, therefore, respecting not only the advantage, but even the quantity, of national wealth, resolves itself finally into one of abstract justice. It is impossible to conclude, of any given mass of acquired wealth, merely by the fact of its existence, whether it signifies good or evil to the nation in the midst of which it exists. Its real value depends on the moral sign attached to it, just as sternly as that of a mathematical quantity depends on the algebraical sign attached to it. Any given accumulation of commercial wealth may be indicative, on the one hand, of faithful industries, progressive energies, and productive ingenuities ; or, on the other, it may be indicative of mortal luxury, merciless tyranny, ruinous chicane. Some treasures are heavy with human tears, as an ill-stored harvest with untimely rain ; and some gold is brighter in sunshine than it is in substance.

And these are not, observe, merely moral or pathetic attributes of riches, which the seeker of riches may, if he chooses, despise ; they are literally and sternly, material attributes of riches, depreciating or exalting, incalculably, the monetary signification of the sum in question. One mass of money is the outcome of action which has created,—another, of action which has annihilated,—ten times as much in the gathering of it ; such and such strong hands have been paralyzed, as if they had been numbed by nightshade : so many strong men's courage broken, so many productive operations hindered ; this and the other false direction given to labour, and lying image of prosperity set up, on Dura plains dug into seven-times-heated furnaces. That which seems to be wealth may in verity be only the gilded index of far-reaching ruin ; a wrecker's handful of coin gleaned from the beach to which he has beguiled an argosy ; a camp-follower's bundle of rags unwrapped from the breasts of goodly soldiers dead ; the purchase-pieces of potter's fields, wherein shall be buried together the citizen and the stranger.

And therefore, the idea that directions can be given for the gaining of wealth, irrespectively of the consideration of its moral sources, or that any general and technical law of purchase and gain can be set down for national practice, is perhaps the most insolently futile of all that ever beguiled men through their vices. So far as I know, there is not in history record of anything so disgraceful to the human intellect as the modern idea that the commercial text, "Buy in the cheapest market and sell in the dearest," represents, or under any circumstances could represent, an available principle of national economy.   Buy in the cheapest market?—yes; but what made your market cheap?   Charcoal may be cheap among your roof timbers after a fire, and bricks may be cheap in your streets after an earthquake; but fire and earthquake may not therefore be national benefits.   Sell in the dearest? —yes, truly; but what made your market dear?   You sold your bread well to-day; was it to a dying man who gave his last coin for it, and will never need bread more, or to a rich man who to-morrow will buy your farm over your head; or to a soldier on his way to pillage the bank in which you have put your fortune?

None of these things you can know.   One thing only you can know, namely, whether this dealing of yours is a just and faithful one, which is all you need concern yourself about respecting it; sure thus to have done your own part in bringing about ultimately in the world a state of things which will not issue in pillage or in death.   And thus every question concerning these things merges itself ultimately in the great question of justice, which, the ground being thus far cleared for it, I will enter upon in the next paper, leaving only, in this, three final points for the reader's consideration.

It has been shown that the chief value and virtue of money consists in its having power over human beings; that, without this power, large material possessions are useless, and to any person possessing such power, comparatively unnecessary. But power over human beings is attainable by other means than by money.   As I said a few pages back, the money power is always imperfect and doubtful; there are many things which cannot be retained by it.   Many joys may be given to men which cannot be bought for gold, and many fidelities found in them which cannot be rewarded with it.

Trite enough,—the reader thinks.   Yes: but it is not so trite,—I wish it were,—that in this moral power, quite inscrutable and immeasurable though it be, there is a monetary value just as real as that represented by more ponderous currencies. A man's hand may be full of invisible gold, and the wave of it, or the grasp, shall do more than another's with a shower of bullion. This invisible gold, also, does not necessarily diminish in spending. Political economists will do well some day to take heed of it, though they cannot take measure.

But farther. Since the essence of wealth consists in its authority over men, if the apparent or nominal wealth fail in this power, it fails in essence ; in fact, ceases to be wealth at all. It does not appear lately in England, that our authority over men is absolute. The servants show some disposition to rush riotously upstairs, under an impression that their wages are not regularly paid. We should augur ill of any gentleman's property to whom this happened every other day in his drawing-room.

So also, the power of our wealth seems limited as respects the comfort of the servants, no less than their quietude. The persons in the kitchen appear to be ill-dressed, squalid, half-starved. One cannot help imagining that the riches of the establishment must be of a very theoretical and documentary character.

Finally. Since the essence of wealth consists in power over men, will it not follow that the nobler and the more in number the persons are over whom it has power, the greater the wealth ? Perhaps it may even appear after some consideration, that the persons themselves *are* the wealth—that these pieces of gold with which we are in the habit of guiding them, are, in fact, nothing more than a kind of Byzantine harness or trappings, very glittering and beautiful in barbaric sight, wherewith we bridle the creatures ; but that if these same living creatures could be guided without the fretting and jingling of the Byzants in their mouths and ears, they might themselves be more valuable than their bridles. In fact, it may be discovered that the true veins of wealth are purple—and not in Rock, but in Flesh—perhaps even that the final outcome and consummation of all wealth is in the producing as many as possible full-breathed, bright-eyed, and happy-hearted human creatures. Our modern wealth, I think, has rather a tendency the other way ;—most political economists appearing to consider multitudes of human creatures not conducive to wealth, or at best conducive to it only by remaining in a dim-eyed and narrow-chested state of being.

Nevertheless, it is open, I repeat, to serious question, which I leave to the reader's pondering, whether, among national manufactures, that of Souls of a good quality may not at last turn out a quite leadingly lucrative one? Nay, in some far-away and yet undreamt-of hour, I can even imagine that England may cast all thoughts of possessive wealth back to the barbaric nations among whom they first arose ; and that, while the sands of the Indus and adamant of Golconda may yet stiffen the housings of the charger, and flash from the turban of the slave, she, as a Christian mother, may at last attain to the virtues and the treasures of a Heathen one. and be able to lead forth her Sons, saying,—

"These are MY Jewels."

SOME centuries before the Christian era, a Jew merchant largely engaged in business on the Gold Coast, and reported to have made one of the largest fortunes of his time (held also in repute for much practical sagacity), left among his ledgers some general maxims concerning wealth, which have been preserved, strangely enough, even to our own days. They were held in considerable respect by the most active traders of the middle ages, especially by the Venetians, who even went so far in their admiration as to place a statue of the old Jew on the angle of one of their principal public buildings. Of late years these writings have fallen into disrepute, being opposed in every particular to the spirit of modern commerce. Nevertheless I shall reproduce a passage or two from them here, partly because they may interest the reader by their novelty ; and chiefly because they will show him that it is possible for a very practical and acquisitive tradesman to hold, through a not unsuccessful career, that principle of distinction between well-gotten and ill-gotten wealth, which, partially insisted on in my last paper, it must be our work more completely to examine in this.

He says, for instance, in one place : " The getting of treasure by a lying tongue is a vanity tossed to and fro of them that seek death :" adding in another, with the same meaning (he has a curious way of doubling his sayings): "Treasures of wickedness profit nothing; but justice delivers from death." Both these passages are notable for their assertion of death as the only real issue and sum of attainment by any unjust scheme of wealth. If we read, instead of "lying tongue," "lying label, title, pretence, or advertisement," we shall more clearly perceive the bearing of the words on modern business. The seeking of death is a grand expression of the true course of men's toil in such business. We usually speak as if death pursued us, and we fled from him; but that is only so in rare instances. Ordinarily, he masks himself—makes himself beautiful—all-glorious; not like the King's daughter, all-glorious within, but outwardly: his clothing of wrought gold. We pursue him frantically all our days, he flying or hiding from us. Our crowning success at three-score and ten is utterly and perfectly to seize, and hold him in his eternal integrity—robes, ashes, and sting.

Again: the merchant says, "He that oppresseth the poor to increase his riches, shall surely come to want." And again, more strongly: "Rob not the poor because he is poor; neither oppress the afflicted in the place of business. For God shall spoil the soul of those that spoiled them."

This "robbing the poor because he is poor," is especially the mercantile form of theft, consisting in taking advantage of a man's necessities in order to obtain his labour or property at a reduced price. The ordinary highwayman's opposite form of robbery—of the rich, because he is rich—does not appear to occur so often to the old merchant's mind; probably because, being less profitable and more dangerous than the robbery of the poor, it is rarely practised by persons of discretion.

But the two most remarkable passages in their deep general significance are the following:—

"The rich and the poor have met. God is their maker."

"The rich and the poor have met. God is their light."

They "have met:" more literally, have stood in each other's way (*obviaverunt*). That is to say, as long as the world lasts, the action and counteraction of wealth and poverty, the meeting, face to face, of rich and poor, is just as appointed and necessary a law of that world as the flow of stream to sea, or the interchange of power among the electric clouds:—"God is their maker." But, also, this action may be either gentle and just, or convulsive and destructive: it may be by rage of devouring flood, or by lapse of serviceable wave;—in blackness of thunderstroke, or continual force of vital fire, soft, and shapeable into love-syllables from far away. And which of these it shall be depends on both rich and poor knowing that God is their light; that in the mystery of human life, there is no other light than this by which they can see each other's faces, and live;—light, which is called in another of the books among which the merchant's maxims have been preserved, the "sun of justice," * of which it is promised that it shall rise at last with "healing" (health-giving or helping, making whole or setting at one) in its wings. For truly this healing is only possible by means of justice; no love, no faith, no hope will do it; men will be unwisely fond—vainly faithful, unless primarily they are just; and the mistake of the best men through generation after generation, has been that great one of thinking to help the poor by almsgiving, and by preaching of patience or of hope, and by every other means, emollient or consolatory, except the one thing which God orders for them, justice. But this justice, with its accompanying holiness or helpfulness, being even by the best men denied in its trial time, is by the mass of men hated wherever it appears: so that, when the choice was one day fairly put to them, they denied the Helpful One and the Just;† and desired a murderer, sedition-raiser, and robber, to be granted to them;—the murderer instead of the Lord of Life, the sedition-raiser instead

---

* More accurately, Sun of Justness; but, instead of the harsh word "Justness," the old English "Righteousness" being commonly employed, has, by getting confused with "godliness," or attracting about it various vague and broken meanings, prevented most persons from receiving the force of the passages in which it occurs. The word "righteousness" properly refers to the justice of rule, or right, as distinguished from "equity," which refers to the justice of balance. More broadly, Righteousness is King's justice; and Equity, Judge's justice; the King guiding or ruling all, the Judge dividing or discerning between opposites (therefore, the double question, "Man, who made me a ruler—δικαστής —or a divider—μεριστής—over you?") Thus, with respect to the Justice of Choice (selection, the feebler and passive justice), we have from lego,—lex, legal, loi, and loyal; and with respect to the Justice of Rule (direction, the stronger and active justice), we have from rego,—rex, regal, roi, and royal.

† In another place written with the same meaning. "Just, and having salvation."

of the Prince of Peace, and the robber instead of the Just Judge of all the world.

I have just spoken of the flowing of streams to the sea as a partial image of the action of wealth. In one respect it is not a partial, but a perfect image. The popular economist thinks himself wise in having discovered that wealth, or the forms of property in general, must go where they are required; that where demand is, supply must follow. He farther declares that this course of demand and supply cannot be forbidden by human laws. Precisely in the same sense, and with the same certainty, the waters of the world go where they are required. Where the land falls, the water flows. The course neither of clouds nor rivers can be forbidden by human will. But the disposition and administration of them can be altered by human forethought. Whether the stream shall be a curse or a blessing, depends upon man's labour, and administrating intelligence. For centuries after centuries, great districts of the world, rich in soil, and favoured in climate, have lain desert under the rage of their own rivers; nor only desert, but plague-struck. The stream which, rightly directed, would have flowed in soft irrigation from field to field—would have purified the air, given food to man and beast, and carried their burdens for them on its bosom—now overwhelms the plain, and poisons the wind; its breath pestilence, and its work famine. In like manner this wealth "goes where it is required." No human laws can withstand its flow. They can only guide it : but this, the leading trench and limiting mound can do so thoroughly, that it shall become water of life—the riches of the hand of wisdom ; * or, on the contrary, by leaving it to its own lawless flow, they may make it, what it has been too often, the last and deadliest of national plagues : water of Marah—the water which feeds the roots of all evil.

The necessity of these laws of distribution or restraint is curiously overlooked in the ordinary political economist's definition of his own "science." He calls it, shortly, the "science of getting rich." But there are many sciences, as well as many arts, of getting rich. Poisoning people of large

* "Length of days in her right hand ; in her left, riches and honour. "

estates, was one employed largely in the middle ages; adulteration of food of people of small estates, is one employed
largely now. The ancient and honourable Highland method
of blackmail; the more modern and less honourable system
of obtaining goods on credit, and the other variously im-
proved methods of appropriation—which, in major and minor
scales of industry, down to the most artistic pocket-picking,
we owe to recent genius,—all come under the general head of
sciences, or arts, of getting rich.

So that it is clear the popular economist, in calling his
science the science *par excellence* of getting rich, must attach
some peculiar ideas of limitation to its character. I hope I
do not misrepresent him, by assuming that he means *his*
science to be the science of "getting rich by legal or just
means." In this definition, is the word "just," or "legal,"
finally to stand? For it is possible among certain nations, or
under certain rulers, or by help of certain advocates, that proceedings may be legal which are by no means just. If, therefore, we leave at last only the word "just" in that place of
our definition, the insertion of this solitary and small word
will make a notable difference in the grammar of our science.
For then it will follow that, in order to grow rich scientifically, we must grow rich justly; and, therefore, know what is
just; so that our economy will no longer depend merely on
prudence, but on jurisprudence—and that of divine, not human law. Which prudence is indeed of no mean order, holding itself, as it were, high in the air of heaven, and gazing for
ever on the light of the sun of justice; hence the souls which
have excelled in it are represented by Dante as stars forming
in heaven for ever the figure of the eye of an eagle: they having been in life the discerners of light from darkness; or to
the whole human race, as the light of the body, which is the
eye; while those souls which form the wings of the bird
(giving power and dominion to justice, "healing in its wings")
trace also in light the inscription in heaven: "DILIGITE JUSTI-
TIAM QUI JUDICATIS TERRAM." "Ye who judge the earth, give"
(not, observe, merely love, but) "diligent love to justice:" the
love which seeks diligently, that is to say, choosingly, and by

preference to all things else. Which judging or doing judg
ment in the earth is, according to their capacity and position,
required not of judges only, nor of rulers only, but of all
men : * a truth sorrowfully lost sight of even by those who are
ready enough to apply to themselves passages in which Christian
men are spoken of as called to be " saints " (*i.e.* to helpful or
healing functions) ; and " chosen to be kings " (*i.e.* to knowing or directing functions) ; the true meaning of these titles
having been long lost through the pretences of unhelpful and
unable persons to saintly and kingly character ; also through
the once popular idea that both the sanctity and royalty are
to consist in wearing long robes and high crowns, instead of
in mercy and judgment ; whereas all true sanctity is saving
power, as all true royalty is ruling power ; and injustice is
part and parcel of the denial of such power, which " makes
men as the creeping things, as the fishes of the sea, that have
no ruler over them." †

Absolute justice is indeed no more attainable than absolute
truth ; but the righteous man is distinguished from the un-
righteous by his desire and hope of justice, as the true man
from the false by his desire and hope of truth. And though
absolute justice be unattainable, as much justice as we need
for all practical use is attainable by all those who make it
their aim.

We have to examine, then, in the subject before us, what
are the laws of justice respecting payment of labour—no
small part, these, of the foundations of all jurisprudence.

* I hear that several of our lawyers have been greatly amused by the
statement in the first of these papers that a lawyer's function was to do
justice.   I do not intend it for a jest ; nevertheless it will be seen that
in the above passage neither the determination nor doing of justice are
contemplated as functions wholly peculiar to the lawyer.   Possibly, the
more our standing armies, whether of soldiers, pastors, or legislators
(the generic term " pastor " including all teachers, and the generic term
" lawyer " including makers as well as interpreters of law), can be superseded by the force of national heroism, wisdom, and honesty, the better
it may be for the nation.

† It being the privilege of the fishes, as it is of rats and wolves, to
live by the laws of demand and supply ; but the distinction of humanity, to live by those of right.

I reduced, in my last paper, the idea of money payment to its simplest or radical terms. In those terms its nature, and the conditions of justice respecting it, can be best ascertained.

Money payment, as there stated, consists radically in a promise to some person working for us, that for the time and labour he spends in our service to-day we will give or procure equivalant time and labour in his service at any future time when he may demand it.*

If we promise to give him less labour than he has given us, we under-pay him. If we promise to give him more labour than he has given us, we over-pay him. In practice, according to the laws of demand and supply, when two men are ready to do the work, and only one man wants to have it done, the two men underbid each other for it; and the one who gets it to do, is under-paid. But when two men want the work done, and there is only one man ready to do it, the two men who want it done over-bid each other, and the workman is over-paid.

I will examine these two points of injustice in succession ; but first I wish the reader to clearly understand the central principle, lying between the two, of right or just payment.

When we ask a service of any man, he may either give it us freely, or demand payment for it. Respecting free gift of service, there is no question at present, that being a matter of affection—not of traffic. But if he demand payment for it, and we wish to treat him with absolute equity, it is evident that this equity can only consist in giving time for time,

---

* It might appear at first that the market price of labour expressed such an exchange: but this is a fallacy, for the market price is the momentary price of the kind of labour required, but the just price is its equivalent of the productive labour of mankind. This difference will be analyzed in its place. It must be noted also that I speak here only of the exchangeable value of labour, not of that of commodities. The exchangeable value of a commodity is that of the labour required to produce it, multiplied into the force of the demand for it. If the value of the labour $= x$ and the force of the demand $= y$, the exchangeable value of the commodity is $x\,y$, in which if either $x = 0$, or $y = 0$, $xy = 0$.

strength for strength, and skill for skill. If a man works an hour for us, and we only promise to work half-an-hour for him in return, we obtain an unjust advantage. If, on the contrary, we promise to work an hour and a half for him in return, he has an unjust advantage. The justice consists in absolute exchange ; or, if there be any respect to the stations of the parties, it will not be in favour of the employer : there is certainly no equitable reason in a man's being poor, that if he give me a pound of bread to-day, I should return him less than a pound of bread to-morrow ; or any equitable reason in a man's being uneducated, that if he uses a certain quantity of skill and knowledge in my service, I should use a less quantity of skill and knowledge in his. Perhaps, ultimately, it may appear desirable, or, to say the least, gracious, that I should give in return somewhat more than I received. But at present, we are concerned on the law of justice only, which is that of perfect and accurate exchange ;—one circumstance only interfering with the simplicity of this radical idea of just payment—that inasmuch as labour (rightly directed) is fruitful just as seed is, the fruit (or " interest," as it is called) of the labour first given, or "advanced," ought to be taken into account, and balanced by an additional quantity of labour in the subsequent repayment. Supposing the repayment to take place at the end of a year, or of any other given time, this calculation could be approximately made ; but as money (that is to say, cash) payment involves no reference to time (it being optional with the person paid to spend what he receives at once or after any number of years), we can only assume, generally, that some slight advantage must in equity be allowed to the person who advances the labour, so that the typical form of bargain will be : If you give me an hour to-day, I will give you an hour and five minutes on demand. If you give me a pound of bread to-day, I will give you seventeen ounces on demand, and so on. All that it is necessary for the reader to note is, that the amount returned is at least in equity not to be *less* than the amount given.

The abstract idea, then, of just or due wages, as respects the labourer, is that they will consist in a sum of money which

will at any time procure for him at least as much labour as he
has given, rather more than less. And this equity or justice
of payment is, observe, wholly independent of any reference
to the number of men who are willing to do the work. I
want a horseshoe for my horse. Twenty smiths, or twenty
thousand smiths, may be ready to forge it; their number
does not in one atom's weight affect the question of the equitable payment of the one who *does* forge it. It costs him a
quarter of an hour of his life, and so much skill and strength
of arm to make that horseshoe for me. Then at some future
time I am bound in equity to give a quarter of an hour, and
some minutes more, of my life (or of some other person's at
my disposal), and also as much strength of arm and skill, and
a little more, in making or doing what the smith may have
need of.

Such being the abstract theory of just remunerative payment, its application is practically modified by the fact that
the order for labour, given in payment, is general, while labour
received is special. The current coin or document is practically
an order on the nation for so much work of any kind ; and this
universal applicability to immediate need renders it so much
more valuable than special labour can be, that an order for a
less quantity of this general toil will always be accepted as a
just equivalent for a greater quantity of special toil. Any
given craftsman will always be willing to give an hour of his
own work in order to receive command over half-an-hour, or
even much less, of national work. This source of uncertainty,
together with the difficulty of determining the monetary value of skill,* renders the ascertainment (even approximate) of

---

* Under the term "skill" I mean to include the united force of experience, intellect, and passion in their operation on manual labour: and
under the term " passion," to include the entire range and agency of the
moral feelings ; from the simple patience and gentleness of mind which
will give continuity and fineness to the touch, or enable one person to
work without fatigue, and with good effect, twice as long as another, up
to the qualities of character which render science possible—(the retarda-
tion of science by envy is one of the most tremendous losses in the
economy of the present century)—and to the incommunicable emotion

the proper wages of any given labour in terms of a currency, matter of considerable complexity. But they do not affect the principle of exchange. The worth of the work may not be easily known ; but it *has* a worth, just as fixed and real as the specific gravity of a substance, though such specific gravity may not be easily ascertainable when the substance is united with many others. Nor is there any difficulty or chance in determining it as in determining the ordinary maxima and minima of vulgar political economy. There are few bargains in which the buyer can ascertain with anything like precision that the seller would have taken no less ;—or the seller acquire more than a comfortable faith that the purchaser would have given no more. This impossibility of precise knowledge prevents neither from striving to attain the desired point of

and imagination which are the first and mightiest sources of all value in art.

It is highly singular that political economists should not yet have perceived, if not the moral, at least the passionate element, to be an inextricable quantity in every calculation. I cannot conceive, for instance, how it was possible that Mr. Mill should have followed the true clue so far as to write,—"No limit can be set to the importance—even in a purely productive and material point of view—of mere thought," without seeing that it was logically necessary to add also, " and of mere feeling." And this the more, because in his first definition of labour he includes in the idea of it " all feelings of a disagreeable kind connected with the employment of one's thoughts in a particular occupation. " True; but why not also, "feelings of an agreeable kind ? " It can hardly be supposed that the feelings which retard labour are more essentially a part of the labour than those which accelerate it. The first are paid for as pain, the second as power. The workman is merely indemnified for the first ; but the second both produce a part of the exchangeable value of the work, and materially increase its actual quantity.

"Fritz is with us. *He* is worth fifty thousand men." Truly, a large addition to the material force ;—consisting, however, be it observed, not more in operations carried on in Fritz's head, than in operations carried on in his armies' heart. " No limit can be set to the importance of *mere* thought " Perhaps not ! Nay, suppose some day it should turn out that " mere' thought was in itself a recommendable object of production, and that all Material production was only a step towards this more precious Immaterial one ?

greatest vexation and injury to the other, nor from accepting it for a scientific principle that he is to buy for the least and sell for the most possible, though what the real least or most may be he cannot tell. In like manner, a just person lays it down for a scientific principle that he is to pay a just price, and, without being able precisely to ascertain the limits of such a price, will nevertheless strive to attain the closest possible approximation to them. A practically serviceable approximation he *can* obtain. It is easier to determine scientifically what a man ought to have for his work, than what his necessities will compel him to take for it. His necessities can only be ascertained by empirical, but his due by analytical investigation. In the one case, you try your answer to the sum like a puzzled schoolboy—till you find one that fits ; in the other, you bring out your result within certain limits, by process of calculation.

Supposing, then, the just wages of any quantity of given labour to have been ascertained, let us examine the first results of just and unjust payment, when in favour of the purchaser or employer; *i. e.* when two men are ready to do the work, and only one wants to have it done.

The unjust purchaser forces the two to bid against each other till he has reduced their demand to its lowest terms. Let us assume that the lowest bidder offers to do the work at half its just price.

The purchaser employs him, and does not employ the other. The first or *apparent* result is, therefore, that one of the two men is left out of employ, or to starvation, just as definitely as by the just procedure of giving fair price to the best workman. The various writers who endeavoured to invalidate the positions of my first paper never saw this, and assumed that the unjust hirer employed *both.* He employs both no more than the just hirer. The only difference (in the outset) is that the just man pays sufficiently, the unjust man insufficiently, for the labour of the single person employed.

I say, "in the outset ;" for this first or apparent difference is not the actual difference. By the unjust procedure, half the proper price of the work is left in the hands of the employer

This enables him to hire another man at the same unjust rate, on some other kind of work; and the final result is that he has two men working for him at half price, and two are out of employ.

By the just procedure, the whole price of the first piece of work goes in the hands of the man who does it. No surplus being left in the employer's hands, *he* cannot hire another man for another piece of labour. But by precisely so much as his power is diminished, the hired workman's power is increased; that is to say, by the additional half of the price he has received; which additional half *he* has the power of using to employ another man in *his* service. I will suppose, for the moment, the least favourable, though quite probable, case— that, though justly treated himself, he yet will act unjustly to his subordinate; and hire at half-price, if he can. The final result will then be, that one man works for the employer, at just price; one for the workman, at half-price; and two, as in the first case, are still out of employ. These two, as I said before, are out of employ in *both* cases. The difference between the just and unjust procedure does not lie in the number of men hired, but in the price paid to them, and the *persons by whom* it is paid. The essential difference, that which I want the reader to see clearly, is, that in the unjust case, two men work for one, the first hirer. In the just case, one man works for the first hirer, one for the person hired, and so on, down or up through the various grades of service; the influence being carried forward by justice, and arrested by injustice. The universal and constant action of justice in this matter is therefore to diminish the power of wealth, in the hands of one individual, over masses of men, and to distribute it through a chain of men. The actual power exerted by the wealth is the same in both cases; but by injustice it is put all in one man's hands, so that he directs at once and with equal force the labour of a circle of men about him; by the just procedure, he is permitted to touch the nearest only, through whom, with diminished force, modified by new minds, the energy of the wealth passes on to others, and so till it exhausts itself.

The immediate operation of justice in this respect is there-fore to diminish the power of wealth, first in acquisition of luxury, and, secondly, in exercise of moral influence. The employer cannot concentrate so multitudinous labour on his own interests, nor can he subdue so multitudinous mind to his own will. But the secondary operation of justice is not less important. The insufficient payment of the group of men working for one, places each under a maximum of diffi-culty in rising above his position. The tendency of the sys-tem is to check advancement. But the sufficient or just pay-ment, distributed through a descending series of offices or grades of labour,* gives each subordinated person fair and sufficient means of rising in the social scale, if he chooses to use them ; and thus not only diminishes the immediate power of wealth, but removes the worst disabilities of poverty.

It is on this vital problem that the entire destiny of the labourer is ultimately dependent. Many minor interests may sometimes appear to interfere with it, but all branch from it.

* I am sorry to lose time by answering, however curtly, the equivo-cations of the writers who sought to obscure the instances given of reg-ulated labour in the first of these papers, by confusing kinds, ranks, and quantities of labour with its qualities. I never said that a colonel should have the same pay as a private, nor a bishop the same pay as a curate. Neither did I say that more work ought to be paid as less work (so that the curate of a parish of two thousand souls should have no more than the curate of a parish of five hundred). But I said that, so far as you employ it at all, bad work should be paid no less than good work ; as a bad clergyman yet takes his tithes, a bad physician takes his fee, and a bad lawyer his costs. And this, as will be farther shown in the conclusion, I said, and say, partly because the best work never was nor ever will be, done for money at all ; but chiefly because, the moment people know they have to pay the bad and good alike, they will try to discern the one from the other, and not use the bad. A sagacious writer in the *Scotsman* asks me if I should like any common scribbler to be paid by Messrs. Smith, Elder and Co. as their good authors are. I should, if they employed him —but would seriously rec-ommend them, for the scribbler's sake, as well as their own, *not* to employ him. The quantity of its money which the country at present invests in scribbling is not, in the outcome of it, economically spent; and even the highly ingenious person to whom this question occurred, might perhaps have been more beneficially employed than in printing it.

For instance, considerable agitation is often caused in the minds of the lower classes when they discover the share which they nominally, and, to all appearance, actually, pay out of their wages in taxation (I believe thirty-five or forty per cent.). This sounds very grievous; but in reality the labourer does not pay it, but his employer. If the workman had not to pay it, his wages would be less by just that sum : competition would still reduce them to the lowest rate at which life was possible. Similarly the lower orders agitated for the repeal of the corn laws,* thinking they would be bet-

---

* I have to acknowledge an interesting communication on the subject of free trade from Paisley (for a short letter from " A Well-wisher " at ——, my thanks are yet more due). But the Scottish writer will, I fear, be disagreeably surprised to hear, that I am, and always have been, an utterly fearless and unscrupulous free-trader. Seven years ago, speaking of the various signs of infancy in the European mind (*Stones of Venice*, vol. iii. p. 168), I wrote : " The first principles of commerce were acknowledged by the English parliament only a few months ago, and in its free-trade measures, and are still so little understood by the million, that *no nation dares to abolish its custom-houses.*"

It will be observed that I do not admit even the idea of reciprocity. Let other nations, if they like, keep their ports shut ; every wise nation will throw its own open. It is not the opening them, but a sudden, inconsiderate, and blunderingly experimental manner of opening them, which does the harm. If you have been protecting a manufacture for long series of years, you must not take protection off in a moment, so as to throw every one of its operatives at once out of employ, any more than you must take all its wrappings off a feeble child at once in cold weather, though the cumber of them may have been radically injuring its health. Little by little, you must restore it to freedom and to air.

Most people's minds are in curious confusion on the subject of free trade, because they suppose it to imply enlarged competition. On the contrary, free trade puts an end to all competition. "Protection" (among various other mischievous functions) endeavours to enable one country to compete with another in the production of an article at a disadvantage. When trade is entirely free, no country can be competed with in the articles for the production of which it is naturally calculated ; nor can it compete with any other in the production of articles for which it is not naturally calculated. Tuscany, for instance, cannot compete with England in steel, nor England with Tuscany in oil. They must exchange their steel and oil. Which exchange should be as frank and free as honesty and the sea-winds can make it. Competition, in-

ter off if bread were cheaper ; never perceiving that as soon
as bread was permanently cheaper, wages would permanently
fall in precisely that proportion. The corn laws were rightly
repealed ; not, however, because they directly oppressed the
poor, but because they indirectly oppressed them in causing
a large quantity of their labour to be consumed unproduc-
tively. So also unnecessary taxation oppresses them, through
destruction of capital, but the destiny of the poor depends
primarily always on this one question of dueness of wages.
Their distress (irrespectively of that caused by sloth, minor
error, or crime) arises on the grand scale from the two react-
ing forces of competition and oppression. There is not yet,
nor will yet for ages be, any real over-population in the world :
but a local over-population, or, more accurately, a degree of
population locally unmanageable under existing circumstances
for want of forethought and sufficient machinery, necessarily
shows itself by pressure of competition ; and the taking advantage of this competition by the purchaser to obtain their
labour unjustly cheap, consummates at once their suffering
and his own ; for in this (as I believe in every other kind of
slavery) the oppressor suffers at last more than the oppressed,
and those magnificent lines of Pope, even in all their force,
fall short of the truth—

> " Yet, to be just to these poor men of pelf,
>   Each does but HATE HIS NEIGHBOUR AS HIMSELF :
>   Damned to the mines, an equal fate betides
>   The slave that digs it, and the slave that hides."

The collateral and reversionary operations of justice in this
matter I shall examine hereafter (it being needful first to define the nature of value) ; proceeding then to consider within
what practical terms a juster system may be established ; and
ultimately the vexed question of the destinies of the unemployed workmen.* Lest, however, the reader should be

---

deed, arises at first, and sharply, in order to prove which is strongest in
any given manufacture possible to both ; this point once ascertained,
competition is at an end.

* I should be glad if the reader would first clear the ground for himself so far as to determine whether the difficulty lies in getting the work

alarmed at some of the issues to which our investigations seem to be tending, as if in their bearing against the power of wealth they had something in common with those of socialism, I wish him to know, in accurate terms, one or two of the main points which I have in view.

Whether socialism has made more progress among the army and navy (where payment is made on my principles), or among the manufacturing operatives (who are paid on my opponents' principles), I leave it to those opponents to ascertain and declare. Whatever their conclusion may be, I think it necessary to answer for myself only this : that if there be any one point insisted on throughout my works more frequently than another, that one point is the impossibility of Equality. My continual aim has been to show the eternal superiority of some men to others, sometimes even of one man to all others ; and to show also the advisability of appointing more such persons or person to guide, to lead, or on occasion even to compel and subdue, their inferiors, according to their own better knowledge and wiser will. My principles of Political Economy were all involved in a single phrase spoken three years ago at

or getting the pay for it. Does he consider occupation itself to be an expensive luxury, difficult of attainment, of which too little is to be found in the world ? or is it rather that, while in the enjoyment even of the most athletic delight, men must nevertheless be maintained, and this maintenance is not always forthcoming ? We must be clear on this head before going farther, as most people are loosely in the habit of talking of the difficulty of "finding employment." Is it employment that we want to find, or support during employment ? Is it idleness we wish to put an end to, or hunger ? We have to take up both questions in succession, only not both at the same time. No doubt that work *is* a luxury, and a very great one. It is, indeed, at once a luxury and a necessity ; no man can retain either health of mind or body without it. So profoundly do I feel this, that, as will be seen in the sequel, one of the principal objects I would recommend to benevolent and practical persons, is to induce rich people to seek for a larger quantity of this luxury than they at present possess. Nevertheless, it appears by experience that even this healthiest of pleasures may be indulged in to excess, and that human beings are just as liable to surfeit of labour as to surfeit of meat ; so that, as on the one hand, it may be charitable to provide, for some people, lighter dinner, and more work,—for others it may be equally expedient to provide lighter work, and more dinner.

Manchester : "Soldiers of the Ploughshare as well as soldiers of the Sword :" and they were all summed in a single sentence in the last volume of *Modern Painters*—" Government and co-operation are in all things the Laws of Life ; Anarchy and competition the Laws of Death."

And with respect to the mode in which these general principles affect the secure possession of property, so far am I from invalidating such security, that the whole gist of these papers will be found ultimately to aim at an extension in its range ; and whereas it has long been known and declared that the poor have no right to the property of the rich, I wish it also to be known and declared that the rich have no right to the property of the poor.

But that the working of the system which I have undertaken to develop would in many ways shorten the apparent and direct, though not the unseen and collateral, power, both of wealth, as the Lady of Pleasure, and of capital as the Lord of Toil, I do not deny : on the contrary, I affirm it in all joyfulness ; knowing that the attraction of riches is already too strong, as their authority is already too weighty, for the reason of mankind. I said in my last paper that nothing in history had ever been so disgraceful to human intellect as the acceptance among us of the common doctrines of political economy as a science. I have many grounds for saying this, but one of the chief may be given in few words. I know no previous instance in history of a nation's establishing a systematic disobedience to the first principles of its professed religion. The writings which we (verbally) esteem as divine, not only denounce the love of money as the source of all evil, and as an idolatry abhorred of the Deity, but declare mammon service to be the accurate and irreconcileable opposite of God's service : and, whenever they speak of riches absolute, and poverty absolute, declare woe to the rich, and blessing to the poor. Whereupon we forthwith investigate a science of becoming rich, as the shortest road to national prosperity.

> " Tai Cristian dannerà l'Etiòpe,
> Quando si partiranno i due collegi,
> L'UNO IN ETERNO RICCO, E L'ALTRO INÒPE.'

ESSAY IV.

In the last paper we saw that just payment of labour consisted in a sum of money which would approximately obtain
equivalent labour at a future time : we have now to examine
the means of obtaining such equivalence. Which question
involves the definition of Value, Wealth, Price, and Produce.

None of these terms are yet defined so as to be understood
by the public. But the last, Produce, which one might have
thought the clearest of all, is, in use, the most ambiguous ;
and the examination of the kind of ambiguity attendant
on its present employment will best open the way to our
work.

In his chapter on Capital,* Mr. J. S. Mill instances, as a
capitalist, a hardware manufacturer, who, having intended to
spend a certain portion of the proceeds of his business in buying plate and jewels, changes his mind, and " pays it as wages
to additional workpeople." The effect is stated by Mr. Mill
to be, that " more food is appropriated to the consumption of
productive labourers."

Now, I do not ask, though, had I written this paragraph, it
would surely have been asked of me, What is to become of
the silversmiths ? If they are truly unproductive persons, we
will acquiesce in their extinction. And though in another
part of the same passage, the hardware merchant is supposed
also to dispense with a number of servants, whose " food is
thus set free for productive purposes," I do not inquire what
will be the effect, painful or otherwise, upon the servants, of

* Book I. chap. iv. s. 1. To save space, my future references to Mr.
Mill's work will be by numerals only, as in this instance, I. iv. 1. **Ed**
in 2 vols. 8vo. Parker, 1848.

this emancipation of their food. But I very seriously inquire why ironware is produce, and silverware is not? That the merchant consumes the one, and sells the other, certainly does not constitute the difference, unless it can be shown (which, indeed, I perceive it to be becoming daily more and more the aim of tradesmen to show) that commodities are made to be sold, and not to be consumed. The merchant is an agent of conveyance to the consumer in one case, and is himself the consumer in the other: * but the labourers are in either case equally productive, since they have produced goods to the same value, if the hardware and the plate are both goods.

And what distinction separates them? It is indeed possible that in the " comparative estimate of the moralist," with which Mr. Mill says political economy has nothing to do (III. i. 2) a steel fork might appear a more substantial production than a silver one : we may grant also that knives, no less than forks, are good produce ; and scythes and ploughshares serviceable articles. But, how of bayonets? Supposing the hardware merchant to effect large sales of *these*, by help of the " setting free " of the food of his servants and his silversmith,—is he still employing productive labourers, or, in Mr. Mill's words, labourers who increase " the stock of permanent means of en- joyment " (I. iii. 4). Or if, instead of bayonets, he supply bombs, will not the absolute and final " enjoyment" of even these energetically productive articles (each of which costs ten pounds)† be dependent on a proper choice of time and

* If Mr. Mill had wished to show the difference in result between consumption and sale, he should have represented the hardware mer- chant as consuming his own goods instead of selling them ; similarly, the silver merchant as consuming his own goods instead of selling them. Had he done this, he would have made his position clearer, though less tenable ; and perhaps this was the position he really intended to take, tacitly involving his theory, elsewhere stated, and shown in the sequel of this paper to be false, that demand for commodities is not demand for labour. But by the most diligent scrutiny of the paragraph now under examination, I cannot determine whether it is a fallacy pure and simple, or the half of one fallacy supported by the whole of a greater one ; so that I treat it here on the kinder assumption that it is one fallacy only.

† I take Mr. Helps' estimate in his essay on War.

place for their *enfantement* ; choice, that is to say, depending on those philosophical considerations with which political economy has nothing to do ? *

I should have regretted the need of pointing out inconsistency in any portion of Mr. Mill's work, had not the value of his work proceeded from its inconsistencies. He deserves honour among economists by inadvertently disclaiming the principles which he states, and tacitly introducing the moral considerations with which he declares his science has no connection. Many of his chapters are, therefore, true and valuable ; and the only conclusions of his which I have to dispute are those which follow from his premises.

Thus, the idea which lies at the root of the passage we have just been examining, namely, that labour applied to produce luxuries will not support so many persons as labour applied to produce useful articles, is entirely true ; but the instance given fails—and in four directions of failure at once—because Mr. Mill has not defined the real meaning of usefulness. The definition which he has given—" capacity to satisfy a desire, or serve a purpose " (III. i. 2)—applies equally to the iron and silver ; while the true definition—which he has not given, but which nevertheless underlies the false verbal definition in his mind, and comes out once or twice by accident (as in the words "any support to life or strength" in I. i. 5) —applies to some articles of iron, but not to others, and to some articles of silver, but not to others. It applies to ploughs, but not to bayonets ; and to forks, but not to filigree.†

The eliciting of the true definition will give us the reply to

---

* Also when the wrought silver vases of Spain were dashed to fragments by our custom-house officers, because bullion might be imported free of duty, but not brains, was the axe that broke them productive ?— the artist who wrought them unproductive ? Or again. If the woodman's axe is productive, is the executioner's ? as also, if the hemp of a cable be productive, does not the productiveness of hemp in a halter depend on its moral more than on its material application ?

† Filigree : that is to say, generally, ornament dependent on complexity, not on art.

our first question, " What is value ? " respecting which, however, we must first hear the popular statements.

" The word 'value,' when used without adjunct, always
means, in political economy, value in exchange " (Mill, III. i.
3). So that, if two ships cannot exchange their rudders, their
rudders are, in politico-economic language, of no value to
either.

But " the subject of political economy is wealth."—(Preliminary remarks, page 1.)

And wealth "consists of all useful and agreeable objects
which possess exchangeable value."—(Preliminary remarks,
page 10.)

It appears, then, according to Mr. Mill, that usefulness and
agreeableness underlie the exchange value, and must be ascertained to exist in the thing, before we can esteem it an object of wealth.

Now, the economical usefulness of a thing depends not
merely on its own nature, but on the number of people who
can and will use it. A horse is useless, and therefore unsale-
able, if no one can ride,—a sword if no one can strike, and
meat, if no one can eat. Thus every material utility depends
on its relative human capacity.

Similarly : The agreeableness of a thing depends not merely
on its own likeableness, but on the number of people who can
be got to like it. The relative agreeableness, and therefore
saleableness, of " a pot of the smallest ale," and of " Adonis
painted by a running brook," depends virtually on the opinion
of Demos, in the shape of Christopher Sly. That is to say,
the agreeableness of a thing depends on its relative human
disposition.* Therefore, political economy, being a science of

* These statements sound crude in their brevity ; but will be found
of the utmost importance when they are developed. Thus, in the above
instance, economists have never perceived that disposition to buy is a
wholly *moral* element in demand : that is to say, when you give a man
half-a-crown, it depends on his disposition whether he is rich or poor
with it—whether he will buy disease, ruin, and hatred, or buy health,
advancement, and domestic love. And thus the agreeableness or exchange value of every offered commodity depends on production, not
merely of the commodity, but of buyers of it ; therefore on the educa-

wealth, must be a science respecting human capacities and dispositions. But moral considerations have nothing to do with political economy (III. i. 2). Therefore, moral consider-ations have nothing to do with human capacities and disposi-tions.

I do not wholly like the look of this conclusion from Mr Mill's statements :—let us try Mr. Ricardo's.

" Utility is not the measure of exchangeable value, though it is absolutely essential to it."—(Chap. I. sect. i.) Essential in what degree, Mr. Ricardo ? There may be greater and less degrees of utility. Meat, for instance, may be so good as to be fit for any one to eat, or so bad as to be fit for no one to eat. What is the exact degree of goodness which is " essen-tial " to its exchangeable value, but not " the measure " of it ? How good must the meat be, in order to possess any exchange-able value ; and how bad must it be—(I wish this were a set-tled question in London markets)—in order to possess none ?

There appears to be some hitch, I think, in the working even of Mr. Ricardo's principles ; but let him take his own example. " Suppose that in the early stages of society the bows and arrows of the hunter were of equal value with the implements of the fisherman. Under such circumstances the value of the deer, the produce of the hunter's day's labour, would be *exactly* " (italics mine) " equal to the value of the fish, the product of the fisherman's day's labour. The com-parative value of the fish and game would be *entirely* regulated by the quantity of labour realized in each." (Ricardo, chap. iii. On Value).

Indeed ! Therefore, if the fisherman catches one sprat, and the huntsman one deer, one sprat will be equal in value to one

sion of buyers and on all the moral elements by which their disposition to buy this, or that, is formed. I will illustrate and expand into final consequences every one of these definitions in its place : at present they can only be given with extremest brevity ; for in order to put the sub-ject at once in a connected form before the reader, I have thrown into one, the opening definitions of four chapters ; namely, of that on Value (" Ad Valorem "); on Price (" Thirty Pieces ") ; on Production (" De-meter ") ; and on Economy (" The Law of the House ").

deer; but if the fisherman catches no sprat, and the huntsman two deer, no sprat will be equal in value to two deer?

Nay; but—Mr. Ricardo's supporters may say—he means, on an average;—if the average product of a day's work of fisher and hunter be one fish and one deer, the one fish will always be equal in value to the one deer.

Might I inquire the species of fish. Whale? or whitebait?*

It would be waste of time to pursue these fallacies farther; we will seek for a true definition.

---

* Perhaps it may be said, in farther support of Mr. Ricardo, that he meant, "when the utility is constant or given, the price varies as the quantity of labour." If he meant this, he should have said it; but, had he meant it, he could have hardly missed the necessary result, that utility would be one measure of price (which he expressly denies it to be); and that, to prove saleableness, he had to prove a given quantity of utility, as well as a given quantity of labour; to wit, in his own instance, that the deer and fish would each feed the same number of men, for the same number of days, with equal pleasure to their palates. The fact is, he did not know what he meant himself. The general idea which he had derived from commercial experience, without being able to analyse it, was, that when the demand is constant, the price varies as the quantity of labour required for production; or,—using the formula I gave in last paper—when y is constant, $x y$ varies as x. But demand never is, nor can be, ultimately constant, if x varies distinctly; for, as price rises, consumers fall away; and as soon as there is a monopoly (and all scarcity is a form of monopoly; so that every commodity is affected occasionally by some colour of monopoly), y becomes the most influential condition of the price. Thus the price of a painting depends less on its merits than on the interest taken in it by the public; the price of singing less on the labour of the singer than the number of persons who desire to hear him; and the price of gold less on the scarcity which affects it in common with cerium or iridium, than on the sunlight colour and unalterable purity by which it attracts the admiration and answers the trusts of mankind.

It must be kept in mind, however, that I use the word "demand" in a somewhat different sense from economists usually. They mean by it "the quantity of a thing sold." I mean by it "the force of the buyer's capable intention to buy." In good English, a person's "demand" signifies, not what he gets, but what he asks for.

Economists also do not notice that objects are not valued by absolute bulk or weight, but by such bulk and weight as is necessary to bring them into use. They say, for instance, that water bears no price in the

Much store has been set for centuries upon the use of our English classical education. It were to be wished that our well-educated merchants recalled to mind always this much of their Latin schooling,—that the nominative of *valorem* (a word already sufficiently familiar to them) is *valor ;* a word which, therefore, ought to be familiar to them. *Valor,* from *valere,* to be well, or strong (ὑγιαίνω) ;—strong, *in* life (if a man), or valiant ; strong, *for* life (if a thing), or valuable. To be " valuable," therefore, is to " avail towards life." A truly valuable or availing thing is that which leads to life with its whole strength. In proportion as it does not lead to life, or as its strength is broken, it is less valuable ; in proportion as it leads away from life, it is unvaluable or malignant.

The value of a thing, therefore, is independent of opinion, and of quantity. Think what you will of it, gain how much you may of it, the value of the thing itself is neither greater nor less. For ever it avails, or avails not ; no estimate can raise, no disdain depress, the power which it holds from the Maker of things and of men.

The real science of political economy, which has yet to be distinguished from the bastard science, as medicine from witchcraft, and astronomy from astrology, is that which teaches nations to desire and labour for the things that lead to life ; and which teaches them to scorn and destroy the things that lead to destruction. And if, in a state of infancy, they suppose indifferent things, such as excrescences of shell-fish, and pieces of blue and red stone, to be valuable, and spend large measure of the labour which ought to be employed for the extension and ennobling of life, in diving or digging for them, and cutting them into various shapes,—or if, in the same state of infancy, they imagine precious and beneficent things, such as air, light, and cleanliness, to be valueless,—or if, finally, they imagine the conditions of their

market. It is true that a cupful does not, but a lake does ; just as a handful of dust does not, but an acre does. And were it possible to make even the possession of the cupful or handful permanent (*i. e.* to find a place for them,) the earth and sea would be bought up by handfuls and cupfuls.

own existence, by which alone they can truly possess or use anything, such, for instance, as peace, trust, and love, to be prudently exchangeable, when the market offers, for gold, iron, or excrescences of shells—the great and only science of Political Economy teaches them, in all these cases, what is vanity, and what substance ; and how the service of Death, the Lord of Waste, and of eternal emptiness, differs from the service of Wisdom, the Lady of Saving, and of eternal fulness ; she who has said, "I will cause those that love me to inherit SUBSTANCE ; and I will FILL their treasures."

The "Lady of Saving," in a profounder sense than that of the savings' bank, though that is a good one : Madonna della Salute,—Lady of Health—which, though commonly spoken of as if separate from wealth, is indeed a part of wealth. This word, "wealth," it will be remembered, is the next we have to define.

"To be wealthy," says Mr. Mill, is "to have a large stock of useful articles."

I accept this definition. Only let us perfectly understand it. My opponents often lament my not giving them enough logic : I fear I must at present use a little more than they will like ; but this business of Political Economy is no light one, and we must allow no loose terms in it.

We have, therefore, to ascertain in the above definition, first, what is the meaning of "having," or the nature of Possession. Then what is the meaning of "useful," or the nature of Utility.

And first of possession. At the crossing of the transepts of Milan Cathedral has lain, for three hundred years, the embalmed body of St. Carlo Borromeo. It holds a golden crosier, and has a cross of emeralds on its breast. Admitting the crosier and emeralds to be useful articles, is the body to be considered as "having" them ? Do they, in the politico-economical sense of property, belong to it ? If not, and if we may, therefore, conclude generally that a dead body cannot possess property, what degree and period of animation in the body will render possession possible ?

As thus : lately in a wreck of a Californian ship, one of the passengers fastened a belt about him with two hundred pounds of gold in it, with which he was found afterwards at the bottom. Now, as he was sinking—had he the gold? or had the gold him?*

And if, instead of sinking him in the sea by its weight, the gold had struck him on the forehead, and thereby caused incurable disease—suppose palsy or insanity,—would the gold in that case have been more a "possession" than in the first? Without pressing the inquiry up through instances of gradual increasing vital power over the gold (which I will, however, give, if they are asked for), I presume the reader will see that possession, or "having," is not an absolute, but a gradated, power; and consists not only in the quantity or nature of the thing possessed, but also (and in a greater degree) in its suitableness to the person possessing it, and in his vital power to use it.

And our definition of Wealth, expanded, becomes: "The possession of useful articles, *which we can use.*" This is a very serious change. For wealth, instead of depending merely on a "have," is thus seen to depend on a "can." Gladiator's death, on a "habet;" but soldier's victory, and state's salvation, on a "quo plurimum posset." (Liv. VII. 6.) And what we reasoned of only as accumulation of material, is seen to demand also accumulation of capacity.

So much for our verb. Next for our adjective. What is the meaning of "useful?"

The inquiry is closely connected with the last. For what is capable of use in the hands of some persons, is capable, in the hands of others, of the opposite of use, called commonly, "from-use or ab-use." And it depends on the person, much more than on the article, whether its usefulness or ab-usefulness will be the quality developed in it. Thus, wine, which the Greeks, in their Bacchus, made, rightly, the type of all passion, and which, when used, "cheereth god and man" (that is to say, strengthens both the divine life, or reasoning power, and the earthly, or carnal power, of man); yet, when abused, becomes "Dionusos," hurtful especially to the divine

* Compare GEORGE HERBERT, *The Church Porch,* Stanza 28.

part of man, or reason. And again, the body itself, being equally liable to use and to abuse, and, when rightly disciplined, serviceable to the State, both for war and labour;— but when not disciplined, or abused, valueless to the State, and capable only of continuing the private or single existence of the individual (and that but feebly)—the Greeks called such a body an "idiotic" or "private" body, from their word signifying a person employed in no way directly useful to the State; whence, finally, our "idiot," meaning a person entirely occupied with his own concerns.

Hence, it follows, that if a thing is to be useful, it must be not only of an availing nature, but in availing hands. Or, in accurate terms, usefulness is value in the hands of the valiant; so that this science of wealth being, as we have just seen, when regarded as the science of Accumulation, accumulative of capacity as well as of material,—when regarded as the Science of Distribution, is distribution not absolute, but discriminate; not of every thing to every man, but of the right thing to the right man. A difficult science, dependent on more than arithmetic.

Wealth, therefore, is "THE POSSESSION OF THE VALUABLE BY THE VALIANT;" and in considering it as a power existing in a nation, the two elements, the value of the thing, and the valour of its possessor, must be estimated together. Whence it appears that many of the persons commonly considered wealthy, are in reality no more wealthy than the locks of their own strong boxes are; they being inherently and eternally incapable of wealth; and operating for the nation, in an economical point of view, either as pools of dead water, and eddies in a stream (which, so long as the stream flows, are useless, or serve only to drown people, but may become of importance in a state of stagnation, should the stream dry); or else, as dams in a river, of which the ultimate service depends not on the dam, but the miller; or else, as mere accidental stays and impediments, acting, not as wealth, but (for we ought to have a correspondent term) as "illth," causing various devastation and trouble around them in all directions; or lastly, act not at all, but are merely animated conditions of delay, (no use being possible of anything they have until they are dead,) in which last condition they are nevertheless often useful *as* delays, and "impedimenta," if a nation is apt to move too fast.

This being so, the difficulty of the true science of Political Economy lies not merely in the need of developing manly character to deal with material value, but in the fact, that while the manly character and material value only form wealth by their conjunction, they have nevertheless a mutually destructive operation on each other. For the manly character is apt to ignore, or even cast away, the material value :— whence that of Pope :—

> " Sure, of qualities demanding praise
> More go to ruin fortunes, than to raise,"

And on the other hand, the material value is apt to undermine the manly character ; so that it must be our work, in the issue, to examine what evidence there is of the effect of wealth on the minds of its possessors ; also, what kind of person it is who usually sets himself to obtain wealth, and succeeds in doing so ; and whether the world owes more gratitude to rich or to poor men, either for their moral influence upon it, or for chief goods, discoveries, and practical advancements. I may, however, anticipate future conclusion so far as to state that in a community regulated only by laws of demand and supply, and protected from open violence, the persons who become rich are, generally speaking, industrious, resolute, proud, covetous, prompt, methodical, sensible, unimaginative, insensitive, and ignorant. The persons who remain poor are the entirely foolish, the entirely wise,* the idle, the reckless, the humble, the thoughtful, the dull, the imaginative, the sensitive, the well-informed, the improvident, the irregularly and impulsively wicked, the clumsy knave, the open thief, and the entirely merciful, just, and godly person.

Thus far then of wealth. Next, we have to ascertain the

---

* " ὁ Ζεὺς δήπου πένεται."—*Arist. Plut.* 582. It would but weaken the grand words to lean on the preceding ones :—" ὅτι τοῦ Πλούτου παρέχει βελτίονας, ἄνδρας, καὶ τὴν γνώμην, καὶ τὴν ἰδέαν."

nature of PRICE ; that is to say, of exchange value, and its expression by currencies.

Note first, of exchange, there can be no *profit* in it. It is only in labour there can be profit—that is to say a " making in advance," or "making in favour of " (from proficio). In exchange, there is only advantage, *i.e.* a bringing of vantage or power to the exchanging persons. Thus, one man, by sowing and reaping, turns one measure of corn into two measures. That is Profit. Another by digging and forging, turns one spade into two spades. That is Profit. But the man who has two measures of corn wants sometimes to dig ; and the man who has two spades wants sometimes to eat :— They exchange the gained grain for the gained tool ; and both are the better for the exchange ; but though there is much advantage in the transaction, there is no profit. Nothing is constructed or produced. Only that which had been before constructed is given to the person by whom it can be used. If labour is necessary to effect the exchange, that labour is in reality involved in the production, and, like all other labour, bears profit. Whatever number of men are concerned in the manufacture, or in the conveyance, have share in the profit ; but neither the manufacture nor the conveyance are the exchange, and in the exchange itself there is no profit.

There may, however, be acquisition, which is a very different thing. If, in the exchange, one man is able to give what cost him little labour for what has cost the other much, he " acquires " a certain quantity of the produce of the other's labour. And precisely what he acquires, the other loses. In mercantile language, the person who thus acquires is commonly said to have "made a profit ; " and I believe that many of our merchants are seriously under the impression that it is possible for everybody, somehow, to make a profit in this manner. Whereas, by the unfortunate constitution of the world we live in, the laws both of matter and motion have quite rigorously forbidden universal acquisition of this kind. Profit, or material gain, is attainable only by construction or by discovery ; not by exchange. Whenever material gain follows exchange, for every *plus* there is a precisely equal *minus.*

Unhappily for the progress of the science of Political Economy, the plus quantities, or,—if I may be allowed to coin an awkward plural—the pluses, make a very positive and venerable appearance in the world, so that every one is eager to learn the science which produces results so magnificent; whereas the minuses have, on the other hand, a tendency to retire into back streets, and other places of shade,—or even to get themselves wholly and finally put out of sight in graves: which renders the algebra of this science peculiar, and difficultly legible : a large number of its negative signs being written by the account-keeper in a kind of red ink, which starvation thins, and makes strangely pale, or even quite invisible ink, for the present.

The Science of Exchange, or, as I hear it has been proposed to call it, of "Catallactics," considered as one of gain, is, therefore, simply nugatory ; but considered as one of acquisition, it is a very curious science, differing in its data and basis from every other science known. Thus :—If I can exchange a needle with a savage for a diamond, my power of doing so depends either on the savage's ignorance of social arrangements in Europe, or on his want of power to take advantage of them, by selling the diamond to any one else for more needles. If, farther, I make the bargain as completely advantageous to myself as possible, by giving to the savage a needle with no eye in it (reaching, thus, a sufficiently satisfactory type of the perfect operation of catallactic science), the advantage to me in the entire transaction depends wholly upon the ignorance, powerlessness, or heedlessness of the person dealt with. Do away with these, and catallactic advantage becomes impossible. So far, therefore, as the science of exchange relates to the advantage of one of the exchanging persons only, it is founded on the ignorance or incapacity of the opposite person. Where these vanish, it also vanishes. It is therefore a science founded on nescience, and an art founded on artlessness. But all other sciences and arts, except this, have for their object the doing away with their opposite nescience and artlessness. *This* science, alone of sciences, must, by all available means, promulgate and prolong its opposite nescience; otherwise the science itself is impossible. It is, therefore, peculiarly and alone, the science of darkness; probably a bastard science—not by any means a *divina scientia*, but one begotten of another father, that father who, advising his children to turn stones into bread, is himself employed in turning bread into stones, and who, if you ask a fish of him (fish not being producible on his estate), can but give you a serpent.

The general law, then, respecting just or economical exchange, is simply this:—There must be advantage on both sides (or if only advantage on one, at least no disadvantage on the other) to the persons exchanging; and just payment for his time, intelligence, and labour, to any intermediate person effecting the transaction (commonly called a merchant): and whatever advantage there is on either side, and whatever pay is given to the intermediate person, should be thoroughly known to all concerned. All attempt at concealment implies some practice of the opposite, or undivine science, founded on nescience. Whence another saying of the Jew merchant's — "As a nail between the stone joints, so doth sin stick fast between buying and selling." Which peculiar riveting of stone and timber, in men's dealings with each other, is again set forth in the house which was to be destroyed—timber and stones together—when Zechariah's roll (more probably "curved sword") flew over it: "the curse that goeth forth over all the earth upon every one that stealeth and holdeth himself guiltless," instantly followed by the vision of the Great Measure; —the measure "of the injustice of them in all the earth" (αὕτη ἡ ἀδικία αὐτῶν ἐκ πάσῃ τῇ γῇ), with the weight of lead for its lid, and the woman, the spirit of wickedness, within it; —that is to say, Wickedness hidden by Dulness, and formalized, outwardly, into ponderously established cruelty. "It shall be set upon its own base in the land of Babel."*

I have hitherto carefully restricted myself, in speaking of exchange, to the use of the term "advantage;" but that term includes two ideas; the advantage, namely, of getting what

* Zech. v. 11. See note on the passage, at page 120.

we *need*, and that of getting what we *wish* for. Three-fourths of the demands existing in the world are romantic ; founded on visions, idealisms, hopes, and affections ; and the regulation of the purse is, in its essence, regulation of the imagination and the heart. Hence, the right discussion of the nature of price is a very high metaphysical and physical problem ; sometimes to be solved only in a passionate manner, as by David in his counting the price of the water of the well by the gate of Bethlehem ; but its first conditions are the following :—The price of anything is the quantity of labour given by the person desiring it, in order to obtain possession of it. This price depends on four variable quantities. *A.* The quantity of wish the purchaser has for the thing ; opposed to *a*, the quantity of wish the seller has to keep it. *B.* The quantity of labour the purchaser can afford, to obtain the thing ; opposed to β, the quantity of labour the seller can afford, to keep it. These quantities are operative only in excess ; *i.e.* the quantity of wish (*A*) means the quantity of wish for this thing, above wish for other things ; and the quantity of work (*B*) means the quantity which can be spared to get this thing from the quantity needed to get other things.

Phenomena of price, therefore, are intensely complex, curious, and interesting—too complex, however, to be examined yet ; every one of them, when traced far enough, showing itself at last as a part of the bargain of the Poor of the Flock (or "flock of slaughter"), "If ye think good give ME my price, and if not, forbear"—Zech. xi. 12 ; but as the price of everything is to be calculated finally in labour, it is necessary to define the nature of that standard.

Labour is the contest of the life of man with an opposite ; —the term "life" including his intellect, soul, and physical power, contending with question, difficulty, trial, or material force.

Labour is of a higher or lower order, as it includes more or fewer of the elements of life : and labour of good quality, in any kind, includes always as much intellect and feeling as will fully and harmoniously regulate the physical force.

In speaking of the value and price of labour, it is necessary always to understand labour of a given rank and quality, as we should speak of gold or silver of a given standard. Bad (that is, heartless, inexperienced, or senseless) labour cannot be valued ; it is like gold of uncertain alloy, or flawed iron.*

The quality and kind of labour being given, its value, like that of all other valuable things, is invariable.   But the quantity of it which must be given for other things is variable ; and in estimating this variation, the price of other things must always be counted by the quantity of labour ; not the price of labour by the quantity of other things.

Thus, if we want to plant an apple sapling in rocky ground, it may take two hours' work ; in soft ground, perhaps only half an hour.   Grant the soil equally good for the tree in each case.   Then the value of the sapling planted by two hours' work is nowise greater than that of the sapling planted in half an hour.   One will bear no more fruit than the other. Also, one half-hour of work is as valuable as another half-hour ; nevertheless the one sapling has cost four such pieces of work, the other only one.   Now the proper statement of this fact is, not that the labour on the hard ground is cheaper than on the soft ; but that the tree is dearer.   The exchange value may, or may not, afterwards depend on this fact.   If other people have plenty of soft ground to plant in, they will take no cognizance of our two hours' labour, in the price they will offer for the plant on the rock.   And if, through want of

---

* Labour which is entirely good of its kind, that is to say, effective, or efficient, the Greeks called " weighable," or ἄξιος, translated usually " worthy," and because thus substantial and true, they called its price τιμή, the "honourable estimate " of it (honorarium) : this word being founded on their conception of true labour as a divine thing, to be honoured with the kind of honour given to the gods ; whereas the price of false labour, or of that which led away from life, was to be, not honour, but vengeance ; for which they reserved another word, attributing the exaction of such price to a peculiar goddess, called Tisiphone, the " requiter (or quittance-taker) of death ; " a person versed in the highest branches of arithmetic, and punctual in her habits ; with whom accounts current have been opened also in modern days.

sufficient botanical science, we have planted an upas-tree instead of an apple, the exchange-value will be a negative quantity; still less proportionate to the labour expended.

What is commonly called cheapness of labour, signifies, therefore, in reality, that many obstacles have to be overcome by it; so that much labour is required to produce a small result. But this should never be spoken of as cheapness of labour, but as dearness of the object wrought for. It would be just as rational to say that walking was cheap, because we had ten miles to walk home to our dinner, as that labour was cheap, because we had to work ten hours to earn it.

The last word which we have to define is "Production."

I have hitherto spoken of all labour as profitable; because it is impossible to consider under one head the quality or value of labour, and its aim. But labour of the best quality may be various in aim. It may be either constructive ("gathering," from con and struo), as agriculture; nugatory, as jewel-cutting; or destructive ("scattering," from de and struo), as war. It is not, however, always easy to prove labour, apparently nugatory, to be actually so;[*] generally, the formula holds good: "he that gathereth not, scattereth;" thus, the jeweller's art is probably very harmful in its ministering to a clumsy and inelegant pride. So that, finally, I believe nearly all labour may be shortly divided into positive and negative labour: positive, that which produces life; negative, that which produces death; the most directly negative labour being murder, and the most directly positive, the bearing and rearing of children; so that in the precise degree which murder is

---

[*] The most accurately nugatory labour is, perhaps, that of which not enough is given to answer a purpose effectually, and which, therefore, has all to be done over again Also, labour which fails of effect through non-co-operation. The curé of a little village near Bellinzona, to whom I had expressed wonder that the peasants allowed the Ticino to flood their fields, told me that they would not join to build an effectual embankment high up the valley, because everybody said "that would help his neighbours as much as himself." So every proprietor built a bit of low embankment about his own field; and the Ticino, as soon as it had a mind, swept away and swallowed all up together.

hateful, on the negative side of idleness, in that exact degree
child-rearing is admirable, on the positive side of idleness.
For which reason, and because of the honour that there is in
rearing* children, while the wife is said to be as the vine (for
cheering), the children are as the olive-branch, for praise ; nor
for praise only, but for peace (because large families can only
be reared in times of peace) : though since, in their spreading
and voyaging in various directions, they distribute strength,
they are, to the home strength, as arrows in the hand of a
giant—striking here and there, far away.

Labour being thus various in its result, the prosperity of
any nation is in exact proportion to the quantity of labour
which it spends in obtaining and employing means of life.
Observe,—I say, obtaining and employing ; that is to say, not
merely wisely producing, but wisely distributing and consuming. Economists usually speak as if there were no good
in consumption absolute.† So far from this being so, consumption absolute is the end, crown, and perfection of production ; and wise consumption is a far more difficult art than
wise production. Twenty people can gain money for one
who can use it ; and the vital question, for individual and for
nation, is, never "how much do they make?" but "to what
purpose do they spend?"

The reader may, perhaps, have been surprised at the slight
reference I have hitherto made to "capital," and its functions.
It is here the place to define them.

Capital signifies "head, or source, or root material"—it is
material by which some derivative or secondary good, is pro-

* Observe, I say, "rearing," not "begetting." The praise is in the
seventh season, not in σπορητός, nor in φυτλαιὰ, but in ὀπώρα. It is
strange that men always praise enthusiastically any person who, by a
momentary exertion, saves a life ; but praise very hesitatingly a person
who, by exertion and self-denial prolonged through years, creates one.
We give the crown "ob civem servatum ;"—why not "ob civem natum ?"
Born, I mean, to the full, in soul as well as body. England has oak
enough, I think, for both chaplets.

† When Mr. Mill speaks of productive consumption, he only means
consumption which results in increase of capital, or material wealth.
See I. iii. 4, and I. iii. 5.

duced. It is only capital proper (caput vivum, not caput mortuum) when it is thus producing something different from itself. It is a root, which does not enter into vital function till it produces something else than a root ; namely, fruit. That fruit will in time again produce roots ; and so all living capital issues in reproduction of capital; but capital which produces nothing but capital is only root producing root ; bulb issuing in bulb, never in tulip ; seed issuing in seed, never in bread. The Political Economy of Europe has hitherto devoted itself wholly to the multiplication, or (less even) the aggregation, of bulbs. It never saw nor conceived such a thing as a tulip. Nay, boiled bulbs they might have been —glass bulbs—Prince Rupert's drops, consummated in powder (well, if it were glass-powder and not gunpowder), for any end or meaning the economists had in defining the laws of aggregation. We will try and get a clearer notion of them.

The best and simplest general type of capital is a well-made ploughshare. Now, if that ploughshare did nothing but beget other ploughshares, in a polypous manner,—however the great cluster of polypous plough might glitter in the sun, it would have lost its function of capital. It becomes true capital only by another kind of splendour,—when it is seen, "splendescere sulco," to grow bright in the furrow : rather with diminution of its substance, than addition, by the noble friction. And the true home question, to every capitalist and to every nation, is not, "how many ploughs have you ?"—but, "where are your furrows ?" not—"how quickly will this capital reproduce itself?"—but, "what will it do during reproduction ?" What substance will it furnish, good for life ? what work construct, protective of life ? if none, its own reproduction is useless—if worse than none,—(for capital may destroy life as well as support it), its own reproduction is worse than useless ; it is merely an advance from Tisiphone, on mortgage —not a profit by any means.

Not a profit, as the ancients truly saw, and showed in the type of Ixion ; for capital is the head, or fountain head, of wealth—the "well-head" of wealth, as the clouds are the well

heads of rain : but when clouds are without water, and only
beget clouds, they issue in wrath at last, instead of rain, and
in lightning instead of harvest; whence Ixion is said first to
have invited his guests to a banquet, and then made them fall
into a pit filled with fire ; which is the type of the temptation
of riches issuing in imprisoned torment,—torment in a pit,
(as also Demas' silver mine,) after which, to show the rage
of riches passing from lust of pleasure to lust of power, yet
power not truly understood, Ixion is said to have desired
Juno, and instead, embracing a cloud (or phantasm), to have
begotten the Centaurs; the power of mere wealth being, in
itself, as the embrace of a shadow,—comfortless (so also
" Ephraim feedeth on wind and followth after the east wind ;"
or "that which is not"—Prov. xxiii. 5 ; and again Dante's
Geryon, the type of avaricious fraud, as he flies, gathers the
air up with retractile claws,—" l'aer a se raccolse,"*) but in
its offspring, a mingling of the brutal with the human nature :
human in sagacity—using both intellect and arrow ; but brutal in its body and hoof, for consuming and trampling down.
For which sin Ixion is at last bound upon a wheel—fiery and
toothed, and rolling perpetually in the air ;—the type of human labour when selfish and fruitless (kept far into the middle ages in their wheel of fortune) ; the wheel which has in it
no breath or spirit, but is whirled by chance only ; whereas of

---

* So also in the vision of the women bearing the ephah, before quoted,
"the wind was in their wings," not wings "of a stork," as in our version ; but "*milvi*," of a kite, in the Vulgate, or perhaps more accurately
still in the Septuagint, "hoopoe," a bird connected typically with
the power of riches by many traditions, of which that of its petition for
a crest of gold is perhaps the most interesting. The "Birds" of Aristophanes, in which its part is principal, are full of them ; note especially
the "fortification of the air with baked bricks, like Babylon," l. 550 ;
and, again, compare the Plutus of Dante, who (to show the influence of
riches in destroying the reason) is the only one of the powers of the Inferno who cannot speak intelligibly ; and also the cowardliest ; he is
not merely quelled or restrained, but literally "collapses" at a word ;
the sudden and helpless operation of mercantile panic being all told in
the brief metaphor, "as the sails, swollen with the wind, fall, when
the mast breaks."

all true work the Ezekiel vision is true, that the spirit of the living creature is in the wheels, and where the angels go, the wheels go by them; but move no otherwise.

This being the real nature of capital, it follows that there are two kinds of true production, always going on in an active State ; one of seed, and one of food or production for the Ground, and for the Mouth ; both of which are by covetous persons thought to be production only for the granary ; whereas the function of the granary is but intermediate and conservative, fulfilled in distribution ; else it ends in nothing but mildew, and nourishment of rats and worms. And since production for the Ground is only useful with future hope of harvest, all *essential* production is for the Mouth ; and is finally measured by the mouth ; hence, as I said above, consumption is the crown of production ; and the wealth of a nation is only to be estimated by what it consumes.

The want of any clear sight of this fact is the capital error, issuing in rich interest and revenue of error, among the political economists. Their minds are continually set on money-gain, not on mouth gain ; and they fall into every sort of net and snare, dazzled by the coin-glitter as birds by the fowler's glass ; or rather (for there is not much else like birds in them) they are like children trying to jump on the heads of their own shadows ; the money-gain being only the shadow of the true gain, which is humanity.

The final object of political economy, therefore, is to get good method of consumption, and great quantity of consumption : in other words, to use everything, and to use it nobly ; whether it be substance, service, or service perfecting substance. The most curious error in Mr. Mill's entire work (provided for him originally by Ricardo), is his endeavour to distinguish between direct and indirect service, and consequent assertion that a demand for commodities is not demand for labour (I. v. 9, *et seq.*). He distinguishes between labourers employed to lay out pleasure grounds, and to manufacture velvet ; declaring that it makes material difference to the labouring classes in which of these two ways a capitalist spends his money ; because the employment of the gardeners is a deman⁴ for labour, but the purchase of velvet is not.* Error colossal as well as strange. It will, indeed, make a difference to the labourer whether he bid him swing his scythe in the spring winds, or drive the loom in pestilential air : but, so far as his pocket is concerned, it makes to him absolutely no difference whether we order him to make green velvet, with seed and a scythe, or red velvet, with silk and scissors. Neither does it anywise concern him whether, when the velvet is made, we consume it by walking on it, or wearing it, so long as our consumption of it is wholly selfish. But if our consumption is to be in anywise unselfish, not only our mode of consuming the articles we require interests him, but also the *kind* of article we require with a view to consumption. As thus (returning for a moment to Mr. Mill's great hardware theory †) : it matters, so far as the labourer's immediate profit is concerned, not an iron filing whether I employ him in growing a peach, or forging a bombshell ; but my probable mode of consumption of those articles matters seriously. Admit that it is to be in both cases "unselfish," and the difference, to him, is final, whether when his child is ill, I walk it into his cottage and give it the

---

* The value of raw material, which has, indeed, to be deducted from the price of the labour, is not contemplated in the passages referred to, Mr. Mill having fallen into the mistake solely by pursuing the collateral results of the payment of wages to middlemen. He says—"The consumer does not, with his own funds, pay the weaver for his day's work." Pardon me ; the consumer of the velvet pays the weaver with his own funds as much as he pays the gardener. He pays, probably, an intermediate ship-owner, velvet merchant, and shopman ; pays carriage money, shop rent, damage money, time money, and care money ; all these are above and beside the velvet price (just as the wages of a head gardener would be above the grass price) ; but the velvet is as much produced by the consumer's capital, though he does not pay for it till six months after production, as the grass is produced by his capital, though he does not pay the man who mowed and rolled it on Monday, till Saturday afternoon. I do not know if Mr. Mill's conclusion,—"the capital cannot be dispensed with, the purchasers can " (p. 98), has yet been reduced to practice in the City on any large scale.

† Which, observe, is the precise opposite of the one under examination. The hardware theory required us to discharge our gardeners and engage manufacturers ; the velvet theory requires us to discharge our manufacturers and engage gardeners

peach, or drop the shell down his chimney, and blow his roof off.

The worst of it, for the peasant, is, that the capitalist's consumption of the peach is apt to be selfish, and of the shell, distributive ;* but, in all cases, this is the broad and general fact, that on due catallactic commercial principles, *somebody's* roof must go off in fulfilment of the bomb's destiny. You may grow for your neighbour, at your liking, grapes or grapeshot ; he will also, catallactically, grow grapes or grapeshot for you, and you will each reap what you have sown.

It is, therefore, the manner and issue of consumption which are the real tests of production. Production does not consist in things laboriously made, but in things serviceably consumable ; and the question for the nation is not how much labour it employs, but how much life it produces. For as consumption is the end and aim of production, so life is the end and aim of consumption.

I left this question to the reader's thought two months ago, choosing rather that he should work it out for himself than have it sharply stated to him. But now, the ground being sufficiently broken (and the details into which the sev-

---

* It is one very awful form of the operation of wealth in Europe that it is entirely capitalists' wealth which supports unjust wars. Just wars do not need so much money to support them ; for most of the men who wage such, wage them gratis ; but for an unjust war, men's bodies and souls have both to be bought; and the best tools of war for them besides ; which makes such war costly to the maximum ; not to speak of the cost of base fear, and angry suspicion, between nations which have not grace nor honesty enough in all their multitudes to buy an hour's peace of mind with : as, at present, France and England, purchasing of each other ten millions sterling worth of consternation annually, (a remarkably light crop, half thorns and half aspen leaves,—sown, reaped, and granaried by the "science" of the modern political economist, teaching covetousness instead of truth.) And all unjust war being supportable, if not by pillage of the enemy, only by loans from capitalists, these loans are repaid by subsequent taxation of the people, who appear to have no will in the matter, the capitalists' will being the primary root of the war ; but its real root is the covetousness of the whole nation, rendering it incapable of faith, frankness, or justice, and bringing about, therefore, in due time, his own separate loss and punishment to each person.

eral questions, here opened, must lead us, being too complex for discussion in the pages of a periodical, so that I must pursue them elsewhere), I desire, in closing the series of introductory papers, to leave this one great fact clearly stated. THERE IS NO WEALTH BUT LIFE. Life, including all its powers of love, of joy, and of admiration. That country is the richest which nourishes the greatest number of noble and happy human beings ; that man is richest who, having perfected the functions of his own life to the utmost, has also the widest helpful influence, both personal, and by means of his possessions, over the lives of others.

A strange political economy ; the only one, nevertheless, that ever was or can be : all political economy founded on self-interest * being but the fulfilment of that which once brought schism into the Policy of angels, and ruin into the Economy of Heaven.

" The greatest number of human beings noble and happy." But is the nobleness consistent with the number ? Yes, not only consistent with it, but essential to it. The maximum of life can only be reached by the maximum of virtue. In this respect the law of human population differs wholly from that of animal life. The multiplication of animals is checked only by want of food, and by the hostility of races ; the population of the gnat is restrained by the hunger of the swallow, and that of the swallow by the scarcity of gnats. Man, considered as an animal, is indeed limited by the same laws ; hunger, or plague, or war, are the necessary and only restraints upon his increase,—effectual restraints hitherto,—his principal study having been how most swiftly to destroy himself, or ravage his dwelling-places, and his highest skill directed to give range to the famine, seed to the plague, and sway to the sword. But, considered as other than an animal, his increase is not limited by these laws. It is limited only by the limits of his courage and his love. Both of these *have* their bounds ; and

* " In all reasoning about prices, the proviso must be understood, 'supposing all parties to take care of their own interest ' "—Mill, III i. 5.

ought to have : his race has its bounds also ; but these have not yet been reached, nor will be reached for ages.

In all the ranges of human thought I know none so melancholy as the speculations of political economists on the population question. It is proposed to better the condition of the labourer by giving him higher wages. " Nay," says the economist, " if you raise his wages, he will either people down to the same point of misery at which you found him, or drink your wages away." He will. I know it. Who gave him this will ? Suppose it were your own son of whom you spoke, declaring to me that you dared not take him into your firm, nor even give him his just labourer's wages, because if you did, he would die of drunkenness, and leave half a score of children to the parish. "Who gave your son these dispositions?"—I should inquire. Has he them by inheritance or by education ? By one or other they *must* come ; and as in him, so also in the poor. Either these poor are of a race essentially different from ours, and unredeemable (which, however often implied, I have heard none yet openly say), or else by such care as we have ourselves received, we may make them continent and sober as ourselves—wise and dispassionate as we are—models arduous of imitation. " But," it is answered, "they cannot receive education." Why not? That is precisely the point at issue. Charitable persons suppose the worst fault of the rich is to refuse the people meat ; and the people cry for their meat, kept back by fraud, to the Lord of Multitudes.* Alas ! it is not meat of which the refusal is

---

* James v. 4. Observe, in these statements I am not taking up, nor countenancing one whit, the common socialist idea of division of property ; division of property is its destruction ; and with it the destruction of all hope, all industry, and all justice : it is simply chaos—a chaos towards which the believers in modern political economy are fast tending, and from which I am striving to save them. The rich man does not keep back meat from the poor by retaining his riches ; but by basely using them. Riches are a form of strength ; and a strong man does not injure others by keeping his strength, but by using it injuriously. The socialist, seeing a strong man oppress a weak one, cries out—" Break the strong man's arms ; " but I say, " Teach him to use them to better purpose." The fortitude and intelligence which acquire riches are in

cruelest, or to which the claim is validest. The life is more
than the meat. The rich not only refuse food to the poor;
they refuse wisdom; they refuse virtue; they refuse salvation. Ye sheep without shepherd, it is not the pasture that
has been shut from you, but the presence. Meat! perhaps
your right to that may be pleadable; but other rights have
to be pleaded first. Claim your crumbs from the table, if you
will; but claim them as children, not as dogs; claim your
right to be fed, but claim more loudly your right to be holy,
perfect, and pure.

Strange words to be used of working people: "What!
holy; without any long robes nor anointing oils; these rough-
jacketed, rough-worded persons; set to nameless and dis-
honoured service? Perfect!—these, with dim eyes and
cramped limbs, and slowly wakening minds? Pure—these,
with sensual desire and grovelling thought; foul of body,
and coarse of soul?" It may be so; nevertheless, such as
they are, they are the holiest, perfectest, purest persons the
earth can at present show. They may be what you have said;
but if so, they yet are holier than we, who have left them
thus.

But what can be done for them? Who can clothe—who
teach—who restrain their multitudes? What end can there
be for them at last, but to consume one another?

I hope for another end, though not, indeed, from any of

---

ended, by the Giver of both, not to scatter. nor to give away, but to
employ those riches in the service of mankind; in other words, in the
redemption of the erring and aid of the weak—that is to say, there is
first to be the work to gain money; then the Sabbath of use for it—the
Sabbath, whose law is, not to lose life, but to save. It is continually
the fault or the folly of the poor that they are poor, as it is usually a
child s fault if it falls into a pond, and a cripple's weakness that slips
at a crossing; nevertheless, most passers-by would pull the child out,
or help up the cripple. Put it at the worst, that all the poor of the
world are but disobedient children, or careless cripples, and that all
rich people are wise and strong, and you will see at once that neither is
the socialist right in desiring to make everybody poor, powerless, and
foolish as he is himself, nor the rich man right in leaving the children
in the mire.

the three remedies for over-population commonly suggested by economists.

These three are, in brief—Colonization ; Bringing in of waste lands; or Discouragement of Marriage.

The first and second of these expedients merely evade or delay the question. It will, indeed, be long before the world has been all colonized, and its deserts all brought under cultivation. But the radical question is not how much habitable land is in the world, but how many human beings ought to be maintained on a given space of habitable land.

Observe, I say, *ought* to be, not how many *can* be. Ricardo, with his usual inaccuracy, defines what he calls the "natural rate of wages" as "that which will maintain the labourer." Maintain him ! yes ; but how?—the question was instantly thus asked of me by a working girl, to whom I read the passage. I will amplify her question for her. "Maintain him, how ? " As first, to what length of life ? Out of a given number of fed persons how many are to be old—how many young ; that is to say, will you arrange their maintenance so as to kill them early—say at thirty or thirty-five on the average, including deaths of weakly or ill-fed children ?—or so as to enable them to live out a natural life? You will feed a greater number, in the first case,* by rapidity of succession ; probably a happier number in the second : which does Mr. Ricardo mean to be their natural state, and to which state belongs the natural rate of wages ?

Again : A piece of land which will only support ten idle, ignorant, and improvident persons, will support thirty or forty intelligent and industrious ones. Which of these is their natural state, and to which of them belongs the natural rate of wages ?

Again : If a piece of land support forty persons in industrious ignorance ; and if, tired of this ignorance, they set apart ten of their number to study the properties of cones, and the sizes of stars ; the labour of these ten, being withdrawn from the ground, must either tend to the increase of food in some

---

* The quantity of life is the same in both cases ; but it is differently allotted.

transitional manner, or the persons set apart for siderial and conic purposes must starve, or some one else starve instead of them. What is, therefore, the rate natural of wages of the scientific persons, and how does this rate relate to, or measure, their reverted or transitional productiveness?

Again: If the ground maintains, at first, forty labourers in a peaceable and pious state of mind, but they become in a few years so quarrelsome and impious that they have to set apart five, to meditate upon and settle their disputes;—ten, armed to the teeth with costly instruments, to enforce the decisions; and five to remind everybody in an eloquent manner of the existence of a God;—what will be the result upon the general power of production, and what is the "natural rate of wages" of the meditative, muscular, and oracular labourers?

Leaving these questions to be discussed, or waived, at their pleasure, by Mr. Ricardo's followers, I proceed to state the main facts bearing on that probable future of the labouring classes which has been partially glanced at by Mr. Mill. That chapter and the preceding one differ from the common writing of political economists in admitting some value in the aspect of nature, and expressing regret at the probability of the destruction of natural scenery. But we may spare our anxieties on this head. Men can neither drink steam, nor eat stone. The maximum of population on a given space of land implies also the relative maximum of edible vegetable, whether for men or cattle; it implies a maximum of pure air; and of pure water. Therefore: a maximum of wood, to transmute the air, and of sloping ground, protected by herbage from the extreme heat of the sun, to feed the streams. All England may, if it so chooses, become one manufacturing town; and Englishmen, sacrificing themselves to the good of general humanity, may live diminished lives in the midst of noise, of darkness, and of deadly exhalation. But the world cannot become a factory, nor a mine. No amount of ingenuity will ever make iron digestible by the million, nor substitute hydrogen for wine. Neither the avarice nor the rage of men will ever feed them, and however the apple of Sodom and the grape of Gomorrah may spread their table for a time with dainties of ashes, and nectar of asps,—so long as men live by bread, the far away valleys must laugh as they are covered with the gold of God, and the shouts of His happy multitudes ring round the wine-press and the well.

Nor need our more sentimental economists fear the too wide spread of the formalities of a mechanical agriculture. The presence of a wise population implies the search for felicity as well as for food ; nor can any population reach its maximum but through that wisdom which "rejoices" in the habitable parts of the earth. The desert has its appointed place and work ; the eternal engine, whose beam is the earth's axle, whose beat is its year, and whose breath is its ocean, will still divide imperiously to their desert kingdoms, bound with unfurrowable rock, and swept by unarrested sand, their powers of frost and fire : but the zones and lands between, habitable, will be loveliest in habitation. The desire of the heart is also the light of the eyes. No scene is continually and untiringly loved, but one rich by joyful human labour ; smooth in field, fair in garden ; full in orchard ; trim, sweet, and frequent in homestead ; ringing with voices of vivid existence. No air is sweet that is silent ; it is only sweet when full of low currents of under sound—triplets of birds, and murmur and chirp of insects, and deep-toned words of men, and wayward trebles of childhood. As the art of life is learned, it will be found at last that all lovely things are also necessary :—the wild flower by the wayside, as well as the tended corn ; and the wild birds and creatures of the forest, as well as the tended cattle ; because man doth not live by bread only, but also by the desert manna ; by every wondrous word and unknowable work of God. Happy, in that he knew them not, nor did his fathers know ; and that round about him reaches yet into the infinite, the amazement of his existence.

Note, finally, that all effectual advancement towards this true felicity of the human race must be by individual, not public effort. Certain general measures may aid, certain revised laws guide, such advancement ; but the measure and law which have first to be determined are those of each man's home. We continually hear it recommended by sagacious people to complaining neighbours (usually less well placed in the world than themselves), that they should "remain content in the station in which Providence has placed them." There are perhaps some circumstances of life in which Providence has no intention that people *should* be content. Nevertheless, the maxim is on the whole a good one ; but it is peculiarly for home use. That your neighbour should, or should not, remain content with *his* position, is not your business ; but it is very much your business to remain content with your own. What is chiefly needed in England at the present day is to show the quantity of pleasure that may be obtained by a consistent, well-administered competence. modest, confessed, and laborious. We need examples of people who, leaving Heaven to decide whether they are to rise in the world, decide for themselves that they will be happy in it, and have resolved to seek—not greater wealth, but simpler pleasure ; not higher fortune, but deeper felicity ; making the first of possessions, self-possession ; and honouring themselves in the harmless pride and calm pursuits of peace.

Of which lowly peace it is written that "justice and peace have kissed each other ; " and that the fruit of justice is "sown in peace of them that make peace ; " not "peace-makers " in the common understanding—reconcilers of quarrels ; (though that function also follows on the greater one ;) but peace-Creators ; Givers of Calm. Which you cannot give, unless you first gain ; nor is this gain one which will follow assuredly on any course of business, commonly so called. No form of gain is less probable, business being (as is shown in the language of all nations—$\pi\omega\lambda\epsilon\hat{\iota}\nu$ from $\pi\epsilon\lambda\omega$, $\pi\rho\hat{a}\sigma\iota s$ from $\pi\epsilon\rho\acute{a}\omega$, venire, vendre, and venal, from venio, &c.) essentially restless—and probably contentious ;—having a raven-like mind to the motion to and fro, as to the carrion food ; whereas the olive-feeding and bearing birds look for rest for their feet : thus it is said of Wisdom that she "hath builded her house, and hewn out her seven pillars ; " and even when, though apt to wait long at the doorposts, she has to leave her house and go abroad, her paths are peace also.

For us, at all events, her work must begin at the entry of

the doors : all true economy is "Law of the house." **Strive** to make that law strict, simple, generous : waste nothing, and grudge nothing. Care in nowise to make more of money, but care to make much of it ; remembering always the great, palpable, inevitable fact—the rule and root of all economy—that what one person has, another cannot have ; and that every atom of substance, of whatever kind, used or consumed, is so much human life spent ; which, if it issue in the saving present life, or gaining more, is well spent, but if not, is either so much life prevented, or so much slain. In all buying, consider, first, what condition of existence you cause in the producers of what you buy ; secondly, whether the sum you have paid is just to the producer, and in due proportion, lodged in his hands ;* thirdly, to how much clear use, for food, knowledge, or joy, this that you have bought can be put ; and fourthly, to whom and in what way it can be most speedily and serviceably distributed : in all dealings whatsoever insisting on entire openness and stern fulfilment ; and in all doings, on perfection and loveliness of accomplishment ; especially on fineness and purity of all marketable commodity : watching at the same time for all ways of gaining, or teaching, powers of simple pleasure ; and of showing " ὅσον ἐν ἀσφοδέλῳ γέγ᾽ ὄνειαρ "—the sum of enjoyment depending not on the quantity of things tasted, but on the vivacity and patience of taste.

And if, on due and honest thought over these things, it seems that the kind of existence to which men are now summoned by every plea of pity and claim of right, may, for some time at least, not to be a luxurious one ;—consider whether, even supposing it guiltless, luxury would be desired by any of us,

---

* The proper offices of middle-men, namely, overseers (or authoritative workmen), conveyancers (merchants, sailors, retail dealers, &c.), and ordertakers (persons employed to receive directions from the consumer), must, of course, be examined before I can enter farther into the question of just payment of the first producer. But I have not spoken of them in these introductory papers, because the evils attendant on the abuse of such intermediate functions result not from any alleged principle of modern political economy, but from private careless ness or iniquity.

if we saw clearly at our sides the suffering which accompanies it in the world. Luxury is indeed possible in the future—innocent and exquisite ; luxury for all, and by the help of all : but luxury at present can only be enjoyed by the ignorant ; the cruelest man living could not sit at his feast, unless he sat blindfold. Raise the veil boldly ; face the light ; and if, as yet, the light of the eye can only be through tears, and the light of the body through sackcloth, go thou forth weeping, bearing precious seed, until the time come, and the kingdom, when Christ's gift of bread and bequest of peace shall be Unto this last as unto thee ; and when, for earth's severed multitudes of the wicked and the weary, there shall be holier reconciliation than that of the narrow home, and calm economy where the Wicked cease—not from trouble, but from troubling- and the Weary are at rest.

THE END.

THE QUEEN OF THE AIR

BEING

A STUDY OF THE GREEK MYTHS

OF

CLOUD AND STORM

PREFACE.

My days and strength have lately been much broken; and I never more felt the insufficiency of both than in preparing for the press the following desultory memoranda on a most noble subject. But I leave them now as they stand, for no time nor labour would be enough to complete them to my contentment; and I believe that they contain suggestions which may be followed with safety, by persons who are beginning to take interest in the aspects of mythology, which only recent investigation has removed from the region of conjecture into that of rational inquiry. I have some advantage, also, from my field work, in the interpretation of myths relating to natural phenomena; and I have had always near me, since we were at college together, a sure, and unweariedly kind, guide, in my friend Charles Newton, to whom we owe the finding of more treasure in mines of marble, than, were it rightly estimated, all California could buy. I must not, however, permit the chance of his name being in any wise associated with my errors. Much of my work has been done obstinately in my own way; and he is never responsible for me, though he has often kept me right, or at least enabled me to advance in a right direction. Absolutely right no one can be in such matters; nor does a day pass without convincing every honest student of antiquity of some partial error, and showing him better how to think, and where to look. But I knew that there was no hope of my being able to enter with advantage on the fields of history opened by the splendid investigation of recent philologists; though I could qualify myself, by attention and sympathy, to understand here and there, a verse of Homer's or Hesiod's, as the simple people did for whom they sang.

Even while I correct these sheets for press, a lecture by Professor Tyndall has been put into my hands, which I ought to have heard last 16th of January, but was hindered by mischance ; and which, I now find, completes, in two important particulars, the evidence of an instinctive truth in ancient symbolism ; showing, first, that the Greek conception of an ætherial element pervading space is justified by the closest reasoning of modern physicists ; and, secondly, that the blue of the sky, hitherto thought to be caused by watery vapour, is, indeed, reflected from the divided air itself ; so that the bright blue of the eyes of Athena, and the deep blue of her ægis, prove to be accurate mythic expressions of natural phenomena which it is an uttermost triumph of recent science to have revealed.

Indeed, it would be very difficult to imagine triumph more complete. To form, "within an experimental tube, a bit of more perfect sky than the sky itself !" here is magic of the finest sort ! singularly reversed from that of old time, which only asserted its competency to enclose in bottles elemental forces that were—not of the sky.

Let me, in thanking Professor Tyndall for the true wonder of this piece of work, ask his pardon, and that of all masters in physical science, for any words of mine, either in the following pages or elsewhere, that may ever seem to fail in the respect due to their great powers of thought, or in the admiration due to the far scope of their discovery. But I will be judged by themselves, if I have not bitter reason to ask them to teach us more than yet they have taught.

This first day of May, 1869, I am writing where my work was begun thirty-five years ago,—within sight of the snows of the higher Alps. In that half of the permitted life of man, I have seen strange evil brought upon every scene that I best loved, or tried to make beloved by others. The light which once flushed those pale summits with its rose at dawn, and purple at sunset, is now umbered and faint ; the air which once inlaid the clefts of all their golden crags with azure, is now defiled with languid coils of smoke, belched from worse than volcanic fires ; their very glacier waves are ebbing, and their snows fading, as if Hell had breathed on them ; the waters that once sank at their feet into crystalline rest, are now dimmed and foul, from deep to deep, and shore to shore. These are no careless words—they are accurately—horribly— true. I know what the Swiss lakes were ; no pool of Alpine fountain at its source was clearer. This morning, on the Lake of Geneva, at half a mile from the beach, I could scarcely see my oar-blade a fathom deep.

The light, the air, the waters, all defiled! How of the earth itself? Take this one fact for type of honour done by the modern Swiss to the earth of his native land. There used to be a little rock at the end of the avenue by the port of Neuchâtel ; there, the last marble of the foot of Jura, sloping to the blue water, and (at this time of year) covered with bright pink tufts of Saponaria. I went, three days since, to gather a blossom at the place. The goodly native rock and its flowers were covered with the dust and refuse of the town ; but, in the middle of the avenue, was a newly-constructed artificial rockery, with a fountain twisted through a spinning spout, and an inscription on one of its loose-tumbled stones,—

> " Aux Botanistes,
> Le club Jurassique."

Ah, masters of modern science, give me back my Athena out of your vials, and seal, if it may be, once more, Asmodeus therein. You have divided the elements, and united them ; enslaved them upon the earth, and discerned them in the stars. Teach us, now, but this of them, which is all that man need know,—that the Air is given to him for his life ; and the Rain to his thirst, and for his baptism ; and the Fire for warmth ; and the Sun for sight ; and the Earth for his meat—and his Rest.

Vevay, May 1, 1869.

THE QUEEN OF THE AIR.

I.

ATHENA CHALINITIS.*

(Athena in the Heavens.)

Lecture on the Greek Myths of Storm, given (partly) in University College, London, March 9th, 1869.

1. I WILL not ask your pardon for endeavouring to interest you in the subject of Greek Mythology; but I must ask your permission to approach it in a temper differing from that in which it is frequently treated. We cannot justly interpret the religion of any people, unless we are prepared to admit that we ourselves, as well as they, are liable to error in matters of faith; and that the convictions of others, however singular, may in some points have been well founded, while our own, however reasonable, may in some particulars be mistaken. You must forgive me, therefore, for not always distinctively calling the creeds of the past "superstition," and the creeds of the present day "religion;" as well as for assuming that a faith now confessed may sometimes be superficial, and that a faith long forgotten may once have been sincere. It is the task of the Divine to condemn the errors of antiquity, and of the Philologist to account for them: I will only pray you to read, with patience, and human sympathy, the thoughts of men who lived without blame in a darkness they could not dispel; and to remember that, whatever charge of folly may justly attach to the saying,—"There is no God," the folly is

---

* "Athena the Restrainer." The name is given to her as having helped Bellerophon to bridle Pegasus, the flying cloud.

prouder, deeper, and less pardonable, in saying, "There is no God but for me."

2. A Myth, in its simplest definition, is a story with a meaning attached to it, other than it seems to have at first; and the fact that it has such a meaning is generally marked by some of its circumstances being extraordinary, or, in the common use of the word, unnatural. Thus, if I tell you that Hercules killed a water-serpent in the lake of Lerna, and if I mean, and you understand, nothing more than that fact, the story, whether true or false, is not a myth. But if by telling you this, I mean that Hercules purified the stagnation of many streams from deadly miasmata, my story, however simple, is a true myth; only, as, if I left it in that simplicity, you would probably look for nothing beyond, it will be wise in me to surprise your attention by adding some singular circumstance; for instance, that the water-snake had several heads, which revived as fast as they were killed, and which poisoned even the foot that trode upon them as they slept. And in proportion to the fulness of intended meaning I shall probably multiply and refine upon these improbabilities; as, suppose, if, instead of desiring only to tell you that Hercules purified a marsh, I wished you to understand that he contended with the venom and vapour of envy and evil ambition, whether in other men's souls or in his own, and choked *that* malaria only by supreme toil,—I might tell you that this serpent was formed by the Goddess whose pride was in the trial of Hercules; and that its place of abode was by a palm-tree; and that for every head of it that was cut off, two rose up with renewed life; and that the hero found at last he could not kill the creature at all by cutting its heads off or crushing them; but only by burning them down; and that the midmost of them could not be killed even that way, but had to be buried alive. Only in proportion as I mean more, I shall certainly appear more absurd in my statement; and at last, when I get unendurably significant, all practical persons will agree that I was talking mere nonsense from the beginning, and never meant anything at all.

3. It is just possible, however, also, that the story-teller

may all along have meant nothing but what he said ; and that, incredible as the events may appear, he himself literally believed—and expected you also to believe—all this about Hercules, without any latent moral or history whatever. And it is very necessary, in reading traditions of this kind, to deter-mine, first of all, whether you are listening to a simple person, who is relating what, at all events, he believes to be true (and may, therefore, possibly have been so to some extent), or to a reserved philosopher, who is veiling a theory of the universe under the grotesque of a fairy tale. It is, in general, more likely that the first supposition should be the right one :— simple and credulous persons are, perhaps fortunately, more common than philosophers : and it is of the highest impor- tance that you should take their innocent testimony as it was meant, and not efface, under the graceful explanation which your cultivated ingenuity may suggest, either the evidence their story may contain (such as it is worth) of an extra-ordinary event having really taken place, or the unquestion-able light which it will cast upon the character of the person by whom it was frankly believed. And to deal with Greek religion honestly, you must at once understand that this lit-eral belief was, in the mind of the general people, as deeply rooted as ours in the legends of our own sacred book ; and that a basis of unmiraculous event was as little suspected, and an explanatory symbolism as rarely traced, by them, as by us.

You must, therefore, observe that I deeply degrade the position which such a myth as that just referred to occupied in the Greek mind, by comparing it (for fear of offending you) to our story of St. George and the Dragon. Still, the analogy is perfect in minor respects ; and though it fails to give you any notion of the vitally religious earnestness of the Greek faith, it will exactly illustrate the manner in which faith laid hold of its objects.

4. This story of Hercules and the Hydra, then, was to the general Greek mind, in its best days, a tale about a real hero and a real monster. Not one in a thousand knew anything of the way in which the story had arisen, any more than the English peasant generally is aware of the plebeian origin of

St. George ; or supposes that there were once alive in the world, with sharp teeth and claws, real, and very ugly, flying dragons. On the other hand, few persons traced any moral or symbolical meaning in the story, and the average Greek was as far from imagining any interpretation like that I have just given you, as an average Englishman is from seeing in St. George the Red Cross Knight of Spenser, or in the Dragon the Spirit of Infidelity. But, for all that, there was a certain undercurrent of consciousness in all minds, that the figures meant more than they at first showed ; and, according to each man's own faculties of sentiment, he judged and read them ; just as a Knight of the Garter reads more in the jewel on his collar than the George and Dragon of a public-house expresses to the host or to his customers. Thus, to the mean person the myth always meant little ; to the noble person, much : and the greater their familiarity with it, the more contemptible it became to the one, and the more sacred to the other : until vulgar commentators explained it entirely away, while Virgil made it the crowning glory of his choral hymn to Hercules—

> " Around thee, powerless to infect thy soul,
> Rose, in his crested crowd, the Lerna worm."

> " Non te rationis egentem
> Lernæus turbâ capitum circumstetit anguis."

And although, in any special toil of the hero's life, the moral interpretation was rarely with definiteness attached to its event, yet in the whole course of the life, not only a symbolical meaning, but the warrant for the existence of a real spiritual power, was apprehended of all men. Hercules was no dead hero, to be remembered only as a victor over monsters of the past—harmless now, as slain. He was the perpetual type and mirror of heroism, and its present and living aid against every ravenous form of human trial and pain.

5. But, if we seek to know more than this, and to ascertain the manner in which the story first crystallized into its shape, we shall find ourselves led back generally to one or other of two sources—either to actual historical events, represented by

the fancy under figures personifying them ; or else to natural phenomena similarly endowed with life by the imaginative power, usually more or less under the influence of terror. The historical myths we must leave the masters of history to follow ; they, and the events they record, being yet involved in great, though attractive and penetrable, mystery. But the stars, and hills, and storms are with us now, as they were with others of old ; and it only needs that we look at them with the earnestness of those childish eyes to understand the first words spoken of them by the children of men. And then, in all the most beautiful and enduring myths, we shall find, not only a literal story of a real person,—not only a parallel imagery of moral principle,—but an underlying worship of natural phenomena, out of which both have sprung, and in which both forever remain rooted. Thus, from the real sun, rising and setting ; from the real atmosphere, calm in its dominion of unfading blue, and fierce in its descent of tempest,—the Greek forms first the idea of two entirely personal and corporeal gods, whose limbs are clothed in divine flesh and whose brows are crowned with divine beauty ; yet so real that the quiver rattles at their shoulder, and the chariot bends beneath their weight. And, on the other hand, collaterally with these corporeal images, and never for one instant separated from them, he conceives also two omnipresent spiritual influences, of which one illuminates, as the sun, with a constant fire, whatever in humanity is skilful and wise ; and the other, like the living air, breathes the calm of heavenly fortitude, and strength of righteous anger, into every human breast that is pure and brave.

6. Now, therefore, in nearly every myth of importance, and certainly in every one of those of which I shall speak to-night, you have to discern these three structural parts—the root and the two branches :—the root, in physical existence, sun, or sky, or cloud, or sea ; then the personal incarnation of that ; becoming a trusted and companionable deity, with whom you may walk hand in hand, as a child with its brother or its sister ; and, lastly, the moral significance of the image, which is in all the great myths eternally and beneficently true.

7. The great myths; that is to say, myths made by great people. For the first plain fact about myth-making is one which has been most strangely lost sight of,—that you cannot make a myth unless you have something to make it of. You cannot tell a secret which you don't know. If the myth is about the sky, it must have been made by somebody who had looked at the sky. If the myth is about justice and fortitude, it must have been made by some one who knew what it was to be just or patient. According to the quantity of understanding in the person will be the quantity of significance in his fable; and the myth of a simple and ignorant race must necessarily mean little, because a simple and ignorant race have little to mean. So the great question in reading a story is always, not what wild hunter dreamed, or what childish race first dreaded it; but what wise man first perfectly told, and what strong people first perfectly lived by it. And the real meaning of any myth is that which it has at the noblest age of the nation among whom it is current. The farther back you pierce, the less significance you will find, until you come to the first narrow thought, which, indeed, contains the germ of the accomplished tradition; but only as the seed contains the flower. As the intelligence and passion of the race develop, they cling to and nourish their beloved and sacred legend; leaf by leaf it expands under the touch of more pure affections, and more delicate imagination, until at last the perfect fable burgeons out into symmetry of milky stem, and honied bell.

8. But through whatever changes it may pass, remember that our right reading of it is wholly dependent on the materials we have in our own minds for an intelligent answering sympathy. If it first arose among a people who dwelt under stainless skies, and measured their journeys by ascending and declining stars, we certainly cannot read their story, if we have never seen anything above us in the day, but smoke; nor anything round us in the night but candles. If the tale goes on to change clouds or planets into living creatures,—to invest them with fair forms—and inflame them with mighty passions, we can only understand the story of the human-hearted

things, in so far as we ourselves take pleasure in the perfectness of visible form, or can sympathize, by an effort of imagination, with the strange people who had other loves than that
of wealth, and other interests than those of commerce. And,
lastly, if the myth complete itself to the fulfilled thoughts of
the nation, by attributing to the gods, whom they have carved
out of their fantasy, continual presence with their own souls ;
and their every effort for good is finally guided by the sense of
the companionship, the praise, and the pure will of Immortals,
we shall be able to follow them into this last circle of their
faith only in the degree in which the better parts of our own
beings have been also stirred by the aspects of nature, or
strengthened by her laws. It may be easy to prove that the
ascent of Apollo in his chariot signifies nothing but the rising
of the sun. But what does the sunrise itself signify to us ?
If only languid return to frivolous amusement, or fruitless
labour, it will, indeed, not be easy for us to conceive the
power, over a Greek, of the name of Apollo. But if, for us
also, as for the Greek, the sunrise means daily restoration to
the sense of passionate gladness and of perfect life—if it
means the thrilling of new strength through every nerve,—the
shedding over us of a better peace than the peace of night, in
the power of the dawn,—and the purging of evil vision and fear
by the baptism of its dew ;—if the sun itself is an influence,
to us also, of spiritual good—and becomes thus in reality, not
in imagination, to us also, a spiritual power,—we may then
soon over-pass the narrow limit of conception which kept
that power impersonal, and rise with the Greek to the thought
of an angel who rejoiced as a strong man to run his course,
whose voice, calling to life and to labour, rang round the
earth, and whose going forth was to the ends of heaven.

9. The time, then, at which I shall take up for you, as well
as I can decipher it, the tradition of the Gods of Greece, shall
be near the beginning of its central and formed faith,—about
500 B.C.,—a faith of which the character is perfectly represented by Pindar and Æschylus, who are both of them out-
spokenly religious, and entirely sincere men ; while we may
always look back to find the less developed thought of the

preceding epoch given by Homer, in a more occult, subtle half-instinctive and involuntary way.

10. Now, at that culminating period of the Greek religion we find, under one governing Lord of all things, four subordinate elemental forces, and four spiritual powers living in them, and commanding them. The elements are of course the well-known four of the ancient world—the earth, the waters, the fire, and the air ; and the living powers of them are Demeter, the Latin Ceres; Poseidon, the Latin Neptune ; Apollo, who has retained always his Greek name ; and Athena, the Latin Minerva. Each of these are descended from, or changed from, more ancient, and therefore more mystic deities of the earth and heaven, and of a finer element of æther supposed to be beyond the heavens ; * but at this time we find the four quite definite, both in their kingdoms and in their personalities. They are the rulers of the earth that we tread upon, and the air that we breathe ; and are with us as closely, in their vivid humanity, as the dust that they animate, and the winds that they bridle. I shall briefly define for you the range of their separate dominions, and then follow, as far as we have time, the most interesting of the legends which relate to the queen of the air.

11. The rule of the first spirit, Demeter, the earth mother, is over the earth, first, as the origin of all life—the dust from whence we were taken ; secondly, as the receiver of all things back at last into silence—" Dust thou art, and unto dust shalt thou return." And, therefore, as the most tender image of this appearing and fading life, in the birth and fall of flowers, her daughter Proserpine plays in the fields of Sicily, and thence is torn away into darkness, and becomes the Queen of Fate—not merely of death, but of the gloom which closes over and ends, not beauty only, but sin ; and chiefly of sins the sin against the life she gave : so that she is, in her highest power, Persephone, the avenger and purifier of blood, —" The voice of thy brother's blood cries to me *out of the ground.*" Then, side by side with this queen of the earth, we

* And by modern science now also asserted, and with probability argued, to exist.

find a demigod of agriculture by the plough—the lord of grain, or of the thing ground by the mill. And it is a singular proof of the simplicity of Greek character at this noble time, that of all representations left to us of their deities by their art, few are so frequent, and none perhaps so beautiful, as the symbol of this spirit of agriculture.

12. Then the dominant spirit of the element of water is Neptune, but subordinate to him are myriads of other water spirits, of whom Nereus is the chief, with Palæmon, and Leucothea, the "white lady" of the sea ; and Thetis, and nymphs innumerable, who, like her, could "suffer a sea change," while the river deities had each independent power, according to the preciousness of their streams to the cities fed by them,—the "fountain Arethuse, and thou, honored flood, smooth sliding Mincius, crowned with vocal reeds." And, spiritually, this king of the waters is lord of the strength and daily flow of human life—he gives it material force and victory ; which is the meaning of the dedication of the hair, as the sign of the strength of life, to the river of the native land.

13. Demeter, then, over the earth, and its giving and receiving of life. Neptune over the waters, and the flow and force of life,—always among the Greeks typified by the horse, which was to them as a crested sea-wave, animated and bridled. Then the third element, fire, has set over it two powers : over earthly fire, the assistant of human labour, is set Hephæstus, lord of all labour in which is the flush and the sweat of the brow ; and over heavenly fire, the source of day, is set Apollo, the spirit of all kindling, purifying, and illuminating intellectual wisdom ; each of these gods having also their subordinate or associated powers—servant, or sister, or companion muse.

14. Then, lastly, we come to the myth which is to be our subject of closer inquiry—the story of Athena and of the deities subordinate to her. This great goddess, the Neith of the Egyptians, the Athena or Athenaia of the Greeks, and, with broken power, half usurped by Mars, the Minerva of the Latins, is, physically, the queen of the air ; having supreme

power both over its blessing of calm, and wrath of storm, and, spiritually, she is the queen of the breath of man, first of the bodily breathing which is life to his blood, and strength to his arm in battle ; and then of the mental breathing, or inspiration, which is his moral health and habitual wisdom ; wisdom of conduct and of the heart, as opposed to the wisdom of imagination and the brain ; moral, as distinct from intellectual ; inspired, as distinct from illuminated.

15. By a singular, and fortunate, though I believe wholly accidental coincidence, the heart-virtue, of which she is the spirit, was separated by the ancients into four divisions, which have since obtained acceptance from all men as rightly discerned, and have received, as if from the quarters of the four winds of which Athena is the natural queen, the name of " Cardinal " virtues : namely, Prudence, (the right seeing, and foreseeing, of events through darkness) ; Justice, (the righteous bestowal of favour and of indignation) ; Fortitude, (patience under trial by pain) ; and Temperance, (patience under trial by pleasure). With respect to these four virtues, the attributes of Athena are all distinct. In her prudence, or sight in darkness, she is " Glaukopis," " owl-eyed." * In her justice, which is the dominant virtue, she wears two robes, one of light and one of darkness ; the robe of light, saffron colour, or the colour of the daybreak, falls to her feet, covering her wholly with favour and love,—the calm of the sky in blessing ; it is embroidered along its edge with her victory over the giants, (the troublous powers of the earth,) and the likeness of it was woven yearly by the Athenian maidens and carried to the temple of their own Athena,—not to the Parthenon, that was the temple of all the world's Athena,— but this they carried to the temple of their own only one, who loved them, and stayed with them always. Then her robe of indignation is worn on her breast and left arm only, fringed with fatal serpents, and fastened with Gorgonian cold, turning men to stone ; physically, the lightning and the hail of chastisement by storm. Then in her fortitude she

* There are many other meanings in the epithet ; see, farther on, § 31, p. 71.

wears the crested and unstooping helmet;* and lastly, in her temperance, she is the queen of maidenhood—stainless as the air of heaven.

16. But all these virtues mass themselves in the Greek mind into the two main ones—of Justice, or noble passion, and Fortitude, or noble patience ; and of these, the chief powers of Athena, the Greeks had divinely written for them, and for all men after them, two mighty songs,—one, of the Menis,† mens, passion, or zeal, of Athena, breathed into a mortal whose name is "Ache of heart," and whose short life is only the incarnate brooding and burst of storm ; and the other is of the foresight and fortitude of Athena, maintained by her in the heart of a mortal whose name is given to him from a longer grief, Odysseus, the full of sorrow, the much-endur-ing, and the long-suffering.

17. The minor expressions by the Greeks in word, in sym-bol, and in religious service, of this faith, are so many and so beautiful, that I hope some day to gather at least a few of them into a separate body of evidence respecting the power of Athena, and its relations to the ethical conception of the Homeric poems, or, rather, to their ethical nature ; for they are not conceived didactically, but are didactic in their es-sence, as all good art is. There is an increasing insensibility to this character, and even an open denial of it, among us, now, which is one of the most curious errors of modernism, —the peculiar and judicial blindness of an age which, having long practised art and poetry for the sake of pleasure only, has become incapable of reading their language when they were both didactic : and also, having been itself accustomed to a professedly didactic teaching, which yet, for private in-terests, studiously avoids collision with every prevalent vice of its day, (and especially with avarice), has become equally

* I am compelled, for clearness' sake, to mark only one meaning at a time. Athena's helmet is sometimes a mask—sometimes a sign of anger—sometimes of the highest light of æther ; but I cannot speak of all this at once.

† This first word of the Iliad, Menis, afterwards passes into the Latin Mens ; is the root of the Latin name for Athena, "Minerva,' and so of the English " mind."

2

dead to the intensely ethical conceptions of a race which habitually divided all men into two broad classes of worthy or worthless ;—good, and good for nothing. And even the celebrated passage of Horace about the Iliad is now misread or disbelieved, as if it was impossible that the Iliad could be instructive because it is not like a sermon. Horace does not say that it is like a sermon, and would have been still less likely to say so, if he ever had had the advantage of hearing a sermon. "I have been reading that story of Troy again" (thus he writes to a noble youth of Rome whom he cared for), "quietly at Præneste, while you have been busy at Rome ; and truly I think that what is base and what is noble, and what useful and useless, may be better learned from that, than from all Chrysippus' and Crantor's talk put together."* Which is profoundly true, not of the Iliad only, but of all other great art whatsoever ; for all pieces of such art are didactic in the purest way, indirectly and occultly, so that, first, you shall only be bettered by them if you are already hard at work in bettering yourself ; and when you *are* bettered by them, it shall be partly with a general acceptance of their influence, so constant and subtle that you shall be no more conscious of it than of the healthy digestion of food ; and partly by a gift of unexpected truth, which you shall only find by slow mining for it ;—which is withheld on purpose, and close-locked, that you may not get it till you have forged the key of it in a furnace of your own heating. And this withholding of their meaning is continual, and confessed, in the great poets. Thus Pindar says of himself : "There is many an arrow in my quiver, full of speech to the wise, but, for the many, they need interpreters." And neither Pindar, nor Æschylus, nor Hesiod, nor Homer, nor any of the greater poets or teachers of any nation or time, ever spoke but with intentional reservation : nay, beyond this, there is often a meaning which they themselves cannot interpret,—which it may be for ages long after them to interpret,—in what they

* Note, once for all, that unless when there is question about some particular expression, I never translate literally, but give the real force of what is said, as I best can, freely.

said, so far as it recorded true imaginative vision. For all the greatest myths have been seen, by the men who tell them, involuntarily and passively,—seen by them with as great distinctness (and in some respects, though not in all, under conditions as far beyond the control of their will) as a dream sent to any of us by night when we dream clearest ; and it is this veracity of vision that could not be refused, and of moral that could not be foreseen, which in modern historical inquiry has been left wholly out of account : being indeed the thing which no merely historical investigator can understand, or even believe ; for it belongs exclusively to the creative or artistic group of men, and can only be interpreted by those of their race, who themselves in some measure also see visions and dream dreams.

So that you may obtain a more truthful idea of the nature of Greek religion and legend from the poems of Keats, and the nearly as beautiful, and, in general grasp of subject, far more powerful, recent work of Morris, than from frigid scholarship, however extensive. Not that the poet's impressions or renderings of things are wholly true, but their truth is vital, not formal. They are like sketches from the life by Reynolds or Gainsborough, which may be demonstrably inaccurate or imaginary in many traits, and indistinct in others, yet will be in the deepest sense like, and true ; while the work of historical analysis is too often weak with loss, through the very labour of its miniature touches, or useless in clumsy and vapid veracity of externals, and complacent security of having done all that is required for the portrait, when it has measured the breadth of the forehead, and the length of the nose.

18. The first of requirements, then, for the right reading of myths, is the understanding of the nature of all true vision by noble persons ; namely, that it is founded on constant laws common to all human nature ; that it perceives, however darkly, things which are for all ages true ;—that we can only understand it so far as we have some perception of the same truth ;—and that its fulness is developed and manifested more and more by the reverberation of it from minds of the same

mirror-temper, in succeeding ages. You will understand Homer better by seeing his reflection in Dante, as you may trace new forms and softer colours in a hill-side, redoubled by a lake.

I shall be able partly to show you, even to-night, how much, in the Homeric vision of Athena, has been made clearer by the advance of time, being thus essentially and eternally true; but I must in the outset indicate the relation to that central thought of the imagery of the inferior deities of storm.

19. And first I will take the myth of Æolus, (the "sage Hippotades" of Milton), as it is delivered pure by Homer from the early times.

Why do you suppose Milton calls him "sage?" One does not usually think of the winds as very thoughtful or deliberate powers. But hear Homer: "Then we came to the Æolian island, and there dwelt Æolus Hippotades, dear to the death-less gods: there he dwelt in a floating island, and around it was a wall of brass that could not be broken; and the smooth rock of it ran up sheer. To whom twelve children were born in the sacred chambers—six daughters and six strong sons; and they dwell for ever with their beloved father, and their mother strict in duty; and with them are laid up a thousand benefits; and the misty house around them rings with fluting all the day long." Now, you are to note first, in this descrip-tion, the wall of brass and the sheer rock. You will find, throughout the fables of the tempest-group, that the brazen wall and precipice (occurring in another myth as the brazen tower of Danae) are always connected with the idea of the towering cloud lighted by the sun, here truly described as a floating island. Secondly, you hear that all treasures were laid up in them; therefore, you know this Æolus is lord of the beneficent winds ("he bringeth the wind out of his treas-uries"); and presently afterwards Homer calls him the "stew-ard" of the winds, the master of the storehouse of them. And this idea of gifts and preciousness in the winds of heaven is carried out in the well-known sequel of the fable:—Æolus gives them to Ulysses, all but one, bound in leathern bags, with a glittering cord of silver; and so like bags of treasure

that the sailors think they are so, and open them to see.
And when Ulysses is thus driven back to Æolus, and prays
him again to help him, note the deliberate words of the King's
refusal,—" Did I not," he says, " send thee on thy way heartily, that thou mightest reach thy country, thy home, and
whatever is dear to thee? It is not lawful for me again to
send forth favourably on his journey a man hated by the
happy gods." This idea of the beneficence of Æolus remains
to the latest times, though Virgil, by adopting the vulgar
change of the cloud island into Lipari, has lost it a little ; but
even when it is finally explained away by Diodorus, Æolus is
still a kind-hearted monarch, who lived on the coast of Sor-
rento, invented the use of sails, and established a system of
storm signals.

20. Another beneficent storm-power, Boreas, occupies an
important place in early legend, and a singularly principal
one in art ; and I wish I could read to you a passage of Plato
about the legend of Boreas and Oreithyia,* and the breeze and
shade of the Ilissus—notwithstanding its severe reflection
upon persons who waste their time on mythological studies :
but I must go on at once to the fable with which you are all
generally familiar, that of the Harpies.

This is always connected with that of Boreas or the north
wind, because the two sons of Boreas are enemies of the
Harpies, and drive them away into frantic flight. The myth
in its first literal form means only the battle between the fair
north wind and the foul south one : the two Harpies, " Storm-
swift" and " Swiftfoot," are the sisters of the rainbow—that is
to say, they are the broken drifts of the showery south wind,
and the clear north wind drives them back ; but they quickly
take a deeper and more malignant significance. You know
the short, violent, spiral gusts that lift the dust before coming
rain : the Harpies get identified first with these, and then
with more violent whirlwinds, and so they are called " Harpies,"
" the Snatchers," and are thought of as entirely destructive ;
their manner of destroying being twofold—by snatching

* Translated by Max Müller in the opening of his essay on " Com-
parative Mythology." (*Chips from a German Workshop*, vol. ii.)

away, and by defiling and polluting. This is a month in which you may really see a small Harpy at her work almost whenever you choose. The first time that there is threatening of rain after two or three days of fine weather, leave your window well open to the street, and some books or papers on the table ; and if you do not, in a little while, know what the Harpies mean ; and how they snatch, and how they defile, I'll give up my Greek myths.

21. That is the physical meaning. It is now easy to find the mental one. You must all have felt the expression of ignoble anger in those fitful gusts of sudden storm. There is a sense of provocation and apparent bitterness of purpose in their thin and senseless fury, wholly different from the noble anger of the greater tempests. Also, they seem useless and unnatural, and the Greek thinks of them always as vile in malice, and opposed, therefore, to the sons of Boreas, who are kindly winds, that fill sails, and wave harvests,—full of bracing health and happy impulses. From this lower and merely malicious temper, the Harpies rise into a greater terror, always associated with their whirling motion, which is indeed indicative of the most destructive winds : and they are thus related to the nobler tempests, as Charybdis to the sea ; they are devouring and desolating, merciless, making all things disappear that come in their grasp : and so, spiritually, they are the gusts of vexatious, fretful, lawless passion, vain and overshadowing, discontented and lamenting, meagre and insane,—spirits of wasted energy, and wandering disease, and unappeased famine, and unsatisfied hope. So you have, on the one side, the winds of prosperity and health, on the other, of ruin and sickness. Understand that, once, deeply—any who have ever known the weariness of vain desires ; the piti- ful, unconquerable, coiling and recoiling and self-involved returns of some sickening famine and thirst of heart :—and you will know what was in the sound of the Harpy Celæno's shriek from her rock ; and why, in the seventh circle of the "Inferno," the Harpies make their nests in the warped branches of the trees that are the souls of suicides.

22. Now you must always be prepared to read Greek le-

gends as you trace threads through figures on a silken damask:
the same thread runs through the web, but it makes part of
different figures. Joined with other colours you hardly recognize it, and in different lights, it is dark or light. Thus
the Greek fables blend and cross curiously in different directions, till they knit themselves into an arabesque where sometimes you cannot tell black from purple, nor blue from emerald—they being all the truer for this, because the truths of
emotion they represent are interwoven in the same way, but
all the more difficult to read, and to explain in any order.
Thus the Harpies, as they represent vain desire, are connected with the Sirens, who are the spirits of constant desire:
so that it is difficult sometimes in early art to know which
are meant, both being represented alike as birds with
women's heads; only the Sirens are the great constant desires—the infinite sicknesses of heart—which, rightly placed,
give life, and wrongly placed, waste it away; so that there
are two groups of Sirens, one noble and saving, as the other
is fatal. But there are no animating or saving Harpies; their
nature is always vexing and full of weariness, and thus they
are curiously connected with the whole group of legends
about Tantalus.

23. We all know what it is to be tantalized; but we do not
often think of asking what Tantalus was tantalized for—what
he had done, to be for ever kept hungry in sight of food?
Well; he had not been condemned to this merely for being a
glutton. By Dante the same punishment is assigned to simple gluttony, to purge it away;—but the sins of Tantalus
were of a much wider and more mysterious kind. There are
four great sins attributed to him—one, stealing the food of
the Gods to give it to men; another, sacrificing his son to
feed the Gods themselves (it may remind you for a moment
of what I was telling you of the earthly character of Demeter,
that, while the other Gods all refuse, she, dreaming about her
lost daughter, eats part of the shoulder of Pelops before she
knows what she is doing); another sin is, telling the secrets
of the Gods; and only the fourth—stealing the golden dog of
Pandareos—is connected with gluttony. The special sense

of this myth is marked by Pandareos receiving the happy privilege of never being troubled with indigestion ; the dog, in general, however, mythically represents all utterly senseless and carnal desires ; mainly that of gluttony ; and in the mythic sense of Hades—that is to say, so far as it represents spiritual ruin in this life, and not a literal hell—the dog Cerberus is its gate-keeper—with this special marking of his character of sensual passion, that he fawns on all those who descend, but rages against all who would return, (the Virgilian "facilis descensus" being a later recognition of this mythic character of Hades :) the last labour of Hercules is the dragging him up to the light ; and in some sort, he represents the voracity or devouring of Hades itself ; and the mediæval representation of the mouth of hell perpetuates the same thought. Then, also, the power of evil passion is partly associated with the red and scorching light of Sirius, as opposed to the pure light of the sun :—he is the dog-star of ruin ; and hence the continual Homeric dwelling upon him, and comparison of the flame of anger to his swarthy light ; only, in his scorching, it is thirst, not hunger, over which he rules physically ; so that the fable of Icarius, his first master, corresponds, among the Greeks, to the legend of the drunkenness of Noah.

The story of Actæon, the raging death of Hecuba, and the tradition of the white dog which ate part of Hercules' first sacrifice, and so gave name to the Cynosarges, are all various phases of the same thought—the Greek notion of the dog being throughout confused between its serviceable fidelity, its watchfulness, its foul voracity, shamelessness, and deadly madness, while, with the curious reversal or recoil of the meaning which attaches itself to nearly every great myth—and which we shall presently see notably exemplified in the relations of the serpent to Athena,—the dog becomes in philosophy a type of severity and abstinence.

24. It would carry us too far aside were I to tell you the story of Pandareos' dog—or rather, of Jupiter's dog, for Pandareos was its guardian only ; all that bears on our present purpose is that the guardian of this golden dog had three daughters, one of whom was subject to the power of the Si-

rens, and is turned into the nightingale ; and the other two were subject to the power of the Harpies, and this was what happened to them. They were very beautiful, and they were beloved by the gods in their youth, and all the great goddesses were anxious to bring them up rightly. Of all types of young ladies' education, there is nothing so splendid as that of the younger daughters of Pandareos. They have literally the four greatest goddesses for their governesses. Athena teaches them domestic accomplishments ; how to weave, and sew, and the like ; Artemis teaches them to hold themselves up straight ; Hera, how to behave proudly and oppressively to company ; and Aphrodite—delightful governess—feeds them with cakes and honey all day long. All goes well, until just the time when they are going to be brought out ; then there is a great dispute whom they are to marry, and in the midst of it they are carried off by the Harpies, given by them to be slaves to the Furies, and never seen more. But of course there is nothing in Greek myths ; and one never heard of such things as vain desires, and empty hopes, and clouded passions, defiling and snatching away the souls of maidens, in a London season.

I have no time to trace for you any more harpy legends, though they are full of the most curious interest ; but I may confirm for you my interpretation of this one, and prove its importance in the Greek mind, by noting that Polygnotus painted these maidens, in his great religious series of paintings at Delphi, crowned with flowers, and playing at dice ; and that Penelope remembers them in her last fit of despair, just before the return of Ulysses ; and prays bitterly that she may be snatched away at once into nothingness by the Harpies, like Pandareos' daughters, rather than be tormented longer by her deferred hope, and anguish of disappointed love.

25. I have hitherto spoken only of deities of the winds. We pass now to a far more important group, the Deities of Cloud. Both of these are subordinate to the ruling power of the air, as the demigods of the fountains and minor seas are to the great deep : but, as the cloud-firmament detaches itself

more from the air, and has a wider range of ministry than the minor streams and seas, the highest cloud deity, Hermes, has a rank more equal with Athena than Nereus or Proteus with Neptune ; and there is greater difficulty in tracing his character, because his physical dominion over the clouds can, of course, be asserted only where clouds are ; and, therefore, scarcely at all in Egypt : * so that the changes which Hermes undergoes in becoming a Greek from an Egyptian and Phœnician god, are greater than in any other case of adopted tradition. In Egypt Hermes is a deity of historical record, and a conductor of the dead to judgment ; the Greeks take away much of this historical function, assigning it to the Muses ; but, in investing him with the physical power over clouds, they give him that which the Muses disdain, the power of concealment, and of theft. The snatching away by the Harpies is with brute force ; but the snatching away by the clouds is connected with the thought of hiding, and of making things seem to be what they are not ; so that Hermes is the god of lying, as he is of mist ; and yet with this ignoble function of making things vanish and disappear, is connected the remnant of his grand Egyptian authority of leading away souls in the cloud of death (the actual dimness of sight caused by mortal wounds physically suggesting the darkness and descent of clouds, and continually being so described in the Iliad) , while the sense of the need of guidance on the untrodden road follows necessarily. You cannot but remember how this thought of cloud guidance, and cloud receiving of souls at death, has been elsewhere ratified.

26. Without following that higher clue, I will pass to the lovely group of myths connected with the birth of Hermes on the Greek mountains. You know that the valley of Sparta is

---

* I believe that the conclusions of recent scholarship are generally opposed to the Herodotean ideas of any direct acceptance by the Greeks of Egyptian myths : and very certainly, Greek art is developed by giving the veracity and simplicity of real life to Eastern savage grotesque ; and not by softening the severity of pure Egyptian design. But it is of no consequence whether one conception was, or was not, in this case, derived from the other : my object is only to mark the essential differences between them.

one of the noblest mountain ravines in the world, and that the western flank of it is formed by an unbroken chain of crags, forty miles long, rising, opposite Sparta, to a height of 8,000 feet, and known as the chain of Taygetus. Now, the nymph from whom that mountain ridge is named, was the mother of Lacedæmon; therefore, the mythic ancestress of the Spartan race. She is the nymph Taygeta, and one of the seven stars of spring; one of those Pleiades of whom is the question to Job,—"Canst thou bind the sweet influences of Pleiades, or loose the bands of Orion?" "The sweet influences of Pleiades," of the stars of spring,—nowhere sweeter than among the pine-clad slopes of the hills of Sparta and Arcadia, when the snows of their higher summits, beneath the sunshine of April, fell into fountains, and rose into clouds; and in every ravine was a newly-awakened voice of waters,— soft increase of whisper among its sacred stones: and on every crag its forming and fading veil of radiant cloud; temple above temple, of the divine marble that no tool can pollute, nor ruin undermine. And, therefore, beyond this central valley, this great Greek vase of Arcadia, on the "*hollow*" mountain, Cyllene, or "pregnant" mountain, called also "cold," because there the vapours rest,* and born of the eldest of those stars of Spring, that Maia, from whom your own month of May has its name, bringing to you, in the green of her garlands, and the white of her hawthorn, the unrecognized symbols of the pastures and the wreathed snows of Arcadia, where long ago she was queen of stars: there, first cradled and wrapt in swaddling-clothes; then raised, in a moment of surprise, into his wandering power,—is born the shepherd of the clouds, winged-footed and deceiving,—blinding the eyes of Argus,—escaping from the grasp of Apollo—restless messenger between the highest sky and topmost earth—"the herald Mercury, new lighted on a heaven-kissing hill."

27. Now, it will be wholly impossible, at present, to trace for you any of the minor Greek expressions of this thought,

* On the altar of Hermes on its summit, as on that of the Lacinian Hera, no wind ever stirred the ashes. By those altars, the Gods of Heaven were appeased; and all their storms at rest.

except only that Mercury, as the cloud shepherd, is especially called Eriophoros, the wool-bearer. You will recollect the name from the common woolly rush "eriophorum" which has a cloud of silky seed; and note also that he wears distinctively the flat cap, *petasos,* named from a word meaning to expand; which shaded from the sun, and is worn on journeys. You have the epithet of mountains "cloud-capped" as an established form with every poet, and the Mont Pilate of Lucerne is named from a Latin word signifying specially a *woollen* cap; but Mercury has, besides, a general Homeric epithet, curiously and intensely concentrated in meaning, "the profitable or serviceable by wool," * that is to say, by shepherd wealth; hence, "pecuniarily," rich, or serviceable, and so he passes at last into a general mercantile deity; while yet the cloud sense of the wool is retained by Homer always, so that he gives him this epithet when it would otherwise have been quite meaningless, (in Iliad, xxiv. 440,) when he drives Priam's chariot, and breathes force into his horses, precisely as we shall find Athena drive Diomed: and yet the serviceable and profitable sense,—and something also of gentle and soothing character in the mere wool-softness, as used for dress, and religious rites, —is retained also in the epithet, and thus the gentle and serviceable Hermes is opposed to the deceitful one.

28. In connection with this driving of Priam's chariot, remember that as Autolycus is the son of Hermes the Deceiver, Myrtilus (the Auriga of the Stars) is the son of Hermes the Guide. The name Hermes itself means Impulse; and he is especially the shepherd of the flocks of the sky, in driving, or guiding, or stealing them; and yet his great name, Argeiphontes, not only—as in different passages of the olden poets—means "Shining White," which is said of him as being himself the silver cloud lighted by the sun; but "Argus-Killer," the killer of brightness, which is said of him as he

* I am convinced that the ἐρι in ἐριούνιος is not intensitive; but retained from ἔριον: but even if I am wrong in thinking this, the mistake is of no consequence with respect to the general force of the term as meaning the *profitableness* of Hermes. Athena's epithet of ἀγελεία has a parallel significance.

veils the sky, and especially the stars, which are the eyes of Argus ; or, literally, eyes of brightness, which Juno, who is, with Jupiter, part of the type of highest heaven, keeps in her peacock's train. We know that this interpretation is right, from a passage in which Euripides describes the shield of Hippomedon, which bore for its sign, "Argus the all-seeing, covered with eyes ; open towards the rising of the stars, and closed towards their setting."

And thus Hermes becomes the spirit of the movement of the sky or firmament ; not merely the fast flying of the transi-tory cloud, but the great motion of the heavens and stars themselves. Thus, in his highest power, he corresponds to the "primo mobile" of the later Italian philosophy, and, in his simplest, is the guide of all mysterious and cloudy move-ment, and of all successful subtleties. Perhaps the prettiest minor recognition of his character is when, on the night foray of Ulysses and Diomed, Ulysses wears the helmet stolen by Autolycus, the son of Hermes.

29. The position in the Greek mind of Hermes as the Lord of cloud is, however, more mystic and ideal than that of any other deity, just on account of the constant and real presence of the cloud itself under different forms, giving rise to all kinds of minor fables. The play of the Greek imagination in this direction is so wide and complex, that I cannot even give you an outline of its range in my present limits. There is first a great series of storm-legends connected with the family of the historic Æolus, centralized by the story of Athamas, with his two wives, "the Cloud" and the "White Goddess," ending in that of Phrixus and Helle, and of the golden fleece (which is only the cloud-burden of Hermes Eriophoros). With this, there is the fate of Salmoneus, and the destruction of Glaucus by his own horses ; all these minor myths of storm concen-trating themselves darkly into the legend of Bellerophon and the Chimæra, in which there is an under story about the vain subduing of passion and treachery, and the end of life in fad-ing melancholy,—which, I hope, not many of you could un-derstand even were I to show it you : (the merely physical meaning of the Chimæra is the cloud of volcanic lightning,

connected wholly with earth-fire, but resembling the heavenly
cloud in its height and its thunder). Finally, in the Æolic
group, there is the legend of Sisyphus, which I mean to work
out thoroughly by itself : its root is in the position of Corinth
as ruling the isthmus and the two seas — the Corinthian
Acropolis, two thousand feet high, being the centre of the
crossing currents of the winds, and of the commerce of Greece.
Therefore, Athena, and the fountain cloud Pegasus, are more
closely connected with Corinth than even with Athens in their
material, though not in their moral power ; and Sisyphus
founds the Isthmian games in connection with a melancholy
story about the sea gods ; but he himself is κέρδιστος ἀνδρῶν,
the most " gaining " and subtle of men ; who, having the key
of the Isthmus, becomes the type of transit, transfer, or trade,
as such ; and of the apparent gain from it, which is not gain :
and this is the real meaning of his punishment in hell—eternal
toil and recoil (the modern idol of capital being, indeed, the
stone of Sisyphus with a vengeance, *crushing* in its recoil).
But, throughout, the old ideas of the cloud power and cloud
feebleness,—the deceit of its hiding,—and the emptiness of
its vanishing,—the Autolycus enchantment of making black
seem white,—and the disappointed fury of Ixion (taking
shadow for power), mingle in the moral meaning of this and
its collateral legends ; and give an aspect, at last, not only of
foolish cunning, but of impiety or literal " idolatry," " imagination worship," to the dreams of avarice and injustice, until
this notion of atheism and insolent blindness becomes principal ; and the " Clouds " of Aristophanes, with the personified
" just " and " unjust" sayings in the latter part of the play,
foreshadow, almost feature by feature, in all that they were
written to mock and to chastise, the worst elements of the impious " δῖνος " and tumult in men's thoughts, which have followed on their avarice in the present day, making them alike
forsake the laws of their ancient gods, and misapprehend or
reject the true words of their existing teachers.

30. All this we have from the legends of the historic Æolus
only ; but, besides these, there is the beautiful story of
Semele, the Mother of Bacchus. She is the cloud with the

strength of the vine in its bosom, consumed by the light which matures the fruit ; the melting away of the cloud into the clear air at the fringe of its edges being exquisitely rendered by Pindar's epithet for her, Semele, " with the stretched-out hair " (ταννέθειρα). Then there is the entire tradition of the Danaides, and of the tower of Danae and golden shower ; the birth of Perseus connecting this legend with that of the Gorgons and Graiæ, who are the true clouds of thunderous and ruinous tempest. I must, in passing, mark for you that the form of the sword or sickle of Perseus, with which he kills Medusa, is another image of the whirling harpy vortex, and belongs especially to the sword of destruction or annihilation ; whence it is given to the two angels who gather for destruction the evil harvest and evil vintage of the earth (Rev. xiv. 15). I will collect afterwards and complete what I have already written respecting the Pegasean and Gorgonian legends, noting here only what is necessary to explain the central myth of Athena herself, who represents the ambient air, which included all cloud, and rain, and dew, and darkness, and peace, and wrath of heaven. Let me now try to give you, however briefly, some distinct idea of the several agencies of this great goddess.

31. I. She is the air giving life and health to all animals.

II. She is the air giving vegetative power to the earth.

III. She is the air giving motion to the sea, and rendering navigation possible.

IV. She is the air nourishing artificial light, torch or lamplight ; as opposed to that of the sun, on one hand, and of *consuming* * fire on the other.

V. She is the air conveying vibration of sound.

I will give you instances of her agency in all these functions.

32. First, and chiefly, she is air as the spirit of life, giving vitality to the blood. Her psychic relation to the vital force in matter lies deeper. and we will examine it afterwards ; but a great number of the most interesting passages in Homer regard her as flying over the earth in local and transitory strength, simply and merely the goddess of fresh air.

* Not a scientific, but a very practical and expressive distinction.

It is curious that the British city which has somewhat sau cily styled itself the Modern Athens, is indeed more under her especial tutelage and favour in this respect than perhaps any other town in the island. Athena is first simply what in the Modern Athens you so practically find her, the breeze of the mountain and the sea ; and wherever she comes, there is purification, and health, and power. The sea-beach round this isle of ours is the frieze of our Parthenon ; every wave that breaks on it thunders with Athena's voice ; nay, when-ever you throw your window wide open in the morning, you let in Athena, as wisdom and fresh air at the same instant ; and whenever you draw a pure, long, full breath of right heaven, you take Athena into your heart, through your blood; and, with the blood, into the thoughts of your brain.

Now this giving of strength by the air, observe, is mechani-cal as well as chemical. You cannot strike a good blow but with your chest full ; and in hand to hand fighting, it is not the muscle that fails first, it is the breath ; the longest-breathed will, on the average, be the victor,—not the strong-est. Note how Shakspeare always leans on this. Of Morti-mer, in " changing hardiment with great Glendower : "—

> "Three times they breathed, and three times did they drink,
> Upon agreement, of swift Severn's flood."

And again, Hotspur sending challenge to Prince Harry :—

> "That none might draw short breath to-day
> But I and Harry Monmouth."

Again, of Hamlet, before he receives his wound :—

> " He's fat, and scant of breath."

Again, Orlando in the wrestling :—

> " Yes; I beseech your grace
> I am not yet well breathed."

Now of all people that ever lived, the Greeks knew best what breath meant, both in exercise and in battle ; and there-fore the queen of the air becomes to them at once the queen of bodily strength in war ; not mere brutal muscular strength,

-that belongs to Ares,—but the strength of young lives passed in pure air and swift exercise,—Camilla's virginal force, that "flies o'er the unbending corn, and skims along the main."

33. Now I will rapidly give you two or three instances of her direct agency in this function. First, when she wants to make Penelope bright and beautiful ; and to do away with the signs of her waiting and her grief. "Then Athena thought of another thing ; she laid her into deep sleep, and loosed all her limbs, and made her taller, and made her smoother, and fatter, and whiter than swan ivory ; and breathed ambrosial brightness over her face ; and so she left her and went up to heaven." Fresh air and sound sleep at night, young ladies ! You see you may have Athena for lady's maid whenever you choose. Next, hark how she gives strength to Achilles when he is broken with fasting and grief. Jupiter pities him and says to her,—"'Daughter mine, are you forsaking your own soldier, and don't you care for Achilles any more? see how hungry and weak he is,—go and feed him with ambrosia.' So he urged the eager Athena ; and she leaped down out of heaven like a harpy falcon, shrill voiced ; and she poured nectar and ambrosia, full of delight, into the breast of Achilles, that his limbs might not fail with famine : then she returned to the solid dome of her strong father." And then comes the great passage about Achilles arming—for which we have no time. But here is again Athena giving strength to the whole Greek army. She came as a falcon to Achilles, straight at him ;—a sudden drift of breeze ; but to the army she must come wide-ly,—she sweeps round them all. "As when Jupiter spreads the purple rainbow over heaven, portending battle or cold storm, so Athena, wrapping herself round with a purple cloud, stooped to the Greek soldiers, and raised up each of them." Note that purple, in Homer's use of it, nearly always means "fiery," "full of light." It is the light of the rainbow, not the colour of it, which Homer means you to think of.

34. But the most curious passage of all, and fullest of meaning, is when she gives strength to Menelaus, that he may stand unwearied against Hector. He prays to her : "And blue-eyed

Athena was glad that he prayed to her, first ; and she gave him strength in his shoulders, and in his limbs, and she gave him the courage "—of what animal, do you suppose? Had it been Neptune or Mars, they would have given him the courage of a bull, or a lion ; but Athena gives him the courage of the most fearless in attack of all creatures—small or great—and very small it is, but wholly incapable of terror,—she gives him the courage of a fly.

35. Now this simile of Homer's is one of the best instances I can give you of the way in which great writers seize truths unconsciously which are for all time. It is only recent science which has completely shown the perfectness of this minute symbol of the power of Athena ; proving that the insect's flight and breath are co-ordinated ; that its wings are actually forcing-pumps, of which the stroke compels the thoracic respiration ; and that it thus breathes and flies simultaneously by the action of the same muscles, so that respiration is carried on most vigorously during flight, " while the air-vessels, supplied by many pairs of lungs instead of one, traverse the organs of flight in far greater numbers than the capillary blood-vessels of our own system, and give enormous and untiring muscular power, a rapidity of action measured by thousands of strokes in the minute, and an endurance, by miles and hours of flight." *

Homer could not have known this ; neither that the buzzing of the fly was produced as in a wind instrument, by a constant current of air through the trachea. But he had seen, and, doubtless, meant us to remember, the marvellous strength and swiftness of the insect's flight (the glance of the swallow itself is clumsy and slow compared to the darting of common house-flies at play) ; he probably attributed its murmur to the wings, but in this also there was a type of what we shall presently find recognized in the name of Pallas,—the vibratory power of the air to convey sound,—while, as a purifying creature, the fly holds its place beside the old symbol of Athena in Egypt, the vulture ; and as a venomous and tormenting creature, has more than the strength of the serpent in propor-

* Ormerod. *Natural History of Wasps.*

tion to its size, being thus entirely representative of the influence of the air both in purification and pestilence ; and its
courage is so notable that, strangely enough, forgetting
Homer's simile, I happened to take the fly for an expression
of the audacity of freedom in speaking of quite another subject.* Whether it should be called courage, or mere mechanical instinct, may be questioned, but assuredly no other animal, exposed to continual danger, is so absolutely without
sign of fear.

36. You will, perhaps, have still patience to hear two instances, not of the communication of strength, but of the personal agency of Athena as the air.   When she comes down to
help Diomed against Ares, she does not come to fight instead
of him, but she takes his charioteer's place.

> "She snatched the reins, she lashed with all her force,
> And full on Mars impelled the foaming horse."

Ares is the first to cast his spear ; then, note this, Pope
says :—

> " Pallas opposed her hand, and caused to glance,
> Far from the car, the strong immortal lance."

She does not oppose her hand in the Greek—the wind could
not meet the lance straight—she catches it in her hand, and
throws it off.   There is no instance in which a lance is so
parried by a mortal hand in all the Iliad, and it is exactly the
way the wind would parry it, catching it, and turning it aside.
If there are any good rifleshots here—they know something
about Athena's parrying—and in old times the English masters of feathered artillery knew more yet.   Compare also the
turning of Hector's lance from Achilles : Iliad xx. 439.

37. The last instance I will give you is as lovely as it is
subtle.   Throughout the Iliad, Athena is herself the will or
Menis of Achilles.   If he is to be calmed, it is she who calms
him ; if angered, it is she who inflames him.   In the first
quarrel with Atrides, when he stands at pause, with the great
sword half drawn, " Athena came from heaven, and stood behind him, and caught him by the yellow hair."   Another god

* See farther on, § 148, pp. 112, 113.

would have stayed his hand upon the hilt, but Athena only
lifts his hair. "And he turned and knew her, and her dreadful eyes shone upon him." There is an exquisite tenderness
in this laying her hand upon his hair, for it is the talisman of
his life, vowed to his own Thessalian river if he ever returned
to its shore, and cast upon Patroclus' pile, so ordaining that
there should be no return.

38. Secondly—Athena is the air giving vegetative impulse
to the earth. She is the wind and the rain—and yet more
the pure air itself, getting at the earth fresh turned by spade
or plough—and, above all, feeding the fresh leaves; for
though the Greeks knew nothing about carbonic acid, they
did know that trees fed on the air.

Now, note first in this, the myth of the air getting at
ploughed ground. You know I told you the Lord of all
labour by which man lived was Hephæstus ; therefore Athena
adopts a child of his, and of the Earth,—Erichthonius,—
literally, "the tearer up of the ground"—who is the head
(though not in direct line,) of the kings of Attica ; and having
adopted him, she gives him to be brought up by the three
nymphs of the dew. Of these, Aglauros, the dweller in the
fields, is the envy or malice of the earth ; she answers nearly
to the envy of Cain, the tiller of the ground, against his shepherd brother, in her own envy against her two sisters, Herse,
the cloud dew, who is the beloved of the shepherd Mercury ;
and Pandrosos, the diffused dew, or dew of heaven. Literally, you have in this myth the words of the blessing of
Esau—"Thy dwelling shall be of the fatness of the earth,
and of the dew of heaven from above." Aglauros is for her
envy turned into a black stone ; and hers is one of the voices,
—the other being that of Cain,—which haunts the circle of
envy in the Purgatory :—

"Io sono Aglauro, chi divenne sasso."

But to her two sisters, with Erichthonius, (or the hero Erec-
theus,) is built the most sacred temple of Athena in Athens ;
the temple to their own dearest Athena—to her, and to the
dew together : so that it was divided into two parts : one,

the temple of Athena of the city, and the other that of the dew. And this expression of her power, as the air bringing the dew to the hill pastures, in the central temple of the central city of the heathen, dominant over the future intellectual world, is, of all the facts connected with her worship as the spirit of life, perhaps the most important. I have no time now to trace for you the hundredth part of the different ways in which it bears both upon natural beauty, and on the best order and happiness of men's lives. I hope to follow out some of these trains of thought in gathering together what I have to say about field herbage ; but I must say briefly here that the great sign, to the Greeks, of the coming of spring in the pastures, was not, as with us, in the primrose, but in the various flowers of the asphodel tribe (of which I will give you some separate account presently) ; therefore it is that the earth answers with crocus flame to the cloud on Ida ; and the power of Athena in eternal life is written by the light of the asphodel on the Elysian fields.

But farther, Athena is the air, not only to the lilies of the field, but to the leaves of the forest. We saw before the reason why Hermes is said to be the son of Maia, the eldest of the sister stars of spring. Those stars are called not only Pleiades, but Vergiliæ, from a word mingling the ideas of the turning or returning of spring-time with the outpouring of rain. The mother of Virgil bearing the name of Maia, Virgil himself received his name from the seven stars ; and he, in forming, first, the mind of Dante, and through him that of Chaucer (besides whatever special minor influence came from the Pastorals and Georgics), became the fountain-head of all the best literary power connected with the love of vegetative nature among civilized races of men. Take the fact for what it is worth ; still it is a strange seal of coincidence, in word and in reality, upon the Greek dream of the power over human life, and its purest thoughts, in the stars of spring. But the first syllable of the name of Virgil has relation also to another group of words, of which the English ones, virtue, and virgin, bring down the force to modern days. It is a group containing mainly the idea of " spring," or increase of life in vegetation—the rising of the new branch of the tree out of the bud, and of the new leaf out of the ground. It involves, secondarily, the idea of greenness and of strength, but primarily, that of living increase of a new rod from a stock, stem, or root; ("There shall come forth a rod out of the stem of Jesse;") and chiefly the stem of certain plants—either of the rose tribe, as in the budding of the almond rod of Aaron; or of the olive tribe, which has triple significance in this symbolism, from the use of its oil for sacred anointing, for strength in the gymnasium, and for light. Hence, in numberless divided and reflected ways, it is connected with the power of Hercules and Athena: Hercules plants the wild olive, for its shade, on the course of Olympia, and it thenceforward gives the Olympic crown, of consummate honour and rest; while the prize at the Panathenaic games is a vase of its oil, (meaning encouragement to continuance of effort); and from the paintings on these Panathenaic vases we get the most precious clue to the entire character of Athena. Then to express its propagation by slips, the trees from which the oil was to be taken were called "Moriai," trees of division (being all descendants of the sacred one in the Erechtheum). And thus, in one direction, we get to the "children like olive plants round about thy table" and the olive grafting of St. Paul; while the use of the oil for anointing gives chief name to the rod itself of the stem of Jesse, and to all those who were by that name signed for his disciples first in Antioch. Remember, farther, since that name was first given, the influence of the symbol, both in extreme unction, and in consecration of priests and kings to their "divine right;" and think, if you can reach with any grasp of thought, what the influence on the earth has been, of those twisted branches whose leaves give grey bloom to the hill-sides under every breeze that blows from the midland sea. But, above and beyond all, think how strange it is that the chief Agonia of humanity, and the chief giving of strength from heaven for its fulfilment, should have been under its night shadow in Palestine.

39. Thirdly—Athena is the air in its power over the sea.

On the earliest Panathenaic vase known—the "Burgon"

vase in the British Museum—Athena has a dolphin on her
shield. The dolphin has two principal meanings in Greek
symbolism. It means, first, the sea; secondarily, the ascending and descending course of any of the heavenly bodies from
one sea horizon to another—the dolphins' arching rise and
replunge (in a summer evening, out of calm sea, their black
backs roll round with exactly the slow motion of a water-
wheel; but I do not know how far Aristotle's exaggerated account of their leaping or their swiftness has any foundation,)
being taken as a type of the emergence of the sun or stars
from the sea in the east, and plunging beneath in the west.
Hence, Apollo, when in his personal power he crosses the sea,
leading his Cretan colonists to Pytho, takes the form of a dolphin, becomes Apollo Delphinius, and names the founded
colony "Delphi." The lovely drawing of the Delphic Apollo
on the hydria of the Vatican (Le Normand and De Witte, vol.
ii. p. 6), gives the entire conception of this myth. Again, the
beautiful coins of Tarentum represent Taras coming to found
the city, riding on a dolphin, whose leaps and plunges have
partly the rage of the sea in them, and partly the spring of the
horse, because the splendid riding of the Tarentines had made
their name proverbial in Magna Græcia. The story of Arion
is a collateral fragment of the same thought; and, again, the
plunge before their transformation, of the ships of Æneas.
Then, this idea of career upon, or conquest of the sea, either
by the creatures themselves, or by dolphin-like ships, (compare the Merlin prophecy,—

> "They shall ride
> Over ocean wide
> With hempen bridle, and horse of tree,)"

connects itself with the thought of undulation, and of the wave-
power in the sea itself, which is always expressed by the serpentine bodies either of the sea-gods or of the sea-horse; and
when Athena carries, as she does often in later work, a serpent for her shield-sign, it is not so much the repetition of
her own ægis-snakes as the farther expression of her power
over the sea-wave; which, finally, Virgil gives in its perfect

unity with her own anger, in the approach of the serpents against Laocoon from the sea; and then, finally, when her own storm-power is fully put forth on the ocean also, and the madness of the ægis-snake is given to the wave-snake, the sea-wave becomes the devouring hound at the waist of Scylla, and Athena takes Scylla for her helmet-crest; while yet her benef icent and essential power on the ocean, in making navigation possible, is commemorated in the Panathenaic festival by her peplus being carried to the Erechtheum suspended from the mast of a ship.

In Plate cxv. of vol. ii., Le Normand, are given two sides of a vase, which, in rude and childish way, assembles most of the principal thoughts regarding Athena in this relation. In the first, the sunrise is represented by the ascending chariot of Apollo, foreshortened; the light is supposed to blind the eyes, and no face of the god is seen (Turner, in the Ulysses and Polyphemus sunrises, loses the form of the god in light, giving the chariot-horses only; rendering in his own manner, after 2,200 years of various fall and revival of the arts, pre-cisely the same thought as the old Greek potter). He ascends out of the sea; but the sea itself has not yet caught the light. In the second design, Athena as the morning breeze, and Hermes as the morning cloud, fly over the sea before the sun. Hermes turns back his head; his face is unseen in the cloud, as Apollo's in the light; the grotesque appearance of an ani-mal's face is only the cloud-phantasm modifying a frequent form of the hair of Hermes beneath the back of his cap. Un-der the morning breeze, the dolphins leap from the rippled sea, and their sides catch the light.

The coins of the Lucanian Heracleia give a fair representa-tion of the helmed Athena, as imagined in later Greek art, with the embossed Scylla.

40. Fourthly—Athena is the air nourishing artificial light —unconsuming fire. Therefore, a lamp was always kept burning in the Erechtheum; and the torch-race belongs chiefly to her festival, of which the meaning is to show the danger of the perishing of the light even by excess of the air that nourishes it; and so that the race is not to the swift, but

to the wise. The household use of her constant light is symbolized in the lovely passage in the Odyssey, where Ulysses
and his son move the armour while the servants are shut in
their chambers, and there is no one to hold torches for them;
but Athena herself, "having a golden lamp," fills all the rooms
with light. Her presence in war-strength with her favourite
heroes is always shown by the "unwearied" fire hovering on
their helmets and shields; and the image gradually becomes
constant and accepted, both for the maintenance of household watchfulness, as in the parable of the ten virgins, or as
the symbol of direct inspiration, in the rushing wind and
divided flames of Pentecost: but, together with this thought
of unconsuming and constant fire, there is always mingled in
the Greek mind the sense of the consuming by excess, as of
the flame by the air, so also of the inspired creature by its
own fire (thus, again, "the zeal of thine house hath eaten me
up"—"my zeal hath consumed me, because of thine enemies,"
and the like); and especially Athena has this aspect towards
the truly sensual and bodily strength; so that to Ares, who
is himself insane and consuming, the opposite wisdom seems
to be insane and consuming: "All we the other gods have
thee against us, O Jove! when we would give grace to men;
for thou hast begotten the maid without a mind—the mischievous creature, the doer of unseemly evil. All we obey
thee, and are ruled by thee. Her only thou wilt not resist in
anything she says or does, because thou didst bear her—consuming child as she is."

41. Lastly—Athena is the air, conveying vibration of
sound.

In all the loveliest representations in central Greek art of
the birth of Athena, Apollo stands close to the sitting Jupiter,
singing, with a deep, quiet joyfulness, to his lyre. The sun
is always thought of as the master of time and rhythm, and
as the origin of the composing and inventive discovery of
melody; but the air, as the actual element and substance of
the voice, the prolonging and sustaining power of it, and the
symbol of its moral passion. Whatever in music is measured
and designed, belongs therefore to Apollo and the Muses;

whatever is impulsive and passionate, to Athena: hence her constant strength of voice or cry (as when she aids the shout of Achilles) curiously opposed to the dumbness of Demeter. The Apolline lyre, therefore, is not so much the instrument producing sound, as its measurer and divider by length or tension of string into given notes; and I believe it is, in a double connection with its office as a measurer of time or motion, and its relation to the transit of the sun in the sky, that Hermes forms it from the tortoise-shell, which is the image of the dappled concave of the cloudy sky. Thenceforward all the limiting or restraining modes of music belong to the Muses; but the passionate music is wind music, as in the Doric flute. Then, when this inspired music becomes degraded in its passion, it sinks into the pipe of Pan, and the double pipe of Marsyas, and is then rejected by Athena. The myth which represents her doing so is that she invented the double pipe from hearing the hiss of the Gorgonian serpents; but when she played upon it, chancing to see her face reflected in the water, she saw that it was distorted, whereupon she threw down the flute, which Marsyas found. Then, the strife of Apollo and Marsyas represents the enduring contest between music in which the words and thought lead, and the lyre measures or melodizes them, (which Pindar means when he calls his hymns "kings over the lyre,") and music in which the words are lost, and the wind or impulse leads,— generally, therefore, between intellectual, and brutal, or meaningless, music. Therefore, when Apollo prevails, he flays Marsyas, taking the limit and external bond of his shape from him, which is death, without touching the mere muscular strength; yet shameful and dreadful in dissolution.

42. And the opposition of these two kinds of sound is continually dwelt upon by the Greek philosophers, the real fact at the root of all their teaching being this,—that true music is the natural expression of a lofty passion for a right cause; that in proportion to the kinglyness and force of any personality, the expression either of its joy or suffering becomes measured, chastened, calm, and capable of interpretation only by the majesty of ordered, beautiful, and worded sound. Ex-

actly in proportion to the degree in which we become narrow in the cause and conception of our passions, incontinent in the utterance of them, feeble of perseverance in them, sullied or shameful in the indulgence of them, their expression by musical sound becomes broken, mean, fatuitous, and at last impossible ; the measured waves of the air of heaven will not lend themselves to expression of ultimate vice, it must be for ever sunk into discordance or silence. And since, as before stated, every work of right art has a tendency to reproduce the ethical state which first developed it, this, which of all the arts is most directly ethical in origin, is also the most direct in power of discipline ; the first, the simplest, the most effect- ive of all instruments of moral instruction ; while in the failure and betrayal of its functions, it becomes the subtlest aid of moral degradation. Music is thus, in her health, the teacher of perfect order, and is the voice of the obedience of angels, and the companion of the course of the spheres of heaven ; and in her depravity she is also the teacher of per- fect disorder and disobedience, and the Gloria in Excelsis be- comes the Marseillaise. In the third section of this volume, I reprint two chapters from another essay of mine, ("The Cestus of Aglaia,") on modesty or measure, and on liberty, containing farther reference to music in her two powers; and I do this now, because, among the many monstrous and mis- begotten fantasies which are the spawn of modern licence, perhaps the most impishly opposite to the truth is the con- ception of music which has rendered possible the writing, by educated persons, and, more strangely yet, the tolerant criticism, of such words as these :—" *This so persuasive art is the only one that has no didactic efficacy, that engenders no emo- tions save such as are without issue on the side of moral truth, that expresses nothing of God, nothing of reason, nothing of human liberty.*" I will not give the author's name ; the pas- sage is quoted in the *Westminster Review* for last January, p. 153.

43. I must also anticipate something of what I have to say respecting the relation of the power of Athena to organic life, so far as to note that her name, Pallas, probably refers to

the quivering or vibration of the air; and to its power whether as vital force, or communicated wave, over every kind of matter, in giving it vibratory movement; first, and most intense, in the voice and throat of the bird; which is the air incarnate; and so descending through the various orders of animal life to the vibrating and semi-voluntary murmur of the insect; and, lower still, to the hiss, or quiver of the tail, of the half-lunged snake and deaf adder; all these, nevertheless, being wholly under the rule of Athena as representing either breath, or vital nervous power; and, therefore, also, in their simplicity, the "oaten pipe and pastoral song," which belong to her dominion over the asphodel meadows, and breathe on their banks of violets.

Finally, is it not strange to think of the influence of this one power of Pallas in vibration; (we shall see a singular mechanical energy of it presently in the serpent's motion;) in the voices of war and peace? How much of the repose—how much of the wrath, folly, and misery of men, has literally depended on this one power of the air;—on the sound of the trumpet and of the bell—on the lark's song, and the bee's murmur.

44. Such is the general conception in the Greek mind of the physical power of Athena. The spiritual power associated with it is of two kinds;—first, she is the Spirit of Life in material organism; not strength in the blood only, but formative energy in the clay: and, secondly, she is inspired and impulsive wisdom in human conduct and human art, giving the instinct of infallible decision, and of faultless invention.

It is quite beyond the scope of my present purpose—and, indeed, will only be possible for me at all after marking the relative intention of the Apolline myths—to trace for you the Greek conception of Athena as the guide of moral passion. But I will at least endeavor, on some near occasion,* to define some of the actual truths respecting the vital force in created organism, and inventive fancy in the works of man, which are

* I have tried to do this in mere outline in the two following sections of this volume.

more or less expressed by the Greeks, under the personality
of Athena. You would, perhaps, hardly bear with me if I
endeavoured farther to show you—what is nevertheless perfectly true—the analogy between the spiritual power of
Athena in her gentle ministry, yet irresistible anger, with the
ministry of another Spirit whom we also, holding for the
universal power of life, are forbidden, at our worst peril, to
quench or to grieve.

45. But, I think, to-night, you should not let me close,
without requiring of me an answer on one vital point, namely,
how far these imaginations of Gods—which are vain to us—
were vain to those who had no better trust? and what real
belief the Greek had in these creations of his own spirit,
practical and helpful to him in the sorrow of earth? I am
able to answer you explicitly in this. The origin of his
thoughts is often obscure, and we may err in endeavouring to
account for their form of realization; but the effect of that
realization on his life is not obscure at all. The Greek creed
was, of course, different in its character, as our own creed is,
according to the class of persons who held it. The common
people's was quite literal, simple, and happy: their idea of
Athena was as clear as a good Roman Catholic peasant's idea
of the Madonna. In Athens itself, the centre of thought and
refinement, Pisistratus obtained the reins of government
through the ready belief of the populace that a beautiful
woman, armed like Athena, was the goddess herself. Even
at the close of the last century some of this simplicity
remained among the inhabitants of the Greek islands; and
when a pretty English lady first made her way into the grotto
of Antiparos, she was surrounded, on her return, by all
the women of the neighbouring village, believing her to be
divine, and praying her to heal them of their sicknesses.

46. Then, secondly, the creed of the upper classes was more
refined and spiritual, but quite as honest, and even more
forcible in its effect on the life. You might imagine that the
employment of the artifice just referred to implied utter unbe-
lief in the persons contriving it; but it really meant only that
the more worldly of them would play with a popular faith for

their own purposes, as doubly-minded persons have often done since, all the while sincerely holding the same ideas themselves in a more abstract form ; while the good and un- worldly men, the true Greek heroes, lived by their faith as firmly as St. Louis, or the Cid, or the Chevalier Bayard.

47. Then, thirdly, the faith of the poets and artists was, necessarily, less definite, being continually modified by the involuntary action of their own fancies ; and by the necessity of presenting, in clear verbal or material form, things of which they had no authoritative knowledge. Their faith was, in some respects, like Dante's or Milton's : firm in general con- ception, but not able to vouch for every detail in the forms they gave it : but they went considerably farther, even in that minor sincerity, than subsequent poets ; and strove with all their might to be as near the truth as they could. Pindar says, quite simply, " I cannot think so-and-so of the Gods. It must have been this way—it cannot have been that way— that the thing was done." And as late among the Latins as the days of Horace, this sincerity remains. Horace is just as true and simple in his religion as Wordsworth ; but all power of understanding any of the honest classic poets has been taken away from most English gentlemen by the mechanical drill in verse writing at school. Throughout the whole of their lives afterwards, they never can get themselves quit of the notion that all verses were written as an exercise, and that Minerva was only a convenient word for the last of an hex- ameter, and Jupiter for the last but one.

48. It is impossible that any notion can be more fallacious or more misleading in its consequences. All great song, from the first day when human lips contrived syllables, has been sincere song. With deliberate didactic purpose the tragedi- ans—with pure and native passion the lyrists—fitted their perfect words to their dearest faiths. " Operosa parvus car- mina fingo." " I, little thing that I am, weave my laborious songs " as earnestly as the bee among the bells of thyme on the Matin mountains. Yes, and he dedicates his favourite pine to Diana, and he chants his autumnal hymn to the Faun that guards his fields, and he guides the noble youths **and**

maids of Rome in their choir to Apollo, and he tells the
farmer's little girl that the Gods will love her, though she has
only a handful of salt and meal to give them—just as earnestly
as ever English gentleman taught Christian faith to English
youth in England's truest days.

49. Then, lastly, the creed of the philosophers or sages
varied according to the character and knowledge of each;—
their relative acquaintance with the secrets of natural science
—their intellectual and sectarian egotism—and their mystic
or monastic tendencies, for there is a classic as well as a mediæval monasticism. They ended in losing the life of Greece
in play upon words ; but we owe to their early thought some
of the soundest ethics, and the foundation of the best practical
laws, yet known to mankind.

50. Such was the general vitality of the heathen creed in
its strength. Of its direct influence on conduct, it is, as I
said, impossible for me to speak now ; only, remember
always, in endeavouring to form a judgment of it, that what
of good or right the heathens did, they did looking for no reward. The purest forms of our own religion have always
consisted in sacrificing less things to win greater ;—time, to
win eternity,—the world, to win the skies. The order, " sell
that thou hast," is not given without the promise,—" thou
shalt have treasure in heaven ; " and well for the modern
Christian if he accepts the alternative as his Master left it—
and does not practically read the command and promise thus :
" Sell that thou hast in the best market, and thou shalt have
treasure in eternity also." But the poor Greeks of the great
ages expected no reward from heaven but honour, and no reward from earth but rest ;—though, when, on those conditions, they patiently, and proudly, fulfilled their task of the
granted day, an unreasoning instinct of an immortal benediction broke from their lips in song : and they, even they, had
sometimes a prophet to tell them of a land " where there is
sun alike by day, and alike by night—where they shall need
no more to trouble the earth by strength of hands for daily
bread—but the ocean breezes blow around the blessed islands,
and golden flowers burn on their bright trees for evermore."

II.

ATHENA KERAMITIS.*

(*Athena in the Earth.*)

Study, supplementary to the preceding lecture, of the supposed, and ~~actual~~ relations of Athena to the vital force in material organism.

51. It has been easy to decipher approximately the Greek conception of the physical power of Athena in cloud and sky, because we know ourselves what clouds and skies are, and what the force of the wind is in forming them. But it is not at all easy to trace the Greek thoughts about the power of Athena in giving life, because we do not ourselves know clearly what life is, or in what way the air is necessary to it, or what there is, besides the air, shaping the forms that it is put into. And it is comparatively of small consequence to find out what the Greeks thought or meant, until we have determined what we ourselves think, or mean, when we translate the Greek word for "breathing" into the Latin-English word "spirit."

52. But it is of great consequence that you should fix in your minds—and hold, against the baseness of mere materialism on the one hand, and against the fallacies of controversial speculation on the other—the certain and practical sense of this word "spirit;"—the sense in which you all know that its reality exists, as the power which shaped you into your shape, and by which you love, and hate, when you have received that shape. You need not fear, on the one hand, that either the sculpturing or the loving power can ever be beaten down by the philosophers into a metal, or evolved by them into a gas: but on the other hand, take care that you your selves, in trying to elevate your conception of it, do not lose

* "Athena, fit for being made into pottery." I coin the expression as a counterpart of γῆ παρθενία, "Clay intact."

its truth in a dream, or even in a word. Beware always of contending for words : you will find them not easy to grasp, if
you know them in several languages. This very word, which
is so solemn in your mouths, is one of the most doubtful. In
Latin it means little more than breathing, and may mean
merely accent ; in French it is not breath, but wit, and our
neighbours are therefore obliged, even in their most solemn
expressions, to say "wit" when we say "ghost." In Greek,
"pneuma," the word we translate "ghost," means either wind
or breath, and the relative word "psyche" has, perhaps, a
more subtle power ; yet St. Paul's words "pneumatic body"
and "psychic body" involve a difference in his mind which
no words will explain. But in Greek and in English, and in
Saxon and in Hebrew, and in every articulate tongue of humanity the "spirit of man" truly means his passion and
virtue, and is stately according to the height of his conception, and stable according to the measure of his endurance.

53. Endurance, or patience, that is the central sign of spirit ;
a constancy against the cold and agony of death ; and as,
physically, it is by the burning power of the air that the heat
of the flesh is sustained, so this Athena, spiritually, is the
queen of all glowing virtue, the unconsuming fire and inner
lamp of life. And thus, as Hephæstus is lord of the fire of
the hand and Apollo of the fire of the brain, so Athena of the
fire of the heart ; and as Hercules wears for his chief armour
the skin of the Nemean lion, his chief enemy, whom he slew ;
and Apollo has for his highest name "the Pythian," from his
chief enemy, the Python, slain ; so Athena bears always on
her breast the deadly face of her chief enemy slain, the Gorgonian cold, and venomous agony, that turns living men to
stone.

54. And so long as you have that fire of the heart within
you, and know the reality of it, you need be under no alarm
as to the possibility of its chemical or mechanical analysis.
The philosophers are very humorous in their ecstasy of hope
about it ; but the real interest of their discoveries in this direction is very small to human-kind. It is quite true that
the tympanum of the ear vibrates under sound, and that the

surface of the water in a ditch vibrates too : but the ditch
hears nothing for all that ; and my hearing is still to me as
blessed a mystery as ever, and the interval between the ditch
and me, quite as great. If the trembling sound in my ears
was once of the marriage-bell which began my happiness, and
is now of the passing-bell which ends it, the difference between those two sounds to me cannot be counted by the
number of concussions. There have been some curious speculations lately as to the conveyance of mental consciousness
by " brain-waves." What does it matter how it is conveyed ?
The consciousness itself is not a wave. It may be accompanied here or there by any quantity of quivers and shakes,
up or down, of anything you can find in the universe that is
shakeable - what is that to me ? My friend is dead, and my
—according to modern views—vibratory sorrow is not one
whit less, or less mysterious, to me, than my old quiet one.

55. Beyond, and entirely unaffected by, any questionings
of this kind, there are, therefore, two plain facts which we
should all know : first, that there is a power which gives their
several shapes to things, or capacities of shape ; and, secondly,
a power which gives them their several feelings, or capacities
of feeling ; and that we can increase or destroy both of these
at our will. By care and tenderness, we can extend the range
of lovely life in plants and animals ; by our neglect and
cruelty, we can arrest it, and bring pestilence in its stead.
Again, by right discipline we can increase our strength of
noble will and passion, or destroy both. And whether these
two forces are local conditions of the elements in which they
appear, or are part of a great force in the universe, out of
which they are taken, and to which they must be restored, is
not of the slightest importance to us in dealing with them :
neither is the manner of their connection with light and air.
What precise meaning we ought to attach to expressions such
as that of the prophecy to the four winds that the dry bones
might be breathed upon, and might live, or why the presence
of the vital power should be dependent on the chemical action
of the air, and its awful passing away materially signified by
the rendering up of that breath or ghost, we cannot at pres-

ent know, and need not at any time dispute. What we assuredly know is that the states of life and death are different,
and the first more desirable than the other, and by effort attainable, whether we understand being "born of the spirit"
to signify having the breath of heaven in our flesh, or its
power in our hearts.

56. As to its power on the body, I will endeavor to tell you,
having been myself much led into studies involving necessary
reference both to natural science and mental phenomena, what,
at least, remains to us after science has done its worst;—what
the Myth of Athena, as a Formative and Decisive power—a
Spirit of Creation and Volition, must eternally mean for all of
us.

57. It is now (I believe I may use the strong word) "ascertained" that heat and motion are fixed in quantity, and measurable in the portions that we deal with. We can measure
out portions of power, as we can measure portions of space
while yet, as far as we know, space may be infinite, and force
infinite. There may be heat as much greater than the sun's,
as the sun's heat is greater than a candle's; and force as much
greater than the force by which the world swings, as that is
greater than the force by which a cobweb trembles. Now, on
heat and force, life is inseparably dependent; and I believe,
also, on a form of substance, which the philosophers call
"protoplasm." I wish they would use English instead of
Greek words. When I want to know why a leaf is green, they
tell me it is coloured by "chlorophyll," which at first sounds
very instructive; but if they would only say plainly that a
leaf is coloured green by a thing which is called "green leaf,"
we should see more precisely how far we had got. However,
it is a curious fact that life is connected with a cellular structure called protoplasm, or, in English, "first stuck together:"
whence, conceivably through deuteroplasms, or second stickings, and tritoplasms, or third stickings,* we reach the high-

---

* Or, perhaps, we may be indulged with one consummating gleam of
"glycasm"—visible "Sweetness,"—according to the good old monk
"Full moon," or "All moonshine." I cannot get at his original Greek,
but am content with M. Durand's clear French (Manuel d'Iconographie

est plastic phase in the human pottery, which differs from common chinaware, primarily, by a measurable degree of heat, developed in breathing, which it borrows from the rest of the universe while it lives, and which it as certainly returns to the rest of the universe, when it dies.

58. Again, with this heat certain assimilative powers are connected, which the tendency of recent discovery is to simplify more and more into modes of one force ; or finally into mere motion, communicable in various states, but not destructible. We will assume that science has done its utmost ; and that every chemical or animal force is demonstrably resolvable into heat or motion, reciprocally changing into each other. I would myself like better, in order of thought, to consider motion as a mode of heat than heat as a mode of motion : still, granting that we have got thus far, we have yet to ask, What is heat ? or what motion ? What is this "primo mobile," this transitional power, in which all things live, and move, and have their being ? It is by definition something different from matter, and we may call it as we choose— "first cause," or "first light," or "first heat ;" but we can show no scientific proof of its not being personal, and coinciding with the ordinary conception of a supporting spirit in all things.

59. Still, it is not advisable to apply the word "spirit" or "breathing" to it, while it is only enforcing chemical affinities ; but, when the chemical affinities are brought under the influence of the air, and of the sun's heat, the formative force enters an entirely different phase. It does not now merely crystallize indefinite masses, but it gives to limited portions of matter the power of gathering, selectively, other elements proper to them, and binding these elements into their own peculiar and adopted form.

This force, now properly called life, or breathing, or spirit,

Chrétienne. Paris, 1845) :—"Lorsque vous aurez fait le proplasme, et esquissé un visage, vous ferez les chairs avec le glycasme dont nous avons donné la recette. Chez les vieillards, vous indiquerez les rides, et chez les jeunes gens, les angles des yeux. C'est ainsi que l'on fait les chairs, suivant Panselinos."

is continually creating its own shells of definite shape out of the wreck round it : and this is what I meant by saying, in the "Ethics of the Dust : "—" you may always stand by form against force." For the mere force of junction is not spirit ; but the power that catches out of chaos charcoal, water, lime, or what not and fastens them down into a given form, is properly called "spirit ; " and we shall not diminish, but strengthen our conception of this creative energy by recognizing its presence in lower states of matter than our own ;—such recognition being enforced upon us by a delight we instinctively receive from all the forms of matter which manifest it ; and yet more, by the glorifying of those forms, in the parts of them that are most animated, with the colours that are pleasantest to our senses. The most familiar instance of this is the best, and also the most wonderful : the blossoming of plants.

60. The Spirit in the plant,—that is to say, its power of gathering dead matter out of the wreck round it, and shaping it into its own chosen shape,—is of course strongest at the moment of its flowering, for it then not only gathers, but forms, with the greatest energy.

And where this Life is in it at full power, its form becomes invested with aspects that are chiefly delightful to our own human passions ; namely, first, with the loveliest outlines of shape ; and, secondly, with the most brilliant phases of the primary colours, blue, yellow, and red or white, the unison of all ; and, to make it all more strange, this time of peculiar and perfect glory is associated with relations of the plants or blossoms to each other, correspondent to the joy of love in human creatures, and having the same object in the continuance of the race. Only, with respect to plants, as animals, we are wrong in speaking as if the object of this strong life were only the bequeathing of itself. The flower is the end or proper object of the seed, not the seed of the flower. The reason for seeds is that flowers may be ; not the reason of flowers that seeds may be. The flower itself is the creature which the spirit makes ; only, in connection with its perfectness, is placed the giving birth to its successor.

61. The main fact, then, about a flower is that it is the part

of the plant's form developed at the moment of its intensest
life : and this inner rapture is usually marked externally for
us by the flush of one or more of the primary colours. What
the character of the flower shall be, depends entirely upon the
portion of the plant into which this rapture of spirit has been
put. Sometimes the life is put into its outer sheath, and then
the outer sheath becomes white and pure, and full of strength
and grace ; sometimes the life is put into the common leaves,
just under the blossom, and they become scarlet or purple ;
sometimes the life is put into the stalks of the flower, and
they flush blue ; sometimes into its outer enclosure or calyx ;
mostly into its inner cup ; but, in all cases, the presence of
the strongest life is asserted by characters in which the human
sight takes pleasure, and which seem prepared with distinct
reference to us, or rather, bear, in being delightful, evidence
of having been produced by the power of the same spirit as
our own.

62. And we are led to feel this still more strongly, because
all the distinctions of species,* both in plants and animals, appear to have similar connection with human character. Whatever the origin of species may be, or however those species,
once formed, may be influenced by external accident, the
groups into which birth or accident reduce them have distinct
relation to the spirit of man. It is perfectly possible, and
ultimately conceivable, that the crocodile and the lamb may
have descended from the same ancestral atom of protoplasm ;
and that the physical laws of the operation of calcareous slime
and of meadow grass, on that protoplasm, may in time have
developed the opposite natures and aspects of the living
frames ; but the practically important fact for us is the existence of a power which creates that calcareous earth itself ;—
which creates, that separately—and quartz, separately ; and

* The facts on which I am about to dwell are in nowise antagonistic
to the theories which Mr. Darwin's unwearied and unerring investigations are every day rendering more probable. The æsthetic relations
of species are independent of their origin. Nevertheless, it has always
seemed to me, in what little work I have done upon organic forms, as
if the species mocked us by their deliberate imitation of each other
when they met : yet did not pass one into another.

gold, separately; and charcoal, separately; and then so directs the relation of these elements as that the gold shall destroy the souls of men by being yellow; and the charcoal
destroy their souls by being hard and bright; and the quartz
represent to them an ideal purity; and the calcareous earth,
soft, shall beget crocodiles, and dry and hard, sheep; and
that the aspects and qualities of these two products, crocodiles
and lambs, shall be, the one repellent to the spirit of man, the
other attractive to it, in a quite inevitable way; representing
to him states of moral evil and good; and becoming myths
to him of destruction or redemption, and, in the most literal
sense, "words" of God.

63. And the force of these facts cannot be escaped from by
the thought that there are species innumerable, passing into
each other by regular gradations, out of which we choose
what we most love or dread, and say they were indeed prepared for us. Species are not innumerable; neither are they
now connected by consistent gradation. They touch at certain points only; and even then are connected, when we examine them deeply, in a kind of reticulated way, not in chains,
but in chequers; also, however connected, it is but by a touch
of the extremities, as it were, and the characteristic form of the
species is entirely individual. The rose nearly sinks into a
grass in the sanguisorba; but the formative spirit does not
the less clearly separate the ear of wheat from the dog-rose,
and oscillate with tremulous constancy round the central
forms of both, having each their due relation to the mind of
man. The great animal kingdoms are connected in the same
way. The bird through the penguin drops towards the fish,
and the fish in the cetacean reascends to the mammal, yet
there is no confusion of thought possible between the perfect
forms of an eagle, a trout, and a war-horse, in their relations
to the elements, and to man.

64. Now we have two orders of animals to take some note
of in connection with Athena, and one vast order of plants,
which will illustrate this matter very sufficiently for us.

The orders of animals are the serpent and the bird; the
serpent, in which the breath or spirit is less than in any other

creature, and the earth-power greatest :—the bird, in which the breath or spirit is more full than in any other creature, and the earth power least.

65. We will take the bird first. It is little more than a drift of the air brought into form by plumes ; the air is in all its quills, it breathes through its whole frame and flesh, and glows with air in its flying, like blown flame : it rests upon the air, subdues it, surpasses it, outraces it ;—*is* the air, con-scious of itself, conquering itself, ruling itself.

Also, into the throat of the bird is given the voice of the air. All that in the wind itself is weak, wild, useless in sweet-ness, is knit together in its song. As we may imagine the wild form of the cloud closed into the perfect form of the bird's wings, so the wild voice of the cloud into its ordered and commanded voice ; unwearied, rippling through the clear heaven in its gladness, interpreting all intense passion through the soft spring nights, bursting into acclaim and rapture of choir at daybreak, or lisping and twittering among the boughs and hedges through heat of day, like little winds that only make the cowslip bells shake, and ruffle the petals of the wild rose.

66. Also, upon the plumes of the bird are put the colours of the air : on these the gold of the cloud, that cannot be gathered by any covetousness ; the rubies of the clouds, that are not the price of Athena, but *are* Athena ; the vermilion of the cloud-bar, and the flame of the cloud-crest, and the snow of the cloud, and its shadow, and the melted blue of the deep wells of the sky—all these, seized by the creating spirit, and woven by Athena herself into films and threads of plume ; with wave on wave following and fading along breast, and throat, and opened wings, infinite as the dividing of the foam and the sifting of the sea-sand ;—even the white down of the cloud seeming to flutter up between the stronger plumes, seen, but too soft for touch.

And so the Spirit of the Air is put into, and upon, this created form ; and it becomes, through twenty centuries, the symbol of divine help, descending, as the Fire, to speak, but as the Dove, to bless.

67. Next, in the serpent, we approach the source of a group

of myths, world-wide, founded on great and common human instincts, respecting which I must note one or two points which bear intimately on all our subject. For it seems to me that the scholars who are at present occupied in interpretation of human myths have most of them forgotten that there are any such things as natural myths ; and that the dark sayings of men may be both difficult to read, and not always worth reading ; but the dark sayings of nature will probably become clearer for the looking into, and will very certainly be worth reading. And, indeed, all guidance to the right sense of the human and variable myths will probably depend on our first getting at the sense of the natural and invariable ones. The dead hieroglyph may have meant this or that—the living hieroglyph means always the same ; but remember, it is just as much a hieroglyph as the other ; nay, more,—a "sacred or reserved sculpture," a thing with an inner language. The serpent crest of the king's crown, or of the god's, on the pillars of Egypt, is a mystery; but the serpent itself, gliding past the pillar's foot, is it less a mystery? Is there, indeed, no tongue, except the mute forked flash from its lips, in that running brook of horror on the ground ?

68. Why that horror? We all feel it, yet how imaginative it is, how disproportioned to the real strength of the creature ! There is more poison in an ill-kept drain,—in a pool of dish-washings at a cottage-door, than in the deadliest asp of Nile. Every back-yard which you look down into from the railway, as it carries you out by Vauxhall or Deptford, holds its coiled serpent : all the walls of those ghastly suburbs are enclosures of tank temples for serpent-worship ; yet you feel no horror in looking down into them, as you would if you saw the livid scales, and lifted head. There is more venom, mortal, inevitable, in a single word, sometimes, or in the gliding entrance of a wordless thought, than ever "vanti Libia con sua rena." But that horror is of the myth, not of the creature. There are myriads lower than this, and more loathsome, in the scale of being ; the links between dead matter and animation drift everywhere unseen. But it is the strength of the base element that is so dreadful in the ser-

pent; it is the very omnipotence of the earth. That rivulet of smooth silver—how does it flow, think you? It literally rows on the earth, with every scale for an oar; it bites the dust with the ridges of its body. Watch it, when it moves slowly :—A wave, but without wind! a current, but with no fall! all the body moving at the same instant, yet some of it to one side, some to another, or some forward, and the rest of the coil backwards; but all with the same calm will and equal way—no contraction, no extension; one soundless, causeless, march of sequent rings, and spectral procession of spotted dust, with dissolution in its fangs, dislocation in its coils. Startle it ;—the winding stream will become a twisted arrow ;—the wave of poisoned life will lash through the grass like a cast lance.* It scarcely breathes with its one lung (the other shrivelled and abortive); it is passive to the sun and shade, and is cold or hot like a stone; yet "it can out-climb the monkey, outswim the fish, outleap the zebra, out-wrestle the athlete, and crush the tiger." † It is a divine hieroglyph of the demoniac power of the earth,—of the entire earthly nature. As the bird is the clothed power of the air, so this is the clothed power of the dust; as the bird the symbol of the spirit of life, so this of the grasp and sting of death.

69. Hence the continual change in the interpretation put upon it in various religions. As the worm of corruption, it is the mightiest of all adversaries of the gods—the special ad-

---

* I cannot understand this swift forward motion of serpents. The seizure of prey by the constrictor, though invisibly swift, is quite simple in mechanism; it is simply the return to its coil of an opened watch spring, and is just as instantaneous. But the steady and continuous motion, without a visible fulcrum (for the whole body moves at the same instant, and I have often seen even small snakes glide as fast as I could walk), seems to involve a vibration of the scales quite too rapid to be conceived. The motion of the crest and dorsal fin of the hippocampus, which is one of the intermediate types between serpent and fish, perhaps gives some resemblance of it, dimly visible, for the quivering turns the fin into a mere mist. The entrance of the two barbs of a bee's sting by alternate motion, "the teeth of one barb acting as a fulcrum for the other," must be something like the serpent motion on a small scale.

† Richard Owen.

versary of their light and creative power—Python against Apollo. As the power of the earth against the air, the giants are serpent-bodied in the Giganto-machia ; but as the power of the earth upon the seed—consuming it into new life ("that which thou sowest is not quickened except it die ")—serpents sustain the chariot of the spirit of agriculture.

70. Yet, on the other hand, there is a power in the earth to take away corruption, and to purify, (hence the very fact of burial, and many uses of earth, only lately known) ; and in this sense, the serpent is a healing spirit,—the representative of Æsculapius, and of Hygieia ; and is a sacred earth-type in the temple of the Dew ;—being there especially a symbol of the native earth of Athens ; so that its departure from the temple was a sign to the Athenians that they were to leave their homes. And then, lastly, as there is a strength and dealing in the earth, no less than the strength of air, so there is conceived to be a wisdom of earth no less than a wisdom of the spirit ; and when its deadly power is killed, its guiding power becomes true ; so that the Python serpent is killed at Delphi, where yet the oracle is from the breath of the earth.

71. You must remember, however, that in this, as in every other instance, I take the myth at its central time. This is only the meaning of the serpent to the Greek mind which could conceive an Athena. Its first meaning to the nascent eyes of men, and its continued influence over degraded races, are subjects of the most fearful mystery. Mr. Fergusson has just collected the principal evidence bearing on the matter in a work of very great value, and if you read his opening chapters, they will put you in possession of the circumstances needing chiefly to be considered. I cannot touch upon any of them here, except only to point out that, though the doctrine of the so-called " corruption of human nature," asserting that there is nothing but evil in humanity, is just as blasphemous and false as a doctrine of the corruption of physical nature would be, asserting there was nothing but evil in the earth,—there is yet the clearest evidence of a disease, plague, or cre-tinous imperfection of development, hitherto allowed to pre vail against the greater part of the races of men ; and this in

monstrous ways, more full of mystery than the serpent-being itself. I have gathered for you to-night only instances of what is beautiful in Greek religion ; but even in its best time there were deep corruptions in other phases of it, and degraded forms of many of its deities, all originating in a misunderstood worship of the principle of life ; while in the religions of lower races, little else than these corrupted forms of devotion can be found ;—all having a strange and dreadful consistency with each other, and infecting Christianity, even at its strongest periods, with fatal terror of doctrine, and ghastliness of symbolic conception, passing through fear into frenzied grotesque, and thence into sensuality.

In the Psalter of St. Louis itself, half of its letters are twisted snakes ; there is scarcely a wreathed ornament, employed in Christian dress, or architecture, which cannot be traced back to the serpent's coil ; and there is rarely a piece of monkish decorated writing in the world, that is not tainted with some ill-meant vileness of grotesque—nay, the very leaves of the twisted ivy-pattern of the fourteenth century can be followed back to wreaths for the foreheads of bacchanalian gods. And truly, it seems to me, as I gather in my mind the evidences of insane religion, degraded art, merciless war, sullen toil, detestable pleasure, and vain or vile hope, in which the nations of the world have lived since first they could bear record of themselves—it seems to me, I say, as if the race itself were still half-serpent, not extricated yet from its clay ; a lacertine breed of bitterness—the glory of it emaciate with cruel hunger, and blotted with venomous stain : and the track of it, on the leaf a glittering slime, and in the sand a useless furrow.

72. There are no myths, therefore, by which the moral state and fineness of intelligence of different races can be so deeply tried or measured, as by those of the serpent and the bird ; both of them having an especial relation to the kind of remorse for sin, or grief in fate, of which the national minds that spoke by them had been capable. The serpent and vulture are alike emblems of immortality and purification among races which desired to be immortal and pure : and as they

recognize their own misery, the serpent becomes to them the scourge of the Furies, and the vulture finds its eternal prey in their breast. The bird long contests among the Egyptians with the still received serpent symbol of power. But the Draconian image of evil is established in the serpent Apap; while the bird's wings, with the globe, become part of a better symbol of deity, and the entire form of the vulture, as an em‑ blem of purification, is associated with the earliest conception of Athena. In the type of the dove with the olive branch, the conception of the spirit of Athena in renewed life prevailing over ruin, is embodied for the whole of futurity; while the Greeks, to whom, in a happier climate and higher life than that of Egypt, the vulture symbol of cleansing became unin‑ telligible, took the eagle, instead, for their hieroglyph of supreme spiritual energy, and it thenceforward retains its hold on the human imagination, till it is established among Christian myths as the expression of the most exalted form of evangelistic teaching. The special relation of Athena to her favourite bird we will trace presently : the peacock of Hera, and dove of Aphrodite, are comparatively unimportant myths : but the bird power is soon made entirely human by the Greeks in their flying angel of victory (partially human, with modified meaning of evil, in the Harpy and Siren) ; and thenceforward it associates itself with the Hebrew cherubim, and has had the most singular influence on the Christian re‑ ligion by giving its wings to render the conception of angels mysterious and untenable, and check rational endeavour to determine the nature of subordinate spiritual agency ; while yet it has given to that agency a vague poetical influence of the highest value in its own imaginative way.

73. But with the early serpent worship there was associated another—that of the groves—of which you will also find the evidence exhaustively collected in Mr. Fergusson's work. This tree-worship may have taken a dark form when asso‑ ciated with the Draconian one ; or opposed, as in Judea, to a purer faith ; but in itself, I believe, it was always healthy, and though it retains little definite hieroglyphic power in subse‑ quent religion, it becomes, instead of symbolic, real ; the

flowers and trees are themselves beheld and beloved with a
half-worshipping delight, which is always noble and healthful.

And it is among the most notable indications of the volition
of the animating power, that we find the ethical signs of good
and evil set on these also, as well as upon animals ; the venom
of the serpent, and in some respects its image also, being associated even with the passionless growth of the leaf out of
the ground ; while the distinctions of species seem appointed
with more definite ethical address to the intelligence of man
as their material products become more useful to him.

74. I can easily show this, and, at the same time, make clear
the relation to other plants of the flowers which especially belong to Athena, by examining the natural myths in the groups
of the plants which would be used at any country dinner, over
which Athena would, in her simplest household authority,
cheerfully rule, here, in England. Suppose Horace's favourite
dish of beans, with the bacon ; potatoes ; some savoury stuffing of onions and herbs with the meat ; celery, and a radish
or two, with the cheese ; nuts and apples for dessert, and
brown bread.

75. The beans are, from earliest time, the most important
and interesting of the seeds of the great tribe of plants from
which came the Latin and French name for all kitchen vege-
tables,—things that are gathered with the hand—podded
seeds that cannot be reaped, or beaten, or shaken down, but
must be gathered green. "Leguminous" plants, all of them
having flowers like butterflies, seeds in (frequently pendent)
pods,—"lætum siliqua quassante legumen "—smooth and tender leaves, divided into many minor ones ; strange adjuncts of
tendril, for climbing (and sometimes of thorn) ;—exquisitely
sweet, yet pure, scents of blossom, and almost always harmless, if not serviceable, seeds. It is, of all tribes of plants, the
most definite ; its blossoms being entirely limited in their
parts, and not passing into other forms. It is also the most
usefully extended in range and scale ; familar in the height of
the forest—acacia, laburnum, Judas-tree ; familiar in the sown
field—bean and vetch and pea ; familiar in the pasture—in

every form of clustered clover and sweet trefoil tracery ; the most entirely serviceable and human of all orders of plants.

76. Next, in the potato, we have the scarcely innocent underground stem of one of a tribe set aside for evil; having the deadly nightshade for its queen, and including the henbane, the witch's mandrake and the worst natural curse of modern civilization — tobacco.* And the strange thing about this tribe is, that though thus set aside for evil, they are not a group distinctly separate from those that are happier in function. There is nothing in other tribes of plants like the form of the bean blossom ; but there is another family with forms and structure closely connected with this venomous one. Examine the purple and yellow bloom of the common hedge nightshade; you will find it constructed exactly like some of the forms of the cyclamen; and, getting this clue, you will find at last the whole poisonous and terrible group to be — sisters of the primulas!

The nightshades are, in fact, primroses with a curse upon them ; and a sign set in their petals, by which the deadly and condemned flowers may always be known from the innocent ones, — that the stamens of the nightshades are between the lobes, and of the primulas, opposite the lobes, of the corolla.

77. Next, side by side, in the celery and radish, you have the two great groups of umbelled and cruciferous plants ; alike in conditions of rank among herbs : both flowering in clusters; but the umbelled group, flat, the crucifers, in spires : — both of them mean and poor in the blossom, and losing what beauty they have by too close crowding : — both of them having the most curious influence on human character in the temperate zones of the earth, from the days of the parsley crown, and hemlock drink, and mocked Euripidean chervil, until now : but chiefly among the northern nations, being especially plants that are of some humble beauty, and (the crucifers) of endless use, when they are chosen and cultivated ; but that run to wild waste, and are the signs of neglected

* It is not easy to estimate the demoralizing effect on the youth of Europe of the cigar, in enabling them to pass their time happily in idleness.

ground, in their rank or ragged leaves, and meagre stalks, and
pursed or podded seed clusters. Capable, even under cultivation, of no perfect beauty, though reaching some subdued delightfulness in the lady's smock and the wallflower; for the
most part, they have every floral quality meanly, and in vain,
—they are white, without purity; golden, without preciousness; redundant, without richness; divided, without fineness;
massive, without strength; and slender, without grace. Yet
think over that useful vulgarity of theirs; and of the relations
of German and English peasant character to its food of kraut
and cabbage, (as of Arab character to its food of palm-fruit,)
and you will begin to feel what purposes of the forming spirit
are in these distinctions of species.

78. Next we take the nuts and apples,—the nuts representing one of the groups of catkined trees, whose blossoms are
only tufts and dust; and the other, the rose tribe, in which
fruit and flower alike have been the types, to the highest races
of men, of all passionate temptation, or pure delight, from the
coveting of Eve to the crowning of the Madonna, above the

> " Rosa sempiterna,
> Che si dilata, rigrada, e ridole
> Odor di lode al Sol."

We have no time now for these, we must go on to the hum-
blest group of all, yet the most wonderful, that of the grass,
which has given us our bread; and from that we will go back
to the herbs.

79. The vast family of plants which, under rain, make the
earth green for man, and, under sunshine, give him bread,
and, in their springing in the early year, mixed with their
native flowers, have given us (far more than the new leaves of
trees) the thought and word of "spring," divide themselves
broadly into three great groups—the grasses, sedges, and
rushes. The grasses are essentially a clothing for healthy and
pure ground, watered by occasional rain, but in itself dry,
and fit for all cultivated pasture and corn. They are distinctively plants with round and jointed stems, which have
long green flexible leaves, and heads of seed, independently

emerging from them. The sedges are essentially the clothing of waste and more or less poor or uncultivable soils, coarse in their structure, frequently triangular in stem—hence called "acute" by Virgil—and with their heads of seed not extricated from their leaves. Now, in both the sedges and grasses, the blossom has a common structure, though undeveloped in the sedges, but composed always of groups of double husks, which have mostly a spinous process in the centre, sometimes projecting into a long awn or beard ; this central process being characteristic also of the ordinary leaves of mosses, as if a moss were a kind of ear of corn made permanently green on the ground, and with a new and distinct fructification. But the rushes differ wholly from the sedge and grass in their blossom structure. It is not a dual cluster, but a twice three-fold one, so far separate from the grasses, and so closely connected with a higher order of plants, that I think you will find it convenient to group the rushes at once with that higher order, to which, if you will for the present let me give the general name of Drosidæ, or dew-plants, it will enable me to say what I have to say of them much more shortly and clearly.

80. These Drosidæ, then, are plants delighting in interrupted moisture—moisture which comes either partially or at certain seasons—into dry ground. They are not water-plants ; but the signs of water resting among dry places. Many of the true water-plants have triple blossoms, with a small triple calyx holding them ; in the Drosidæ, the floral spirit passes into the calyx also, and the entire flower becomes a six-rayed star, bursting out of the stem laterally, as if it were the first of flowers, and had made its way to the light by force through the unwilling green. They are often required to retain moisture or nourishment for the future blossom through long times of drought ; and this they do in bulbs under ground, of which some become a rude and simple, but most wholesome, food for man.

81. So now, observe, you are to divide the whole family of the herbs of the field into three great groups—Drosidæ, Carices,*

* I think Carex will be found ultimately better that Cyperus for the generic name, being the Virgilian word, and representing a larger sub-species

Gramineæ — dew-plants, sedges, and grasses. Then, the Drosidæ are divided into five great orders—lilies, asphodels, amaryllids, irids, and rushes. No tribes of flowers have had so great, so varied, or so healthy an influence on man as this great group of Drosidæ, depending, not so much on the whiteness of some of their blossoms, or the radiance of others, as on the strength and delicacy of the substance of their petals; enabling them to take forms of faultless elastic curvature, either in cups, as the crocus, or expanding bells, as the true lily, or heath-like bells, as the hyacinth, or bright and perfect stars, like the star of Bethlehem, or, when they are affected by the strange reflex of the serpent nature which forms the labiate group of all flowers, closing into forms of exquisitely fantastic symmetry in the gladiolus. Put by their side their Nereid sisters, the water-lilies, and you have in them the origin of the loveliest forms of ornamental design, and the most powerful floral myths yet recognized among human spirits, born by the streams of Ganges, Nile, Arno, and Avon.

82. For consider a little what each of those five tribes* has been to the spirit of man. First, in their nobleness: the Lilies gave the lily of the Annunciation; the Asphodels, the flower of the Elysian fields; the Irids, the fleur-de-lys of chivalry; and the Amaryllids, Christ's lily of the field: while the rush, trodden always under foot, became the emblem of humility. Then take each of the tribes, and consider the extent of their lower influence. Perdita's "The crown imperial, lilies of all kinds," are the first tribe; which, giving the type of perfect purity in the Madonna's lily, have, by their lovely form, influenced the entire decorative design of Italian sacred art; while ornament of war was continually enriched by the curves of the triple petals of the Florentine "giglio," and French fleur-de-lys; so that it is impossible to count their in-

---

* Take this rough distinction of the four tribes:—Lilies, superior ovary, white seeds; Asphodels, superior ovary, black seeds; Irids, inferior ovary, style (typically) rising into central crest; Amaryllids, inferior ovary, stamens (typically) joined in central cup. Then the rushes are a dark group, through which they stoop to the grasses.

fluence for good in the middle ages, partly as a symbol of womanly character, and partly of the utmost brightness and refinement of chivalry in the city which was the flower of cities.

Afterwards, the group of the turban-lilies, or tulips, did some mischief, (their splendid stains having made them the favourite caprice of florists ;) but they may be pardoned all such guilt for the pleasure they have given in cottage gardens, and are yet to give, when lowly life may again be possible among us; and the crimson bars of the tulips in their trim beds, with their likeness in crimson bars of morning above them, and its dew glittering heavy, globed in their glossy cups, may be loved better than the gray nettles of the ash heap, under gray sky, unveined by vermilion or by gold.

83. The next great group, of the Asphodels, divides itself also into two principal families ; one, in which the flowers are like stars, and clustered characteristically in balls, though opening sometimes into looser heads ; and the other, in which the flowers are in long bells, opening suddenly at the lips, and clustered in spires on a long stem, or drooping from it, when bent by their weight.

The star-group, of the squills, garlics, and onions, has always caused me great wonder. I cannot understand why its beauty, and serviceableness, should have been associated with the rank scent which has been really among the most powerful means of degrading peasant life, and separating it from that of the higher classes.

The belled group, of the hyacinth and convallaria, is as delicate as the other is coarse : the unspeakable azure light along the ground of the wood hyacinth in English spring ; the grape hyacinth, which is in south France, as if a cluster of grapes and a hive of honey had been distilled and compressed together into one small boss of celled and beaded blue ; the lilies of the valley everywhere, in each sweet and wild recess of rocky lands ;—count the influences of these on childish and innocent life ; then measure the mythic power of the hyacinth and asphodel as connected with Greek thoughts of immortality ; finally take their useful and nour-

ishing power in ancient and modern peasant life, and it wi
be strange if you do not feel what fixed relation exists between the agency of the creating spirit in these, and in us
who live by them.

84. It is impossible to bring into any tenable compass for
our present purpose, even hints of the human influence of the
two remaining orders of Amaryllids and Irids;—only note
this generally, that while these in northern countries share
with the Primulas the fields of spring, it seems that in Greece,
the primulaceæ are not an extended tribe, while the crocus,
narcissus, and Amaryllis lutea, the "lily of the field" (I suspect also that the flower whose name we translate "violet"
was in truth an Iris) represented to the Greek the first coming of the breath of life on the renewed herbage ; and became
in his thoughts the true embroidery of the saffron robe of
Athena.   Later in the year, the dianthus (which, though belonging to an entirely different race of plants, has yet a strange
look of having been made out of the grasses by turning the
sheath-membrane at the root of their leaves into a flower,)
seems to scatter, in multitudinous families, its crimson stars
far and wide.   But the golden lily and crocus, together with
the asphodel, retain always the old Greek's fondest thoughts
—they are only "golden" flowers that are to burn on the
trees, and float on the streams of paradise.

85. I have but one tribe of plants more to note at our
country feasts—the savoury herbs ; but must go a little out
of my way to come at them rightly.   All flowers whose petals
are fastened together, and most of those whose petals are
loose, are best thought of first as a kind of cup or tube opening at the mouth.   Sometimes the opening is gradual, as in
the convolvulus or campanula ; oftener there is a distinct
change of direction between the tube and expanding lip, as
in the primrose ; or even a contraction under the lip, making
the tube into a narrow-necked phial or vase, as in the heaths,
but the general idea of a tube expanding into a quatrefoil,
cinquefoil, or sixfoil, will embrace most of the forms.

86. Now it is easy to conceive that flowers of this kind,
growing in close clusters, may, in process of time, have ex

tended their outside petals rather than the interior ones (as the outer flowers of the clusters of many umbellifers actually do), and thus, elongated and variously distorted forms have established themselves ; then if the stalk is attached to the side instead of the base of the tube, its base becomes a spur, and thus all the grotesque forms of the mints, violets, and larkspurs, gradually might be composed. But, however this may be, there is one great tribe of plants separate from the rest, and of which the influence seems shed upon the rest in different degrees : and these would give the impression, not so much of having been developed by change, as of being stamped with a character of their own, more or less serpentine or dragon-like. And I think you will find it convenient to call these generally, *Draconidæ ;* disregarding their present ugly botanical name, which I do not care even to write once— you may take for their principal types the Foxglove, Snapdragon, and Calceolaria ; and you will find they all agree in a tendency to decorate themselves by spots, and with bosses or swollen places in their leaves, as if they had been touched by poison. The spot of the Foxglove is especially strange, because it draws the colour out of the tissue all around it, as if it had been stung, and as if the central colour was really an inflamed spot, with paleness round. Then also they carry to its extreme the decoration by bulging or pouting the petal ; —often beautifully used by other flowers in a minor degree, like the beating out of bosses in hollow silver, as in the kalmia, beaten out apparently in each petal by the stamens instead of a hammer ; or the borage, pouting inwards ; but the snapdragons and calceolarias carry it to its extreme.

87. Then the spirit of these Draconidæ seems to pass more or less into other flowers, whose forms are properly pure vases ; but it affects some of them slightly,—others not at all. It never strongly affects the heaths ; never once the roses ; but it enters like an evil spirit into the buttercup, and turns it into a larkspur, with a black, spotted, grotesque centre, and a strange, broken blue, gorgeous and intense, yet impure, glittering on the surface as if it were strewn with broken glass, and stained or darkening irregularly into red. **And**

then at last the serpent charm changes the ranunculus into
monkshood ; and makes it poisonous. It enters into the for-
get-me-not, and the star of heavenly turquoise is corrupted
into the viper's bugloss, darkened with the same strange red
as the larkspur, and fretted into a fringe of thorn ; it enters,
together with a strange insect-spirit, into the asphodels, and
(though with a greater interval between the groups,) they
change into spotted orchideæ : it touches the poppy, it becomes a fumaria ; the iris, and it pouts into a gladiolus ; the
lily, and it chequers itself into a snake's-head, and secretes in
the deep of its bell, drops, not of venom indeed, but honey-
dew, as if it were a healing serpent. For there is an Æscu-
lapian as well as an evil serpentry among the Draconidæ, and
the fairest of them, the "erba della Madonna" of Venice,
(Linaria Cymbalaria,) descends from the ruins it delights in
to the herbage at their feet, and touches it ; and behold, instantly, a vast group of herbs for healing,—all draconid in
form,—spotted, and crested, and from their lip-like corollas
named "labiatæ ;" full of various balm, and warm strength
for healing, yet all of them without splendid honour or perfect beauty, "ground ivies," richest when crushed under the
foot ; the best sweetness and gentle brightness of the robes
of the field,—thyme, and marjoram, and Euphrasy.

88. And observe, again and again, with respect to all these
divisions and powers of plants ; it does not matter in the least
by what concurrences of circumstance or necessity they may
gradually have been developed : the concurrence of circumstance is itself the supreme and inexplicable fact. We always
come at last to a formative cause, which directs the circumstance, and mode of meeting it. If you ask an ordinary
botanist the reason of the form of a leaf, he will tell you it is
a "developed tubercle," and that its ultimate form "is owing
to the directions of its vascular threads." But what directs
its vascular threads ? "They are seeking for something they
want," he will probably answer. What made them want that ?
What made them seek for it thus ? Seek for it, in five fibres
or in three ? Seek for it, in serration, or in sweeping curves ?
Seek for it, in servile tendrils, cr impetuous spray ? Seek for

it, in woollen wrinkles rough with stings, or in glossy surfaces, green with pure strength, and winterless delight?

89. There is no answer. But the sum of all is, that over the entire surface of the earth and its waters, as influenced by the power of the air under solar light, there is developed a series of changing forms, in clouds, plants, and animals, all of which have reference in their action, or nature, to the human intelligence that perceives them ; and on which, in their aspects of horror and beauty, and their qualities of good and evil, there is engraved a series of myths, or words of the forming power, which, according to the true passion and energy of the human race, they have been enabled to read into religion. And this forming power has been by all nations partly confused with the breath or air through which it acts, and partly understood as a creative wisdom, proceeding from the Supreme Deity ; but entering into and inspiring all intelligences that work in harmony with Him. And whatever intellectual results may be in modern days obtained by regarding this effluence only as a motion of vibration, every formative human art hitherto, and the best states of human happiness and order, have depended on the apprehension of its mystery (which is certain), and of its personality, which is probable.

90. Of its influence on the formative arts, I have a few words to say separately : my present business is only to interpret, as we are now sufficiently enabled to do, the external symbols of the myth under which it was represented by the Greeks as a goddess of counsel, taken first into the breast of their supreme Deity, then created out of his thoughts, and abiding closely beside him ; always sharing and consummating his power.

91. And in doing this we have first to note the meaning of the principal epithet applied to Athena, "Glaukopis," "with eyes full of light," the first syllable being connected, by its root, with words signifying sight, not with words signifying colour. As far as I can trace the colour perception of the Greeks, I find it all founded primarily on the degree of connection between colour and light ; the most important fact to them in the colour of red being its connection with fire and

sunshine; so that "purple" is, in its original sense, "fire colour," and the scarlet, or orange, of dawn, more than any other fire-colour. I was long puzzled by Homer's calling the sea purple; and misled into thinking he meant the colour of cloud shadows on green sea; whereas he really means the gleaming blaze of the waves under wide light. Aristotle's idea (partly true) is that light, subdued by blackness, becomes red; and blackness, heated or lighted, also becomes red. Thus, a colour may be called purple because it is light sub-dued (and so death is called "purple" or "shadowy" death); or else it may be called purple as being shade kindled with fire, and thus said of the lighted sea; or even of the sun it-self, when it is thought of as a red luminary opposed to the whiteness of the moon: " purpureos inter soles et candida lunæ sidera ;" or of golden hair: " pro purpureo pœnam sol-vens scelerata capillo ;" while both ideas are modified by the influence of an earlier form of the word, which has nothing to do with fire at all, but only with mixing or staining; and then, to make the whole group of thoughts inextricably com-plex, yet rich and subtle in proportion to their intricacy, the various rose and crimson colours of the murex-dye,—the crimson and purple of the poppy, and fruit of the palm,—and the association of all these with the hue of blood ;—partly di-rect, partly through a confusion between the word signifying "slaughter" and "palm-fruit colour," mingle themselves in, and renew the whole nature of the old word; so that, in later literature, it means a different colour, or emotion of colour, in almost every place where it occurs; and casts forever around the reflection of all that has been dipped in its dyes.

92. So that the word is really a liquid prism, and stream of opal. And then, last of all, to keep the whole history of it in the fantastic course of a dream, warped here and there into wild grotesque, we moderns, who have preferred to rule over coal-mines instead of the sea (and so have turned the everlast-ing lamp of Athena into a Davy's safety-lamp in the hand of Britannia, and Athenian heavenly lightning into British sub-terranean "damp"), have actually got our purple out of coal instead of the sea! And thus, grotesquely, we have had en-

forced on us the doubt that held the old word between black-ness and fire, and have completed the shadow, and the fear of it, by giving it a name from battle, "Magenta."

93. There is precisely a similar confusion between light and colour in the word used for the blue of the eyes of Athena —a noble confusion, however, brought about by the intensity of the Greek sense that the heaven is light, more than it is blue. I was not thinking of this when I wrote, in speaking of pictorial chiaroscuro, "The sky is not blue colour merely; it is blue fire, and cannot be painted" (Mod. P. iv. p. 36); but it was this that the Greeks chiefly felt of it, and so " Glau-kopis" chiefly means gray-eyed: gray standing for a pale or lu-minous blue; but it only means "owl-eyed" in thought of the roundness and expansion, not from the colour; this breadth and brightness being, again, in their moral sense typical of the breadth, intensity, and singleness of the sight in prudence ("if thine eye be single, thy whole body shall be full of light"). Then the actual power of the bird to see in twilight enters into the type, and perhaps its general fineness of sense. " Before the human form was adopted, her (Athena's) proper symbol was the owl, a bird which seems to surpass all other creatures in acuteness of organic perception, its eye being cal-culated to observe objects which to all others are enveloped in darkness, its ear to hear sounds distinctly, and its nostrils to discriminate effluvia with such nicety that it has been deemed prophetic, from discovering the putridity of death even in the first stages of disease." *

I cannot find anywhere an account of the first known occur-rence of the type; but, in the early ones on Attic coins, the wide round eyes are clearly the principal things to be made manifest.

94. There is yet, however, another colour of great impor-tance in the conception of Athena—the dark blue of her ægis. Just as the blue or gray of her eyes was conceived as more light than colour, so her ægis was dark blue, because the

---

* Payne Knight in his " Inquiry into the Symbolical Language of Ancient Art," not trustworthy, being little more than a mass of conjec-tural memoranda, but the heap is suggestive, if well sifted.

Greeks thought of this tint more as shade than colour, and, while they used various materials in ornamentation, lapislazuli, carbonate of copper, or perhaps, smalt, with real enjoyment of the blue tint, it was yet in their minds as distinctly repre-sentative of darkness as scarlet was of light, and therefore, anything dark,* but especially the colour of heavy thunder cloud, was described by the same term.   The physical power

* In the breastplate and shield of Atrides the serpents and bosses are all of this dark colour, yet the serpents are said to be like rainbows; but through all this splendour and opposition of hue, I feel distinctly tnat the literal "splendour," with its relative shade, are prevalent in the concep-tion ; and that there is always a tendency to look through the nue to its cause.   And in this feeling about colour the Greeks are separated from the eastern nations, and from the best designers of Christian times.   I cannot find that they take pleasure in colour for its own sake ; it may be in something more than colour, or better ; but it is not in the hue it-self.   When Homer describes cloud breaking from a mountain summit, the crags became visible in light, not in colour ; he feels only their flashing out in bright edges and trenchant shadows : above, the "in-finite," "unspeakable" æther is torn open—but not the *blue* of it.   He has scarcely any abstract pleasure in blue, or green, or gold; but only in their shade or flame.

I have yet to trace the causes of this (which will be a long task, be-l, nging to art questions, not to mythological ones); but it is, I believe, much connected with the brooding of the shadow of death over the Greeks without any clear hope of immortality.   The restriction of the colour on their vases to dim red (or yellow) with black and white, is greatly connected with their sepulchral use, and with all the melancholy of Greek tragic thought; and in this gloom the failure of colour-percep-tion is partly noble, partly base : noble, in its earnestness, which raises the design of Greek vases as far above the designing of mere colourist nations like the Chinese, as men's thoughts are above children's ; and yet it is partly base and earthly ; and inherently defective in one human faculty : and I believe it was one cause of the perishing of their art so swiftly, for indeed there is no decline so sudden, or down to such utter loss and ludicrous depravity, as the fall of Greek design on its vases from the fifth to the third century, B.C.   On the other hand, the pure coloured-gift, when employed for pleasure only, degrades in another direction ; so that among the Indians, Chinese, and Japanese, all intel-lectual progress in art has been for ages rendered impossible by the prevalence of that faculty : and yet it is, as I have said again and again, the spiritual power of art ; and its true brightness is the essential char-acteristic of all healthy schools.

of this darkness of the ægis, fringed with lightning, is given quite simply when Jupiter himself uses it to overshadow Ida and the Plain of Troy, and withdraws it at the prayer of Ajax for light ; and again when he grants it to be worn for a time by Apollo, who is hidden by its cloud when he strikes down Patroclus : but its spiritual power is chiefly expressed by a word signifying deeper shadow ;—the gloom of Erebus, or of our evening, which, when spoken of the ægis, signifies, not merely the indignation of Athena, but the entire hiding or withdrawal of her help, and beyond even this, her deadliest of all hostility,—the darkness by which she herself deceives and beguiles to final ruin those to whom she is wholly adverse ; this contradiction of her own glory being the uttermost judgment upon human falsehood. Thus it is she who provokes Pandarus to the treachery which purposed to fulfil the rape of Helen by the murder of her husband in time of truce ; and *then* the Greek King, holding his wounded brother's hand, prophesies against Troy the darkness of the ægis which shall be over all, and for ever.*

95. This, then, finally, was the perfect colour-conception of Athena ;—the flesh, snow-white, (the hands, feet, and face of marble, even when the statue was hewn roughly in wood) ; the eyes of keen pale blue, often in statues represented by jewels ; the long robe to the feet, crocus coloured ; and the ægis thrown over it of thunderous purple ; the helmet golden, (Il. v. 744), and I suppose its crest also, as that of Achilles.

If you think carefully of the meaning and character which is now enough illustrated for you in each of these colours ; and remember that the crocus-colour and the purple were both of them developments, in opposite directions, of the great central idea of fire-colour, or scarlet, you will see that this form of the creative spirit of the earth is conceived as robed in the blue, and purple, and scarlet, the white, and the gold, which have been recognized for the sacred chord of colours, from the day when the cloud descended on a Rock more mighty than Ida.

96. I have spoken throughout, hitherto, of the conception

* ἐρεμνὴν Αἰγίδα πᾶσι.—Il. iv. 166.

of Athena, as it is traceable in the Greek mind ; not as it was rendered by Greek art.   It is matter of extreme difficulty, requiring a sympathy at once affectionate and cautious, and a knowledge reaching the earliest springs of the religion of many lands, to discern through the imperfection, and, alas ! more dimly yet, through the triumphs of formative art, what kind of thoughts they were that appointed for it the tasks of its childhood, and watched by the awakening of its strength.

The religious passion is nearly always vividest when the art is weakest ; and the technical skill only reaches its deliberate splendour when the ecstasy which gave it birth has passed away for ever.   It is as vain an attempt to reason out the visionary power or guiding influence of Athena in the Greek heart, from anything we now read, or possess, of the work of Phidias, as it would be for the disciples of some new religion to infer the spirit of Christianity from Titian's " Assumption." The effective vitality of the religious conception can be traced only through the efforts of trembling hands, and strange pleasures of untaught eyes ; and the beauty of the dream can no more be found in the first symbols by which it is expressed, than a child's idea of fairyland can be gathered from its pencil scrawl, or a girl's love for her broken doll explained by the defaced features.   On the other hand, the Athena of Phidias was, in very fact, not so much the deity, as the darling of the Athenian people.   Her magnificence represented their pride and fondness, more than their piety ; and the great artist, in lavishing upon her dignities which might be ended abruptly by the pillage they provoked, resigned, apparently without regret, the awe of her ancient memory ; and (with only the careless remonstrance of a workman too strong to be proud) even the perfectness of his own art.   Rejoicing in the protection of their goddess, and in their own hour of glory, the people of Athena robed her, at their will, with the preciousness of ivory and gems ; forgot or denied the darkness of the breastplate of judgment, and vainly bade its unappeasable serpents relax their coils in gold.

97. It will take me many a day yet—if days, many or few,

are given me—to disentangle in anywise the proud and practised disguises of religious creeds from the instinctive arts
which, grotesquely and indecorously, yet with sincerity, strove
to embody them, or to relate. But I think the reader, by
help even of the imperfect indications already given to him,
will be able to follow, with a continually increasing security,
the vestiges of the Myth of Athena; and to reanimate its almost evanescent shade, by connecting it with the now recognized facts of existent nature, which it, more or less dimly, reflected and foretold. I gather these facts together in brief sum.

98. The deep of air that surrounds the earth enters into union
with the earth at its surface, and with its waters; so as to be
the apparent cause of their ascending into life. First, it warms
them, and shades, at once, staying the heat of the sun's rays
in its own body, but warding their force with its clouds. It
warms and cools at once, with traffic of balm and frost; so
that the white wreaths are withdrawn from the field of the
Swiss peasant by the glow of Libyan rock. It gives its own
strength to the sea; forms and fills every cell of its foam;
sustains the precipices, and designs the valleys of its waves;
gives the gleam to their moving under the night, and the
white fire to their plains under sunrise; lifts their voices along
the rocks, bears above them the spray of birds, pencils through
them the dimpling of unfooted sands. It gathers out of them
a portion in the hollow of its hand: dyes, with that, the hills
into dark blue, and their glaciers with dying rose; inlays with
that, for sapphire, the dome in which it has to set the cloud;
shapes out of that the heavenly flocks: divides them, numbers,
cherishes, bears them on its bosom, calls them to their
journeys, waits by their rest; feeds from them the brooks
that cease not, and strews with them the dews that cease.
It spins and weaves their fleece into wild tapestry, rends it,
and renews; and flits and flames, and whispers, among the
golden threads, thrilling them with a plectrum of strange fire
that traverses them to and fro. and is enclosed in them like life.

It enters into the surface of the earth, subdues it, and falls
together with it into fruitful dust, from which can be moulded
flesh; it joins itself, in dew, to the substance of adamant;

and becomes the green leaf out of the dry ground; it enters into the separated shapes of the earth it has tempered, commands the ebb and flow of the current of their life, fills their limbs with its own lightness, measures their existence by its indwelling pulse, moulds upon their lips the words by which one soul can be known to another; is to them the hearing of the ear, and the beating of the heart; and, passing away, leaves them to the peace that hears and moves no more.

99. This was the Athena of the greatest people of the days of old. And opposite to the temple of this Spirit of the breath, and life-blood, of man and of beast, stood, on the Mount of Justice, and near the chasm which was haunted by the goddess-Avengers, an altar to a God unknown;—proclaimed at last to them, as one who, indeed, gave to all men, life, and breath, and all things; and rain from heaven, filling their hearts with food and gladness;—a God who had made of one blood all nations of men who dwell on the face of all the earth, and had determined the times of their fate, and the bounds of their habitation.

100. We ourselves, fretted here in our narrow days, know less, perhaps, in very deed, than they, what manner of spirit we are of, or what manner of spirit we ignorantly worship. Have we, indeed, desired the Desire of all nations? and will the Master whom we meant to seek, and the Messenger in whom we thought we delighted, confirm, when He comes to His temple,—or not find in its midst,—the tables heavy with gold for bread, and the seats that are bought with the price of the dove? Or is our own land also to be left by its angered Spirit;—left among those, where sunshine vainly sweet, and passionate folly of storm, waste themselves in the silent places of knowledge that has passed away, and of tongues that have ceased?

This only we may discern assuredly: this, every true light of science, every mercifully-granted power, every wisely-restricted thought, teach us more clearly day by day, that in the heavens above, and the earth beneath, there is one continual and omnipotent presence of help, and of peace, for all men who know that they Live, and remember that they Die.

ATHENA ERGANE.*

(Athena in the Heart.)

Various Notes relating to the Conception of Athena as the Directress of the Imagination and Will.

101. I HAVE now only a few words to say, bearing on what seems to me present need, respecting the third function of Athena, conceived as the directress of human passion, resolution, and labour.

Few words, for I am not yet prepared to give accurate distinction between the intellectual rule of Athena and that of the Muses : but, broadly, the Muses, with their king, preside over meditative, historical, and poetic arts, whose end is the discovery of light or truth, and the creation of beauty : but Athena rules over moral passion, and practically useful art. She does not make men learned, but prudent and subtle : she does not teach them to make their work beautiful, but to make it right.

In different places of my writings, and through many years of endeavour to define the laws of art, I have insisted on this rightness in work, and on its connection with virtue of character, in so many partial ways, that the impression left on the reader's mind—if, indeed, it was ever impressed at all—has been confused and uncertain. In beginning the series of my corrected works, I wish this principle (in my own mind the foundation of every other) to be made plain, if nothing else is : and will try, therefore, to make it so, as far as, by any effort, I can put it into unmistakable words. And, first, here is a very simple statement of it, given lately in a lecture on the Architecture of the Valley of the Somme, which will be

---

* " Athena the worker, or having rule over work." The name was first given to her by the Athenians.

better read in this place than in its incidental connection **with** my account of the porches of Abbeville.

102. I had used, in a preceding part of the lecture, the expression, "by what faults" this Gothic architecture fell. We continually speak thus of works of art. We talk of their faults and merits, as of virtues and vices. What do we mean by talking of the faults of a picture, or the merits of a piece of stone?

The faults of a work of art are the faults of its workmen, and its virtues his virtues.

Great art is the expression of the mind of a great man, and mean art, that of the want of mind of a weak man. A foolish person builds foolishly, and a wise one, sensibly; a virtuous one, beautifully; and a vicious one, basely. If stone work is well put together, it means that a thoughtful man planned it, and a careful man cut it, and an honest man cemented it. If it has too much ornament, it means that its carver was too greedy of pleasure; if too little, that he was rude, or insensitive, or stupid, and the like. So that when once you have learned how to spell these most precious of all legends,—pictures and buildings,—you may read the characters of men, and of nations, in their art, as in a mirror;—nay, as in a microscope, and magnified a hundredfold; for the character becomes passionate in the art, and intensifies itself in all its noblest or meanest delights. Nay, not only as in a microscope, but as under a scalpel, and in dissection; for a man may hide himself from you, or misrepresent himself to you, every other way; but he cannot in his work: there, be sure, you have him to the inmost. All that he likes, all that he sees,—all that he can do,—his imagination, his affections, his perseverance, his impatience, his clumsiness, cleverness, everything is there. If the work is a cobweb, you know it was made by a spider; if a honeycomb, by a bee; a worm-cast is thrown up by a worm, and a nest wreathed by a bird; and a house built by a man, worthily, if he is worthy, and ignobly, if he is ignoble.

And always, from the least to the greatest, as the made thing is good or bad, so is the maker of it.

103. You all use this faculty of judgment more or less, whether you theoretically admit the principle or not. Take that floral gable ;* you don't suppose the man who built Stonehenge could have built that, or that the man who built that, *would* have built Stonehenge? Do you think an old Roman would have liked such a piece of filigree work? or that Michael Angelo would have spent his time in twisting these stems of roses in and out? Or, of modern handicrafts-men, do you think a burglar, or a brute, or a pickpocket could have carved it? Could Bill Sykes have done it? or the Dodger, dexterous with finger and tool? You will find in the end, that *no man could have done it but exactly the man who did it ;* and by looking close at it, you may, if you know your letters, read precisely the manner of man he was.

104. Now I must insist on this matter, for a grave reason. Of all facts concerning art, this is the one most necessary to be known, that, while manufacture is the work of hands only, art is the work of the whole spirit of man ; and as that spirit is, so is the deed of it : and by whatever power of vice or vir-tue any art is produced, the same vice or virtue it reproduces and teaches. That which is born of evil begets evil ; and that which is born of valour and honour, teaches valour and hon-our. All art is either infection or education. It *must* be one or other of these.

105. This, I repeat, of all truths respecting art, is the one of which understanding is the most precious, and denial the most deadly. And I assert it the more, because it has of late been repeatedly, expressly, and with contumely, denied ; and that by high authority : and I hold it one of the most sorrow-ful facts connected with the decline of the arts among us, that English gentlemen, of high standing as scholars and artists, should have been blinded into the acceptance, and betrayed into the assertion of a fallacy which only authority such as theirs could have rendered for an instant credible. For the contrary of it is written in the history of all great nations ; it

* The elaborate pediment above the central porch at the west end of Rouen Cathedral, pierced into a transparent web of tracery, and en-riched with a border of " twisted eglantine."

is the one sentence always inscribed on the steps of their thrones; the one concordant voice in which they speak to us out of their dust.

All such nations first manifest themselves as a pure and beautiful animal race, with intense energy and imagination. They live lives of hardship by choice, and by grand instinct of manly discipline: they become fierce and irresistible soldiers; the nation is always its own army, and their king, or chief head of government, is always their first soldier. Pharaoh, or David, or Leonidas, or Valerius, or Barbarossa, or Cœur de Lion, or St. Louis, or Dandolo, or Frederick the Great:—Egyptian, Jew, Greek, Roman, German, English, French, Venetian,—that is inviolable law for them all; their king must be their first soldier, or they cannot be in progressive power. Then, after their great military period, comes the domestic period; in which, without betraying the discipline of war, they add to their great soldiership the delights and possessions of a delicate and tender home-life: and then, for all nations, is the time of their perfect art, which is the fruit, the evidence, the reward of their national idea of character, developed by the finished care of the occupations of peace. That is the history of all true art that ever was, or can be: palpably the history of it,—unmistakably,—written on the forehead of it in letters of light,—in tongues of fire, by which the seal of virtue is branded as deep as ever iron burnt into a convict's flesh the seal of crime. But always, hitherto, after the great period, has followed the day of luxury, and pursuit of the arts for pleasure only. And all has so ended.

106. Thus far of Abbeville building. Now I have here asserted two things,—first, the foundation of art in moral character; next, the foundation of moral character in war. I must make both these assertions clearer, and prove them.

First, of the foundation of art in moral character. Of course art-gift and amiability of disposition are two different things; a good man is not necessarily a painter, nor does an eye for colour necessarily imply an honest mind. But great art implies the union of both powers: it is the expression, by an art-gift, of a pure soul. If the gift is not there, we can have no art at all; and if the soul—and a right soul too—is not there, the art is bad, however dexterous.

107. But also, remember, that the art-gift itself is only the result of the moral character of generations. A bad woman may have a sweet voice; but that sweetness of voice comes of the past morality of her race. That she can sing with it at all, she owes to the determination of laws of music by the morality of the past. Every act, every impulse, of virtue and vice, affects in any creature, face, voice, nervous power, and vigour and harmony of invention, at once. Perseverance in rightness of human conduct, renders, after a certain number of generations, human art possible; every sin clouds it, be it ever so little a one; and persistent vicious living and following of pleasure render, after a certain number of generations, all art impossible. Men are deceived by the long-suffering of the laws of nature; and mistake, in a nation, the reward of the virtue of its sires for the issue of its own sins. The time of their visitation will come, and that inevitably; for, it is always true, that if the fathers have eaten sour grapes, the children's teeth are set on edge. And for the individual, as soon as you have learned to read, you may, as I said, know him to the heart's core, through his art. Let his art-gift be never so great, and cultivated to the height by the schools of a great race of men; and it is still but a tapestry thrown over his own being and inner soul; and the bearing of it will show, infallibly, whether it hangs on a man, or on a skeleton. If you are dim-eyed, you may not see the difference in the fall of the folds at first, but learn how to look, and the folds themselves will become transparent, and you shall see through them the death's shape, or the divine one, making the tissue above it as a cloud of light, or as a winding-sheet.

108. Then farther, observe, I have said (and you will find it true, and that to the uttermost) that, as all lovely art is rooted in virtue, so it bears fruit of virtue, and is didactic in its own nature. It is often didactic also in actually expressed thought, as Giotto's, Michael Angelo's, Dürer's, and hundreds more; but that is not its special function.—it is didactic chiefly by being beautiful; but beautiful with haunting

thought, no less than with form, and full of myths that can be read only with the heart.

For instance, at this moment there is open beside me as 1 write, a page of Persian manuscript, wrought with wreathed azure and gold, and soft green, and violet, and ruby and scar let, into one field of pure resplendence. It is wrought to delight the eyes only; and does delight them; and the man who did it assuredly had eyes in his head; but not much more. It is not didactic art, but its author was happy: and it will do the good, and the harm, that mere pleasure can do. But, opposite me, is an early Turner drawing of the lake of Geneva, taken about two miles from Geneva, on the Lausanne road, with Mont Blanc in the distance. The old city is seen lying beyond the waveless waters, veiled with a sweet misty veil of Athena's weaving: a faint light of morning, peaceful exceedingly, and almost colourless, shed from behind the Voirons, increases into soft amber along the slope of the Saleve, and is just seen, and no more, on the fair warm fields of its summit, between the folds of a white cloud that rests upon the grass, but rises, high and tower-like, into the zenith of dawn above.

109. There is not as much colour in that low amber light upon the hill-side as there is in the palest dead leaf. The lake is not blue, but gray in mist, passing into deep shadow beneath the Voirons' pines; a few dark clusters of leaves, a single white flower—scarcely seen—are all the gladness given to the rocks of the shore. One of the ruby spots of the eastern manuscript would give colour enough for all the red that is in Turner's entire drawing. For the mere pleasure of the eye, there is not so much in all those lines of his, throughout the entire landscape, as in half an inch square of the Persian's page. What made him take pleasure in the low colour that is only like the brown of a dead leaf? in the cold gray of dawn —in the one white flower among the rocks—in these—and no more than these?

110. He took pleasure in them because he had been bred among English fields and hills; because the gentleness of a great race was in his heart, and its powers of thought in his

brain ; because he knew the stories of the Alps, and of the cities at their feet ; because he had read the Homeric legends of the clouds, and beheld the gods of dawn, and the givers of dew to the fields ; because he knew the faces of the crags, and the imagery of the passionate mountains, as a man knows the face of his friend ; because he had in him the wonder and sorrow concerning life and death, which are the inheritance of the Gothic soul from the days of its first sea kings ; and also the compassion and the joy that are woven into the innermost fabric of every great imaginative spirit, born now in countries that have lived by the Christian faith with any courage or truth. And the picture contains also, for us, just this which its maker had in him to give ; and can convey it to us, just so far as we are of the temper in which it must be received. It is didactic if we are worthy to be taught, no otherwise. The pure heart, it will make more pure ; the thoughtful, more thoughtful. It has in it no words for the reckless or the base.

111. As I myself look at it, there is no fault nor folly of my life,—and both have been many and great,—that does not rise up against me, and take away my joy, and shorten my power of possession, of sight, of understanding. And every past effort of my life, every gleam of rightness or good in it, is with me now, to help me in my grasp of this art, and its vision. So far as I can rejoice in, or interpret either, my power is owing to what of right there is in me. I dare to say it, that, because through all my life I have desired good, and not evil ; because I have been kind to many ; have wished to be kind to all; have wilfully injured none ; and because I have loved much, and not selfishly ;—therefore, the morning light is yet visible to me on those hills, and you, who read, may trust my thought and word in such work as I have to do for you ; and you will be glad afterwards that you have trusted them.

112. Yet remember,—I repeat it again and yet again,—that I may for once, if possible, make this thing assuredly clear :— the inherited art-gift must be there, as well as the life in some poor measure, or rescued fragment, right. This art-gift of

mine could not have been won by any work or by any con‹ duct : it belongs to me by birthright, and came by Athena's will, from the air of English country villages, and Scottish hills. I will risk whatever charge of folly may come on me, for printing one of my many childish rhymes, written on a frosty day in Glen Farg, just north of Loch Leven. It bears date 1st January, 1828. I was born on the 8th of February, 1819 ; and all that I ever could be, and all that I cannot be, the weak little rhyme already shows.

> " Papa, how pretty those icicles are,
>   That are seen so near,—that are seen so far ;
>   —Those dropping waters that come from the rocks
>   And many a hole, like the haunt of a fox.
>   That silvery stream that runs babbling along,
>   Making a murmuring, dancing song.
>   Those trees that stand waving upon the rock's side
>   And men, that, like spectres, among them glide.
>   And waterfalls that are heard from far,
>   And come in sight when very near.
>   And the water-wheel that turns slowly round,
>   Grinding the corn that—requires to be ground,—

(Political Economy of the future !)

> ——And mountains at a distance seen,
>   And rivers winding through the plain.
>   And quarries with their craggy stones,
>   And the wind among them moans."

So foretelling Stones of Venice, and this essay on Athena.

Enough now concerning myself.

113. Of Turner's life, and of its good and evil, both great, but the good immeasurably the greater, his work is in all things a perfect and transparent evidence. His biography is simply,—" He did this, nor will ever another do its like again." Yet read what I have said of him, as compared with the great Italians, in the passages taken from the " Cestus of Aglaia," farther on, § 158, p. 119.

114. This then is the nature of the connection of morals with art. Now, secondly, I have asserted the foundation of

both these, at least, hitherto, in war. The reason of this too manifest fact is, that, until now, it has been impossible for any nation, except a warrior one, to fix its mind wholly on its men, instead of on their possessions. Every great soldier nation thinks, necessarily, first of multiplying its bodies and souls of men, in good temper and strict discipline. As long as this is its political aim, it does not matter what it temporarily suffers, or loses, either in numbers or in wealth; its morality and its arts, (if it have national art-gift,) advance together; but so soon as it ceases to be a warrior nation, it thinks of its possessions instead of its men; and then the moral and poetic powers vanish together.

115. It is thus, however, absolutely necessary to the virtue of war that it should be waged by personal strength, not by money or machinery. A nation that fights with a mercenary force, or with torpedoes instead of its own arms, is dying. Not but that there is more true courage in modern than even in ancient war; but this is, first, because all the remaining life of European nations is with a morbid intensity thrown into their soldiers; and, secondly, because their present heroism is the culmination of centuries of inbred and traditional valour, which Athena taught them by forcing them to govern the foam of the sea-wave and of the horse,—not the steam of kettles.

116. And farther, note this, which is vital to us in the present crisis: If war is to be made by money and machinery, the nation which is the largest and most covetous multitude will win. You may be as scientific as you choose; the mob that can pay more for sulphuric acid and gunpowder will at last poison its bullets, throw acid in your faces, and make an end of you;—of itself, also, in good time, but of you first. And to the English people the choice of its fate is very near now. It may spasmodically defend its property with iron walls a fathom thick, a few years longer—a very few. No walls will defend either it, or its havings, against the multitude that is breeding and spreading, faster than the clouds, over the habitable earth. We shall be allowed to live by small pedlar's business, and ironmongery—since we have chosen those for our line of life—as long as we are found useful black

servants to the Americans; and are content to dig coals and sit in the cinders; and have still coals to dig,—they once exhausted, or got cheaper elsewhere, we shall be abolished. But if we think more wisely, while there is yet time, and set our minds again on multiplying Englishmen, and not on cheapening English wares; if we resolve to submit to wholesome laws of labour and economy, and, setting our political squabbles aside, try how many strong creatures, friendly and faithful to each other, we can crowd into every spot of English dominion, neither poison nor iron will prevail against us; nor traffic—nor hatred: the noble nation will yet, by the grace of Heaven, rule over the ignoble, and force of heart hold its own against fire-balls.

117. But there is yet a farther reason for the dependence of the arts on war. The vice and injustice of the world are constantly springing anew, and are only to be subdued by battle; the keepers of order and law must always be soldiers. And now, going back to the myth of Athena, we see that though she is first a warrior maid, she detests war for its own sake; she arms Achilles and Ulysses in just quarrels, but she *dis*arms Ares. She contends, herself, continually against disorder and convulsion, in the Earth giants; she stands by Hercules' side in victory over all monstrous evil: in justice only she judges and makes war. But in this war of hers she is wholly implacable. She has little notion of converting criminals. There is no faculty of mercy in her when she has been resisted. Her word is only, "I will mock you when your fear cometh." Note the words that follow: "when your fear cometh as desolation, and your destruction as a whirlwind;" for her wrath is of irresistible tempest: once roused, it is blind and deaf,—rabies—madness of anger—darkness of the Dies Iræ.

And that is, indeed, the sorrowfullest fact we have to know about our own several lives. Wisdom never forgives. Whatever resistance we have offered to her law, she avenges for ever;—the lost hour can never be redeemed, and the accomplished wrong never atoned for. The best that can be done afterwards, but for that, had been better;—the falsest of all the cries of peace, where there is no peace, is that of the pardon of sin, as the mob expect it. Wisdom can "put away " sin, but she cannot pardon it ; and she is apt, in her haste, to put away the sinner as well, when the black ægis is on her breast.

118. And this is also a fact we have to know about our national life, that it is ended as soon as it has lost the power of noble Anger. When it paints over, and apologizes for its pitiful criminalities ; and endures its false weights, and its adulterated food ;—dares not to decide practically between good and evil, and can neither honour the one, nor smite the other, but sneers at the good, as if it were hidden evil, and consoles the evil with pious sympathy, and conserves it in the sugar of its leaden heart,—the end is come.

119. The first sign, then, of Athena's presence with any people, is that they become warriors, and that the chief thought of every man of them is to stand rightly in his rank, and not fail from his brother's side in battle. Wealth, and pleasure, and even love, are all, under Athena's orders, sacrificed to this duty of standing fast in the rank of war.

But farther : Athena presides over industry, as well as battle ; typically, over women's industry; that brings comfort with pleasantness. Her word to us all is :—"Be well exercised, and rightly clothed. Clothed, and in your right minds ; not insane and in rags, nor in soiled fine clothes clutched from each other's shoulders. Fight and weave. Then I myself will answer for the course of the lance, and the colours of the loom."

And now I will ask the reader to look with some care through these following passages respecting modern multitudes and their occupations, written long ago, but left in fragmentary form, in which they must now stay, and be of what use they can.

120. It is not political economy to put a number of strong men down on an acre of ground, with no lodging, and nothing to eat. Nor is it political economy to build a city on good ground, and fill it with store of corn and treasure, and put a score of lepers to live in it. Political economy creates together the means of life, and the living persons who are to

use them ; and of both, the best and the most that it can, but imperatively the best, not the most. A few good and healthy men, rather than a multitude of diseased rogues ; and a little real milk and wine rather than much chalk and petroleum ; but the gist of the whole business is that the men and their property must both be produced together—not one to the loss of the other. Property must not be created in lands desolate by exile of their people, nor multiplied and depraved humanity, in lands barren of bread.

121. Nevertheless, though the men and their possessions are to be increased at the same time, the first object of thought is always to be the multiplication of a worthy people. The strength of the nation is in its multitude, not in its territory ; but only in its sound multitude. It is one thing, both in a man and a nation, to gain flesh, and another to be swollen with putrid humours. Not that multitude ever ought to be inconsistent with virtue. Two men should be wiser than one, and two thousand than two ; nor do I know another so gross fallacy in the records of human stupidity as that excuse for neglect of crime by greatness of cities. As if the first purpose of congregation were not to devise laws and repress crimes ! as if bees and wasps could live honestly in flocks,—men, only in separate dens !—as if it was easy to help one another on the opposite sides of a mountain, and impossible on the opposite sides of a street ! But when the men are true and good, and stand shoulder to shoulder, the strength of any nation is in its quantity of life, not in its land nor gold. The more good men a state has, in proportion to its territory, the stronger the state. And as it has been the madness of economists to seek for gold instead of life, so it has been the madness of kings to seek for land instead of life. They want the town on the other side of the river, and seek it at the spear point : it never enters their stupid heads that to double the honest souls in the town on *this* side of the river, would make them stronger kings ; and that this doubling might be done by the ploughshare instead of the spear, and through happiness instead of misery.

Therefore, in brief, this is the object of all true policy and true economy : "utmost multitude of good men on every given space of ground "—imperatively always, good, sound, honest men, not a mob of white-faced thieves. So that, on the one hand, all aristocracy is wrong which is inconsistent with numbers ; and, on the other, all numbers are wrong which are inconsistent with breeding.

122. Then, touching the accumulation of wealth for the maintenance of such men, observe, that you must never use the terms "money" and "wealth" as synonymous. Wealth consists of the good, and therefore useful, things in the possession of the nation : money is only the written or coined sign of the relative quantities of wealth in each person's possession. All money is a divisible title-deed, of immense importance as an expression of right to property ; but absolutely valueless, as property itself. Thus, supposing a nation isolated from all others, the money in its possession is, at its maximum value, worth all the property of the nation, and no more, because no more can be got for it. And the money of all nations is worth, at its maximum, the property of all nations, and no more, for no more can be got for it. Thus, every article of property produced increases, by its value, the value of all the money in the world, and every article of property destroyed, diminishes the value of all the money in the world. If ten men are cast away on a rock, with a thousand pounds in their pockets, and there is on the rock neither food nor shelter, their money is worth simply nothing; for nothing is to be had for it : if they build ten huts, and recover a cask of biscuit from the wreck, then their thousand pounds, at its maximum value, is worth ten huts and a cask of biscuit. If they make their thousand pounds into two thousand by writing new notes, their two thousand pounds are still only worth ten huts and a cask of biscuit. And the law of relative value is the same for all the world, and all the people in it, and all their property, as for ten men on a rock. Therefore, money is truly and finally lost in the degree in which its value is taken from it, (ceasing in that degree to be money at all) ; and it is truly gained in the degree in which value is added to it. Thus, suppose the money coined by the

nation to be a fixed sum, divided very minutely, (say into francs and cents), and neither to be added to, nor diminished. Then every grain of food and inch of lodging added to its possessions makes every cent in its pockets worth proportionally more, and every grain of food it consumes, and inch of roof it allows to fall to ruin, makes every cent in its pockets worth less ; and this with mathematical precision. The immediate value of the money at particular times and places depends, indeed, on the humours of the possessors of property ; but the nation is in the one case gradually getting richer ; and will feel the pressure of poverty steadily everywhere relaxing, whatever the humours of individuals may be ; and, in the other case, is gradually growing poorer, and the pressure of its poverty will every day tell more and more, in ways that it cannot explain, but will most bitterly feel.

123. The actual quantity of money which it coins, in relation to its real property, is therefore only of consequence for convenience of exchange ; but the proportion in which this quantity of money is divided among individuals expresses their various rights to greater or less proportions of the national property, and must not, therefore, be tampered with. The Government may at any time, with perfect justice, double its issue of coinage, if it gives every man who had ten pounds in his pocket, another ten pounds, and every man who had ten pence, another ten pence ; for it thus does not make any of them richer ; it merely divides their counters for them into twice the number. But if it gives the newly-issued coins to other people, or keeps them itself, it simply robs the former holders to precisely that extent. This most important function of money, as a title-deed, on the non-violation of which all national soundness of commerce and peace of life depend, has been never rightly distinguished by economists from the quite unimportant function of money as a means of exchange. You can exchange goods,—at some inconvenience, indeed, but still you can contrive to do it,—without money at all ; but you cannot maintain your claim to the savings of your past life without a document declaring the amount of them, which the nation and its Government will respect.

124. And as economists have lost sight of this great function of money in relation to individual rights, so they have equally lost sight of its function as a representative of good things. That, for every good thing produced, so much money is put into everybody's pocket—is the one simple and primal truth for the public to know, and for economists to teach How many of them have taught it? Some have ; but only incidentally ; and others will say it is a truism. If it be, do the public know it? Does your ordinary English householder know that every costly dinner he gives has destroyed for ever as much money as it is worth? Does every well-educated girl—do even the women in high political position —know that every fine dress they wear themselves, or cause to be worn, destroys precisely so much of the national money as the labour and material of it are worth? If this be a truism, it is one that needs proclaiming somewhat louder.

125. That, then, is the relation of money and goods. So much goods, so much money ; so little goods, so little money. But, as there is this true relation between money and " goods," or good things, so there is a false relation between money and " bads," or bad things. Many bad things will fetch a price in exchange ; but they do not increase the wealth of the country. Good wine is wealth—drugged wine is not ; good meat is wealth—putrid meat is not ; good pictures are wealth —bad pictures are not. A thing is worth precisely what it can do for you ; not what you choose to pay for it. You may pay a thousand pounds for a cracked pipkin, if you please ; but you do not by that transaction make the cracked pipkin worth one that will hold water, nor that, nor any pipkin whatsoever, worth more than it was before you paid such sum for it. You may, perhaps, induce many potters to manufacture fissured pots, and many amateurs of clay to buy them ; but the nation is, through the whole business so encouraged, rich by the addition to its wealth of so many potsherds—and there an end. The thing is worth what it CAN do for you, not what you think it can ; and most national luxuries, now-a-days, are a form of potsherd, provided for the solace of self-complacent Job, voluntary sedent on his ash-heap.

126. And, also, so far as good things already exist, and have become media of exchange, the variations in their prices are absolutely indifferent to the nation. Whether Mr. A. buys a Titian from Mr. B. for twenty, or for two thousand, pounds, matters not sixpence to the national revenue : that is to say, it matters in nowise to the revenue whether Mr. A. has the picture, and Mr. B. the money, or Mr. B. the picture, and Mr. A. the money. Which of them will spend the money most wisely, and which of them will keep the picture most carefully, is, indeed, a matter of some importance ; but this cannot be known by the mere fact of exchange.

127. The wealth of a nation then, first, and its peace and well-being besides, depend on the number of persons it can employ in making good and useful things. I say its well-being also, for the character of men depends more on their occupations than on any teaching we can give them, or principles with which we can imbue them. The employment forms the habits of body and mind, and these are the constitution of the man ;—the greater part of his moral or persistent nature, whatever effort, under special excitement, he may make to change, or overcome them. Employment is the half, and the primal half, of education—it is the warp of it ; and the fineness or the endurance of all subsequently woven pattern depends wholly on its straightness and strength. And, whatever difficulty there may be in tracing through past history the remoter connections of event and cause, one chain of sequence is always clear : the formation, namely, of the character of nations by their employments, and the determination of their final fate by their character. The moment, and the first direction of decisive revolutions, often depend on accident ; but their persistent course, and their consequences, depend wholly on the nature of the people. The passing of the Reform Bill by the late English Parliament may have been more or less accidental : the results of the measure now rest on the character of the English people, as it has been developed by their recent interests, occupations, and habits of life. Whether, as a body, they employ their new powers for good or evil, will depend, not on their facilities of knowledge, nor even on the general intelligence they may possess ; but on the number of persons among them whom wholesome employ-ments have rendered familiar with the duties, and modest in their estimate of the promises, of Life.

128. But especially in framing laws respecting the treatment or employment of improvident and more or less vicious per-sons, it is to be remembered that as men are not made heroes by the performance of an act of heroism, but must be brave before they can perform it, so they are not made villains by the commission of a crime, but were villains before they com-mitted it ; and that the right of public interference with their conduct begins when they begin to corrupt themselves ;—not merely at the moment when they have proved themselves hopelessly corrupt.

All measures of reformation are effective in exact propor-tion to their timeliness : partial decay may be cut away and cleansed ; incipient error corrected : but there is a point at which corruption can no more be stayed, nor wandering re-called. It has been the manner of modern philanthropy to remain passive until that precise period, and to leave the sick to perish, and the foolish to stray, while it spent itself in frantic exertions to raise the dead, and reform the dust.

The recent direction of a great weight of public opinion against capital punishment is, I trust, the sign of an awaken-ing perception that punishment is the last and worst instru-ment in the hands of the legislator for the prevention of crime. The true instruments of reformation are employment and re-ward ;—not punishment. Aid the willing, honour the vir-tuous, and compel the idle into occupation, and there will be no need for the compelling of any into the great and last in-dolence of death.

129. The beginning of all true reformation among the criminal classes depends on the establishment of institutions for their active employment, while their criminality is still unripe, and their feelings of self-respect, capacities of affec-tion, and sense of justice, not altogether quenched. That those who are desirous of employment should always be able to find it. will hardly, at the present day, be disputed : but

that those who are *un*desirous of employment should of all persons be the most strictly compelled to it, the public are hardly yet convinced ; and they must be convinced. If the danger of the principal thoroughfares in their capital city, and the multiplication of crimes more ghastly than ever yet dis-graced a nominal civilization, are not enough, they will not have to wait long before they receive sterner lessons. For our neglect of the lower orders has reached a point at which it begins to bear its necessary fruit, and every day makes the fields, not whiter, but more sable, to harvest.

130. The general principles by which employment should be regulated may be briefly stated as follows :—

1. There being three great classes of mechanical powers at our disposal, namely, (*a*) vital or muscular power ; (*b*) natural mechanical power of wind, water, and electricity ; and (*c*) artificially produced mechanical power ; it is the first princi-ple of economy to use all available vital power first, then the inexpensive natural forces, and only at last to have recourse to artificial power. And this, because it is always better for a man to work with his own hands to feed and clothe himself, than to stand idle while a machine works for him ; and if he cannot by all the labour healthily possible to him, feed and clothe himself, then it is better to use an inexpensive machine —as a windmill or watermill—than a costly one like a steam-engine, so long as we have natural force enough at our dis-posal. Whereas at present we continually hear economists regret that the water-power of the cascades or streams of a country should be lost, but hardly ever that the muscular power of its idle inhabitants should be lost ; and, again, we see vast districts, as the south of Provence, where a strong wind * blows steadily all day long for six days out of seven throughout the year, without a windmill, while men are con-tinually employed a hundred miles to the north, in digging fuel to obtain artificial power. But the principal point of all to be kept in view is, that in every idle arm and shoulder

---

* In order fully to utilize this natural power, we only require ma-chinery to turn the variable into a constant velocity—no insurmount-able difficulty.

throughout the country there is a certain quantity of force, equivalent to the force of so much fuel; and that it is mere insane waste to dig for coal for our force, while the vital force is unused; and not only unused, but, in being so, corrupting and polluting itself. We waste our coal, and spoil our humanity at one and the same instant. Therefore, wherever there is an idle arm, always save coal with it, and the stores of England will last all the longer. And precisely the same argument answers the common one about "taking employment out of the hands of the industrious labourer." Why, what is "employment" but the putting out of vital force instead of mechanical force? We are continually in search of means of strength,—to pull, to hammer, to fetch, to carry; we waste our future resources to get this strength, while we leave all the living fuel to burn itself out in mere pestiferous breath, and production of its variously noisome forms of ashes! Clearly, if we want fire for force, we want men for force first. The industrious hands must already have so much to do that they can do no more, or else we need not use machines to help them. Then use the idle hands first. Instead of dragging petroleum with a steam-engine, put it on a canal, and drag it with human arms and shoulders. Petroleum cannot possibly be in a hurry to arrive anywhere. We can always order that, and many other things, time enough before we want it. So, the carriage of everything which does not spoil by keeping may most wholesomely and safely be done by water-traction and sailing vessels; and no healthier work can men be put to, nor better discipline, than such active porterage.

131. (2nd.) In employing all the muscular power at our disposal we are to make the employments we choose as educational as possible. For a wholesome human employment is the first and best method of education, mental as well as bodily. A man taught to plough, row, or steer well, and a woman taught to cook properly, and make a dress neatly, are already educated in many essential moral habits. Labour considered as a discipline has hitherto been thought of only for criminals; but the real and noblest function of labour is

7

to prevent crime, and not to be *Re*formatory, but **Forma-**
tory.

132. The third great principle of employment is, that whenever there is pressure of poverty to be met, all enforced occupation should be directed to the production of useful articles
only, that is to say, of food, of simple clothing, of lodging, or
of the means of conveying, distributing, and preserving these.
It is yet little understood by economists, and not at all by the
public, that the employment of persons in a useless business
cannot relieve ultimate distress. The money given to employ
riband-makers at Coventry is merely so much money withdrawn from what would have employed lace-makers at Honiton : or makers of something else, as useless, elsewhere. We
must spend our money in some way, at some time, and it
cannot at any time be spent without employing somebody.
If we gamble it away. the person who wins it must spend it ;
if we lose it in a railroad speculation, it has gone into some
one else's pockets, or merely gone to pay navvies for making
a useless embankment, instead of to pay riband or button
makers for making useless ribands or buttons ; we cannot
lose it (unless by actually destroying it) without giving employment of some kind ; and therefore, whatever quantity of
money exists, the relative quantity of employment must some
day come out of it ; but the distress of the nation signifies
that the employments given have produced nothing that will
support its existence. Men cannot live on ribands, or buttons,
or velvet, or by going quickly from place to place ; and every
coin spent in useless ornament, or useless motion, is so much
withdrawn from the national means of life. One of the most
beautiful uses of railroads is to enable A to travel from the
town of X to take away the business of B in the town of Y ;
while, in the meantime, B travels from the town of Y to take
away A's business in the town of X. But the national wealth
is not increased by these operations. Whereas every coin
spent in cultivating ground, in repairing lodging, in making
necessary and good roads, in preventing danger by sea or
land, and in carriage of food or fuel where they are required,
is so much absolute and direct gain to the whole nation. To

cultivate land round Coventry makes living easier at Honiton, and every acre of sand gained from the sea in Lincolnshire, makes life easier all over England.

4th, and lastly. Since for every idle person, some one else must be working somewhere to provide him with clothes and food, and doing, therefore, double the quantity of work that would be enough for his own needs, it is only a matter of pure justice to compel the idle person to work for his maintenance himself. The conscription has been used in many countries, to take away labourers who supported their families, from their useful work, and maintain them for purposes chiefly of military display at the public expense. Since this has been long endured by the most civilized nations, let it not be thought that they would not much more gladly endure a conscription which should seize only the vicious and idle, already living by criminal procedures at the public expense ; and which should discipline and educate them to labour which would not only maintain themselves, but be serviceable to the commonwealth. The question is simply this :—we *must* feed the drunkard, vagabond, and thief ; —but shall we do so by letting them steal their food, and do no work for it ? or shall we give them their food in appointed quantity, and enforce their doing work which shall be worth it ? and which, in process of time, will redeem their own characters, and make them happy and serviceable members of society ?

I find by me a violent little fragment of undelivered lecture, which puts this, perhaps, still more clearly. Your idle people, (it says,) as they are now, are not merely waste coal-beds. They are explosive coal-beds, which you pay a high annual rent for. You are keeping all these idle persons, remember, at far greater cost than if they were busy. Do you think a vicious person eats less than an honest one? or that it is cheaper to keep a bad man drunk, than a good man sober? There is, I suppose, a dim idea in the mind of the public, that they don't pay for the maintenance of people they don't employ. Those staggering rascals at the street corner, grouped around its splendid angle of public-house, we fancy they are no servants of ours? that we pay them no wages? that no cash out of our pockets is spent over that beer-stained counter !

Whose cash is it then they are spending? It is not got honestly by work. You know that much. Where do they get it from? Who has paid for their dinner and their pot? Those fellows can only live in one of two ways—by pillage or beggary. Their annual income by thieving comes out of the public pocket, you will admit. They are not cheaply fed, so far as they are fed by theft. But the rest of their living—all that they don't steal—they must beg. Not with success from you, you think. Wise as benevolent, you never gave a penny in "indiscriminate charity." Well, I congratulate you on the freedom of your conscience from that sin, mine being bitterly burdened with the memory of many a sixpence given to beggars of whom I knew nothing, but that they had pale faces and thin waists. But it is not that kind of street beggary that the vagabonds of our people chiefly practise. It is home beggary that is the worst beggars' trade. Home alms which it is their worst degradation to receive. Those scamps know well enough that you and your wisdom are worth nothing to them. They won't beg of you. They will beg of their sisters, and mothers, and wives, and children, and of any one else who is enough ashamed of being of the same blood with them to pay to keep them out of sight. Every one of those blackguards is the bane of a family. *That* is the deadly "indiscriminate charity"—the charity which each household pays to maintain its own private curse.

133. And you think that is no affair of yours? and that every family ought to watch over and subdue its own living plague? Put it to yourselves this way, then: suppose you knew every one of those families kept an idol in an inner room—a big-bellied bronze figure, to which daily sacrifice and oblation was made; at whose feet so much beer and brandy was poured out every morning on the ground: and before which, every night, good meat, enough for two men's keep, was set, and left, till it was putrid, and then carried out and thrown on the dunghill;—you would put an end to that form of idolatry with your best diligence, I suppose. You would understand then that the beer, and brandy, and meat, were wasted: and that the burden imposed by each household on

itself lay heavily through them on the whole community?
But, suppose farther, that this idol were not of silent and
quiet bronze only ;—but an ingenious mechanism, wound up
every morning, to run itself down in automatic blasphemies ;
that it struck and tore with its hands the people who set food
before it ; that it was anointed with poisonous unguents and
infected the air for miles round. You would interfere with
the idolatry then, straightway? Will you not interfere with
it now, when the infection that the venomous idol spreads is
not merely death—but sin ?

134. So far the old lecture. Returning to cool English, the
end of the matter is, that sooner or later, we shall have to
register our people ; and to know how they live ; and to make
sure, if they are capable of work, that right work is given
them to do.

The different classes of work for which bodies of men could
be consistently organized, might ultimately become numerous;
these following divisions of occupation may at once be suggested :—

1. *Road-making.*—Good roads to be made, wherever needed,
and kept in repair ; and the annual loss on unfrequented
roads, in spoiled horses, strained wheels, and time, done
away with.

2. *Bringing in of waste land.*—All waste lands not necessary
for public health, to be made accessible and gradually re-
claimed ; chiefly our wide and waste seashores. Not our
mountains nor moorland. Our life depends on them more
than on the best arable we have.

3. *Harbour-making.*—The deficiencies of safe or convenient
harbourage in our smaller ports to be remedied ; other har-
bours built at dangerous points of coast, and a disciplined
body of men always kept in connection with the pilot and
life-boat services. There is room for every order of intelligence in this work, and for a large body of superior officers.

4. *Porterage.*—All heavy goods, not requiring speed in transit,
to be carried (under preventive duty on transit by railroad) by
canal-boats, employing men for draught ; and the merchant-
shipping service extended by sea ; so that no ships may be

wrecked for want of hands, while there are idle ones in mischief on shore.

5. *Repair of buildings.*—A body of men in various trades to be kept at the disposal of the authorities in every large town, for repair of buildings, especially the houses of the poorer orders, who, if no such provision were made, could not employ workmen on their own houses, but would simply live with rent walls and roofs.

6. *Dressmaking.*—Substantial dress, of standard material and kind, strong shoes, and stout bedding, to be manufactured for the poor, so as to render it unnecessary for them, unless by extremity of improvidence, to wear cast clothes, or be without sufficiency of clothing.

7. *Works of Art.*—Schools to be established on thoroughly sound principles of manufacture, and use of materials, and with sample and, for given periods, unalterable modes of work ; first, in pottery, and embracing gradually metal work, sculpture, and decorative painting ; the two points insisted upon, in distinction from ordinary commercial establishments, being perfectness of material to the utmost attainable degree ; and the production of everything by hand-work, for the special purpose of developing personal power and skill in the workman.

The two last departments, and some subordinate branches of the others, would include the service of women and children.

I give now, for such farther illustration as they contain of the points I desire most to insist upon with respect both to education and employment, a portion of the series of notes published some time ago in the *Art Journal*, on the opposition of Modesty and Liberty, and the unescapable law of wise restraint. I am sorry that they are written obscurely ;—and it may be thought affectedly :—but the fact is, I have always had three different ways of writing ; one, with the single view of making myself understood, in which I necessarily omit a great deal of what comes into my head :—another, in which I say what I think ought to be said, in what I suppose to be the best words I can find for it ; (which is in reality an affected style—be it good or bad ;) and my third way of writing is to say all that comes into my head for my own pleasure, in the first words that come, retouching them afterwards into (approximate) grammar. These notes for the *Art Journal* were so written ; and I like them myself, of course ; but ask the reader's pardon for their confusedness.

135. "Sir, it cannot be better done."

We will insist, with the reader's permission, on this comfortful saying of Albert Durer's, in order to find out, if we may, what Modesty is ; which it will be well for painters, readers, and especially critics, to know, before going farther. What it is ; or, rather, who she is ; her fingers being among the deftest in laying the ground-threads of Aglaia's Cestus.

For this same opinion of Albert's is entertained by many other people respecting their own doings—a very prevalent opinion, indeed, I find it ; and the answer itself, though rarely made with the Nuremberger's crushing decision, is nevertheless often enough intimated, with delicacy, by artists of all countries, in their various dialects. Neither can it always be held an entirely modest one, as it assuredly was in the man who would sometimes estimate a piece of his unconquerable work at only the worth of a plate of fruit, or a flask of wine—would have taken even one "fig for it," kindly offered ; or given it royally for nothing, to show his hand to a fellow-king of his own, or any other craft—as Gainsborough gave the "Boy at the Stile" for a solo on the violin. An entirely modest saying, I repeat, in him—not always in us. For Modesty is "the measuring virtue," the virtue of *modes* or limits. She is, indeed, said to be only the third or youngest of the children of the cardinal virtue, Temperance ; and apt to be despised, being more given to arithmetic, and other vulgar studies (Cinderella-like) than her elder sisters : but she is useful in the household, and arrives at great results with her yard-measure and slate-pencil—a pretty little Marchande des Modes, cutting her dress always according to the silk (if this be the proper feminine reading of "coat according to the cloth"), so that, consulting with her carefully of a morning, men get to know not only their income, but their inbeing—to know *themselves*, that is, in a gauger's manner, round, and up and down—surface and contents; what is in them, and what may be got out of them; and, in fine, their entire canon of weight and capacity. That yard-measure of Modesty's lent to those who will use it, is a curious musical reed, and will go round and round waists that are slender enough, with latent melody in every joint of it, the dark root only being soundless, moist from the wave wherein

> " Null' altra pianta che facesse fronda
> O indurasse, puote aver vita." *

But when the little sister herself takes it in hand, to measure things outside of us with, the joints shoot out in an amazing manner: the four-square walls even of celestial cities being measurable enough by that reed; and the way pointed to them, though only to be followed, or even seen, in the dim starlight shed down from worlds amidst which there is no name of Measure any more, though the reality of it always. For, indeed, to all true modesty the necessary business is not inlook, but outlook, and especially *up*look: it is only her sister, Shamefacedness, who is known by the drooping lashes —Modesty, quite otherwise, by her large eyes full of wonder; for she never contemns herself, nor is ashamed of herself, but forgets herself—at least until she has done something worth memory. It is easy to peep and potter about one's own deficiencies in a quiet immodest discontent; but Modesty is so pleased with other people's doings, that she has no leisure to lament her own: and thus, knowing the fresh feeling of contentment, unstained with thought of self, she does not fear being pleased, when there is cause, with her own rightness, as with another's, saying calmly, "Be it mine, or yours, or whose else's it may, it is no matter;—this also is well." But the right to say such a thing depends on continual reverence, and manifold sense of failure. If you have known yourself to have failed, you may trust, when it comes, the strange consciousness of success; if you have faithfully loved the noble work of others, you need not fear to speak with respect of things duly done, of your own.

* *Purgatorio,* i. 103.

136. But the principal good that comes of art's being followed in this reverent feeling, is vitally manifest in the associative conditions of it. Men who know their place, can take
it and keep it, be it low or high, contentedly and firmly,
neither yielding nor grasping ; and the harmony of hand and
thought follows, rendering all great deeds of art possible—
deeds in which the souls of men meet like the jewels in the
windows of Aladdin's palace, the little gems and the large all
equally pure, needing no cement but the fitting of facets ;
while the associative work of immodest men is all jointless,
and astir with wormy ambition ; putridly dissolute, and for
ever on the crawl : so that if it come together for a time, it
can only be by metamorphosis through flash of volcanic fire
out of the vale of Siddim, vitrifying the clay of it, and fastening the slime, only to end in wilder scattering ; according to
the fate of those oldest, mightiest, immodestest of builders, of
whom it is told in scorn, " They had brick for stone, and slime
had they for mortar."

137. The first function of Modesty, then, being this recognition of place, her second is the recognition of law, and delight in it, for the sake of law itself, whether her part be to
assert it, or obey. For as it belongs to all immodesty to defy
or deny law, and assert privilege and licence, according to its
own pleasure (it being therefore rightly called " in*solent*," that
is, "custom-breaking," violating some usual and appointed
order to attain for itself greater forwardness or power), so it
is the habit of all modesty to love the constancy and " *solemnity*," or, literally, " accustomedness," of law, seeking first
what are the solemn, appointed, inviolable customs and general orders of nature, and of the Master of nature, touching
the matter in hand ; and striving to put itself, as habitually
and inviolably, in compliance with them. Out of which habit,
once established, arises what is rightly called " conscience,"
not " science " merely, but " with-science," a science " with
us," such as only modest creatures can have—with or within
them—and within all creation besides, every member of it,
strong or weak, witnessing together, and joining in the happy
consciousness that each one's work is good ; the bee also being

profoundly of that opinion ; and the lark ; and the swallow, in that noisy, but modestly upside-down, Babel of hers, under the eaves, with its unvolcanic slime for mortar ; and the two ants who are asking of each other at the turn of that little ant's-foot-worn path through the moss, " lor via e lor fortuna ; " and the builders also, who built yonder pile of cloud-marble in the west, and the gilder who gilded it, and is gone down behind it.

138. But I think we shall better understand what we ought of the nature of Modesty, and of her opposite, by taking a simple instance of both, in the practice of that art of music which the wisest have agreed in thinking the first element of education ; only I must ask the reader's patience with me through a parenthesis.

Among the foremost men whose power has had to assert itself, though with conquest, yet with countless loss, through peculiarly English disadvantages of circumstance, are assuredly to be ranked together, both for honour and for mourning, Thomas Bewick and George Cruikshank. There is, however, less cause for regret in the instance of Bewick. We may understand that it was well for us once to see what an entirely powerful painter's genius, and an entirely keen and true man's temper, could achieve, together, unhelped, but also unharmed, among the black banks and wolds of Tyne. But the genius of Cruikshank has been cast away in an utterly ghastly and lamentable manner : his superb line-work, worthy of any class of subject, and his powers of conception and composition, of which I cannot venture to estimate the range in their degraded application, having been condemned, by his fate, to be spent either in rude jesting, or in vain war with conditions of vice too low alike for record or rebuke, among the dregs of the British populace. Yet perhaps I am wrong in regretting even this : it may be an appointed lesson for futurity, that the art of the best English etcher in the nineteenth century, spent on illustrations of the lives of burglars and drunkards, should one day be seen in museums beneath Greek vases fretted with drawings of the wars of Troy, or side by side with Durer's " Knight and Death."

139. Be that as it may, I am at present glad to be able to refer to one of these perpetuations, by his strong hand, of such human character as our faultless British constitution occasionally produces, in out-of-the-way corners. It is among his illustrations of the Irish Rebellion, and represents the pillage and destruction of a gentleman's house by the mob. They have made a heap in the drawing-room of the furniture and books, to set first fire to; and are tearing up the floor for its more easily kindled planks : the less busily-disposed meanwhile hacking round in rage, with axes, and smashing what they can with butt-ends of guns. I do not care to follow with words the ghastly truth of the picture into its detail ; but the most expressive incident of the whole, and the one immediately to my purpose, is this, that one fellow has sat himself at the piano, on which, hitting down fiercely with his clenched fists, he plays, grinning, such tune as may be so producible, to which melody two of his companions, flourishing knotted sticks, dance, after their manner, on the top of the instrument.

140. I think we have in this conception as perfect an instance as we require of the lowest supposable phase of immodest or licentious art in music ; the "inner consciousness of good" being dim, even in the musician and his audience ; and wholly unsympathized with, and unacknowledged, by the Delphian, Vestal, and all other prophetic and cosmic powers. This represented scene came into my mind suddenly, one evening, a few weeks ago, in contrast with another which I was watching in its reality ; namely, a group of gentle school-girls, leaning over Mr. Charles Hallè as he was playing a variation on "Home, sweet Home." They had sustained with unwonted courage the glance of subdued indignation with which, having just closed a rippling melody of Sebastian Bach's (much like what one might fancy the singing of nightingales would be if they fed on honey instead of flies), he turned to the slight, popular air. But they had their own associations with it, and besought for, and obtained it ; and pressed close, at first, in vain, to see what no glance could follow, the traversing of the fingers. They soon thought no

more of seeing. The wet eyes, round-open, and the little scarlet upper lips, lifted, and drawn slightly together, in passionate glow of utter wonder, became picture-like,—porcelain-like,—in motionless joy, as the sweet multitude of low notes fell in their timely infinities, like summer rain. Only La Robbia himself (nor even he, unless with tenderer use of colour than is usual in his work) could have rendered some image of that listening.

141. But if the reader can give due vitality in his fancy to these two scenes, he will have in them representative types, clear enough for all future purpose, of the several agencies of debased and perfect art. And the interval may easily and continuously be filled by mediate gradations. Between the entirely immodest, unmeasured, and (in evil sense) unmannered, execution with the fist ; and the entirely modest, measured, and (in the noblest sense) mannered, or moral'd, execution with the finger ; between the impatient and unpractised doing, containing in itself the witness of lasting impatience and idleness through all previous life, and the patient and practised doing, containing in itself the witness of self-restraint and unwearied toil through all previous life ; —between the expressed subject and sentiment of home violation, and the expressed subject and sentiment of home love ; —between the sympathy of audience, given in irreverent and contemptuons rage, joyless as the rabidness of a dog, and the sympathy of audience given in an almost appalled humility of intense, rapturous, and yet entirely reasoning and reasonable pleasure ;—between these two limits of octave, the reader will find he can class, according to its modesty, usefulness, and grace, or becomingness all other musical art. For although purity of purpose and fineness of execution by no means go together, degree to degree, (since fine, and indeed all but the finest, work is often spent in the most wanton purpose—as in all our modern opera—and the rudest execution is again often joined with purest purpose, as in a mother's song to her child), still the entire accomplishment of music is only in the union of both. For the difference between that "all but" finest and "finest" is an infinite one ; and besides this, how-

ever the power of the performer, once attained, may be afterwards misdirected, in slavery to popular passion or childish-
ness, and spend itself, at its sweetest, in idle melodies, cold
and ephemeral (like Michael Angelo's snow statue in the other
art), or else in vicious difficulty and miserable noise—crack-
ling of thorns under the pot of public sensuality—still, the attainment of this power, and the maintenance of it, involve always in the executant some virtue or courage of high kind ;
the understanding of which, and of the difference between the
discipline which develops it and the disorderly efforts of the
amateur, it will be one of our first businesses to estimate
rightly. And though not indeed by degree to degree, yet in
essential relation (as of winds to waves, the one being always
the true cause of the other, though they are not necessarily of
equal force at the same time), we shall find vice in its varieties, with art-failure,—and virtue in its varieties, with art-suc-
cess,—fall and rise together : the peasant-girl's song at her
spinning-wheel, the peasant-labourer's "to the oaks and rills,"
—domestic music, feebly yet sensitively skilful,—music for
the multitude, of beneficent, or of traitorous power,—dance-
melodies, pure and orderly, or foul and frantic,—march-music,
blatant in mere fever of animal pugnacity, or majestic with
force of national duty and memory,—song-music, reckless,
sensual, sickly, slovenly, forgetful even of the foolish words it
effaces with foolish noise,—or thoughtful, sacred, healthful,
artful, for ever sanctifying noble thought with separately distinguished loveliness of belonging sound,—all these families
and gradations of good or evil, however mingled, follow, in so far
as they are good, one constant law of virtue (or "life-strength,"
which is the literal meaning of the word, and its intended one,
in wise men's mouths), and in so far as they are evil, are evil
by outlawry and unvirtue, or death-weakness. Then, passing
wholly beyond the domain of death, we may still imagine the
ascendant nobleness of the art, through all the concordant life
of incorrupt creatures, and a continually deeper harmony of
"*puissant* words and murmurs made to bless," until we reach

> "The undisturbed song of pure consent,
> Aye sung before the sapphire-coloured throne."

142. And so far as the sister arts can be conceived to have place or office, their virtues are subject to a law absolutely the same as that of music, only extending its authority into more various conditions, owing to the introduction of a distinctly representative and historical power, which acts under logical as well as mathematical restrictions, and is capable of endlessly changeful fault, fallacy, and defeat, as well as of endlessly manifold victory.

143. Next to Modesty, and her delight in measures, let us reflect a little on the character of her adversary, the Goddess of Liberty, and her delight in absence of measures, or in false ones. It is true that there are liberties and liberties. Yonder torrent, crystal-clear, and arrow-swift, with its spray leaping into the air like white troops of fawns, is free enough. Lost, presently, amidst bankless, boundless marsh—soaking in slow shallowness, as it will, hither and thither, listless, among the poisonous reeds and unresisting slime—it is free also. We may choose which liberty we like,—the restraint of voiceful rock, or the dumb and edgeless shore of darkened sand. Of that evil liberty, which men are now glorifying, and proclaiming as essence of gospel to all the earth, and will presently, I suppose, proclaim also to the stars, with invitation to them *out* of their courses,—and of its opposite continence, which is the clasp and χρυσέη περόνη of Aglaia's cestus, we must try to find out something true. For no quality of Art has been more powerful in its influence on public mind ; none is more frequently the subject of popular praise, or the end of vulgar effort, than what we call "Freedom." It is necessary to determine the justice or injustice of this popular praise.

144. I said, a little while ago, that the practical teaching of the masters of Art was summed by the O of Giotto. "You may judge my masterhood of craft," Giotto tells us, "by seeing that I can draw a circle unerringly." And we may safely believe him, understanding him to mean, that—though more may be necessary to an artist than such a power—at least *this* power is necessary. The qualities of hand and eye needful to do this are the first conditions of artistic craft.

145. Try to draw a circle yourself with the "free" hand, and with a single line. You cannot do it if your hand trembles, nor if it hesitates, nor if it is unmanageable, nor if it is in the common sense of the word "free." So far from being free, it must be under a control as absolute and accurate as if it were fastened to an inflexible bar of steel. And yet it must move, under this necessary control, with perfect, untormented serenity of ease.

146. That is the condition of all good work whatsoever. All freedom is error. Every line you lay down is either right or wrong: it may be timidly and awkwardly wrong, or fearlessly and impudently wrong: the aspect of the impudent wrongness is pleasurable to vulgar persons; and is what they commonly call "free" execution: the timid, tottering, hesitating wrongness is rarely so attractive; yet sometimes, if accompanied with good qualities, and right aims in other directions, it becomes in a manner charming, like the inarticulateness of a child: but, whatever the charm or manner of the error, there is but one question ultimately to be asked respecting every line you draw, Is it right or wrong? If right, it most assuredly is not a "free" line, but an intensely continent, restrained, and considered line; and the action of the hand in laying it is just as decisive, and just as " free " as the hand of a first-rate surgeon in a critical incision. A great operator told me that his hand could check itself within about the two-hundredth of an inch, in penetrating a membrane; and this, of course, without the help of sight, by sensation only. With help of sight, and in action on a substance which does not quiver nor yield, a fine artist's line is measurable in its proposed direction to considerably less than the thousandth of an inch.

A wide freedom, truly!

147. The conditions of popular art which most foster the common ideas about freedom, are merely results of irregularly energetic effort by men imperfectly educated; these conditions being variously mingled with cruder mannerisms resulting from timidity, or actual imperfection of body. Northern hands and eyes are, of course, never so subtle as

Southern; and in very cold countries, artistic execution is palsied. The effort to break through this timidity, or to refine the bluntness, may lead to a licentious impetuosity, or an ostentatious minuteness. Every man's manner has this kind of relation to some defect in his physical powers or modes of thought; so that in the greatest work there is no manner visible. It is at first uninteresting from its quietness; the majesty of restrained power only dawns gradually upon us, as we walk towards its horizon.

There is, indeed, often great delightfulness in the innocent manners of artists who have real power and honesty, and draw, in this way or that, as best they can, under such and such untoward circumstances of life. But the greater part of the looseness, flimsiness, or audacity of modern work is the expression of an inner spirit of licence in mind and heart, connected, as I said, with the peculiar folly of this age, its hope of, and trust in, "liberty." Of which we must reason a little in more general terms.

148. I believe we can nowhere find a better type of a perfectly free creature than in the common house fly. Nor free only, but brave; and irreverent to a degree which I think no human republican could by any philosophy exalt himself to. There is no courtesy in him; he does not care whether it is king or clown whom he teases; and in every step of his swift mechanical march, and in every pause of his resolute observation, there is one and the same expression of perfect egotism, perfect independence and self-confidence, and conviction of the world's having been made for flies. Strike at him with your hand; and to him, the mechanical fact and external aspect of the matter is, what to you it would be, if an acre of red clay, ten feet thick, tore itself up from the ground in one massive field, hovered over you in the air for a second, and came crashing down with an aim. That is the external aspect of it; the inner aspect, to his fly's mind, is of a quite natural and unimportant occurrence—one of the momentary conditions of his active life. He steps out of the way of your hand, and alights on the back of it. You cannot terrify him, nor govern him, nor persuade him, nor convince him. He

has his own positive opinion on all matters; not an unwise
one, usually, for his own ends; and will ask no advice of
yours. He has no work to do—no tyrannical instinct to
obey. The earthworm has his digging; the bee her gathering and building; the spider her cunning net-work; the ant
her treasury and accounts. All these are comparatively slaves,
or people of vulgar business. But your fly, free in the air,
free in the chamber—a black incarnation of caprice—wandering, investigating, flitting, flirting, feasting at his will, with
rich variety of choice in feast, from the heaped sweets in the
grocer's window to those of the butcher's back-yard, and from
the galled place on your cab-horse's back, to the brown
spot in the road, from which, as the hoof disturbs him, he
rises with angry republican buzz — what freedom is like
his?

149. For captivity, again, perhaps your poor watch-dog is
as sorrowful a type as you will easily find. Mine certainly is.
The day is lovely, but I must write this, and cannot go out
with him. He is chained in the yard, because I do not like
dogs in rooms, and the gardener does not like dogs in
gardens. He has no books,—nothing but his own weary
thoughts for company, and a group of those free flies, whom
he snaps at, with sullen ill success. Such dim hope as he
may have that I may yet take him out with me, will be, hour
by hour, wearily disappointed; or, worse, darkened at once
into a leaden despair by an authoritative " No "—too well
understood. His fidelity only seals his fate; if he would not
watch for me, he would be sent away, and go hunting with
some happier master: but he watches, and is wise, and faithful, and miserable: and his high animal intellect only gives
him the wistful powers of wonder, and sorrow, and desire,
and affection, which embitter his captivity. Yet of the two,
would we rather be watch-dog, or fly?

150. Indeed, the first point we have all to determine is not
how free we are, but what kind of creatures we are. It is of
small importance to any of us whether we get liberty; but of
the greatest that we deserve it. Whether we can win it, fate
must determine; but that we will be worthy of it, we may

8

ourselves determine ; and the sorrowfullest fate, of all that we can suffer, is to have it, *without* deserving it.

151. I have hardly patience to hold my pen and go on writing, as I remember (I would that it were possible for a few consecutive instances to forget) the infinite follies of modern thought in this matter, centred in the notion that liberty is good for a man, irrespectively of the use he is likely to make of it. Folly unfathomable ! unspeakable ! unendurable to look in the full face of, as the laugh of a cretin. You will send your child, will you, into a room where the table is loaded with sweet wine and fruit—some poisoned, some not? —you will say to him, " Choose freely, my little child ! It is so good for you to have freedom of choice : it forms your character—your individuality ! If you take the wrong cup, or the wrong berry, you will die before the day is over, but you will have acquired the dignity of a Free child ? "

152. You think that puts the case too sharply ? I tell you, lover of liberty, there is no choice offered to you, but it is similarly between life and death. There is no act, nor option of act, possible, but the wrong deed or option has poison in it which will stay in your veins thereafter forever. Never more to all eternity can you be as you might have been, had you not done that—chosen that. You have " formed your character," forsooth ! No ; if you have chosen ill, you have De-formed it, and that forever ! In some choices, it had been better for you that a red hot iron bar had struck you aside, scarred and helpless, than that you had so chosen. " You will know better next time ! " No. Next time will never come. Next time the choice will be in quite another aspect —between quite different things,—you, weaker than you were by the evil into which you have fallen ; it, more doubtful than it was, by the increased dimness of your sight. No one ever gets wiser by doing wrong, nor stronger. You will get wiser and stronger only by doing right, whether forced or not ; the prime, the one need is to do *that*, under whatever compulsion, until you can do it without compulsion. And then you are a Man.

153. " What ! " a wayward youth might perhaps answer, in-

credulously ; "no one ever gets wiser by doing wrong? Shall
I not know the world best by trying the wrong of it, and re-
penting? Have I not, even as it is, learned much by many of
my errors ?" Indeed, the effort by which partially you recov-
ered yourself was precious ; that part of your thought by
which you discerned the error was precious. What wisdom
and strength you kept, and rightly used, are rewarded ; and
in the pain and the repentance, and in the acquaintance with
the aspects of folly and sin, you have learned *something ;*
how much less than you would have learned in right paths,
can never be told, but that it *is* less is certain. Your liberty
of choice has simply destroyed for you so much life and
strength, never regainable. It is true you now know the
habits of swine, and the taste of husks : do you think your
father could not have taught you to know better habits and
pleasanter tastes, if you had stayed in his house ; and that the
knowledge you have lost would not have been more, as well
as sweeter, than that you have gained? But "it so forms my
individuality to be free !" Your individuality was given you
by God, and in your race ; and if you have any to speak of,
you will want no liberty. You will want a den to work in,
and peace, and light—no more,—in absolute need ; if more,
in anywise, it will still not be liberty, but direction, instruction, reproof, and sympathy. But if you have no individuality, if there is no true character nor true desire in you, then
you will indeed want to be free. You will begin early ; and,
as a boy, desire to be a man ; and, as a man, think yourself as
good as every other. You will choose freely to eat, freely to
drink, freely to stagger and fall, freely, at last, to curse yourself and die. Death is the only real freedom possible to us :
and that is consummate freedom,—permission for every particle in the rotting body to leave its neighbour particle, and
shift for itself. You call it "corruption" in the flesh ; but
before it comes to that, all liberty is an equal corruption in
mind. You ask for freedom of thought ; but if you have not
sufficient grounds for thought, you have no business to think ;
and if you have sufficient grounds, you have no business to
think wrong. Only one thought is possible to you, if you are

wise—your liberty is geometrically proportionate to your folly.

154. "But all this glory and activity of our age ; what are they owing to, but to our freedom of thought?" In a measure, they are owing—what good is in them—to the discovery of many lies, and the escape from the power of evil. Not to liberty, but to the deliverance from evil or cruel masters. Brave men have dared to examine lies which had long been taught, not because they were *free*-thinkers, but because they were such stern and close thinkers that the lie could no longer escape them. Of course the restriction of thought, or of its expression, by persecution, is merely a form of violence, justifiable or not, as other violence is, according to the character of the persons against whom it is exercised, and the divine and eternal laws which it vindicates or violates. We must not burn a man alive for saying that the Athanasian creed is ungrammatical, nor stop a bishop's salary because we are getting the worst of an argument with him ; neither must we let drunken men howl in the public streets at night. There is much that is true in the part of Mr. Mill's essay on Liberty which treats of freedom of thought ; some important truths are there beautifully expressed, but many, quite vital, are omitted ; and the balance, therefore, is wrongly struck. The liberty of expression, with a great nation, would become like that in a well-educated company, in which there is indeed freedom of speech, but not of clamour ; or like that in an orderly senate, in which men who deserve to be heard, are heard in due time, and under determined restrictions. The degree of liberty you can rightly grant to a number of men is in the inverse ratio of their desire for it ; and a general hush, or call to order, would be often very desirable in this England of ours. For the rest, of any good or evil extant, it is impossible to say what measure is owing to restraint, and what to licence, where the right is balanced between them. I was not a little provoked one day, a summer or two since, in Scotland, because the Duke of Athol hindered me from examining the gneiss and slate junctions in Glen Tilt, at the hour convenient to me ; but I saw them at last, and in quietness ; and to the

very restriction that annoyed me, owed, probably, the fact of their being in existence, instead of being blasted away by a mob-company ; while the " free " paths and inlets of Loch Katrine and the Lake of Geneva are for ever trampled down and destroyed, not by one duke, but by tens of thousands of ignorant tyrants.

155. So, a Dean and Chapter may, perhaps, unjustifiably charge me twopence for seeing a cathedral ;—but your free mob pulls spire and all down about my ears, and I can see it no more for ever. And even if I cannot get up to the granite junctions in the glen, the stream comes down from them pure to the Garry ; but in Beddington Park I am stopped by the newly erected fence of a building speculator ; and the bright Wandel, divine of waters as Castaly, is filled by the free pub- lic with old shoes, obscene crockery, and ashes.

156. In fine, the arguments for liberty may in general be summed in a few very simple forms, as follows :—

Misguiding is mischievous : therefore guiding is.

If the blind lead the blind, both fall into the ditch : there- fore, nobody should lead anybody.

Lambs and fawns should be left free in the fields ; much more bears and wolves.

If a man's gun and shot are his own, he may fire in any direction he pleases.

A fence across a road is inconvenient ; much more one at the side of it.

Babes should not be swaddled with their hands bound down to their sides : therefore they should be thrown out to roll in the kennels naked.

None of these arguments are good, and the practical issues of them are worse. For there are certain eternal laws for human conduct which are quite clearly discernible by human reason. So far as these are discovered and obeyed, by what- ever machinery or authority the obedience is procured, there follow life and strength. So far as they are disobeyed, by whatever good intention the disobedience is brought about, there follow ruin and sorrow. And the first duty of every man in the world is to find his true master, and, for his own good, submit to him ; and to find his true inferior, and, for that inferior's good, conquer him. The punishment is sure, if we either refuse the reverence, or are too cowardly and indolent to enforce the compulsion. A base nation crucifies or poisons its wise men, and lets its fools rave and rot in its streets. A wise nation obeys the one, restrains the other, and cherishes all.

157. The best examples of the results of wise normal discipline in Art will be found in whatever evidence remains respecting the lives of great Italian painters, though, unhappily, in eras of progress, but just in proportion to the admirableness and efficiency of the life, will be usually the scantiness of its history. The individualities and liberties which are causes of destruction may be recorded ; but the loyal conditions of daily breath are never told. Because Leonardo made models of machines, dug canals, built fortifications, and dissipated half his art-power in capricious ingenuities, we have many anecdotes of him ;—but no picture of importance on canvas, and only a few withered stains of one upon a wall. But because his pupil, or reputed pupil, Luini, laboured in constant and successful simplicity, we have no anecdotes of him ;—only hundreds of noble works. Luini is, perhaps, the best central type of the highly-trained Italian painter. He is the only man who entirely united the religious temper which was the spirit-life of art, with the physical power which was its bodily life. He joins the purity and passion of Angelico to the strength of Veronese : the two elements, poised in perfect balance, are so calmed and restrained, each by the other, that most of us lose the sense of both. The artist does not see the strength, by reason of the chastened spirit in which it is used; and the religious visionary does not recognize the passion, by reason of the frank human truth with which it is rendered. He is a man ten times greater than Leonardo ;—a mighty colourist, while Leonardo was only a fine draughtsman in black, staining the chiaroscuro drawing, like a coloured print : he perceived and rendered the delicatest types of human beauty that have been painted since the days of the Greeks, while Leonardo depraved his finer instincts by caricature, and re-

mained to the end of his days the slave of an archaic smile : and he is a designer as frank, instinctive, and exhaustless as Tintoret, while Leonardo's design is only an agony of science, admired chiefly because it is painful, and capable of analysis in its best accomplishment. Luini has left nothing behind him that is not lovely ; but of his life I believe hardly anything is known beyond remnants of tradition which murmur about Lugano and Saronno, and which remain ungleaned. This only is certain, that he was born in the loveliest district of North Italy, where hills, and streams, and air, meet in softest harmonies. Child of the Alps, and of their divinest lake, he is taught, without doubt or dismay, a lofty religious creed, and a sufficient law of life, and of its mechanical arts. Whether lessoned by Leonardo himself, or merely one of many, disciplined in the system of the Milanese school, he learns unerringly to draw, unerringly and enduringly to paint. His tasks are set him without question day by day, by men who are justly satisfied with his work, and who accept it without any harmful praise, or senseless blame. Place, scale, and subject are determined for him on the cloister wall or the church dome ; as he is required, and for sufficient daily bread, and little more, he paints what he has been taught to design wisely, and has passion to realize gloriously : every touch he lays is eternal, every thought he conceives is beautiful and pure : his hand moves always in radiance of blessing ; from day to day his life enlarges in power and peace ; it passes away cloudlessly, the starry twilight remaining arched far against the night.

158. Oppose to such a life as this that of a great painter amidst the elements of modern English liberty. Take the life of Turner, in whom the artistic energy and inherent love of beauty were at least as strong as in Luini : but, amidst the disorder and ghastliness of the lower streets of London, his instincts in early infancy were warped into toleration of evil, or even into delight in it. He gathers what he can of instruction by questioning and prying among half-informed masters ; spells out some knowledge of classical fable ; educates himself, by an admirable force, to the production of wildly ma-

jestic or pathetically tender and pure pictures, by which he cannot live. There is no one to judge them, or to command him : only some of the English upper classes hire him to paint their houses and parks, and destroy the drawings afterwards by the most wanton neglect. Tired of labouring carefully, without either reward or praise, he dashes out into various experimental and popular works—makes himself the servant of the lower public, and is dragged hither and thither at their will ; while yet, helpless and guideless, he indulges his idiosyncrasies till they change into insanities ; the strength of his soul increasing its sufferings, and giving force to its errors ; all the purpose of life degenerating into instinct ; and the web of his work wrought, at last, of beauties too subtle to be understood, his liberty, with vices too singular to be forgiven—all useless, because magnificent idiosyncrasy had become solitude, or contention, in the midst of a reckless populace, instead of submitting itself in loyal harmony to the Art-laws of an understanding nation. And the life passed away in darkness ; and its final work, in all the best beauty of it, has already perished, only enough remaining to teach us what we have lost.

159. These are the opposite effects of Law and of Liberty on men of the highest powers. In the case of inferiors the contrast is still more fatal : under strict law, they become the subordinate workers in great schools, healthily aiding, echoing, or supplying, with multitudinous force of hand, the mind of the leading masters : they are the nameless carvers of great architecture—stainers of glass—hammerers of iron—helpful scholars, whose work ranks round, if not with, their master's and never disgraces it. But the inferiors under a system of licence for the most part perish in miserable effort ;* a few

* As I correct this sheet for press, my *Pall Mall Gazette* of last Saturday, April 17th, is lying on the table by me. I print a few lines out of it :—

"AN ARTIST'S DEATH.—A sad story was told at an inquest held in St. Pancras last night by Dr. Lankester on the body of * * *, aged fifty-nine, a French artist, who was found dead in his bed at his rooms in * * * Street. M. * * *, also an artist, said he had known the deceased for fifteen years He once held a high position, and being anx

struggle into pernicious eminence—harmful alike to themselves
and to all who admire them ; many die of starvation ; many
insane, either in weakness of insolent egotism, like Haydon,
or in a conscientious agony of beautiful purpose and warped
power, like Blake. There is no probability of the persistence
of a licentious school in any good accidentally discovered by
them ; there is an approximate certainty of their gathering,
with acclaim, round any shadow of evil, and following *it* to
whatever quarter of destruction it may lead.

160. Thus far the notes on Freedom. Now, lastly, here is
some talk which I tried at the time to make intelligible ; and
with which I close this volume, because it will serve sufficiently to express the practical relation in which I think the
art and imagination of the Greeks stand to our own ; and will
show the reader that my view of that relation is unchanged,
from the first day on which I began to write, until now.

ious to make a name in the world, he five years ago commenced a large
picture, which he hoped, when completed, to have in the gallery at
Versailles ; and with that view he sent a photograph of it to the French
Emperor. He also had an idea of sending it to the English Royal Acad-
emy. He laboured on this picture, neglecting other work which would
have paid him well, and gradually sank lower and lower into poverty.
His friends assisted him, but being absorbed in his great work, he did
not heed their advice, and they left him. He was, however, assisted
by the French Ambassador, and last Saturday he (the witness) saw deceased, who was much depressed in spirits, as he expected the brokers
to be put in possession for rent. He said his troubles were so great that
he feared his brain would give way. The witness gave him a shilling,
for which he appeared very thankful. On Monday the witness called
upon him, but received no answer to his knock. He went again on
Tuesday, and entered the deceased's bedroom and found him dead.
Dr. George Ross said that when called in to the deceased he had been
dead at least two days. The room was in a filthy dirty condition, and the
picture referred to—certainly a very fine one—was in that room. The
post-mortem examination shewed that the cause of death was fatty de-
generation of the heart, the latter probably having ceased its action
through the mental excitement of the deceased."

The Hercules of Camarina.

Address to the Students of the Art School of South Lambeth, March 15th 1869.

161. Among the photographs of Greek coins which present so many admirable subjects for your study, I must speak for the present of one only : the Hercules of Camarina. You have, represented by a Greek workman, in that coin, the face of a man, and the skin of a lion's head. And the man's face is like a man's face, but the lion's skin is not like a lion's skin.

162. Now there are some people who will tell you that Greek art is fine, because it is true ; and because it carves men's faces as like men's faces as it can.

And there are other people who will tell you that Greek art is fine because it is not true ; and carves a lion's skin so as to look not at all like a lion's skin.

And you fancy that one or other of these sets of people must be wrong, and are perhaps much puzzled to find out which you should believe.

But neither of them are wrong, and you will have eventually to believe, or rather to understand and know, in reconciliation, the truths taught by each ;—but for the present, the teachers of the first group are those you must follow.

It is they who tell you the deepest and usefullest truth, which involves all others in time. *Greek art, and all other art, is fine when it makes a man's face as like a man's face as it can.* Hold to that. All kinds of nonsense are talked to you, now-a-days, ingeniously and irrelevantly about art. Therefore, for the most part of the day, shut your ears, and keep your eyes open : and understand primarily, what you may, I fancy, understand easily, that the greatest masters of all greatest schools —Phidias, Donatello, Titian, Velasquez, or Sir Joshua Reynolds—all tried to make human creatures as like human creatures as they could ; and that anything less like humanity than their work. is not so good as theirs.

Get that well driven into your heads ; and don't let it out again, at your peril.

163. Having got it well in, you may then farther under-stand, safely, that there is a great deal of secondary work in pots, and pans, and floors, and carpets, and shawls, and archi-tectural ornament, which ought, essentially, to be *unlike* real-ity, and to depend for its charm on quite other qualities than imitative ones. But all such art is inferior and secondary— much of it more or less instinctive and animal, and a civilized human creature can only learn its principles rightly, by know-ing those of great civilized art first—which is always the rep-resentation, to the utmost of its power, of whatever it has got to show—made to look as like the thing as possible. Go into the National Gallery, and look at the foot of Correggio's Venus there. Correggio made it as like a foot as he could, and you won't easily find anything liker. Now, you will find on any Greek vase something meant for a foot, or a hand, which is not at all like one. The Greek vase is a good thing in its way, but Correggio's picture is the best work.

164. So, again, go into the Turner room of the National Gallery, and look at Turner's drawing of "Ivy Bridge." You will find the water in it is like real water, and the ducks in it are like real ducks. Then go into the British Museum, and look for an Egyptian landscape, and you will find the water in that constituted of blue zigzags, not at all like water ; and ducks in the middle of it made of red lines, looking not in the least as if they could stand stuffing with sage and onions. They are very good in their way, but Turner's are better.

165. I will not pause to fence my general principle against what you perfectly well know of the due contradiction,— that a thing may be painted very like, yet painted ill. Rest content with knowing that it *must* be like, if it is painted well ; and take this farther general law :—Imitation is like charity. When it is done for love it is lovely ; when it is done for show, hateful.

166. Well, then, this Greek coin is fine, first, because the face is like a face. Perhaps you think there is something particularly handsome in the face, which you can't see in the

photograph, or can't at present appreciate. But there is nothing of the kind. It is a very regular, quiet, commonplace sort of face; and any average English gentleman's, of good descent, would be far handsomer.

167. Fix that in your heads also, therefore, that Greek faces are not particularly beautiful. Of the much nonsense against which you are to keep your ears shut, that which is talked to you of the Greek ideal of beauty, is among the absolutest. There is not a single instance of a very beautiful head left by the highest school of Greek art. On coins, there is even no approximately beautiful one. The Juno of Argos is a virago; the Athena of Athens, grotesque; the Athena of Corinth is insipid; and of Thurium, sensual. The Siren Ligeia, and fountain of Arethusa, on the coins of Terina and Syracuse, are prettier, but totally without expression, and chiefly set off by their well-curled hair. You might have expected something subtle in Mercuries; but the Mercury of Ænus is a very stupid-looking fellow, in a cap like a bowl, with a knob on the top of it. The Bacchus of Thasos is a drayman with his hair pomatum'd. The Jupiter of Syracuse is, however, calm and refined; and the Apollo of Clazomenæ would have been impressive, if he had not come down to us much flattened by friction. But on the whole, the merit of Greek coins does not primarily depend on beauty of features, nor even, in the period of highest art, that of the statues. You may take the Venus of Melos as a standard of beauty of the central Greek type. She has tranquil, regular, and lofty features; but could not hold her own for a moment against the beauty of a simple English girl, of pure race and kind heart.

168. And the reason that Greek art, on the whole, bores you, (and you know it does,) is that you are always forced to look in it for something that is not there; but which may be seen every day, in real life, all round you; and which you are naturally disposed to delight in, and ought to delight in. For the Greek race was not at all one of exalted beauty, but only of general and healthy completeness of form. They were only, and could be only, beautiful in body to the degree that

they were beautiful in soul (for you will find, when you read deeply into the matter, that the body is only the soul made visible). And the Greeks were indeed very good people, much better people than most of us think, or than many of us are; but there are better people alive now than the best of them, and lovelier people to be seen now than the loveliest of them.

169. Then, what *are* the merits of this Greek art, which make it so exemplary for you? Well, not that it is beautiful, but that it is Right.* All that it desires to do, it does, and all that it does, does well. You will find, as you advance in the knowledge of art, that its laws of self-restraint are very marvellous; that its peace of heart, and contentment in doing a simple thing, with only one or two qualities, restrictedly desired, and sufficiently attained, are a most wholesome element of education for you, as opposed to the wild writhing, and wrestling, and longing for the moon, and tilting at wind-mills, and agony of eyes, and torturing of fingers, and general spinning out of one's soul into fiddlestrings, which constitute the ideal life of a modern artist.

Also observe, there is entire masterhood of its business up to the required point. A Greek does not reach after other people's strength, nor out-reach his own. He never tries to paint before he can draw; he never tries to lay on flesh where there are no bones; and he never expects to find the bones of anything in his inner consciousness. Those are his first merits—sincere and innocent purpose, strong common sense and principle, and all the strength that comes of these, and all the grace that follows on that strength.

170. But, secondly, Greek art is always exemplary in disposition of masses, which is a thing that in modern days students rarely look for, artists not enough, and the public never. But, whatever else Greek work may fail of, you may be always sure its masses are well placed, and their placing has been the object of the most subtle care. Look, for instance, at the inscription in front of this Hercules of the name of the town—Camarina. You can't read it, even though you may know Greek, without some pains; for the sculptor knew well

* Compare above, § 101.

enough that it mattered very little whether you read it or not, for the Camarina Hercules could tell his own story ; but what did above all things matter was, that no K or A or M should come in a wrong place with respect to the outline of the head, and divert the eye from it, or spoil any of its lines. So the whole inscription is thrown into a sweeping curve of gradually diminishing size, continuing from the lion's paws, round the neck, up to the forehead, and answering a decorative purpose as completely as the curls of the mane opposite. Of these, again, you cannot change or displace one without mischief : they are almost as even in reticulation as a piece of basket-work ; but each has a different form and a due relation to the rest, and if you set to work to draw that mane rightly, you will find that, whatever time you give to it, you can't get the tresses quite into their places, and that every tress out of its place does an injury. If you want to test your powers of accurate drawing, you may make that lion's mane your *pons asinorum.* I have never yet met with a student who didn't make an ass in a lion's skin of himself, when he tried it.

171. Granted, however, that these tresses may be finely placed, still they are not like a lion's mane. So we come back to the question,—if the face is to be like a man's face, why is not the lion's mane to be like a lion's mane? Well, because it can't be like a lion's mane without too much trouble ;—and inconvenience after that, and poor success, after all. Too much trouble, in cutting the die into fine fringes and jags ; inconvenience after that,—because fringes and jags would spoil the surface of a coin ; poor success after all, —because, though you can easily stamp cheeks and foreheads smooth at a blow, you can't stamp projecting tresses fine at a blow, whatever pains you take with your die.

So your Greek uses his common sense, wastes no time, loses no skill, and says to you, " Here are beautifully set tresses, which I have carefully designed and easily stamped. Enjoy them ; and if you cannot understand that they mean lion's mane, heaven mend your wits."

172. See then, you have in this work, well-founded knowl-

edge, simple and right aims, thorough mastery of handicraft, splended invention in arrangement, unerring common sense in treatment,—merits, these, I think, exemplary enough to justify our tormenting you a little with Greek Art. But it has one merit more than these, the greatest of all. It always means something worth saying. Not merely worth saying for that time only, but for all time. What do you think this helmet of lion's hide is always given to Hercules for? You can't suppose it means only that he once killed a lion, and always carried the skin afterwards to show that he had, as Indian sportsmen send home stuffed rugs, with claws at the corners, and a lump in the middle which one tumbles over every time one stirs the fire. What *was* this Nemean Lion, whose spoils were evermore to cover Hercules from the cold? Not merely a large specimen of Felis Leo, ranging the fields of Nemea, be sure of that. This Nemean cub was one of a bad litter. Born of Typhon and Echidna,—of the whirlwind and the snake,—Cerberus his brother, the Hydra of Lerna his sister,—it must have been difficult to get his hide off him. He had to be found in darkness too, and dealt upon without weapons, by grip at the throat—arrows and club of no avail against him. What does all that mean?

173. It means that the Nemean Lion is the first great adversary of life, whatever that may be—to Hercules, or to any of us, then or now. The first monster we have to strangle, or be destroyed by, fighting in the dark, and with none to help us, only Athena standing by to encourage with her smile. Every man's Nemean Lion lies in wait for him somewhere. The slothful man says, there is a lion in the path. He says well. The quiet *un*slothful man says the same, and knows it too. But they differ in their farther reading of the text. The slothful man says I shall be slain, and the unslothful, IT shall be. It is the first ugly and strong enemy that rises against us, all future victory depending on victory over that. Kill it; and through all the rest of life, what was once dreadful is your armour and you are clothed with that conquest for every other, and helmed with its crest of fortitude for evermore.

Alas, we have most of us to walk bare-headed; but that is

the meaning of the story of Nemea,—worth laying to heart and thinking of, sometimes, when you see a dish garnished with parsley, which was the crown at the Nemean games.

174. How far, then, have we got, in our list of the merits of Greek art now?

Sound knowledge.

Simple aims.

Mastered craft.

Vivid invention.

Strong common sense.

And eternally true and wise meaning.

Are these not enough? Here is one more then, which will find favour, I should think, with the British Lion. Greek art is never frightened at anything, it is always cool.

175. It differs essentially from all other art, past or present, in this incapability of being frightened. Half the power and imagination of every other school depend on a certain feverish terror mingling with their sense of beauty;—the feeling that a child has in a dark room, or a sick person in seeing ugly dreams. But the Greeks never have ugly dreams. They cannot draw anything ugly when they try. Sometimes they put themselves to their wits'-end to draw an ugly thing, —the Medusa's head, for instance,—but they can't do it,— not they,—because nothing frightens them. They widen the mouth, and grind the teeth, and puff the cheeks, and set the eyes a-goggling; and the thing is only ridiculous after all, not the least dreadful, for there is no dread in their hearts. Pensiveness; amazement; often deepest grief and desolateness. All these; but terror never. Everlasting calm in the presence of all fate; and joy such as they could win, not indeed in a perfect beauty, but beauty at perfect rest! A kind of art this, surely, to be looked at, and thought upon sometimes with profit, even in these latter days.

176. To be looked at sometimes. Not continually, and never as a model for imitation. For you are not Greeks; but, for better or worse, English creatures; and cannot do, even if it were a thousand times better worth doing, anything well, except what your English hearts shall prompt, and your Eng·

lish skies teach you. For all good art is the natural utterance of its own people in its own day.

But also, your own art is a better and brighter one than
ever this Greek art was. Many motives, powers, and insights
have been added to those elder ones. The very corruptions
into which we have fallen are signs of a subtle life, higher
than theirs was, and therefore more fearful in its faults and
death. Christianity has neither superseded, nor, by itself,
excelled heathenism ; but it has added its own good, won also
by many a Nemean contest in dark valleys, to all that was
good and noble in heathenism : and our present thoughts
and work, when they are right, are nobler than the heathen's.
And we are not reverent enough to them, because we possess
too much of them. That sketch of four cherub heads from
an English girl, by Sir Joshua Reynolds, at Kensington, is an
incomparably finer thing than ever the Greeks did. Ineffably
tender in the touch, yet Herculean in power ; innocent, yet
exalted in feeling ; pure in colour as a pearl ; reserved and
decisive in design, as this Lion crest,—if *it* alone existed of
such,—if it were a picture by Zeuxis, the only one left in the
world, and you built a shrine for it, and were allowed to see
it only seven days in a year, it alone would teach you all of art
that you ever needed to know. But you do not learn from
this or any other such work, because you have not reverence
enough for them, and are trying to learn from all at once,
and from a hundred other masters besides.

177. Here, then, is the practical advice which I would venture to deduce from what I have tried to show you. Use
Greek art as a first, not a final, teacher. Learn to draw carefully from Greek work ; above all, to place forms correctly,
and to use light and shade tenderly. Never allow yourselves
black shadows. It is easy to make things look round and
projecting ; but the things to exercise yourselves in are the
placing of the masses, and the modelling of the lights. It is
an admirable exercise to take a pale wash of colour for all the
shadows, never reinforcing it everywhere, but drawing the
statue as if it were in far distance, making all the darks one
flat pale tint. Then model from those into the lights, round-

9

ing as well as you can, on those subtle conditions. In your chalk drawings, separate the lights from the darks at once all over ; then reinforce the darks slightly where absolutely necessary, and put your whole strength on the lights and their limits. Then, when you have learned to draw thoroughly, take one master for your painting, as you would have done necessarily in old times by being put into his school (were I to choose for you, it should be among six men only—Titian, Correggio, Paul Veronese, Velasquez, Reynolds, or Holbein). If you are a landscapist, Turner must be your only guide, (for no other great landscape painter has yet lived) ; and having chosen, do your best to understand your own chosen master, and obey *him*, and no one else, till you have strength to deal with the nature itself round you, and then, be your own master, and see with your own eyes. If you have got masterhood or sight in you, that is the way to make the most of them ; and if you have neither, you will at least be sound in your work, prevented from immodest and useless effort, and protected from vulgar and fantastic error.

And so I wish you all, good speed, and the favour of Hercules and of the Muses ; and to those who shall best deserve them, the crown of Parsley first and then of the Laurel.

THE STORM CLOUD OF THE
NINETEENTH CENTURY

TWO LECTURES

DELIVERED AT THE LONDON INSTITUTION,
FEBRUARY 4th AND 11th, 1884.

PREFACE.

THE following lectures, drawn up under the pressure of
more imperative and quite otherwise directed work, contain
many passages which stand in need of support, and some, I
do not doubt, more or less of correction, which I always prefer to receive openly from the better knowledge of friends,
after setting down my own impressions of the matter in clearness as far as they reach, than to guard myself against by
submitting my manuscript, before publication, to annotators
whose stricture or suggestion I might often feel pain in re-
fusing, yet hesitation in admitting.

But though thus hastily, and to some extent incautiously,
thrown into form, the statements in the text are founded on
patient and, in all essential particulars, accurately recorded
observations of the sky, during fifty years of a life of solitude
and leisure ; and in all they contain of what may seem to the
reader questionable, or astonishing, are guardedly and absolutely true.

In many of the reports given by the daily press, my assertion of radical change, during recent years, in weather aspect
was scouted as imaginary, or insane. I am indeed, every day
of my yet spared life, more and more grateful that my mind is
capable of imaginative vision, and liable to the noble dangers
of delusion which separate the speculative intellect of humanity from the dreamless instinct of brutes : but I have been
able, during all active work, to use or refuse my power of
contemplative imagination, with as easy command of it as a
physicist's of his telescope : the times of morbid are just as
easily distinguished by me from those of healthy vision, as by
men of ordinary faculty, dream from waking ; nor is there a

single fact stated in the following pages which I have not ver-
ified with a chemist's analysis, and a geometer's precision.

The first lecture is printed, with only addition here and
there of an elucidatory word or phrase, precisely as it was
given on the 4th February. In repeating it on the 11th, I am-
plified several passages, and substituted for the concluding
one, which had been printed with accuracy in most of the
leading journals, some observations which I thought calculated
to be of more general interest. To these, with the additions in
the first text, I have now prefixed a few explanatory notes, to
which numeral references are given in the pages they explain,
and have arranged the fragments in connection clear enough
to allow of their being read with ease as a second Lecture.

HERNE HILL, 12th March. 1870.

CONTENTS.

THE STORM-CLOUD OF THE NINETEENTH CENTURY.

LECTURE I.

LET me first assure my audience that I have no *arrière pensée* in the title chosen for this lecture. I might, indeed, have meant, and it would have been only too like me to mean, any number of things by such a title ;—but, to-night, I mean simply what I have said, and propose to bring to your notice a series of cloud phenomena, which, so far as I can weigh existing evidence, are peculiar to our own times ; yet which have not hitherto received any special notice or description from meteorologists.

So far as the existing evidence, I say, of former literature can be interpreted, the storm-cloud—or more accurately plague-cloud, for it is not always stormy—which I am about to describe to you, never was seen but by now living, or *lately* living eyes. It is not yet twenty years that this—I may well call it, wonderful, cloud has been, in its essence, recognizable. There is no description of it, so far as I have read, by any ancient observer. Neither Homer nor Virgil, neither Aristophanes nor Horace, acknowledges any such clouds among those compelled by Jove. Chaucer has no word of them, nor Dante ; [1] Milton none, nor Thomson. In modern times, Scott, Wordsworth and Byron are alike unconscious of them ; and the most observant and descriptive of scientific men, De Saussure, is utterly silent concerning them. Taking up the traditions of air from the year before Scott's death, I am able, by my own constant and close observation, to certify you that in the forty following years (1831 to 1871 approximately—for the phenomena in question came on gradually)—no such clouds as these are, and are now often for months without intermission, were ever seen in the skies of England, France, or Italy.

In those old days, when weather was fine, it was luxuriously fine ; when it was bad—it was often abominably bad, but it had its fit of temper and was done with it—it didn't sulk for three months without letting you see the sun,—nor send you one cyclone inside out, every Saturday afternoon, and another outside in, every Monday morning.

In fine weather the sky was either blue or clear in its light ; the clouds, either white or golden, adding to, not abating, the lustre of the sky. In wet weather, there were two different species of clouds,—those of beneficent rain, which for distinction's sake I will call the non-electric rain-cloud, and those of storm, usually charged highly with electricity. The beneficent rain-cloud was indeed often extremely dull and grey for days together, but gracious nevertheless, felt to be doing good, and often to be delightful after drought ; capable also of the most exquisite colouring, under certain conditions ; [a] and continually traversed in clearing by the rainbow:—and, secondly, the storm-cloud, always majestic, often dazzlingly beautiful, and felt also to be beneficent in its own way, affecting the mass of the air with vital agitation, and purging it from the impurity of all morbific elements.

In the entire system of the Firmament, thus seen and understood, there appeared to be, to all the thinkers of those ages, the incontrovertible and unmistakable evidence of a Divine Power in creation, which had fitted, as the air for human breath, so the clouds for human sight and nourishment ;—the Father who was in heaven feeding day by day the souls of His children with marvels, and satisfying them with bread, and so filling their hearts with food and gladness.

Their *hearts*, you will observe, it is said, not merely their bellies,—or indeed not at all, in this sense, their bellies—but the heart itself, with its blood for this life, and its faith for the next. The opposition between this idea and the notions of

our own time may be more accurately expressed by modifica-
tion of the Greek than of the English sentence. The old
Greek is—

ἐμπιπλῶν τροφῆς καὶ εὐφροσύνης
τὰς καρδίας ἡμῶν.

filling with meat, and cheerfulness, our hearts. The modern
Greek should be—

ἐμπιπλῶν ἀνέμου καὶ ἀφροσύνης
τὰς γαστέρας ἡμῶν.

filling with wind, and foolishness, our stomachs.

You will not think I waste your time in giving you two
cardinal examples of the sort of evidence which the higher
forms of literature furnish respecting the cloud-phenomena
of former times.

When, in the close of my lecture on landscape last year at
Oxford, I spoke of stationary clouds as distinguished from
passing ones, some blockheads wrote to the papers to say that
clouds never were stationary. Those foolish letters were so
far useful in causing a friend to write me the pretty one I am
about to read to you, quoting a passage about clouds in Homer
which I had myself never noticed, though perhaps the most
beautiful of its kind in the Iliad. In the fifth book, after the
truce is broken, and the aggressor Trojans are rushing to the
onset in a tumult of clamour and charge, Homer says that the
Greeks, abiding them, "stood like clouds." My correspondent, giving the passage, writes as follows :

"Sir,—Last winter when I was at Ajaccio, I was one day
reading Homer by the open window, and came upon the
lines—

Ἀλλ' ἔμενον, νεφέλῃσιν ἐοικότες ἅς τε Κρονίων
Νηνεμίης ἔστησεν ἐπ' ἀκροπόλοισιν ὄρεσσιν,
Ἀτρέμας, ὄφρ' εὕδῃσι μένος Βορέαο καὶ ἄλλων
Ζαχρειῶν ἀνέμων, οἵτε νέφεα σκιόεντα
Πνοιῇσιν λιγυρῇσι διασκιδνᾶσιν ἀέντες ·
Ὣς Δαναοὶ Τρῶας μένον ἔμπεδον, οὐδ' ἐφέβοντο.

'But they stood, like the clouds which the Son of Kronos
stablishes in calm upon the mountains, motionless, when the

rage of the North and of all the fiery winds is asleep.' As I finished these lines, I raised my eyes, and looking across the gulf, saw a long line of clouds resting on the top of its hills. The day was windless, and there they stayed, hour after hour, without any stir or motion. I remember how I was delighted at the time, and have often since that day thought on the beauty and the truthfulness of Homer's simile.

"Perhaps this little fact may interest you, at a time when you are attacked for your description of clouds.

"I am, sir, yours faithfully,

"G. B. HILL."

With this bit of noonday from Homer, I will read you a sunset and a sunrise from Byron. That will enough express to you the scope and sweep of all glorious literature, from the orient of Greece herself to the death of the last Englishman who loved her.³ I will read you from 'Sardanapalus' the address of the Chaldean priest Beleses to the sunset, and of the Greek slave, Myrrha, to the morning.

> " The sun goes down : methinks he sets more slowly,
> Taking his last look of Assyria's empire.
> How red he glares amongst those deepening clouds,⁴
> Like the blood he predicts.⁵ If not in vain,
> Thou sun that sinkest, and ye stars which rise,
> I have outwatch'd ye, reading ray by ray
> The edicts of your orbs, which make Time tremble
> For what he brings the nations, 't is the furthest
> Hour of Assyria's years. And yet how calm !
> An earthquake should announce so great a fall—
> A summer's sun discloses it. Yon disk
> To the star-red Chaldean, bears upon
> Its everlasting page the end of what
> Seem'd everlasting ; but oh ! thou TRUE sun !
> *The burning oracle of all that live,*
> *As fountain of all life*, and *symbol of*
> *Him who bestows it*, wherefore dost thou limit
> Thy lore unto calamity ?⁶ Why not
> Unfold the rise of days more worthy thine
> All-glorious burst from ocean ? why not dart
> A beam of hope athwart the future years,
> As of wrath to its days ? Hear me ! oh, hear me !
> I am thy worshipper, thy priest, thy servant—

I have gazed on thee at thy rise and fall,
And bow'd my head beneath thy mid-day beams,
When my eye dared not meet thee. I have watch'd
For thee, and after thee, and pray'd to thee,
And sacrificed to thee, and read, and fear'd thee,
And ask'd of thee, and thou hast answer'd—but
Only to thus much. While I speak, he sinks—
Is gone—and leaves his beauty, not his knowledge,
To the delighted west, which revels in
Its hues of dying glory. Yet what is
Death, so it be but glorious? 'T is a sunset;
And mortals may be happy to resemble
The gods but in decay."

Thus the Chaldean priest, to the brightness of the setting sun. Hear now the Greek girl, Myrrha, of his rising.

"The day at last has broken. What a night
Hath usher'd it! How beautiful in heaven!
Though varied with a transitory storm,
More beautiful in that variety: [7]
How hideous upon earth! where peace, and hope,
And love, and revel, in an hour were trampled
By human passions to a human chaos,
Not yet resolved to separate elements:—
'T is warring still! And can the sun so rise,
So bright, so rolling back the clouds into
Vapours more lovely than the unclouded sky,
With golden pinnacles, and snowy mountains,
And billows purpler than the ocean's, making
In heaven a glorious mockery of the earth,
So like,—we almost deem it permanent;
So fleeting,—we can scarcely call it aught
Beyond a vision, 't is so transiently
Scatter'd along the eternal vault: and yet
It dwells upon the soul, and soothes the soul,
And blends itself into the soul, until
Sunrise and sunset form the haunted epoch
Of sorrow and of love."

How often *now*—young maids of London,—do you make *sunrise* the 'haunted epoch' of either?

Thus much, then, of the skies that used to be, and clouds " more lovely than the unclouded sky," and of the temper of their observers.   I pass to the account of clouds that *are,* and—I say it with sorrow—of the *dis*temper of *their* ob-servers.

But the general division which I have instituted between bad-weather and fair-weather clouds must be more carefully carried out in the sub-species, before we can reason of it farther : and before we begin talk either of the sub-genera and sub-species, or super-genera and super-species of cloud, per-haps we had better define what *every* cloud is, and must be, to begin with.

Every cloud that can be, is thus primarily definable : "Vis-ible vapour of water floating at a certain height in the air." The second clause of this definition, you see, at once implies that there is such a thing as visible vapour of water which does *not* float at a certain height in the air.   You are all familiar with one extremely cognizable variety of that sort of vapour—London Particular ; but that especial blessing of metropolitan society is only a strongly-developed and highly-seasoned condition of a form of watery vapour which exists just as generally and widely at the bottom of the air, as the clouds do—on what, for convenience' sake, we may call the top of it ;—only as yet, thanks to the sagacity of scientific men, we have got no general name for the bottom cloud, though the whole question of cloud nature begins in this broad fact, that you have one kind of vapour that lies to a certain depth on the ground, and another that floats at a certain height in the sky.   Perfectly definite, in both cases, the surface level of the earthly vapour, and the roof level of the heavenly vapour, are each of them drawn within the depth of a fathom.   Under *their* line, drawn for the day and for the hour, the clouds will not stoop, and above *theirs,* the mists will not rise.   Each in their own region, high or deep, may expatiate at their pleasure ; within that, they climb, or decline,—within that they congeal or melt away ; but below their assigned horizon the surges of the cloud sea may not sink, and the floods of the mist lagoon may not be swollen.

That is the first idea you have to get well into your minds concerning the abodes of this visible vapour ; next, you have to consider the manner of its visibility. Is it, you have to ask, with cloud vapour, as with most other things, that they are seen when they are there, and not seen when they are not there? or has cloud vapour so much of the ghost in it, that it can be visible or invisible as it likes, and may perhaps be all unpleasantly and malignantly there, just as much when we don't see it, as when we do? To which I answer, comfortably and generally, that, on the whole, a cloud is where you see it, and isn't where you don't; that, when there's an evident and honest thunder-cloud in the north-east, you needn't suppose there's a surreptitious and slinking one in the north-west;—when there's a visible fog at Bermondsey, it doesn't follow there's a spiritual one, more than usual, at the West End : and when you get up to the clouds, and can walk into them or out of them, as you like, you find when you're in them they wet your whiskers, or take out your curls, and when you're out of them, they don't ; and therefore you may with probability assume—not with certainty, observe, but with probability—that there's more water in the air where it damps your curls than where it doesn't. If it gets much denser than that, it will begin to rain ; and then you may assert, certainly with safety, that there is a shower in one place, and not in another ; and not allow the scientific people to tell you that the rain is everywhere, but palpable in Tooley Street, and impalpable in Grosvenor Square.

That, I say, is broadly and comfortably so on the whole,— and yet with this kind of qualification and farther condition in the matter. If you watch the steam coming strongly out of an engine-funnel,[8]—at the top of the funnel it is transparent, —you can't see it, though it is more densely and intensely there than anywhere else. Six inches out of the funnel it becomes snow-white,—you see it, and you see it, observe, exactly where it is,—it is then a real and proper cloud. Twenty yards off the funnel it scatters and melts away ; a little of it sprinkles you with rain if you are underneath it, but the rest disappears ; yet it is still there ;—the surrounding air does not absorb it all into space in a moment; there is a gradually diffusing current of invisible moisture at the end of the visible stream—an invisible, yet quite substantial, vapour ; but not, according to our definition, a cloud, for a cloud is vapour *visible*.

Then the next bit of the question, of course, is, What makes the vapour visible, when it is so? Why is the compressed steam transparent, the loose steam white, the dissolved steam transparent again?

The scientific people tell you that the vapour becomes visible, and chilled, as it expands. Many thanks to them ; but can they show us any reason why particles of water should be more opaque when they are separated than when they are close together, or give us any idea of the difference of the state of a particle of water, which won't *sink* in the air, from that of one that won't *rise* in it? [9]

And here I must parenthetically give you a little word of, I will venture to say, extremely useful, advice about scientific people in general. Their first business is, of course, to tell you things that are so, and do happen,—as that, if you warm water, it will boil ; if you cool it, it will freeze ; and if you put a candle to a cask of gunpowder, it will blow you up. Their second, and far more important business, is to tell you what you had best do under the circumstances,—put the kettle on in time for tea ; powder your ice and salt, if you have a mind for ices ; and obviate the chance of explosion by not making the gunpowder. But if, beyond this safe and beneficial business, they ever try to *explain* anything to you, you may be confident of one of two things,—either that they know nothing (to speak of) about it, or that they have only seen one side of it—and not only haven't seen, but usually have no mind to see, the other. When, for instance, Professor Tyndall explains the twisted beds of the Jungfrau to you by intimating that the Matterhorn is growing flat ; [10] or the clouds on the lee side of the Matterhorn by the wind's rubbing against the windward side of it, [11]—you may be pretty sure the scientific people don't know much (to speak of) yet, either about rock-beds, or cloud-beds. And even if the explanation, so to call it, be sound on one side, windward or lee, you may, as I said, be nearly certain it won't do on the other. Take the very top and centre of scientific interpretation by the greatest of its masters: Newton explained to you—or at least was once supposed to have explained—why an apple fell ; but he never thought of explaining the exactly correlative, but infinitely more difficult question, how the apple got up there !

You will not, therefore, so please you, expect me to explain anything to you,—I have come solely and simply to put before you a few facts, which you can't see by candlelight, or in railroad tunnels, but which are making themselves now so very distinctly felt as well as seen, that you may perhaps have to roof, if not wall, half London afresh before we are many years older.

I go back to my point—the way in which clouds, as a matter of fact, become visible. I have defined the floating or sky cloud, and defined the falling, or earth cloud. But there's a sort of thing between the two, which needs a third definition : namely, Mist. In the 22nd page of his ' Glaciers of the Alps,' Professor Tyndall says that " the marvellous blueness of the sky in the earlier part of the day indicated that the air was charged, almost to saturation, with transparent aqueous vapour." Well, in certain weather that is true. You all know the peculiar clearness which precedes rain,—when the distant hills are looking nigh. I take it on trust from the scientific people that there is then a quantity—almost to saturation— of aqueous vapour in the air, but it is aqueous vapour in a state which makes the air more transparent than it would be without it. What state of aqueous molecule is that, absolutely unreflective [12] of light—perfectly transmissive of light, and showing at once the colour of blue water and blue air on the distant hills ?

I put the question—and pass round to the other side. Such a clearness, though a certain forerunner of rain, is not always its forerunner. Far the contrary. Thick air is a much more frequent forerunner of rain than clear air. In cool weather, you will often get the transparent prophecy : but in hot weather, or in certain not hitherto defined states of atmosphere, the forerunner of rain is mist. In a general way, after you have had two or three days of rain, the air and sky are healthily clear, and the sun bright. If it is hot also, the

next day is a little mistier—the next misty and sultry,—and
the next and the next, getting thicker and thicker—end in
another storm, or period of rain.

I suppose the thick air, as well as the transparent, is in both
cases saturated with aqueous vapour ;—but also in both, observe, vapour that floats everywhere, as if you mixed mud with
the sea ; and it takes no shape anywhere : you may have it with
calm, or with wind, it makes no difference to it. You have a
nasty haze with a bitter east wind, or a nasty haze with not a
leaf stirring, and you may have the clear blue vapour with a
fresh rainy breeze, or the clear vapour as still as the sky
above. What difference is there between *these* aqueous molecules that are clear, and those that are muddy, *these* that must
sink or rise, and those that must stay where they are, *these*
that have form and stature, that are bellied like whales and
backed like weasels, and those that have neither backs nor
fronts, nor feet nor faces, but are a mist—and no more—over
two or three thousand square miles?

I again leave the questions with you, and pass on.

Hitherto I have spoken of all aqueous vapour as if it were
either transparent or white—visible by becoming opaque like
snow, but not by any accession of colour. But even those of
us who are least observant of skies, know that, irrespective of
all supervening colours from the sun, there are white clouds,
brown clouds, grey clouds, and black clouds. Are these indeed—what they appear to be—entirely distinct monastic
disciplines of cloud ; Black Friars, and White Friars, and
Friars of Orders Grey? Or is it only their various nearness to us, their denseness, and the failing of the light
upon them, that makes some clouds look black [13] and others
snowy?

I can only give you qualified and cautious answer. There
are, by differences in their own character, Dominican clouds,
and there are Franciscan ;—there are the Black Hussars of
the Bandiera della Morte, and there are the Scots Greys
whose horses *can* run upon the rock. But if you ask me, as I
would have you ask me, why argent and why sable, how bap-
tized in white like a bride or a novice, and how hooded with

blackness like a Judge of the Vehmgericht Tribunal,—I leave these questions with you, and pass on.

Admitting degrees of darkness, we have next to ask what colour from sunshine can the white cloud receive, and what the black ?

You won't expect me to tell you all that, or even the little that is accurately known about that, in a quarter of an hour ; yet note these main facts on the matter.

On any pure white, and practically opaque, cloud, or thing like a cloud, as an Alp, or Milan Cathedral, you can have cast by rising or setting sunlight, any tints of amber, orange, or moderately deep rose—you can't have lemon yellows, or any kind of green except in negative hue by opposition ; and though by storm-light you may sometimes get the reds cast very deep, beyond a certain limit you cannot go,—the Alps are never vermilion colour, nor flamingo colour, nor canary colour ; nor did you ever see a full scarlet cumulus of thunder-cloud.

On opaque white vapour, then, remember, you can get a glow or a blush of colour, never a flame of it.

But when the cloud is transparent as well as pure, and can be filled with light through all the body of it, you then can have by the light reflected [14] from its atoms any force conceivable by human mind of the entire group of the golden and ruby colours, from intensely burnished gold colour, through a scarlet for whose brightness there are no words, into any depth and any hue of Tyrian crimson and Byzantine purple. These with full blue breathed between them at the zenith, and green blue nearer the horizon, form the scales and chords of colour possible to the morning and evening sky in pure and fine weather ; the keynote of the opposition being vermilion against green blue, both of equal tone, and at such a height and acme of brilliancy that you cannot see the line where their edges pass into each other.

No colours that can be fixed in earth can ever represent to you the lustre of these cloudy ones. But the actual tints may be shown you in a lower key, and to a certain extent their power and relation to each other.

I have painted the diagram here shown you with colours prepared for me lately by Messrs. Newman, which I find brilliant to the height that pigments can be ; and the ready kindness of Mr. Wilson Barrett enables me to show you their effect by a white light as pure as that of the day.   The diagram is enlarged from my careful sketch of the sunset of 1st October, 1868, at Abbeville, which was a beautiful example of what, in fine weather about to pass into storm, a sunset could then be, in the districts of Kent and Picardy unaffected by smoke.   In reality, the ruby and vermilion clouds were, by myriads, more numerous than I have had time to paint : but the general character of their grouping is well enough expressed.   All the illumined clouds are high in the air, and nearly motionless ; beneath them, electric storm-cloud rises in a threatening cumulus on the right, and drifts in dark flakes across the horizon, casting from its broken masses radiating shadows on the upper clouds.   These shadows are traced, in the first place by making the misty blue of the open sky more transparent, and therefore darker ; and secondly, by entirely intercepting the sunbeams on the bars of cloud, which, within the shadowed spaces, show dark on the blue instead of light.

But, mind, all that is done by reflected light—and in that light you never get a *green* ray from the reflecting cloud ; there is no such thing in nature as a green lighted cloud relieved from a red sky,—the cloud is always red, and the sky green, and green, observe, by transmitted, not reflected light.

But now note, there is another kind of cloud, pure white, and exquisitely delicate ; which acts not by reflecting, nor by refracting, but, as it is now called, *dif*fracting, the sun's rays. The particles of this cloud are said—with what truth I know not [15]—to send the sunbeams round them instead of through them ; somehow or other, at any rate, they resolve them into their prismatic elements ; and then you have literally a kaleidoscope in the sky, with every colour of the prism in absolute purity ; but above all in force, now, the ruby red and the *green*,—with purple, and violet-blue, in a virtual equality, more definite than that of the rainbow.   The red in the rainbow is mostly brick red, the violet, though beautiful, often lost at the edge ; but in the prismatic cloud the violet, the green, and the ruby are all more lovely than in any precious stones, and they are varied as in a bird's breast, changing their places, depths, and extent at every instant.

The main cause of this change being, that the prismatic cloud itself is always in rapid, and generally in fluctuating motion. " A light veil of clouds had drawn itself," says Professor Tyndall, in describing his solitary ascent of Monte Rosa, " between me and the sun, and this was flooded with the most brilliant dyes. Orange, red, green, blue—all the hues produced by diffraction—were exhibited in the utmost splendour.

" Three times during my ascent (the short ascent of the last peak) similar veils drew themselves across the sun, and at each passage the splendid phenomena were renewed. There seemed a tendency to form circular zones of colour round the sun ; but the clouds were not sufficiently uniform to permit of this, and they were consequently broken into spaces, each steeped with the colour due to the condition of the cloud at the place."

Three times, you observe, the veil passed, and three times another came, or the first faded and another formed ; and so it is always, as far as I have registered prismatic cloud : and the most beautiful colours I ever saw were on those that flew fastest.

This second diagram is enlarged admirably by Mr. Arthur Severn from my sketch of the sky in the afternoon of the 6th of August, 1880, at Brantwood, two hours before sunset. You are looking west by north, straight towards the sun, and nearly straight towards the wind. From the west the wind blows fiercely towards you out of the blue sky. Under the blue space is a flattened dome of earth-cloud clinging to, and altogether masquing the form of, the mountain, known as the Old Man of Coniston.

The top of that dome of cloud is two thousand eight hundred feet above the sea, the mountain two thousand six hundred, the cloud lying two hundred feet deep on it. Behind it, westward and seaward, all's clear ; but when the wind out of that blue clearness comes over the ridge of the earth-cloud, at that moment and that line, its own moisture congeals into these white—I believe, *ice*-clouds ; threads, and meshes, and tresses, and tapestries, flying, failing, melting, reappearing ; spinning and unspinning themselves, coiling and uncoiling, winding and unwinding, faster than eye or thought can follow : and through all their dazzling maze of frosty filaments shines a painted window in palpitation ; its pulses of colour interwoven in motion, intermittent in fire,— emerald and ruby and pale purple and violet melting into a blue that is not of the sky, but of the sunbeam ;—purer than the crystal, softer than the rainbow, and brighter than the snow.

But you must please here observe that while my first diagram did with some adequateness represent to you the colour facts there spoken of, the present diagram can only *explain*, not reproduce them. The bright reflected colours of clouds *can* be represented in painting, because they are relieved against darker colours, or, in many cases, *are* dark colours, the vermilion and ruby clouds being often much darker than the green or blue sky beyond them. But in the case of the phenomena now under your attention, the colours are all *brighter than pure white,*—the entire body of the cloud in which they show themselves being white by transmitted light, so that I can only show you what the colours are, and where they are,—but leaving them dark on the white ground. Only artificial, and very high illumination would give the real effect of them,—painting cannot.

Enough, however, is here done to fix in your minds the distinction between those two species of cloud,—one, either stationary,[16] or slow in motion, *reflecting unresolved* light ; the other, fast-flying, and *transmitting resolved* light. What difference is there in the nature of the atoms, between those two kinds of clouds ? I leave the question with you for to-day, merely hinting to you my suspicion that the prismatic cloud is of finely-comminuted water, or ice, [17] instead of aqueous vapour ; but the only clue I have to this idea is in the purity of the rainbow formed in frost mist, lying close to water surfaces.

Such mist, however, only becomes prismatic as common rain does, when the sun is behind the spectator, while prismatic clouds are, on the contrary, always between the spectator and the sun.

The main reason, however, why I can tell you nothing yet about these colours of diffraction or interference, is that, whenever I try to find anything firm for you to depend on, I am stopped by the quite frightful inaccuracy of the scientific people's terms, which is the consequence of their always trying to write mixed Latin and English, so losing the grace of the one and the sense of the other. And, in this point of the diffraction of light I am stopped dead by their confusion of idea also, in using the words undulation and vibration as synonyms. "When," says Professor Tyndall, "you are told that the atoms of the sun *vibrate* at different rates, and produce *waves* of different sizes,—your experience of water-waves will enable you to form a tolerably clear notion of what is meant."

'Tolerably clear'!—your toleration must be considerable, then. Do you suppose a water-wave is like a harp-string? Vibration is the movement of a body in a state of tension,—undulation, that of a body absolutely lax. In vibration, not an atom of the body changes its place in relation to another, —in undulation, not an atom of the body remains in the same place with regard to another. In vibration, every particle of the body ignores gravitation, or defies it,—in undulation, every particle of the body is slavishly submitted to it. In undulation, not one wave is like another; in vibration, every pulse is alike. And of undulation itself, there are all manner of visible conditions, which are not true conditions. A flag ripples in the wind, but it does not undulate as the sea does, —for in the sea, the water is taken from the trough to put on to the ridge, but in the flag, though the motion is progressive, the bits of bunting keep their place. You see a field of corn undulating as if it was water,—it is different from the flag, for the ears of corn bow out of their places and return to them, —and yet, it is no more like the undulation of the sea, than the shaking of an aspen leaf in a storm, or the lowering of the lances in a battle.

And the best of the jest is, that after mixing up these two notions in their heads inextricably, the scientific people apply both when neither will fit ; and when all undulation known to us presumes weight, and all vibration, impact,—the undulating theory of light is proposed to you concerning a medium which you can neither weigh nor touch !

All *communicable* vibration—of course I mean—and in dead matter : *You* may fall a shivering on your own account, if you like, but you can't get a billiard-ball to fall a shivering on *its* own account.[18]

Yet observe that in thus signalizing the inaccuracy of the terms in which they are taught, I neither accept, nor assail, the conclusions respecting the oscillatory states of light, heat, and sound, which have resulted from the postulate of an elastic, though impalpable and imponderable ether, possessing the elasticity of air.   This only I desire you to mark with attention,—that both light and sound are *sensations* of the animal frame, which remain, and must remain, wholly inexplicable, whatever manner of force, pulse, or palpitation may be instrumental in producing them : nor does any such force *become* light or sound, except in its rencontre with an animal. The leaf hears no murmur in the wind to which it wavers on the branches, nor can the clay discern the vibration by which it is thrilled into a ruby.   The Eye and the Ear are the creators alike of the ray and the tone ; and the conclusion follows logically from the right conception of their living power,— " He that planted the Ear, shall He not hear ?   He that formed the Eye, shall not He see ? "

For security, therefore, and simplicity of definition of light, you will find no possibility of advancing beyond Plato's "the power that through the eye manifests colour," but on that definition, you will find, alike by Plato and all great subsequent thinkers, a *moral* Science of Light founded, far and away more important to you than all the physical laws ever learned by vitreous revelation.   Concerning which I will refer you to the sixth lecture which I gave at Oxford in 1872, on the relation of Art to the Science of Light ('Eagle's Nest,' p. 75), reading now only the sentence introducing its subject;

—" The 'Fiat lux' of creation is therefore, in the deep sense, 'fiat anima,' and is as much, when you understand it, the ordering of Intelligence as the ordering of Vision. It is the appointment of change of what had been else only a mechanical effluence from things unseen to things unseeing,—from Stars, that did not shine, to Earth, that did not perceive,—the change, I say, of that blind vibration into the glory of the Sun and Moon for human eyes : so making possible the communication out of the unfathomable truth of that portion of truth which is good for us, and animating to us, and is set to rule over the day and over the night of our joy and our sorrow."

Returning now to our subject at the point from which I permitted myself, I trust not without your pardon, to diverge ; you may incidentally, but carefully, observe, that the effect of such a sky as that represented in the second diagram, so far as it can be abstracted or conveyed by painting at all, implies the total absence of any pervading warmth of tint, such as artists usually call 'tone.' Every tint must be the purest possible, and above all the white. Partly, lest you should think, from my treatment of these two phases of effect, that I am insensible to the quality of tone,—and partly to complete the representation of states of weather undefiled by plague-cloud, yet capable of the most solemn dignity in saddening colour, I show you, Diagram 3, the record of an autumn twilight of the year 1845,—sketched while I was changing horses between Verona and Brescia. The distant sky in this drawing is in the glowing calm which is always taken by the great Italian painters for the background of their sacred pictures ; a broad field of cloud is advancing upon it overhead, and meeting others enlarging in the distance ; these are rain-clouds, which will certainly close over the clear sky, and bring on rain before midnight : but there is no power in them to pollute the sky beyond and above them : they do not darken the air, nor defile it, nor in any way mingle with it ; their edges are burnished by the sun like the edges of golden shields, and their advancing march is as deliberate and majestic as the fading of the twilight itself into a darkness full of stars.

These three instances are all I have time to give of the

former conditions of serene weather, and of non-electric rain-cloud. But I must yet, to complete the sequence of my sub-ject, show you one example of a good, old-fashioned, healthy, and mighty, storm.

In Diagram 4, Mr. Severn has beautifully enlarged my sketch of a July thunder-cloud of the year 1858, on the Alps of the Val d'Aosta, seen from Turin, that is to say, some twenty-five or thirty miles distant. You see that no mistake is possible here about what is good weather and what bad, or which is cloud and which is sky ; but I show you this sketch especially to give you the scale of heights for such clouds in the atmo-sphere. These thunder cumuli entirely *hide* the higher Alps. It does not, however, follow that they have buried them, for most of their own aspect of height is owing to the approach of their nearer masses ; but at all events, you have cumulus there rising from its base, at about three thousand feet above the plain, to a good ten thousand in the air.

White cirri, in reality parallel, but by perspective radiating, catch the sunshine above, at a height of from fifteen to twenty thousand feet ; but the storm on the mountains gathers itself into a full mile's depth of massy cloud,—every fold of it in-volved with thunder, but every form of it, every action, every colour, magnificent :—doing its mighty work in its own hour and its own dominion, nor snatching from you for an instant, nor defiling with a stain, the abiding blue of the tran-scendent sky, or the fretted silver of its passionless clouds.

We so rarely now see cumulus cloud of this grand kind, that I will yet delay you by reading the description of its nearer aspect, in the 113th page of 'Eagle's Nest.'

" The rain which flooded our fields the Sunday before last, was followed, as you will remember, by bright days, of which Tuesday the 20th (February, 1872) was, in London, notable for the splendour, towards the afternoon, of its white cumulus clouds. There has been so much black east wind lately, and so much fog and artificial gloom, besides, that I find it is actually some two years since I last saw a noble cumulus cloud under full light. I chanced to be standing under the Victoria Tower at Westminster, when the largest mass of them floated past, that day, from the north-west; and I was more impressed then ever yet by the awfulness of the cloud-form, and its unaccountableness, in the present state of our knowledge. The Victoria Tower, seen against it, had no magnitude: it was like looking at Mont Blanc over a lamp-post. The domes of cloud-snow were heaped as definitely: their broken flanks were as grey and firm as rocks, and the whole mountain, of a compass and height in heaven which only became more and more inconceivable as the eye strove to ascend it, was passing behind the tower with a steady march, whose swiftness must in reality have been that of a tempest: yet, along all the ravines of vapour, precipice kept pace with precipice, and not one thrust another.

"What is it that hews them out? Why is the blue sky pure there,—the cloud solid here; and edged like marble: and why does the state of the blue sky pass into the state of cloud, in that calm advance?

"It is true that you can more or less imitate the forms of cloud with explosive vapour or steam; but the steam melts instantly, and the explosive vapour dissipates itself. The cloud, of perfect form, proceeds unchanged. It is not an explosion, but an enduring and advancing presence. The more you think of it, the less explicable it will become to you."

Thus far then of clouds that were once familiar; now at last, entering on my immediate subject, I shall best introduce it to you by reading an entry in my diary which gives progressive description of the most gentle aspect of the modern plague-cloud.

"Bolton Abbey, 4th July, 1875.

"Half-past eight, morning; the first bright morning for the last fortnight.

"At half-past five it was entirely clear, and entirely calm; the moorlands glowing, and the Wharfe glittering in sacred light, and even the thin-stemmed field-flowers quiet as stars, in the peace in which—

> 'All trees and simples, great and small,
>   That balmy leaf do bear,
> Than they were painted on a wall,
>   No more do move, nor steir.'

But, an hour ago, the leaves at my window first shook slightly. They are now trembling *continuously*, as those of all the trees, under a gradually rising wind, of which the tremulous action scarcely permits the direction to be defined,—but which falls and returns in fits of varying force, like those which precede a thunderstorm—never wholly ceasing ; the direction of its upper current is shown by a few ragged white clouds, moving fast from the north, which rose, at the time of the first leaf-shaking, behind the edge of the moors in the east.

"This wind is the plague-wind of the eighth decade of years in the nineteenth century ; a period which will assuredly be recognised in future meteorological history as one of phenomena hitherto unrecorded in the courses of nature, and characterized pre-eminently by the almost ceaseless action of this calamitous wind. While I have been writing these sentences, the white clouds above specified have increased to twice the size they had when I began to write ; and in about two hours from this time—say by eleven o'clock, if the wind continue,—the whole sky will be dark with them, as it was yesterday, and has been through prolonged periods during the last five years. I first noticed the definite character of this wind, and of the clouds it brings with it, in the year 1871, describing it then in the July number of 'Fors Clavigera ;' but little, at that time, apprehending either its universality, or any probability of its annual continuance. I am able now to state positively that its range of power extends from the North of England to Sicily ; and that it blows more or less during the whole of the year, except the early autumn. This autumnal abdication is, I hope, beginning : it blew but feebly yesterday, though without intermission, from the north, making every shady place cold, while the sun was burning ; its effect on the sky being only to dim the blue of it between masses of ragged cumulus. To-day it has entirely fallen ; and there seems hope of bright weather, the first for me since the end of May, when I had two fine days at Aylesbury ; the third, May 28th, being black again from morning to evening. There seems to be some reference to the blackness caused by the prevalence of this wind in the old French name of Bise, '*grey* wind'; and, indeed, one of the darkest and bitterest days of it I ever saw was at Vevay in 1872."

The first time I recognised the clouds brought by the plague-wind as distinct in character was in walking back from

Oxford, after a hard day's work, to Abingdon, in the early spring of 1871 : it would take too long to give you any account this evening of the particulars which drew my attention to them ; but during the following months I had too frequent opportunities of verifying my first thoughts of them, and on the first of July in that year wrote the description of them which begins the 'Fors Clavigera' of August, thus :—

"It is the first of July, and I sit down to write by the dismallest light that ever yet I wrote by ; namely, the light of this mid-summer morning, in mid-England (Matlock, Derbyshire), in the year 1871.

" For the sky is covered with grey clouds ;—not rain-cloud, but a dry black veil, which no ray of sunshine can pierce; partly diffused in mist, feeble mist, enough to make distant objects unintelligible, yet without any substance, or wreathing, or colour of its own. And everywhere the leaves of the trees are shaking fitfully, as they do before a thunderstorm ; only not violently, but enough to show the passing to and fro of a strange, bitter, blighting wind. Dismal enough, had it been the first morning of its kind that summer had sent. But during all this spring, in London, and at Oxford, through meagre March, through changelessly sullen April, through despondent May, and darkened June, morning after morning has come grey-shrouded thus.

"And it is a new thing to me, and a very dreadful one. I am fifty years old, and more ; and since I was five, have gleaned the best hours of my life in the sun of spring and summer mornings ; and I never saw such as these, till now.

" And the scientific men are busy as ants, examining the sun, and the moon, and the seven stars, and can tell me all about *them*, I believe, by this time ; and how they move, and what they are made of.

" And I do not care, for my part, two copper spangles how they move, nor what they are made of. I can't move them any other way than they go, nor make them of anything else, better than they are made. But I would care much and give much, if I could be told where this bitter wind comes from, and what *it* is made of.

"For, perhaps, with forethought, and fine laboratory science, one might make it of something else.

"It looks partly as if it were made of poisonous smoke; very possibly it may be : there are at least two hundred furnace chimneys in a square of two miles on every side of me. But mere smoke would not blow to and fro in that wild way. It looks more to me as if it were made of dead men's souls— such of them as are not gone yet where they have to go, and may be flitting hither and thither, doubting, themselves, of the fittest place for them.

"You know, if there *are* such things as souls, and if ever any of them haunt places where they have been hurt, there must be many about us, just now, displeased enough ! "

The last sentence refers of course to the battles of the Franco-German campaign, which was especially horrible to me, in its digging, as the Germans should have known, a moat flooded with waters of death between the two nations for a century to come.

Since that Midsummer day, my attention, however otherwise occupied, has never relaxed in its record of the phenomena characteristic of the plague-wind ; and I now define for you, as briefly as possible, the essential signs of it.

1. It is a wind of darkness,—all the former conditions of tormenting winds, whether from the north or east, were more or less capable of co-existing with sunlight, and often with steady and bright sunlight ; but whenever, and wherever the plague-wind blows, be it but for ten minutes, the sky is darkened instantly.

2. It is a malignant *quality* of wind, unconnected with any one quarter of the compass ; it blows indifferently from all, attaching its own bitterness and malice to the worst characters of the proper winds of each quarter. It will blow either with drenching rain, or dry rage, from the south,—with ruinous blasts from the west,—with bitterest chills from the north,— and with venomous blight from the east.

Its own favourite quarter, however, is the south-west, so

that it is distinguished in its malignity equally from the Bise of Provence, which is a north wind always, and from our own old friend, the east.

3. It always blows *tremulously*, making the leaves of the trees shudder as if they were all aspens, but with a peculiar fitfulness which gives them—and I watch them this moment as I write—an expression of anger as well as of fear and distress. You may see the kind of quivering, and hear the ominous whimpering, in the gusts that precede a great thunderstorm; but plague-wind is more panic-struck, and feverish; and its sound is a hiss instead of a wail.

When I was last at Avallon, in South France, I went to see 'Faust' played at the little country theatre: it was done with scarcely any means of pictorial effect, except a few old curtains, and a blue light or two. But the night on the Brocken was nevertheless extremely appalling to me,—a strange ghastliness being obtained in some of the witch scenes merely by fine management of gesture and drapery; and in the phantom scenes, by the half-palsied, half-furious, faltering or fluttering past of phantoms stumbling as into graves; as if of not only soulless, but senseless, Dead, moving with the very action, the rage, the decrepitude, and the trembling of the plague-wind.

4. Not only tremulous at every moment, it is also *intermittent* with a rapidity quite unexampled in former weather. There are, indeed, days—and weeks, on which it blows without cessation, and is as inevitable as the Gulf Stream; but also there are days when it is contending with healthy weather, and on such days it will remit for half an hour, and the sun will begin to show itself, and then the wind will come back and cover the whole sky with clouds in ten minutes; and so on, every half-hour, through the whole day; so that it is often impossible to go on with any kind of drawing in colour, the light being never for two seconds the same from morning till evening.

5. It degrades, while it intensifies, ordinary storm; but before I read you any description of its efforts in this kind, I must correct an impression which has got abroad through the papers, that I speak as if the plague-wind blew now always.

and there were no more any natural weather. On the contrary, the winter of 1878–9 was one of the most healthy and lovely I ever saw ice in ;—Coniston lake shone under the calm clear frost in one marble field, as strong as the floor of Milan Cathedral, half a mile across and four miles down ; and the first entries in my diary which I read you shall be from the 22d to 26th June, 1876, of perfectly lovely and natural weather.

" SUNDAY, 25th June, 1876.

" Yesterday, an entirely glorious sunset, unmatched in beauty since that at Abbeville,—deep scarlet, and purest rose, on purple grey, in bars ; and stationary, plumy, sweeping filaments above in upper sky, like ' *using up the brush*,' said Joanie ; remaining in glory, every moment best, changing from one good into another, (but only in colour or light—*form steady*,) for half an hour full, and the clouds afterwards fading into the grey against amber twilight, *stationary in the same form for about two hours*, at least. The darkening rose tint remained till half-past ten, the grand time being at nine.

" The day had been fine,—exquisite green light on afternoon hills.

" MONDAY, 26th June, 1876.

" Yesterday an entirely perfect summer light on the Old Man ; Lancaster Bay all clear ; Ingleborough and the great Pennine fault as on a map. Divine beauty of western colour on thyme and rose,—then twilight of clearest *warm* amber far into night, of *pale* amber all night long ; hills dark-clear against it.

"And so it continued, only growing more intense in blue and sunlight, all day. After breakfast, I came in from the well under strawberry bed, to say I had never seen anything like it, so pure or intense, in Italy ; and so it went glowing on, cloudless, with soft north wind, all day.

" 16TH JULY.

" The sunset almost too bright *through the blinds* for me to read Humboldt at tea by,—finally, new moon like a lime-light, reflected on breeze-struck water ; traces, across dark calm, of reflected hills."

These extracts are, I hope, enough to guard you against the absurdity of supposing that it all only means that I am myself soured, or doting, in my old age, and always in an ill humour.

Depend upon it, when old men are worth anything, they are better humoured than young ones : and have learned to see what good there is, and pleasantness, in the world they are likely so soon to have orders to quit.

Now then—take the following sequences of accurate description of thunderstorm, *with* plague-wind.

"22ND JUNE, 1876.

"Thunderstorm ; pitch dark, with no *blackness,*—but deep, high, *filthiness* of lurid, yet not sublimely lurid, smoke-cloud ; dense manufacturing mist ; fearful squalls of shivery wind, making Mr. Severn's sail quiver like a man in a fever fit—all about four, afternoon—but only two or three claps of thunder, and feeble, though near, flashes. I never saw such a dirty, weak, foul storm. It cleared suddenly, after raining all afternoon, at half-past eight to nine, into pure, natural weather,—low rain-clouds on quite clear, green, wet hills.

"BRANTWOOD, 13th August, 1879.

"The most terrific and horrible thunderstorm, this morning, I ever remember. It waked me at six, or a little before —then rolling incessantly, like railway luggage trains, quite ghastly in its mockery of them—the air one loathsome mass of sultry and foul fog, like smoke ; scarcely raining at all, but increasing to heavier rollings, with flashes quivering vaguely through all the air, and at last terrific double streams of reddish-violet fire, not forked or zigzag, but rippled rivulets— two at the same instant some twenty to thirty degrees apart, and lasting on the eye at least half a second, with grand artillery-peals following ; not rattling crashes, or irregular cracklings, but delivered volleys. It lasted an hour, then passed off, clearing a little, without rain to speak of,—not a glimpse of blue,—and now, half-past seven, seems settling down again into Manchester devil's darkness.

"Quarter to eight, morning.—Thunder returned, all the air collapsed into one black fog, the hills invisible, and scarcely visible the opposite shore ; heavy rain in short fits, and frequent, though less formidable, flashes, and shorter thunder. While I have written this sentence the cloud has again dissolved itself, like a nasty solution in a bottle, with miraculous and unnatural rapidity, and the hills are in sight again ; a double-forked flash—rippled, I mean, like the others—starts into its frightful ladder of light between me and Wetherlam,

as I raise my eyes.   All black above, a rugged spray cloud on
the Eaglet.   (The 'Eaglet' is my own name for the bold and
elevated crag to the west of the little lake above Coniston
mines.   It had no name among the country people, and is one
of the most conspicuous features of the mountain chain, as
seen from Brantwood.)

"Half-past eight.—Three times light and three times dark
since last I wrote, and the darkness seeming each time as it
settles more loathsome, at last stopping my reading in mere
blindness.   One lurid gleam of white cumulus in upper lead-
blue sky, seen for half a minute through the sulphurous
chimney-pot vomit of blackguardly cloud beneath, where its
rags were thinnest.

"THURSDAY, 22nd Feb., 1883.

" Yesterday a fearfully dark mist all afternoon, with steady,
south plague-wind of the bitterest, nastiest, poisonous blight,
and fretful flutter.   I could scarcely stay in the wood for the
horror of it.   To-day, really rather bright blue, and bright
semi-cumuli, with the frantic Old Man blowing sheaves of lan-
cets and chisels across the lake—not in strength enough, or
whirl enough, to raise it in spray, but tracing every squall's
outline in black on the silver grey waves, and whistling meanly,
and as if on a flute made of a file.

"SUNDAY, 17th August, 1879.

"Raining in foul drizzle, slow and steady ; sky pitch-dark,
and I just get a little light by sitting in the bow-window ; dia-
bolic clouds over everything : and looking over my kitchen
garden yesterday, I found it one miserable mass of weeds gone
to seed, the roses in the higher garden putrefied into brown
sponges, feeling like dead snails ; and the half-ripe strawber-
ries all rotten at the stalks."

6. And now I come to the most important sign of the
plague-wind and the plague-cloud : that in bringing on their
peculiar darkness, they *blanch* the sun instead of reddening
it.   And here I must note briefly to you the uselessness of observation by instruments, or machines, instead of eyes.   In
the first year when I had begun to notice the specialty of the
plague-wind, I went of course to the Oxford observatory to
consult its registrars.   They have their anemometer always on
the twirl, and can tell you the force, or at least the pace, of a

gale,'﹡by day or night. But the anemometer can only record
for you how often it has been driven round, not at all whether
it went round *steadily*, or went round *trembling*. And on that
point depends the entire question whether it is a plague breeze
or a healthy one : and what's the use of telling you whether
the wind's strong or not, when it can't tell you whether it's a
strong medicine, or a strong poison ?

But again—you have your *sun*-measure, and can tell exactly at any moment how strong, or how weak, or how want-
ing, the sun is. But the sun-measurer can't tell you whether
the rays are stopped by a dense *shallow* cloud, or a thin *deep*
one. In healthy weather, the sun is hidden behind a cloud,
as it is behind a tree ; and, when the cloud is past, it comes
out again, as bright as before. But in plague-wind, the sun is
choked out of the whole heaven, all day long, by a cloud
which may be a thousand miles square and five miles deep.

And yet observe : that thin, scraggy, filthy, mangy, miserable cloud, for all the depth of it, can't turn the sun red, as a
good, business-like fog does with a hundred feet or so of itself. By the plague-wind every breath of air you draw is
polluted, half round the world ; in a London fog the air itself
is pure, though you choose to mix up dirt with it, and choke
yourself with your own nastiness.

Now I'm going to show you a diagram of a sunset in entirely pure weather, above London smoke. I saw it and
sketched it from my old post of observation—the top garret
of my father's house at Herne Hill. There, when the wind is
south, we are outside of the smoke and above it ; and this diagram, admirably enlarged from my own drawing by my, now
in all things best aide-de-camp, Mr. Collingwood, shows you
an old-fashioned sunset—the sort of thing Turner and I used to
have to look at,—(nobody else ever would) constantly. Every
sunset and every dawn, in fine weather, had something of the
sort to show us. This is one of the last pure sunsets I ever
saw, about the year 1876,—and the point I want you to note
in it is, that the air being pure, the smoke on the horizon,
though at last it hides the sun, yet hides it through gold and
vermilion. Now, don't go away fancying there's any exagger

8

ation in that study. The *prismatic* colours, I told you, were simply impossible to paint; these, which are transmitted colours, can indeed be suggested, but no more. The brightest pigment we have would look dim beside the truth.

I should have liked to have blotted down for you a bit of plague-cloud to put beside this; but Heaven knows, you can see enough of it nowadays without any trouble of mine; and if you want, in a hurry, to see what the sun looks like through it, you've only to throw a bad half-crown into a basin of soap and water.

Blanched Sun,—blighted grass,—blinded man.—If, in conclusion, you ask me for any conceivable cause or meaning of these things—I can tell you none, according to your modern beliefs; but I can tell you what meaning it would have borne to the men of old time. Remember, for the last twenty years, England, and all foreign nations, either tempting her, or following her, have blasphemed the name of God deliberately and openly; and have done iniquity by proclamation, every man doing as much injustice to his brother as it is in his power to do. Of states in such moral gloom every seer of old predicted the physical gloom, saying, "The light shall be darkened in the heavens thereof, and the stars shall withdraw their shining." All Greek, all Christian, all Jewish prophecy insists on the same truth through a thousand myths; but of all the chief, to former thought, was the fable of the Jewish warrior and prophet, for whom the sun hasted not to go down, with which I leave you to compare at leisure the physical result of your own wars and prophecies, as declared by your own elect journal not fourteen days ago,—that the Empire of England, on which formerly the sun never set, has become one on which he never rises.

What is best to be done, do you ask me? The answer is plain. Whether you can affect the signs of the sky or not, you *can* the signs of the times. Whether you can bring the *sun* back or not, you can assuredly bring back your own cheerfulness, and your own honesty. You may not be able to say to the winds, "Peace; be still," but you can cease from the insolence of your own lips, and the troubling of your own

passions. And all *that* it would be extremely well to do, even though the day *were* coming when the sun should be as darkness, and the moon as blood. But, the paths of rectitude and piety once regained, who shall say that the promise of old time would not be found to hold for us also ?—" Bring ye all the tithes into my storehouse, and prove me now herewith, saith the Lord God, if I will not open you the windows of heaven, and pour you out a blessing, that there shall not be room enough to receive it."

LECTURE II.

MARCH 11th, 1884.

IT was impossible for me, this spring, to prepare, as I wished to have done, two lectures for the London Institution : but finding its members more interested in the subject chosen than I had anticipated, I enlarged my lecture at its second reading by some explanations and parentheses, partly represented, and partly farther developed, in the following notes ; which led me on, however, as I arranged them, into branches of the subject untouched in the former lecture, and it seems to me of no inferior interest.

1. The vapour over the pool of Anger in the 'Inferno,' the clogging stench which rises from Caina, and the fog of the circle of Anger in the 'Purgatorio' resemble, indeed, the cloud of the Plague-wind very closely,—but are conceived only as supernatural. The reader will no doubt observe, throughout the following lecture, my own habit of speaking of beautiful things as 'natural,' and of ugly ones as 'unnatural.' In the conception of recent philosophy, the world is one Kosmos in which diphtheria is held to be as natural as song, and cholera as digestion. To my own mind, and the more distinctly the more I see, know, and feel, the Earth, as prepared for the abode of man, appears distinctly ruled by agencies of health and disease, of which the first may be aided by his industry, prudence, and piety ; while the destroying laws are allowed to

prevail against him, in the degree in which he allows himself in idleness, folly, and vice. Had the point been distinctly indicated where the degrees of adversity necessary for his discipline pass into those intended for his punishment, the world would have been put under a manifest theocracy ; but the declaration of the principle is at least distinct enough to have convinced all sensitive and earnest persons, from the beginning of speculation in the eyes and mind of Man : and it has been put in my power by one of the singular chances which have always helped me in my work when it was in the right direction, to present to the University of Oxford the most distinct expression of this first principle of mediæval Theology which, so far as I know, exists in fifteenth-century art. It is one of the drawings of the Florentine book which I bought for a thousand pounds, against the British Museum, some ten or twelve years since ; being a compendium of classic and mediæval religious symbolism. In the two pages of it, forming one picture, given to Oxford, the delivery of the Law on Sinai is represented on the left hand, (*contrary to the Scriptural narrative*, but in deeper expression of the benediction of the Sacred Law to all nations,) as in the midst of bright and calm light, the figure of the Deity being supported by luminous and level clouds, and attended by happy angels : while opposite, on the right hand, the worship of the Golden Calf is symbolized by a single decorated pillar, with the calf on its summit, surrounded by the clouds and darkness of a furious storm, issuing from the mouths of fiends ;—uprooting the trees, and throwing down the rocks, above the broken tables of the Law, of which the fragments lie in the foreground.

2. These conditions are mainly in the arrangement of the lower rain-clouds in flakes thin and detached enough to be illuminated by early or late sunbeams : their textures are then more softly blended than those of the upper cirri, and have the qualities of painted, instead of burnished or inflamed, colour.

They were thus described in the 4th chapter of the 7th part of ' Modern Painters ' :—

" Often in our English mornings, the rain-clouds in the

dawn form soft level fields, which melt imperceptibly into the blue ; or when of less extent, gather into apparent bars, crossing the sheets of broader cloud above ; and all these bathed throughout in an unspeakable light of pure rose-colour, and purple, and amber, and blue, not shining, but misty-soft, the barred masses, when seen nearer, found to be woven in tresses of cloud, like floss silk, looking as if each knot were a little swathe or sheaf of lighted rain.

No clouds form such skies, none are so tender, various, inimitable ; Turner himself never caught them. Correggio, putting out his whole strength, could have painted them,— no other man."

3. I did not, in writing this sentence, forget Mr. Gladstone's finely scholastic enthusiasm for Homer ; nor Mr. Newton's for Athenian—(I wish it had not been also for Halicarnassian) sculpture. But Byron loved Greece herself—through her death—and *to* his own ; while the subsequent refusal of England to give Greece one of our own princes for a king, has always been held by me the most ignoble, cowardly, and lamentable, of all our base commercial *im*policies.

4. 'Deepening' clouds.—Byron never uses an epithet vainly, —he is the most accurate, and therefore the most powerful, of all modern describers. The deepening of the cloud is essentially necessary to the redness of the orb. Ordinary observers are continually unaware of this fact, and imagine that a red sun can be darker than the sky round it ! Thus Mr. Gould, though a professed naturalist, and passing most of his life in the open air, over and over again, in his ' British Birds,' draws the setting sun dark on the sky !

5. ' Like the blood he predicts.'—The astrological power of the planet Mars was of course ascribed to it in the same connection with its red colour. The reader may be interested to see the notice, in 'Modern Painters,' of Turner's constant use of the same symbol ; partly an expression of his own personal feeling, partly the employment of a symbolic language known to all careful readers of solar and stellar tradition.

" He was very definitely in the habit of indicating the association of any subject with circumstances of death, especially the death of multitudes, by placing it under one of his most deeply *crimsoned* sunset skies.

The colour of blood is thus plainly taken for the leading tone in the storm-clouds above the 'Slave-ship.' It occurs with similar distinctness in the much earlier picture of 'Ulysses and Polypheme,' in that of 'Napoleon at St. Helena,' and, subdued by softer hues, in the 'Old Téméraire.'

The sky of this Goldau is, in its scarlet and crimson, the deepest in tone of all that I know in Turner's drawings.

Another feeling, traceable in several of his former works, is an acute sense of the contrast between the careless interests and idle pleasures of daily life, and the state of those whose time for labour, or knowledge, or delight, is passed for ever. There is evidence of this feeling in the introduction of the boys at play in the churchyard of Kirkby Lonsdale, and the boy climbing for his kite among the thickets above the little mountain churchyard of Brignal-banks ; it is in the same tone of thought that he has placed here the two figures fishing, leaning against these shattered flanks of rock,—the sepulchral stones of the great mountain Field of Death."

6. 'Thy lore unto calamity.'—It is, I believe, recognised by all who have in any degree become interested in the traditions of Chaldean astrology, that its warnings were distinct, —its promises deceitful. Horace thus warns Leuconoe against reading the Babylonian numbers to learn the time of her death,—he does not imply their promise of previous happiness ; and the continually deceptive character of the Delphic oracle itself, tempted always rather to fatal than to fortunate conduct, unless the inquirer were more than wise in his reading. Byron gathers into the bitter question all the sorrow of former superstition, while in the lines italicized, just above, he sums in the briefest and plainest English, all that we yet know, or may wisely think, about the Sun. It is the '*Burning* oracle' (other oracles there are by sound, or feeling, but this by fire) of all that live ; the only means of our accurate knowledge of the things round us, and that affect our lives : it is the *fountain* of all life,—Byron does not say the *origin* ;— the origin of life would be the origin of the sun itself ; but it is

the visible *source* of vital energy, as the spring is of a stream, though the origin is the sea. " And symbol of Him who bestows it."—This the sun has always been, to every one who believes there is a bestower ; and a symbol so perfect and beautiful that it may also be thought of as partly an apocalypse.

7. 'More beautiful in that variety.'—This line, with the one italicized beneath, expresses in Myrrha's mind, the feeling which I said, in the outset, every thoughtful watcher of heaven necessarily had in those old days ; whereas now, the variety is for the most part, only in modes of disagreeableness ; and the vapour, instead of adding light to the unclouded sky, takes away the aspect and destroys the functions of sky altogether.

8. 'Steam out of an engine funnel.'—Compare the sixth paragraph of Professor Tyndall's 'Forms of Water,' and the following seventh one, in which the phenomenon of transparent steam becoming opaque is thus explained. " Every bit of steam shrinks, when chilled, to a much more minute particle of water. The liquid particles thus produced form a kind of water dust of exceeding fineness, which floats in the air, and is called a cloud."

But the author does not tell us, in the first place, what is the shape or nature of a 'bit of steam,' nor, in the second place, how the contraction of the individual bits of steam is effected without any diminution of the whole mass of them, but on the contrary, during its steady *expansion ;* in the third place he assumes that the particles of water dust are solid, not vesicular, which is not yet ascertained ; in the fourth place, he does not tell us how their number and size are related to the quantity of invisible moisture in the air ; in the fifth place, he does not tell us how cool invisible moisture differs from hot invisible moisture ; and in the sixth, he does not tell us why the cool visible moisture stays while the hot visible moisture melts away. So much for the present state of 'scientific' information, or at least communicativeness, on the first and simplest conditions of the problem before us !

In its wider range that problem embraces the total mystery

of volatile power in substance; and of the visible states consequent on sudden—and presumably, therefore, imperfect—
vaporization; as the smoke of frankincense, or the sacred
fume of modern devotion which now fills the inhabited world,
as that of the rose and violet its deserts. What,—it would be
useful to know, is the actual bulk of an atom of orange per-
fume?—what of one of vaporized tobacco, or gunpowder?—
and where do *these* artificial vapours fall back in beneficent
rain? or through what areas of atmosphere exist, as invisible,
though perhaps not innocuous, cloud?

All these questions were put, closely and precisely, four-
and-twenty years ago, in the 1st chapter of the 7th part of
'Modern Painters,' paragraphs 4 to 9, of which I can here
allow space only for the last, which expresses the final difficulties of the matter better than anything said in this lecture :—

"But farther: these questions of volatility, and visibility
and hue, are all complicated with those of shape. How is a
cloud outlined? Granted whatever you choose to ask, concerning its material, or its aspect, its loftiness and luminous-
ness,—how of its limitation? What hews it into a heap, or
spins it into a web? Cold is usually shapeless, I suppose,
extending over large spaces equally, or with gradual diminution. You cannot have in the open air, angles, and wedges,
and coils, and cliffs, of cold. Yet the vapour stops suddenly,
sharp and steep as a rock, or thrusts itself across the gates of
heaven in likeness of a brazen bar; or braids itself in and out,
and across and across, like a tissue of tapestry; or falls into
ripples, like sand; or into waving shreds and tongues, as fire.
On what anvils and wheels is the vapour pointed, twisted,
hammered, whirled, as the potter's clay? By what hands is
the incense of the sea built up into domes of marble?"

9. The opposed conditions of the higher and lower orders
of cloud, with the balanced intermediate one, are beautifully
seen on mountain summits of rock or earth. On snowy ones
they are far more complex: but on rock summits there are
three distinct forms of attached cloud in serene weather; the
first that of cloud veil laid over them, and *falling* in folds

through their ravines, (the obliquely descending clouds of the entering chorus in Aristophanes) ; secondly, the ascending cloud, which develops itself loosely and independently as it rises, and does not attach itself to the hillside, while the falling veil cloud clings to it close all the way down ;—and lastly the throned cloud, which rests indeed on the mountain summit, with its base, but rises high above into the sky, continually changing its outlines, but holding its seat perhaps all day long.

These three forms of cloud belong exclusively to calm weather ; attached drift cloud, (see Note 11) can only be formed in the wind.

10. 'Glaciers of the Alps,' page 10.—" Let a pound weight be placed upon a cube of granite " (size of supposed cube not mentioned), " the cube is flattened, though in an infinitesimal degree. Let the weight be removed, the cube remains a little flattened. Let us call the cube thus flattened No. 1. Starting with No. 1 as a new mass, let the pound weight be laid upon it. We have a more flattened mass, No. 2. . . . Apply this to squeezed rocks, to those, for example, which form the base of an obelisk like the Matterhorn,—the conclusion seems inevitable *that the mountain is sinking by its own weight*, etc., etc. Similarly the Nelson statue must be gradually flattening the Nelson column,—and in time Cleopatra's needle will be as flat as her pincushion.

11. 'Glaciers of the Alps,' page 146.—" The sun was near the western horizon, and I remained alone upon the Grat to see his last beams illuminate the mountains, which, with one exception, were without a trace of cloud.

This exception was the Matterhorn, the appearance of which was extremely instructive. The obelisk appeared to be divided in two halves by a vertical line, drawn from its summit half-way down, to the windward of which we had the bare cliffs of the mountain ; and to the left of it a cloud which appeared to cling tenaciously to the rocks.

In reality, however, there was no clinging ; the condensed vapour incessantly got away, but it was ever renewed, and thus a river of cloud had been sent from the mountain over the valley of Aosta. The wind, in fact, blew lightly up the valley of St. Nicholas, charged with moisture, and when the air that held it *rubbed against the cold cone* of the Matterhorn, the vapour was chilled and precipitated in his lee."

It is not explained, why the wind was not chilled by rubbing against any of the neighbouring mountains, nor why the cone of the Matterhorn, mostly of rock, should be colder than cones of snow. The phenomenon was first described by De Saussure, who gives the same explanation as Tyndall; and from whom, in the first volume of 'Modern Painters,' I adopted it without sufficient examination. Afterwards I re-examined it, and showed its fallacy, with respect to the cap or helmet cloud, in the fifth volume of 'Modern Painters,' page 142, in the terms given in the subjoined note,* but I still retained the explanation of Saussure for the lee-side cloud, engraving in plate 69 the modes of its occurrence on the Aiguille Dru, of which the most ordinary one saw afterwards represented by Tyndall in his 'Glaciers of the Alps,' under the title of 'Banner-cloud.' Its less imaginative title, in 'Modern Painters,' of

---

* "But both Saussure and I ought to have known,—we did know, but did not think of it,—that the covering or cap-cloud forms on hot summits as well as cold ones;—that the red and bare rocks of Mont Pilate, hotter, certainly, after a day's sunshine than the cold storm-wind which sweeps to them from the Alps, nevertheless have been renowned for their helmet of cloud, ever since the Romans watched the cloven summit, grey against the south, from the ramparts of Vindonissa, giving it the name from which the good Catholics of Lucerne have warped out their favourite piece of terrific sacred biography. And both my master and I should also have reflected that if our theory about its formation had been generally true, the helmet cloud ought to form on every cold summit, at the approach of rain, in approximating proportions to the bulk of the glaciers; which is so far from being the case that not only (A) the cap-cloud may often be seen on lower summits of grass or rock, while the higher ones are splendidly clear (which may be accounted for by supposing the wind containing the moisture not to have risen so high); but (B) the cap-cloud always shows a preference for hills of a conical form, such as the Mole or Niesen, which can have very little power in chilling the air, even supposing they were cold themselves; while it will entirely refuse to form huge masses of mountain, which, supposing them of chilly temperament, must have discomforted the atmosphere in their neighbourhood for leagues.

'Lee-side cloud,' is more comprehensive, for this cloud forms often under the brows of far-terraced precipices, where it has no resemblance to a banner. No true explanation of it has ever yet been given; for the first condition of the problem has hitherto been unobserved,—namely, that such cloud is constant in certain states of weather, under precipitous rocks; —but never developed with distinctness by domes of snow.

But my former expansion of Saussure's theory is at least closer to the facts than Professor Tyndall's "rubbing against the rocks," and I therefore allow room for it here, with its illustrative woodcut.

"When a moist wind blows in clear weather over a cold summit, it has not time to get chilled as it approaches the rock, and therefore the air remains clear, and the sky bright on the windward side; but under the lee of the peak, there is partly a back eddy, and partly still air; and in that lull and eddy the wind gets time to be chilled by the rock, and the cloud appears, as a boiling mass of white vapour, rising continually with the return current to the upper edge of the mountain, where it is caught by the straight wind and partly torn, partly melted away in broken fragments.

"In the accompanying figure, the dark mass represents the mountain peak, the arrow the main direction of the wind, the

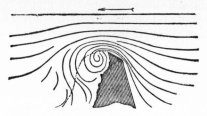

curved lines show the directions of such current and its concentration, and the dotted line encloses the space in which cloud forms densely, floating away beyond and above in irregular tongues and flakes."

12. See below, on the different uses of the word 'reflection,' note 14, and note that throughout this lecture I use the words 'aqueous molecules,' alike of water liquid or vaporized, not

knowing under what conditions or at what temperatures water-dust becomes water-gas ; and still less, supposing pure water-gas blue, and pure air blue, what are the changes in either which make them what sailors call " dirty ; " but it is one of the worst omissions of the previous lecture, that I have not stated among the characters of the plague-cloud that it is *always* dirty,* and *never blue under any conditions,* neither when deep in the distance, nor when in the electric states which produce sulphurous blues in natural cloud. But see the next note.

13. Black clouds.—For the sudden and extreme local black-ness of thundercloud, see Turner's drawing of Winchelsea, (England series), and compare Homer, of the Ajaces, in the 4th book of the Iliad,—(I came on the passage in verifying Mr. Hill's quotation from the 5th.)

> " ἅμα δὲ νέφος εἵπετο πεζῶν.
> Ὡς δ' ὅτ' ἀπὸ σκοπιῆς εἶδεν νέφος αἰπόλος ἀνὴρ
> Ἐρχόμενον κατὰ πόντον ὑπὸ Ζεφύροιο ἰωῆς,
> Τῷ δέ τ', ἄνευθεν ἐόντι, μελάντερον, ἠΰτε πίσσα
> Φαίνετ', ἰὸν κατὰ πόντον, ἄγει δέ τε λαίλαπα πολλήν·
> Ῥίγησέν τε ἰδὼν, ὑπό τε σπέος ἤλασε μῆλα·
> Τοῖαι ἅμ Αἰάντεσσιν ἀρηϊθόων αἰζηῶν
> Δήϊον ἐς πόλεμον πυκιναὶ κίνυντο φάλαγγες
> Κυάνεαι,"

I give Chapman's version—noting only that his *breath* of Zephyrus, ought to have been ' cry ' or ' roar ' of Zephyrus, the blackness of the cloud being as much connected with the wildness of the wind as, in the formerly quoted passage, its brightness with calm of air.

> " Behind them hid the ground
> A cloud of foot, that seemed to smoke.   And as a Goatherd spies
> On some hill top, out of the sea a rainy vapour rise,
> Driven by the breath of Zephyrus, which though far off he rest,
> Comes on as black as pitch, and brings a tempest in his breast
> Whereat he, frighted, drives his herds apace into a den ;
> So, darkening earth, with swords and shields, showed these with all
> their men."

* In my final collation of the lectures given at Oxford last year on the Art of England, I shall have occasion to take notice of the effects of this character of plague-cloud on our younger painters, who have perhaps never in their lives seen a *clean* sky !

I add here Chapman's version of the other passage, which
is extremely beautiful and close to the text, while Pope's is
hopelessly erroneous.

> " Their ground they still made good,
> And in their silence and set powers, like fair still clouds they stood,
> With which Jove crowns the tops of hills in any quiet day
> When Boreas, and the ruder winds that use to drive away
> Air's *dusky vapours, being loose,* in many a whistling gale,
> Are pleasingly bound up and calm, and not a breath exhale."

14. 'Reflected.'—The reader must be warned in this place
of the difference implied by my use of the word 'cast' in
page 17, and 'reflected' here : that is to say, between light
or colour which an object possesses, whatever the angle it is
seen at, and the light which it reverberates at one angle only.
The Alps, under the rose * of sunset, are exactly of the same
colour whether you see them from Berne or Schaffhausen.
But the gilding to our eyes of a burnished cloud depends, I
believe, at least for a measure of its lustre, upon the angle at
which the rays incident upon it are reflected to the eye, just
as much as the glittering of the sea beneath it—or the sparkling of the windows of the houses on the shore.

Previously, at page 15, in calling the molecules of trans-

---

* In speaking, at p. 17 of the first lecture, of the limits of depth in the
rose-colour cast on snow, I ought to have noted the greater strength of
the tint possible under the light of the tropics. The following passage,
in Mr. Cunningham's 'Natural History of the Strait of Magellan,' is to
me of the greatest interest, because of the beautiful effect described as
seen on the occasion of his visit to "the small town of Santa Rosa,"
(near Valparaiso.) "The day, though clear, had not been sunny, so
that, although the snowy heights of the Andes had been distinctly visible throughout the greater part of our journey, they had not been illuminated by the rays of the sun. But now, as we turned the corner of
a street, the chain of the Cordillera suddenly burst on our gaze in such
a blaze of splendour that it almost seemed as if the windows of heaven
had been opened for a moment, permitting a flood of *crimson* light to
stream forth upon the snow. The sight was so unexpected, and so
transcendently magnificent, that a breathless silence fell upon us for a
few moments, while even the driver stopped his horses. This deep red
glow lasted for three or four minutes, and then rapidly faded into that
lovely rosy hue so characteristic of snow at sunset among the Alps."

parent atmospheric 'absolutely' unreflective of light, I mean, in like manner, unreflective from their *surfaces*. Their blue colour seen against a dark ground is indeed a kind of reflection, but one of which I do not understand the nature. It is seen most simply in wood smoke, blue against trees, brown against clear light; but in both cases the colour is communi cated to (or left in) the *transmitted* rays.

So also the green of the sky (p. 18) is said to be given by transmitted light, yellow rays passing through blue air : much yet remains to be known respecting translucent colours of this kind ; only let them always be clearly distinguished in our minds from the firmly possessed colour of opaque substances, like grass or malachite.

15. Diffraction.—Since these passages were written, I have been led, in conversation with a scientific friend, to doubt my statement that the coloured portions of the lighted clouds were brighter than the white ones. He was convinced that the resolution of the rays would diminish their power, and in *thinking* over the matter, I am disposed to agree with him, although my impression at the time has been always that the diffracted colours rose out of the white, as a rainbow does out of the grey. But whatever the facts may be, in this respect the statement in the text of the impossibility of representing diffracted colour in painting is equally true. It may be that the resolved hues are darker than the white, as coloured panes in a window are darker than the colourless glass, but all are alike in a key which no artifice of painting can approach.

For the rest, the phenomena of diffraction are not yet arranged systematically enough to be usefully discussed : some of them involving the resolution of the light, and others merely its intensification. My attention was first drawn to them near St. Laurent, on the Jura mountains, by the vivid reflection, (so it seemed), of the image of the sun from a particular point of a cloud in the west, after the sun itself was beneath the horizon : but in this image there were no prismatic colours, neither is the constantly seen metamorphosis of pine forests into silver filigree on ridges behind which the sun is rising or setting, accompanied with any prismatic hue ; the trees become luminous, but not iridescent : on the other hand, in his great account of his ascent of Mont Blanc with Mr. Huxley, Professor Tyndall thus describes the sun's remarkable behaviour on that occasion :—" As we attained the brow which forms the entrance to the Grand Plateau, he *hung his disk upon a spike of rock* to our left, and, surrounded by a glory of interference spectra of the most gorgeous colours, blazed down upon us." ('Glaciers of the Alps,' p. 76.)

Nothing irritates me more, myself, than having the colour of my own descriptions of phenomena in anywise attributed by the reader to accidental states either of my mind or body ; —but I cannot, for once, forbear at least the innocent question to Professor Tyndall, whether the extreme beauty of these 'interference spectra' may not have been partly owing to the extreme *sobriety* of the observer ? no refreshment, it appears, having been attainable the night before at the Grands Mulets, except the beverage diluted with dirty snow, of which I have elsewhere quoted the Professor's pensive report,—" my memory of that tea is not pleasant."

16. 'Either stationary or slow in motion, reflecting unresolved light.'

The rate of motion is of course not essentially connected with the method of illumination ; their connection, in this instance, needs explanation of some points which could not be dealt with in the time of a single lecture.

It is before said, with reserve only, that " a cloud is where it is seen, and is not where it is not seen." But thirty years ago, in 'Modern Painters,' I pointed out (see the paragraph quoted in note 8th), the extreme difficulty of arriving at the cause of cloud outline, or explaining how, if we admitted at any given moment the atmospheric moisture to be generally diffused, it could be chilled by formal *chills* into formal clouds. How, for instance, in the upper cirri, a thousand little chills, alternating with a thousand little warmths, could stand still as a thousand little feathers.

But the first step to any elucidation of the matter is in the firmly fixing in our minds the difference between windless clouds, unaffected by any conceivable local accident, and windy clouds, affected by some change in their circumstances as they move.

In the sunset at Abbeville, represented in my first diagram, the air is absolutely calm at the ground surface, and the motion of its upper currents extremely slow. There is no local reason assignable for the presence of the cirri above, or of the thundercloud below. There is no conceivable cause either in the geology, or the moral character, of the two sides of the town of Abbeville, to explain why there should be decorative fresco on the sky over the southern suburb, and a muttering heap of gloom and danger over the northern. The electric cloud is as calm in motion as the harmless one : it changes its form, indeed ; but imperceptibly ; and, so far as can be discerned, only at its own will is exalted, and with its own consent abased.

But in my second diagram are shown forms of vapour sustaining at every instant all kinds of varying local influences; beneath, fastened down by mountain attraction, above, flung afar by distracting winds ; here, spread abroad into blanched sheets beneath the sunshine, and presently gathered into strands of coiled cordage in the shade. Their total existence is in metamorphosis, and their every aspect a surprise, or a deceit.

17. 'Finely comminuted water or *ice.*'

My impression that these clouds were glacial was at once confirmed by a member of my audience, Dr. John Rae, in conversation after the lecture, in which he communicated to me the perfectly definite observations which he has had the kindness to set down with their dates for me, in the following letter :—

"4, ADDISON GARDENS, KENSINGTON, 4th Feb., 1884.

DEAR SIR,—I have looked up my old journal of thirty years ago, written in pencil because it was impossible to keep ink unfrozen in the snow-hut in which I passed the winter of 1853–4, at Repulse Bay, on the Arctic Circle.*

* I trust that Dr. Rae will forgive my making the reader better aware of the real value of this communication by allowing him to see also the

On the 1st of February, 1854, I find the following :—

'A beautiful appearance of some cirrus clouds near the sun, the central part of the cloud being of a fine pink or red, then green, and pink fringe. This continued for about a quarter of an hour. The same was observed on the 27th of the month, but not so bright. Distance of clouds from sun, from 3° to 6°.'

On the 1st February the temperature was 38° below zero, and on the 27th February 26° below.

'On the 23rd and 30th (of March) the same splendid appearance of clouds as mentioned in last month's journal was observed. On the first of these days, about 10.30 A.M., it was extremely beautiful. The clouds were about 8° or 10° from the sun, below him and slightly to the eastward,—having a green fringe all round, then pink ; the centre part at first green, and then pink or red.'

The temperature was 21° below zero, Fahrenheit.

There may have been other colours—blue, perhaps—but I merely noted the most prominent ; and what I call green may have been bluish, although I do not mention this last colour in my notes.

From the lowness of the temperature at the time, the clouds *must* have been frozen moisture.

The phenomenon is by no means common, even in the Arctic zone.

The second beautiful cloud-picture shown this afternoon brought so visibly to my memory the appearance seen by me as above described, that I could not avoid remarking upon it.

Believe me, very truly yours,

JOHN RAE," (M.D., F.R.S.)

following passage from the kind private letter by which it was supplemented :—

" Many years in the Hudson's Bay Company's service, I and my men became educated for Arctic work, in which I was five different times employed, in two of which expeditions we lived wholly by our own hunting and fishing for twelve months, once in a stone house (very disagreeable), and another winter in a snow hut (better), *without fire of any kind to warm us.* On the first of these expeditions, 1846–7, my little party, there being no officer but myself, surveyed seven hundred miles of coast of Arctic America by a sledge journey, which Parry, Ross, Bach, and Lyon had failed to accomplish, costing the country about £70,000 or £80,000 at the lowest computation. The total expense of my little party, including my own pay, was under fourteen hundred pounds sterling.

" My Arctic work has been recognised by the award of the founder's gold medal of the Royal Geographical Society (before the completion of the whole of it)."

4

Now this letter enables me to leave the elements of your problem for you in very clear terms.

Your sky—altogether—may be composed of one or more of four things :—

Molecules of water in warm weather.

Molecules of ice in cold weather.

Molecules of water-vapour in warm weather.

Molecules of ice-vapour, in cold weather.

But of the size, distances, or modes of attraction between these different kinds of particles, I find no definite information anywhere, except the somewhat vague statement by Sir William Thomson, that "if a drop of water could be magnified so as to be as large as the earth, and have a diameter of eight thousand miles, then a molecule of this water in it would appear *somewhat larger than a shot*" (What kind of shot?) "*and somewhat smaller than a cricket-ball*" !

And as I finally review the common accounts given of cloud formation, I find it quite hopeless for the general reader to deal with the quantity of points which have to be kept in mind and severally valued, before he can account for any given phenomena. I have myself, in many of the passages of 'Modern Painters' before referred to, conceived of cloud too narrowly as always produced by *cold*, whereas the temperature of a cloud must continually, like that of our visible breath in frosty weather, or of the visible current of steam, or the smoking of a warm lake surface under sudden frost, be above that of the surrounding atmosphere ; and yet I never remember entering a cloud without being chilled by it, and the darkness of the plague-wind, unless in electric states of the air, is always accompanied by deadly chill.

Nor, so far as I can read, has any proper account yet been given of the balance, in serene air, of the warm air under the cold, in which the warm air is at once compressed by weight, and expanded by heat, and the cold air is thinned by its elevation, yet contracted by its cold. There is indeed no possibility of embracing the conditions in a single sentence, any more than in a single thought. But the practical balance is effected in calm air, so that its lower strata have no tendency to rise, like the air in a fire balloon, nor its higher strata to fall, unless they congeal into rain or snow.

I believe it will be an extreme benefit to my younger read-ers if I write for them a little 'Grammar of Ice and Air,' collecting the known facts on all these matters, and I am much minded to put by my ecclesiastical history for a while, in order to relate what is legible of the history of the visible Heaven.

18. 'You can't get a billiard ball to fall a shivering on its own account.'—I am under correction in this statement by the Lucasian professor of Cambridge, with respect to the molecules of bodies capable of 'epipolizing' light. "Nothing seems more natural than to suppose that the incident vibra-tions of the luminiferous ether produce vibratory movements among the ultimate molecules of sensitive substances, and that the molecules in return, *swinging on their own account*, produce vibrations in the luminous ether, and thus cause the sensation of light. The periodic times of these vibrations de-pend upon the periods in which the molecules are *disposed to swing*." ('On the Changes of Refrangibility of Light,' p. 549.)

It seems to me a pleasant conclusion, this, of recent science, and suggestive of a perfectly regenerate theology. The 'Let there be light' of the former Creation is first expanded into 'Let there be a disposition of the molecules to swing,' and the destinies of mankind, no less than the vitality of the uni-verse, depend thereafter upon this amiable, but perhaps ca-pricious, and at all events not easily influenced or anticipated, disposition!

Is it not also strange that in a treatise entering into so high mathematical analysis as that from which I quote, the false word 'swing,' expressing the action of a body liable to con-tinuous arrest by gravitation, should be employed to signify the oscillation, wholly unaffected by gravity, of substance in which the motion once originated, may cease only with the essence of the body?

It is true that in men of high scientific calibre, such as the writer in this instance, carelessness in expression does not affect the security of their conclusions. But in men of lower rank, mental defects in language indicate fatal flaws in thought. And although the constant habit to which I owe my (often foolishly praised) "command of language"—of never allowing a sentence to pass proof in which I have not considered whether, for the vital word in it, a better could be found in the dictionary, makes me somewhat morbidly intolerant of careless diction, it may be taken for an extremely useful and practical rule, that if a man can think clearly he will write well, and that no good science was ever written in bad English. So that, before you consider whether a scientific author says a true or a false thing, you had better first look if he is able properly to say *any*thing,—and secondly, whether his conceit permits him to say anything properly.

Thus, when Professor Tyndall, endeavouring to write poetically of the sun, tells you that "The Lilies of the field are his workmanship," you may observe, first, that since the sun is not a man, nothing that he does is workmanship; while even the figurative statement that he rejoices *as* a strong man to run his course, is one which Professor Tyndall has no intention whatever of admitting. And you may then observe, in the second place, that, if even in that figurative sense, the lilies of the field are the sun's workmanship, in the same sense the lilies of the hothouse are the stove's workmanship,—and in perfectly logical parallel, you, who are alive here to listen to me, because you have been warmed and fed through the winter, are the workmanship of your own coal-scuttles.

Again, when Mr. Balfour Stewart begins a treatise on the 'Conservation of Energy,' which is to conclude, as we shall see presently, with the prophecy of its total extinction as far as the present world is concerned,—by clothing in a "properly scientific garb," our innocent impression that there is some difference between the blow of a rifle stock and a rifle ball; he prepares for the scientific toilette by telling us in italics that "the something which the rifle ball possesses in contradistinction to the rifle stock is clearly the power of overcoming resistance," since "it can penetrate through oak-wood or

through water—or (alas! that it should be so often tried)
through the human body; and *this power of penetration*"
(italics now mine) "*is the distinguishing characteristic of a substance moving with very great velocity.* Let us define by the
term 'Energy,' this power which the rifle ball possesses of
overcoming obstacles, or of doing work."

Now, had Mr. Stewart been a better scholar, he would have
felt, even if he had not known, that the Greek word 'energy'
could only be applied to the living—and of living, with perfect propriety only to the *mental*, action of animals, and that
it could no more be applied as a 'scientific garb,' to the flight
of a rifle ball, than to the fall of a dead body. And, if he had
attained thus much, even of the science of language, it is just
possible that the small forte and faculty of thought he himself
possesses might have been energized so far as to perceive that
the force of all inertly moving bodies, whether rifle stock, rifle
ball, or rolling world, is under precisely one and the same
relation to their weights and velocities; that the effect of
their impact depends—not merely on their pace, but their
constitution; and on the relative forms and stability of the
substances they encounter, and that there is no more quality
of Energy, though much less quality of Art, in the swiftly
penetrating shot, or crushing ball, than in the deliberately
contemplative and administrative puncture by a gnat's pro-
boscis, or a sempstress' needle.

Mistakes of this kind, beginning with affectations of diction, do not always invalidate general statements or conclusions,—for a bad writer often equivocates out of a blun-
der as he equivocates into one,—but I have been strict in
pointing out the confusions of idea admitted in scientific
books between the movement of a swing, that of a sounding
violin chord, and that of an agitated liquid, because these confusions have actually enabled Professor Tyndall to keep the
scientific world in darkness as to the real nature of glacier
motion for the last twenty years; and to induce a resultant
quantity of aberration in the scientific mind concerning glacial erosion, of which another twenty years will scarcely undo
the damage.

19.   'Force and pace.'—Among the nearer questions which the careless terminology on which I have dwelt in the above note has left unsettled, I believe the reader will be surprised, as much as I am myself, to find that of the mode of impulse in a common gust of wind !   Whence is its strength communicated to it, and how gathered in it ? and what is the difference of manner in the impulse between compressible gas and incompressible fluid ?   For instance : The water at the head of a weir is passing every instant from slower into quicker motion ; but (until broken in the air) the fast flowing water is just as dense as the slowly flowing water.   But a fan alternately compresses and rarefies the air between it and the cheek, and the violence of a destructive gust in a gale of wind means a momentary increase in velocity and density of which I cannot myself in the least explain,—and find in no book on dynamics explained,—the mechanical causation.

The following letter, from a friend whose observations on natural history for the last seven or eight years have been consistently valuable and instructive to me, will be found, with that subjoined in the note, in various ways interesting ; but especially in its notice of the inefficiency of ordinary instrumental registry in such matters :—

" 6, MOIRA PLACE, SOUTHAMPTON, Feb. 8th, 1884.

" DEAR MR. RUSKIN,—Some time since I troubled you with a note or two about sea-birds, etc. . . . but perhaps I should never have ventured to trouble you again, had not your lecture on the 'Storm Clouds' touched a subject which has deeply interested me for years past.   I had, of course, no idea that you had noticed this thing, though I might have known that, living the life you do, you must have done so.   As for me, it has been a source of perplexity for years : so much so, that I began to wonder at times whether I was not under some mental delusion about it, until the strange theatrical displays of the last few months, for which I was more or less prepared, led so many to use their eyes, unmuzzled by brass or glass, for a time.   I know you do not bother, or care much to read newspapers, but I have taken the liberty of cutting out and sending a letter of mine, sent on the 1st January to an evening paper,* upon this subject, thinking you might like to know that one person, at any rate, has seen that strange, bleared look about the sun, shining so seldom except through a ghastly glare of pale, persistent haze. May it be that the singular colouring of the sunsets marks an end of this long period of plague-cloud, and that in them we have promise of steadier weather? (No : those sunsets were entirely distinct phenomena, and promised, if anything, only evil.—R.)

"I was glad to see that in your lecture you gave the dependants upon the instrument-makers a warning. On the 26th I had a heavy sailing-boat lifted and blown, from where she lay hauled up, a distance of four feet, which, as the boat has four hundred-weight of iron upon her keel, gives a wind-gust, or force, not easily measured by instruments.

" Believe me, dear Mr. Ruskin,

" Yours sincerely,

" ROBT. C. LESLIE."

* 'THE LOOK OF THE SKY.

' *To the* EDITOR *of the* ST. JAMES'S GAZETTE.

' SIR,—I have been a very constant though not a scientific observer of the sky for a period of forty years; and I confess to a certain feeling of astonishment at the way in which the " recent celestial phenomena " seem to have taken the whole body of scientific observers by surprise. It would even appear that something like these extraordinary sunsets was necessary to call the attention of such observers to what has long been a source of perplexity to a variety of common folk, like sailors, farmers, and fishermen. But to such people the look of the weather, and what comes of that look, is of far more consequence than the exact amount of ozone or the depth or width of a band of the spectrum.

' Now, to all such observers, including myself, it has been plain that of late neither the look of the sky nor the character of the weather has been, as we should say, what it used to be ; and those whose eyes were strong enough to look now and then toward the sun have noticed a very marked increase of what some would call a watery look about him, which might perhaps be better expressed as a white sheen or glare, at times developing into solar halo or mock suns, as noted in your paper of the 2nd of October last year. A fisherman would describe it as " white and davery-like." So far as my observation goes, this appearance was only absent here for a limited period during the present summer, when we had a week or two of nearly normal weather ; the summer before it was seldom absent.

' Again, those whose business or pleasure has depended on the use of wind-power have all remarked the strange persistence of hard westerly and easterly winds, the westerly ones at times partaking of an almost trade-wind-like force and character. The summer of 1882 was especially remarkable for these winds, while each stormy November has been followed by a period about mid-winter of mild calm weather with dense

I am especially delighted, in this letter, by my friend's vigorously accurate expression, eyes "unmuzzled by brass or
glass." I have had occasion continually, in my art-lectures,
to dwell on the great law of human perception and power,
that the beauty which is good for us is prepared for the natural focus of the sight, and the sounds which are delightful
to us for the natural power of the nerves of the ear ; and the
art which is admirable in us, is the exercise of our own bodily
powers, and not carving by sand-blast, nor oratorizing through

fog.   During these strong winds in summer and early autumn the
weather would remain bright and sunny, and to a landsman would be
not remarkable in any way, while the barometer has been little affected by
them ; but it has been often observed by those employed on the water
that when it ceased blowing half a gale the sky at once became overcast,
with damp weather or rain.   This may all seem common enough to
most people ; but to those accustomed to gauge the wind by the number
of reefs wanted in a mainsail or foresail it was not so ; and the number
of consecutive days when two or more reefs have been kept tied down
during the last few summers has been remarkable—alternating at times
with equally persistent spells of calm and fog such as we are now passing through.   Again, we have had an unusually early appearance of ice
in the Atlantic, and most abnormal weather over Central Europe ; while
in a letter I have just received from an old hand on board a large Australian clipper, he speaks of heavy gales and big seas off that coast in
almost the height of their summer.
    ' Now, upon all this, in our season of long twilights, we have bursting
upon us some clear weather ; with a display of cloud-forms or vapour
at such an elevation that, looking at them one day through an opening
in the nearer clouds, they seemed so distant as to resemble nothing but
the delicate grain of ivory upon a billiard-ball.   And yet with the fact
that two-thirds of this earth is covered with water, and bearing in mind
the effect which a very small increase of sun-power would have in producing cloud and lifting it above its normal level for a time, we are
asked to believe that this sheen is all dust of some kind or other, in order
to explain what are now known as the "recent sunsets": though I
venture to think that we shall see more of them yet when the sun comes
our way again.
    ' At first sight, increased sun-power would seem to mean more sun-
shine ; but a little reflection would show us that this would not be for
long, while any considerable addition to the sun's power would be followed by such a vast increase of vapour that we should only see him, in
our latitudes, at very short intervals.   I am aware that all this is most
unscientific ; but I have read column after column of explanation
written by those who are supposed to know all about such things, and
find myself not a jot the wiser for it.   Do you know anybody who is ?—
I am, Sir, your obedient servant,
                                        ' AN UNSCIENTIFIC OBSERVER.   (R. LESLIE.)
    ' *January* 1.'

A speaking trumpet, nor dancing with spring heels. But more recently, I have become convinced that even in matters of science, although every added mechanical power has its proper use and sphere, yet the things which are vital to our happiness and prosperity can only be known by the rational use and subtle skill of our natural powers. We may trust the instrument with the prophecy of storm, or registry of rainfall ; but the conditions of atmospheric change, on which depend the health of animals and fruitfulness of seeds, can only be discerned by the eye and the bodily sense.

Take, for simplest and nearest example, this question of the stress of wind. It is not the actual *power* that is immeasurable, if only it would stand to be measured ! Instruments could easily now be invented which would register not only a blast that could lift a sailing boat, but one that would sink a ship of the line. But, lucklessly—the blast won't pose to the instrument ! nor can the instrument be adjusted to the blast. In the gale of which my friend speaks in his next letter, 26th January, a gust came down the hill above Coniston village upon two old oaks, which were well rooted in the slate rock, and some fifty or sixty feet high—the one, some twenty yards below the other. The blast tore the highest out of the ground, peeling its roots from the rock as one peels an orange —swept the head of the lower tree away with it in one ruin, and snapped the two leader branches of the upper one over the other's stump, as one would break one's cane over some people's heads, if one got the chance. In wind action of this kind the amount of actual force used is the least part of the business ;—it is the suddenness of its concentration, and the lifting and twisting strength, as of a wrestler, which makes the blast fatal ; none of which elements of storm-power can be recognised by mechanical tests. In my friend's next letter, however, he gives us some evidence of the *consistent* strength of this same gale, and of the electric conditions which attended it :—the prefatory notice of his pet bird I had meant for 'Love's Meinie,' but it will help us through the grimness of our studies here.

"MARCH 3rd, 1884.

"My small blackheaded gull Jack is still flourishing, and the time is coming when I look for that singularly sudden change in the plumage of his head which took place last March. I have asked all my ocean-going friends to note whether these little birds are not the gulls *par excellence* of the sea; and so far all I have heard from them confirms this. It seems almost incredible; but my son, a sailor, who met that hurricane of the 26th of January, writes to me to say that out in the Bay of Biscay on the morning after the gale, 'though it was blowing like blazes, I observed some little gulls of Jacky's species, and they followed us half way across the Bay, seeming to find shelter under the lee of our ship. Some alighted now and then, and rested upon the water as if tired.' When one considers that these birds must have been at sea all that night somewhere, it gives one a great idea of their strength and endurance. My son's ship, though a powerful ocean steamer, was for two whole hours battling head to sea off the Eddystone that night, and for that time the lead gave no increase of soundings, so that she could have made no headway during those two hours; while all the time her yards had the St. Elmo's fire at their ends, looking as though a blue light was burning at each yard-arm, and this was about all they could see.

"Yours sincerely,
"ROBT. C. LESLIE."

The next letter, from a correspondent with whom I have the most complete sympathy in some expressions of his post-script which are yet, I consider, more for my own private ear than for the public eye, describes one of the more malignant phases of the plague-wind, which I forgot to notice in my lecture.

"BURNHAM, SOMERSET, Februry 7, 1884.

"DEAR SIR,—I read with great interest your first lecture at Oxford on cloud and wind (very indifferently reported in 'The Times'). You have given a name to a wind I've known for years. You call it the plague—I call it the devil-wind: *e.g.*, on April 29th, 1882, morning warmer, then rain storms from east; afternoon, rain squalls; wind, west by south, rough; barometer falling awfully; 4.30 P.M., tremendous wind.—April 30th, all the leaves of the trees, all plants black and dead, as if a fiery blast had swept over them. *All the hedges on windward side black as black tea.*

"Another devil-wind came towards the end of last summer. The next day, all the leaves were falling sere and yellow, as if it were late autumn.

"I am, dear sir,
"Yours faithfully,
"A. H. BIRKETT."

I remember both these blights well; they were entirely terrific; but only sudden maxima of the constant morbific power of this wind,—which, if Mr. Birkett saw my *personal* notices of, intercalated among the scientific ones, he would find alluded to in terms quite as vigorously damning as he could desire : and the actual effect of it upon my thoughts and work has been precisely that which would have resulted from the visible phantom of an evil spirit, the absolute opponent of the Queen of the Air,—Typhon against Athena,—in a sense of which I had neither the experience nor the conception when I wrote the illustrations of the myth of Perseus in 'Modern Painters.' Not a word of all those explanations of Homer and Pindar could have been written in weather like that of the last twelve years ; and I am most thankful to have got them written before the shadow came, and I could still see what Homer and Pindar saw. I quote one passage only— Vol. v., p. 160—for the sake of a similitude which reminds me of one more thing I have to say here—and a bit of its note—which I think is a precious little piece, not of word-painting, but of simply told feeling—(*that*, if people knew it, is my real power).

"On the Yorkshire and Derbyshire hills, when the rain-cloud is low and much broken, and the steady west wind fills all space with its strength,* the sun-gleams fly like golden vultures ; they are flashes rather than shinings ; the dark spaces and the dazzling race and skim along the acclivities, and dart and *dip from crag to dell, swallow-like.*"

---

* "I have been often at great heights on the Alps in rough weather, and have seen strong gusts of storm in the plains of the south. But, to get full expression of the very heart and meaning of wind, there is no place

The dipping of the shadows here described of course is caused only by that of the dingles they cross ; but I have not in any of my books yet dwelt enough on the difference of character between the dipping and the mounting winds. Our wildest phase of the west wind here at Coniston is 'swallow-like ' with a vengeance, coming down on the lake in swirls which spurn the spray under them as a fiery horse does the dust. On the other hand, the softly ascending winds express themselves in the grace of their cloud motion, as if set to the continuous music of a distant song.*

The reader will please note also that whenever, either in 'Modern Painters ' or elsewhere, I speak of rate of flight in clouds, I am thinking of it as measured by the horizontal distance overpast in given time, and not as apparent only, owing to the nearness of the spectator. All low clouds appear to move faster than high ones, the pace being supposed equal in both : but when I speak of quick or slow cloud, it is always with respect to a given altitude. In a fine summer morning, a cloud will wait for you among the pines, folded to and fro

like a Yorkshire moor. I think Scottish breezes are thinner, very bleak and piercing, but not substantial. If you lean on them they will let you fall, but one may rest against a Yorkshire breeze as one would on a quickset hedge. I shall not soon forget,—having had the good fortune to meet a vigorous one on an April morning, between Hawes and Settle, just on the flat under Wharnside,—the vague sense of wonder *with which I watched Ingleborough stand without rocking.*"

* Compare Wordsworth's

> " Oh beauteous birds, methinks ye measure
>   Your movements to some heavenly tune."

And again—

> " While the mists,
> Flying and rainy vapours, call out shapes,
> And phantoms from the crags and solid earth,
> As fast as a musician scatters sounds
> Out of an instrument."

And again—

> " The Knight had ridden down from Wensley moor,
> With the slow motion of a summer cloud."

among their stems, with a branch or two coming out here, and a spire or two there : you walk through it, and look back to it. At another time on the same spot, the fury of cloud-flood drifts past you like the Rhine at Schaffhausen.

The space even of the double lecture does not admit of my entering into any general statement of the action of the plague cloud in Switzerland and Italy ; but I must not omit the fol-lowing notes of its aspect in the high Alps.

"SALLENCHES, 11th September, 1882.

"This morning, at half-past five, the Mont Blanc summit was clear, and the greater part of the Aiguilles du Plan and Midi clear dark—all, against pure cirri, lighted beneath by sunrise ; the sun of course not visible yet from the valley.

"By seven o'clock, the plague-clouds had formed in *brown* flakes, down to the base of the Aiguille de Bionassay ; entirely covering the snowy ranges; the sun, as it rose to us here, shone only for about ten minutes—gilding in its old glory the range of the Dorons,—before one had time to look from peak to peak of it, the plague-cloud formed from the west, hid Mont Joli, and steadily choked the valley with advancing streaks of dun-coloured mist. Now—twenty minutes to nine —there is not *one ray* of sunshine on the whole valley, or on its mountains, from the Forclaz down to Cluse.

"These phenomena are only the sequel of a series of still more strange and sad conditions of the air, which have con-tinued among the Savoy Alps for the last eight days, (them-selves the sequel of others yet more general, prolonged, and harmful). But the weather was perfectly fine at Dijon, and I doubt not at Chamouni, on the 1st of this month. On the 2nd, in the evening, I saw, from the Jura, heavy thunder-clouds in the west; on the 3rd, the weather broke at Morez, in hot thunder-showers, with intervals of scorching sun ; on the 4th, 5th, and 6th there was nearly continuous rain at St. Cergues, the Alps being totally invisible all the time. The sky cleared on the night of the 6th, and on the 7th I saw from the top of the Dole all the western plateaux of Jura quite clearly ; but *the entire range of the Alps,* from the Moleson to the Salève, and all beyond,—snow, crag, and hill-side,—were wrapped and buried in one unbroken grey-brown winding-sheet, of such cloud *as I had never seen till that day touch an Alpine summit.*

"The wind, from the east, (so that it blew *up* over the edge of the Dole cliff, and admitted of perfect shelter on the slope to the west,) was bitter cold, and extremely violent : the sun overhead, bright enough, and remained so during the afternoon ; the plague-cloud reaching from the Alps only about as far as the southern shore of the lake of Geneva ; but we could not see the Saléve ; nor even the north shore, farther than to Morges! I reached the Col de la Faucille at sunset, when, for a few minutes, the Mont Blanc and Aiguille Verte showed themselves in dull red light, but were buried again, before the sun was quite down, in the rising deluge of cloud-poison. I saw no farther than the Voirons and Brezon—and scarcely those, during the electric heat of the 9th at Geneva ; and last Saturday and Sunday have been mere whirls and drifts of indecisive, but always sullen, storm. This morning I saw the snows clear for the first time, having been, during the whole past week, on steady watch for them.

"I have written that the clouds of the 7th were such as I never before saw on the Alps. Often, during the past ten years, I have seen them on my own hills, and in Italy in 1874 ; but it has always chanced to be fine weather, or common rain and cold, when I have been among the snowy chains ; and now from the Dole for the first time I saw the plague-cloud on *them*."

20. 'Blasphemy.'—If the reader can refer to my papers on Fiction in the 'Nineteenth Century,' he will find this word carefully defined in its Scriptural, and evermore necessary, meaning,—'Harmful speaking'—not against God only, but against man, and against all the good works and purposes of Nature. The word is accurately opposed to 'Euphemy,' the right or well-speaking of God and His world ; and the two modes of speech are those which going out of the mouth sanctify or defile the man.

Going out of the mouth, that is to say, deliberately and of purpose. A French postilion's 'Sacr-r-ré'—loud, with the low 'Nom de Dieu' following between his teeth, is not blasphemy, unless against his horse ;—but Mr. Thackeray's close of his Waterloo chapter in 'Vanity Fair,' "And all the night long Amelia was praying for George, who was lying on his face dead with a bullet through his heart," is blasphemy of the most fatal and subtle kind.

And the universal instinct of blasphemy in the modern vul-gar scientific mind is above all manifested in its love of what is ugly, and natural enthralment by the abominable ;—so that it is ten to one if, in the description of a new bird, you learn much more of it than the enumerated species of vermin that stick to its feathers ; and in the natural history museum of Oxford, humanity has been hitherto taught, not by portraits of great men, but by the skulls of cretins.

But the *deliberate* blasphemy of science, the assertion of its own virtue and dignity against the always implied, and often asserted, vileness of all men and—Gods,—heretofore, is the most wonderful phenomenon, so far as I can read or perceive, that hitherto has arisen in the always marvellous course of the world's mental history.

Take, for brief general type, the following 92nd paragraph of the 'Forms of Water' :—

"But while we thus acknowledge our limits, there is also reason for wonder at the extent to which Science has mastered the system of nature. From age to age and from generation to generation, fact has been added to fact and law to law, the true method and order of the Universe being thereby more and more revealed. In doing this, Science has encountered and overthrown various forms of superstition and deceit, of credulity and imposture. But the world continually produces weak persons and wicked persons, and as long as they con-tinue to exist side by side, as they do in this our day, very debasing beliefs will also continue to infest the world."

The debasing beliefs meant being simply those of Homer, David, and St. John *—as against a modern French gamin's. And what the results of the intended education of English gamins of every degree in that new higher theology will be, England is I suppose by this time beginning to discern.

In the last 'Fors †' which I have written, on education of a

---

* With all who died in Faith, not having received the Promises, nor—according to your modern teachers—ever to receive.

† Hence to the end the text is that read in termination of the lecture on its second delivery, only with an added word or two of comment on Proverbs xvii.

safer kind, still possible, one practical point is insisted on chiefly,—that learning by heart, and repetition with perfect accent and cultivated voice, should be made quite principal branches of school discipline up to the time of going to the university.

And of writings to be learned by heart, among other passages of disputable philosophy and perfect poetry, I include certain chapters of the—now for the most part forgotten—wisdom of Solomon ; and of these, there is one selected portion which I should recommend not only schoolboys and girls, but persons of every age, if they don't know it, to learn forthwith, as the shortest summary of Solomon's wisdom ;—namely, the seventeenth chapter of Proverbs, which being only twenty-eight verses long, may be fastened in the dullest memory at the rate of a verse a day in the shortest month of the year. Out of the twenty-eight verses, I will read you seven, for example of their tenor,—the last of the seven I will with your good leave dwell somewhat upon.   You have heard the verses often before, but probably without remembering that they are all in this concentrated chapter.

1. Verse 1.—Better is a dry morsel, and quietness therewith, than a house full of good eating, with strife.

    (Remember, in reading this verse, that though England has chosen the strife, and set every man's hand against his neighbour, her house is not yet so full of good eating as she expected, even though she gets half of her victuals from America.)

2. Verse 3.—The fining pot is for silver, the furnace for gold, but the Lord tries the heart.

    (Notice the increasing strength of trial for the more precious thing : only the melting-pot for the silver—the fierce furnace for the gold—but the Fire of the Lord for the heart.)

3. Verse 4.—A wicked doer giveth heed to false lips.

    (That means, for *you*, that, intending to live by usury and swindling, you read Mr. Adam Smith and Mr. Stuart Mill, and other such political economists).

4. Verse 5.—Whoso mocketh the poor, reproacheth his Maker.

(Mocketh,—by saying that his poverty is his fault, no less than his misfortune,—England's favourite theory now-a-days.)

5. Verse 12.—Let a bear robbed of her whelps meet a man, rather than a fool in his folly.

(Carlyle is often now accused of false scorn in his calling the passengers over London Bridge, "mostly fools,"—on the ground that men are only to be justly held foolish if their intellect is under, as only wise when it is above, the average. But the reader will please observe that the essential function of modern education is to develope what capacity of mistake a man has. Leave him at his forge and plough,—and those tutors teach him his true value, indulge him in no error, and provoke him to no vice. But take him up to London,—give him her papers to read, and her talk to hear,—and it is fifty to one you send him presently on a fool's errand over London Bridge.)

6. Now listen, for this verse is the question you have mainly to ask yourselves about your beautiful all-over-England system of competitive examination :—

Verse 16. Wherefore is there a price in the hand of a fool to get wisdom, seeing he hath no heart to it?

(You know perfectly well it isn't the wisdom you want, but the "station in life,"—and the money!)

7. Lastly, Verse 24.—Wisdom is before him that hath understanding, but the eyes of a fool are in the ends of the earth.

"And in the beginnings of it"! Solomon would have written, had he lived in our day ; but we will be content with the ends at present. No scientific people, as I told you at first, have taken any notice of the more or less temporary phenomena of which I have to-night given you register. But, from the constant arrangements of the universe, the same respecting which the thinkers of former time came to the conclusion that

they were essentially good, and to end in good, the
modern speculator arrives at the quite opposite and
extremely uncomfortable conclusion that they are essentially evil, and to end—in nothing.

And I have here a volume,* before quoted, by a very foolish
and very lugubrious author, who in his concluding chapter
gives us,—founded, you will observe, on a series of 'ifs,'—the
latest scientific views concerning the order of creation.   "We
have spoken already about a medium pervading space"—this
is the Scientific God, you observe, differing from the unscientific one, in that the purest in heart cannot see—nor the softest in heart feel—this spacious Deity—a *Medium* pervading
space—" the office of which " (italics all mine) " appears to be
to *degrade* and ultimately *extinguish*, all differential motion.
It has been well pointed out by Thomson, that, looked at *in
this light*, the universe is a system that had a beginning and
must have an end, for a process of degradation cannot be
eternal.   If we could view the Universe as a candle not lit,
then it is perhaps conceivable to regard it as having been always in existence ; but if we regard it rather as a candle that
has been lit, we become absolutely certain that it cannot have
been burning from eternity, and that a time will come when
it will cease to burn.   We are led to look to a beginning in
which the particles of matter were in a diffuse chaotic state,
but endowed with the power of gravitation ; and we are led
to look to an end in which the whole Universe will be one
equally heated inert mass, *and from which everything like life,
or motion, or beauty, will have utterly gone away.*"

Do you wish me to congratulate you on this extremely
cheerful result of telescopic and microscopic observation, and
so at once close my lecture ? or may I venture yet to trespass
on your time by stating to you any of the more comfortable
views held by persons who did not regard the universe in
what my author humorously calls " this *light* " ?

In the peculiarly characteristic notice with which the
'Daily News' honoured my last week's lecture, that courte-

* 'The Conservation of Energy.'   King and Co., 1873.

ous journal charged me, in the metaphorical term now classical on Exchange, with "hedging," to conceal my own opinions. The charge was not prudently chosen, since, of all men now obtaining any portion of popular regard, I am pretty well known to be precisely the one who cares least either for hedge or ditch, when he chooses to go across country. It is certainly true that I have not the least mind to pin my heart on my sleeve, for the daily daw, or nightly owl, to peck at ; but the essential reason for my not telling you my own opinions on this matter is—that I do not consider them of material consequence to you.

It *might* possibly be of some advantage for you to know what—were he now living, Orpheus would have thought, or Æschylus, or a Daniel come to judgment, or John the Baptist, or John the Son of Thunder ; but what either you, or I, or any other Jack or Tom of us all, think,—even if we knew what to think,—is of extremely small moment either to the Gods, the clouds, or ourselves.

Of myself, however, if you care to hear it, I will tell you thus much : that had the weather when I was young been such as it is now, no book such as 'Modern Painters' ever would or *could* have been written ; for every argument, and every sentiment in that book, was founded on the personal experience of the beauty and blessing of nature, all spring and summer long ; and on the then demonstrable fact that over a great portion of the world's surface the air and the earth were fitted to the education of the spirit of man as closely as a schoolboy's primer is to his labour, and as gloriously as a lover's mistress is to his eyes.

That harmony is now broken, and broken the world round : fragments, indeed, of what existed still exist, and hours of what is past still return ; but month by month the darkness gains upon the day, and the ashes of the Antipodes glare through the night.*

* Written under the impression that the lurid and prolonged sunsets of last autumn has been proved to be connected with the flight of volcanic ashes. This has been since, I hear, disproved again. Whatever their cause, those sunsets were, in the sense in which I myself use the

What consolation, or what courage, through plague, dan‑ ger or darkness, you can find in the conviction that you are nothing more than brute beasts driven by brute forces, your other tutors can tell you—not I : but *this* I can tell you—and with the authority of all the masters of thought since time was time,—that, while by no manner of vivisection you can learn what a *Beast* is, by only looking into your own hearts you may know what a *Man* is,—and know that his only true happiness is to live in Hope of something to be won by him,

word, altogether ' unnatural ' and terrific : but they have no connection with the far more fearful, because protracted and increasing, power of the Plague‑wind. The letter from White's ' History of Selborne,' quoted by the Rev. W. R. Andrews in his letter to the ' Times,' (dated January 8th) seems to describe aspects of the sky like these of 1883, just a hundred years before, in 1783 : and also some of the circum‑ stances noted, especially the variation of the wind to all quarters with‑ out alteration in the air, correspond with the character of the plague‑ wind ; but the fog of 1783 made the sun dark, with iron‑coloured rays —not pale, with blanching rays. I subjoin Mr. Andrews' letter, ex‑ tremely valuable in its collation of the records of simultaneous volcanic phenomena ; praying the reader also to observe the instantaneous ac‑ knowledgment, by the true ' Naturalist,' of horror in the violation of beneficent natural law.

" THE RECENT SUNSETS AND VOLCANIC ERUPTIONS."

" SIR,—It may, perhaps, be interesting at the present time, when so much attention has been given to the late brilliant sunsets and sun‑ rises, to be reminded that almost identically the same appearances were observed just a hundred years ago.

" Gilbert White writes in the year 1783, in his 109th letter, published in his ' Natural History of Selborne ' :—

" 'The summer of the year 1783 was an amazing and portentous one, and full of horrible phenomena ; for besides the alarming meteors and tremendous thunderstorms that affrighted and distressed the different counties of this kingdom, the peculiar haze or smoky fog that prevailed for many weeks in this island and in every part of Europe, and even beyond its limits, was a most extraordinary appearance, unlike anything known within the memory of man. By my journal I find that I had noticed this strange occurrence from June 23rd to July 20th inclusive. during which period the wind varied to every quarter without making any alteration in the air. The sun at noon looked as black as a clouded in Reverence of something to be worshipped by him, and in Love of something to be cherished by him, and cherished— for ever.

Having these instincts, his only rational conclusion is that the objects which can fulfil them may be by his effort gained, and by his faith discerned; and his only earthly wisdom is to accept the united testimony of the men who have sought these things in the way they were commanded. Of whom no single one has ever said that his obedience or his faith had been

moon, and shed a ferruginous light on the ground and floors of rooms, but was particularly lurid and blood-coloured at rising and setting. The country people began to look with a superstitious awe at the red lowering aspect of the sun ; and, indeed, there was reason for the most enlightened person to be apprehensive, for all the while Calabria and part of the Isle of Sicily were torn and convulsed with earthquakes, and about that juncture a volcano sprang out of the sea on the coast of Norway.'

" Other writers also mention volcanic disturbances in this same year, 1783. We are told by Lyell and Geikie, that there were great volcanic eruptions in and near Iceland. A submarine volcano burst forth in the sea, thirty miles south-west of Iceland, which ejected so much pumice that the ocean was covered with this substance, to the distance of 150 miles, and ships were considerably impeded in their course ; and a new island was formed, from which fire and smoke and pumice were emitted.

" Besides this submarine eruption, the volcano Skaptar-Jokull, on the mainland, on June 11th, 1783, threw out a torrent of lava, so immense as to surpass in magnitude the bulk of Mont Blanc, and ejected so vast an amount of fine dust, that the atmosphere over Iceland continued loaded with it for months afterwards. It fell in such quantities over parts of Caithness—a distance of 600 miles—as to destroy the crops, and that year is still spoken of by the inhabitants as the year of 'the ashie.'

" These particulars are gathered from the text-books of Lyell and Geikie.

" I am not aware whether the coincidence in time of the Icelandic eruptions, and of the peculiar appearance of the sun, described by Gilbert White, has yet been noticed : but this coincidence may very well be taken as some little evidence towards explaining the connexion between the recent beautiful sunsets and the tremendous volcanic explosion of the Isle of Krakatoa in August last.

"W. R. ANDREWS, F.G.S.

" Teffont Ewyas Rectory, Salisbury, January 8th."

vain, or found himself cast out from the choir of the living souls, whether here, or departed, for whom the song was writ-ten : —

> God be merciful unto us, and bless us, and cause His face to shine upon us ;
> That Thy way may be known upon earth, Thy saving health among all nations.
> Oh let the nations rejoice and sing for joy, for Thou shalt judge the people righteously and govern the nations upon earth.
> *Then* shall the earth yield her increase, and God, even our own God, shall bless us.
> God shall bless us, and all the ends of the earth shall fear Him.

INDEX.